SUICIDAL MASS MURDERERS

A Criminological Study of Why They Kill

SUICIDAL MASS MURDERERS

A Criminological Study of Why They Kill

John Liebert and William J. Birnes

CRC Press
Taylor & Francis Group
Boca Raton London New York

CRC Press is an imprint of the
Taylor & Francis Group, an **informa** business

CRC Press
Taylor & Francis Group
6000 Broken Sound Parkway NW, Suite 300
Boca Raton, FL 33487-2742

Printed in the United States of America on acid-free paper
10 9 8 7 6 5 4 3 2 1

International Standard Book Number: 978-1-4200-7678-3 (Paperback)

Library of Congress Cataloging-in-Publication Data

Liebert, John (John A.)
Suicidal mass murderers : a criminological study of why they kill / John Liebert, William J. Birnes.
p. cm.
Includes bibliographical references and index.
ISBN 978-1-4200-7678-3 (pbk. : alk. paper)
1. Mass murderers--Psychology--Case studies. 2. Mass murder--Psychological aspects--Case studies. 3. Suicidal behavior--Case studies. 4. Criminal psychology. 5. Criminal behavior, Prediction of. 6. Violence--Prevention. I. Birnes, William J. II. Title.

HV6515.L38 2011
364.152'34--dc22 2010032789

Visit the Taylor & Francis Web site at
http://www.taylorandfrancis.com

and the CRC Press Web site at
http://www.crcpress.com

Contents

About the Authors

John Liebert, M.D., is a Diplomat of the American Board of Psychiatry and Neurology and is in the private practice of neuropsychiatry, with special interests in both psychopharmacology and forensic problems of children, adults, and the elderly. His career has been focused on the association of trauma and human destructiveness, about which he has extensively lectured and written. He served as special forensic psychiatry consultant to the "Ted" (Bundy), "Green River" (Ridgway), "Atlanta Child" (Williams), and "Charmer" (Russell) cases and was Associate Professor of Psychiatry at the University of Washington Faculty of Medicine. In his latter role he worked closely with Dr. Robert Keppel on development of both his *Murder Book* and thesis in "Solubility Factors in Homicide Investigations." Dr. Liebert's online continuing medical education course, EMPsych, is a major teaching instrument in emergency psychiatry for nonpsychiatric health professionals in emergency services, corrections, and acute care clinics. He developed *The Digital Clinician*, a computerized clinical decision support system for triaging patients; it is currently being integrated into Telenursing for remote Quebec regions by McGill University Faculty of Medicine. Dr. Liebert has extensive experience in high acuity and emergency medicine sites, within both the military and civilian sectors. He completed his premedical training at Amherst College and received his M.D. from McGill University Faculty of Medicine. His postgraduate training in acute and emergency medicine was completed at Santa Clara County/Stanford, San Jose, California, and his psychiatric training at the University of Washington School of Medicine in Seattle. He served as a flight surgeon for the United States Air Force and observer for Georgia Human Relations Council at the Selma March and the Southern Christian Leadership Conference (SCLC) Civil Rights demonstrations in Georgia.

William J. Birnes, J.D., Ph.D., *New York Times* bestselling author is chairman of the Board of Sunrise Community Mental Health Center in Los Angeles. He is an author in the fields of mental health, true crime, human behavior, law and journalism, and science and technology, as well as an editor and book publisher. His first true crime title, *Serial Killers*, is in its 19th printing at Random House. Birnes' book about the O. J. Simpson case in 1994 was made required reading for all first-year law students at Harvard Law School.

Birnes is the editorial director of his own literary imprint at Tor/Forge Books Macmillan Publishing in New York and is the president of the book production company, Shadow Lawn Press. He is also the publisher and president of Filament Books in New York and Los Angeles. A co-author of the *New York Times* bestseller, his *The Day After Roswell* in 1997 is a documentary on the History Channel (May, 2005). Birnes' previous cable feature "The Riverman" that was based on his book, The *Riverman*, which he co-authored with detective Dr. Robert Keppel about how serial killer Ted Bundy helped police track Green River Killer Gary Ridgway, was broadcast on A&E in September 2004.

Birnes is a frequent radio and television talk-show guest, having appeared on *Good Morning America, Dateline, Entertainment Tonight,* and *Coast to Coast AM.* He currently produces and hosts his own documentary series on *The History Channel,* appeared in the feature film *Occam's Razor* in 1999, and was featured in a Canadian Broadcasting Company documentary on the O. J. Simpson murder trial in 1995.

A National Endowment for the Humanities Fellow, grants judge for the National Endowment for the Arts, and law school graduate, William Birnes received his Ph.D. from New York University in 1974 while he was an Instructor of English at Trenton State College. He completed his postdoctoral work under a Lily Foundation Fellowship at the University of Pennsylvania. Birnes has also worked as a member of a grants recipient team from the Bureau of Justice Administration and the United States Department of Justice. In 2007, Dr. Birnes was made the chairman of the board of directors of Sunrise Community Counseling Center in Los Angeles.

Introduction

The Virginia Tech Killings

On April 16, 2007, a young Korean-American student at Virginia Tech, who had a history of mental illness and a skein of red flags popping up since he was a child, became the perpetrator of the most infamous and biggest school or campus shooting in the history of the United States. His name was Cho Seung-Hui, and he was described by his family as very shy and withdrawn, by his teachers as awkward and silent in class, and by his classmates as someone who was likely to go off, one person even saying to a rampage mass murder. And that's exactly what he did, killing thirty people in Norris Hall, the engineering building on the Virginia Tech campus, and two before as a seeming decoy to the Norris Hall massacre, before killing himself. In the aftermath of Cho's mass murder and subsequent suicide and the national television broadcast of his ugly video manifesto on NBC the following evening, only one primary question emerged: Why?

When we look into the timeline of Cho Seung-Hui's descent into the maelstrom from when he was hospitalized as a child to the morning of the massacre, a clearer picture emerges. Cho was a psychotic, even though the severity of his symptoms was overlooked or they were simply not diagnosed at all. Though treated from time to time and repeatedly triaged by campus guidance center personnel as an emotionally troubled student, Cho proceeded through the system until the day of his shooting rampage.

The Cho case is almost an archetype of childhood mental illness and ideations of violence that terminated in a day of apocalyptic suicidal mass murder. Had Cho been diagnosed earlier, the early signs of schizophrenia would have been discovered; people with this condition are self-absorbed in delusional thinking, clinging rigidly to abnormal beliefs—even in the face of obvious evidence to the contrary. They are plagued by auditory and visual hallucinations, voices inside their heads that may command them to do things—sometimes to kill and/or be killed. They also oftentimes have delusions of persecution that can control their lives in both defensive avoidance and isolation—or worse, mass murder. They many times believe that external events, which, in reality, may be totally random, have an intimate connection to their lives, such as the numbers on a digital clock in a big city square giving them a message. These are known as *ideas of reference*, wherein random events, such as a person waving to somebody on the street, are mistakenly "referred to themselves." As with New York's Son of Sam, some people believe that they are commanded to do things by alien voices or even the voices of animals. The main operational focus of schizophrenia is that the victim no longer navigates through reality but through a world inside his mind wired, as experts say, by malfunctioning circuits that mix up signals and misfire due to "diabolical learning" coded and decoded by their own brain DNA. The cause of this diabolical learning within the complex matrix of billions of neurocircuits is unknown, but both external stress and genetic vulnerability are believed to be necessary for such deterioration in brain function, now dramatically visualized and documented in modern imaging studies such as positron emission tomography (PET) scans and functional magnetic resonance imaging (MRI); we need to know more very fast. Schizophrenia appears to hit rather randomly in the prime of earliest adult life at the rate of 1/100 new cases per year. Probably one percent of the entire adult population has schizophrenia and 5 percent of these cases can be traced back to childhood.

Even though it is likely that Cho evidenced antecedents of childhood-onset schizophrenia—perhaps from the time following hospitalization in Korea for an echocardiogram to diagnose what doctors were calling a heart murmur—his terminal apocalyptic vision of the end of his world and the worlds of his victims is very similar to other mass shootings by those who have had paranoid delusions of persecution and extreme grandiosity. Other school shootings—for example, in Littleton, Colorado, or in San Diego, California—were perpetrated by shooters who were ostracized by their peers, probably bullied, but who were already psychotic by the time they created their own delusional worlds over which they were lord and master. The link to other types of mass murders, such as the mass shooting at Luby's cafeteria in Kileen, Texas, in which the killer, George Jo Hennard, also shot himself, lies in the fact that among the symptoms of the killer's psychosis was extreme grandiosity, a false grandeur that the killer projected into his own violence. As evidenced by Cho's video manifesto played on NBC the night following the shootings, Cho portrayed himself as a Christ figure dying for the sins of others like him.

Mass shootings can be perpetrated by those whose sense of being victimized or persecuted goes way beyond any logic and is a manifestation of their own paranoid creation. Sometimes there is real causality, such as relentless bullying that instills fear in the victim or the bullying by a supervisor who is more abusive than he or she is managerial. In Cho's case, his family, teachers, and college roommates insulated him well from the bullying that his sister reported as simply the norm expected for Asian-American children of immigrant parents. Although the bullying might have made Cho's acculturation more difficult—thus the necessary element of external stress—it certainly was not causative of his long slide into darkness. But, causality aside, a perpetrator of a mass homicide and subsequent suicide is usually the victim of a disease that has long since sapped the person's resiliency and left him with a smoldering rage response that builds pressure until it blows. Perhaps, as in the case of Cho, the planning of the event, sometimes driven by the command voices of auditory hallucinations, draws out the timeline. But when it explodes, it explodes. And, in the paranoid type of schizophrenia, a patient can maintain considerable ability to plan and keep track of detail; that is, if you accept the psychotic premise, the action can be considered successfully executed. Most schizophrenic patients, however, are way too disorganized to plan such tragic dramatic disasters in real life, mastering the details too. But, the paranoid schizophrenic patient can, and such apparent skills and planning plague the prosecution of such cases. How can such a sick person carry out such a massive act of violence with such extraordinary planning and mastery of detail in execution?

The archetypal mass murderer most often acts alone and out of his own brooding mental illness. However, clever manipulators, such as terrorist organizations and even organized criminal gangs, can entrap the emotionally at-risk young to their own advantage by feeding their paranoid delusions with targets and logical reasons to fear and hate those targets, providing the access to targets, and providing them the means to carry out their tasks. Thus, organizations such as al-Qaeda can recruit the hopeless and enraged, feed their hatred, train them in the art of exorcising that hatred on high-value targets, and get them to the right spot with the right weapons. The Mumbai massacre, a mass murder/suicide terrorist plot, is an example of this type of psychological control of the psychologically vulnerable, lost youth top-down control.

Other types of hate-/rage-driven mass murder, such as the recent Santa Claus Killer in Covina, California, and George Sodinji in Pittsburgh, are also most often driven by a brooding rage, simmering in an emotional cauldron of mental illness. It could be seeded by guilt, as in the case of the Bruce Jeffrey Pardo Santa Claus killing, but that seed is germinating in the fertile ground of a severe psychosis that may long have preceded the trigger that sets the killer onto his timeline ending in mass murder. Pardo had always been troubled, but when his young son slipped away from him and into the pool, where he injured himself such that he would never walk again, Pardo felt completely responsible. He gave up caring for his son, leaving him in the care of his son's mother, and then remarried. It was during the divorce from his wife that he snapped and killed her and her entire family at a Christmas party, set the house aflame with the gunfire, and then fled to his brother's house, where he killed himself.

Gang murders seem different from mass murder/suicides when looked at from the perspective of the modus operandi but may stem from the same base causality. Some gang murders, especially ones in which entire families, including children, are wiped out, have a psychological calling card to them, which leads observers to believe that these perpetrators have gone beyond the scope of simple contract killers. As in *Helter Skelter*, there is too much psychological interaction with the crime scene and with the victims; too much blood; too little caution exercised about leaving clues or spending too much time at the crime scene for this to be business as usual. These are crimes in which the killer is exorcising something, working out of a delusion or locked in a dangerous and violent psychosis.

This is the relationship between terrorist and gang killings and the homicides perpetrated by Cho Seung-Hui.

The Virginia Tech massacre is marked as well by the failure of the local medical, legal, and educational communities to deal with the problem. Cho, as is evidenced by the revelations in the governor's panel investigation, simply was run recklessly through the local on-campus counseling center and local community mental health system, even though his teachers and his classmates recognized that he was a ticking time bomb, inevitably en route to becoming one of the most dangerous individuals on earth. He appeared hostile and menacing behind his sunglasses and under his ball cap, pulled down low around his head. Yet, as one of his professors noted, when he removed his hat and glasses, his expressionless face revealed a terrible absence of personality—there seemed nothing of a person when unmasked. His students also talked about the danger Cho posed, one ominously predicting the inevitable rampage murder to come.

Cho had been placed into custody by the Virginia Tech police after having stalked women in the residence halls. He was placed under an involuntary commitment order at a psychiatric hospital unit after he told one of his roommates, after the police had confronted him, that he "might as well commit suicide." Yet clinical evaluators let him through the system, a psychiatrist and clinical psychologist both administering quickie evaluations. The court, in fact, found these evaluations of no use, determined Cho to be imminently dangerous, and ordered him into outpatient treatment. He was set free to kill, and nobody to this day knows how Cho even made the trip from that hospital back to the Virginia Tech campus after the magistrate committed him to involuntary treatment. Even though he had been determined to be imminently dangerous, nobody in positions of authority to prevent imminent violence seemed to care. And, although *imminent* means sooner than when Cho exploded, nonetheless, such disregard for the rights of others to be alive constituted what can only be described as reckless endangerment at the time.

No one from the court, from the student counseling services, from the faculty, from the administration, from the police, or from the psychiatric hospital even bothered to call Cho's parents. His parents learned about what Cho had done the same way everyone else in the country learned about it: on the national news. Then the next night, Cho's parents were subjected to an NBC news segment, which was Cho's video manifesto. As they later told the governor's panel, if someone had simply called them or their eldest daughter, who spoke fluent English, they would have come to campus, taken their son home, refused to let him back to campus for the remainder of the semester, placed him under a doctor's care, and none of this would have happened. And, more probably than not, the standard for medical certainty, they were right. They had always been extraordinarily competent and reliable in getting his clinical needs met, despite extreme work responsibilities for both of them and their inability to speak English. It would have only taken one phone call. Where did the system fail?

In evaluating the Cho case, and cases like the Red Lake massacre and even Columbine, healthcare professionals, education professionals, and juvenile justice professionals must ask how do we

- Identify and red flag the potentially dangerous?
- Intervene in their lives early and hard to prevent violence?
- Mitigate the potential damage?
- Sequester, even involuntarily, the violent mentally ill?
- Treat the dangerous mentally ill to bring them back into meaningful lives?

There is a balancing act here between the treatment of serious mental illness and the patient's constitutional rights where the following are concerned:

- Fourth Amendment privacy
- Fourth Amendment search and seizure
- Fifth Amendment due process
- Sixth Amendment legal representation
- Eighth Amendment cruel and inhumane punishment

How does the state, usually called upon to intervene via police action, balance a patient's constitutional rights against its general police powers to provide for domestic tranquility? What kinds of policies are in place to apply the facts of any specific case to the rule of law? In Cho's case the system failed because a dangerous and violent schizophrenic patient, suffering under paranoid delusions, was set free to plan and execute his revenge upon his perceived enemies: women who didn't respond to his apparent erotomanic delusions and both students and teachers upon whom he projected his persecutory wrath.

Erotomania is a specifically defined disease, characterized most infamously by Reagan's would-be assassin John Hinckley, who stalked the actress Jodie Foster at Yale and had a fantasy relationship with her. Erotomania is the false but persistent belief that one is loved by a person, often a famous or prominent person, or the pathologically obsessive pursuit of a disinterested object of love. This was a pursuit Cho engaged in with respect to female students at Virginia Tech, one of whom he wound up shooting to death on the morning of the massacre.

Cho also projected his violence toward them as their violence toward him so as to make himself the victim. In the psychiatric community we know that projective identification is the paranoid defense mechanism that justifies one's aggression toward others. The aggression of this disease likely boils to a point where it is about to boil over, when suddenly there is a cause, in this case Cho's fantasized hero from a story he wrote in a creative writing class, an outcast called "Bud."

In this story, written a year before the massacre, Bud cannot kill. Bud cannot step over a moral line in the sand. But Cho has a solution. In his story, he manages to take Bud over the moral line in a grandiose delusion including the erotomania of a Gothic female hero accomplice. Could this Gothic heroine have been one of the VT (Virginia Tech) girls dressed in black?

In retrospect, all of this makes sense: a paranoid schizophrenic potential killer who cannot kill but who fantasizes about a kind of alter ego or avatar who can walk him across the line to where he can kill. The defensive projective identification that makes the warrior kill enemies is overcome by identification with the aggressor. Like Marlon Brando in *Apocalypse Now,* exclaiming the "horrors" in his final moments, in Cho's the horrors were imaginary. And, like Brando in *Apocalypse Now,* the horrors emanating autistically from inside Cho's mind, rather than from outside in the horrors of combat, provided him the final link—the link to Cho's grandiose delusions of the God of Brutality, carefully communicated for the whole world to watch both in real time and then later in his manifesto.

And a year later he performed the omnipotent massacre constructed in his grandiose delusions. All of this evolved before the watchful eyes of psychologists, the school counseling center, the campus police, and the judicial system, which had already flagged him as dangerous. We must find out what is missing from this picture. Is it the fault of government?

What should the state's policy be, especially in this time of depleted state and local budgets, hiring freezes all across the country, and skeletal emergency services within many local communities such as western Virginia? The mentally ill, the indigent mentally ill, and social services at the public level are all shunted aside for the more visible public services such as police and fire protection, road maintenance, and—everyone's favorite—snow removal.

To discuss the social aspects of serious mental illness, we must first ask whether there is a societal component at all. Are there aspects of modern society that are exacerbating the occurrences of mental illness? If so, is it getting worse? Some would say cynically that we are headed toward a world where everyone needs some kind of counseling. Some would even warn of a brave new world that amounts to a psychiarchy, in which people are treated on a routine basis and, ultimately, a society in which the normalcy dial is ratcheted all the way up the scale to where neurotic used to be twenty-five years ago.

Prevention of Apocalyptic Mass Murder/Suicide

In any study of the Cho case, terrorist and gang murders, Red Lake and other school shootings, and the psychosocial aspects of mass murder, some entity has to ask the basic questions:

- How to prevent it?
- Who does it?
- At what age does the state intervene?

What are the prescriptions for

- School systems at all levels
- Parents and family
- Family physicians, primary care providers
- Hospitals, emergency rooms, and urgent care clinics
- Juvenile justice system
- Criminal justice system

When we look at the timeline of the case of Cho Seung-Hui and other mass murder/suicides and campus shootings, we find that each and every aspect of prevention and each and every prescription caveat rises to the surface in that timeline as if we were shining an ultraviolet light on sensitive ink. But in the middle of that case, as Cho progressed from stage to stage, the duration of his untreated psychosis getting more dangerous with every year and the likelihood of the command voices in his head urging him to strike out getting louder and louder, we still have to ask, when do people in intervention-enabled institutions see the blinking red light for what it is? When does someone cry, "Stop," and who is supposed to listen? This, too, marks the case of Cho Seung-Hui.

In a society in which there are too many people needing too many social services that are too few to distribute and in which the crush of population for limited resources takes its toll on the individual, where do we turn? Similarly, where too many individuals need social mental health services that cannot be supplied because the system is simply overwhelmed, what does the state or local agency do? And if the Mumbai and similar cases are any indicators, where the foot soldiers of apocalyptic mass murder are recruited, like the children of Darfur and in the streets of Baghdad, Jenin, Islamabad, and Gaza City, by ruthless warlords bent only on destruction within a nihilistic but predatory world view, where is the future? Closer to home, gang leaders of the Latin Lords can command 25,000 juveniles and young adults in the Chicago–Milwaukee region from Joliet Prison, a literal Army of the Night, who own entire neighborhoods as younger generations, armed, dangerous, and well financed by drug trafficking proceeds enforce terror. Are we at the tipping point?

These are but some of the questions we raise to discuss, even if the answers are less than comfortable in today's American society.

Chapter 1

Cho Seung-Hui

The Virginia Tech Shootings

It seemed rather early for Cho Seung-Hui to be up, his roommate noticed. It was five in the morning, April 16, 2007, and there he was, leaned over his computer, typing something. What exactly was he finishing up that morning in the dim false-dawn gloaming coming up over the Virginia Tech campus in Blacksburg? It was strange that he was so intent on what he was looking at on the computer screen that early.

In his boxer shorts, Cho stood in front of his bathroom mirror, brushed his teeth, and applied acne cream to his face. Then, without a word to anyone, he got dressed and left the dormitory suite. Cho kept to himself a lot, so it was not unusual for him not to say a word. But, still, 5:30 was out of the ordinary even for Cho.

An hour and fifteen minutes later, a student saw Cho waiting outside West Ambler Johnston residence hall, where Cho had his mailbox. West Ambler was also the residence of Emily Hilscher, an undergraduate who had rebuffed Cho's advances. In Cho's mind, perhaps, he would describe his behavior toward her as soliciting her affections. Others might have described it as stalking, and Cho had been disciplined for it and remanded to the supervision of a psychologist.

The Shootings Begin

Cho was waiting outside West Ambler when Emily Hilscher arrived, dropped off there by her boyfriend just a few minutes after seven. Cho followed her to her room. He was armed. Exactly what the conversation was that the two of them had, we'll never know. All we do know is that Cho had tried to start a relationship with Emily Hilscher, but she had blown him off. Cho was angry. The noise in the room, according to the official reports on the case, aroused the dorm resident advisor, Ryan Christopher Clark, who lived next door. Ryan entered Hilscher's room at some time between 7:05 and 7:15 and found her fatally wounded and Cho in her room. Cho immediately fired a lethal round at Clark and left the dorm, swiping his entry card to leave two minutes later. Whatever psychological precipice Cho Seung-Hui had been standing on, looking into the abyss of his own self-destruction, by the time he left Hilscher's dorm, he had already jumped. What was to come next would only be the denouement of his own life.

Back in his own dorm suite by at least 7:20, Cho changed out of his bloody clothes and sat down at his computer to check e-mail. The university e-mail logs show that Cho was online at 7:25, by which time the Virginia Tech Police Department had been notified, presumably by a resident living near Hilscher's room, that someone in her room had probably fallen out of bed because the noise was evident even down the hall. The emergency dispatcher called in the report to the Virginia Tech ambulance squad and also sent a police officer to accompany the squad, which, the governor's report says, was a standard university public safety procedure.

It took only three minutes for the emergency unit, accompanied by the security officer, to arrive at Hilscher's room, where they found Hilscher and Clark, both of whom had suffered lethal gunshot wounds. At approximately the same time, 7:25 a.m., Cho was back in his room, erasing his e-mail messages and canceling his account. Whatever he had already uploaded, the overnight package he was about to send to NBC news and the acts he was planning to perform would be his final statements, even though his package to NBC would arrive a day after his actions would become known across the nation.

By 7:30 that morning, the Virginia Tech Police Department had opened up a full crime scene investigation. Detectives began examining evidence and interviewing residents on the floor, asking them whether they had seen anyone leaving Hilscher's room after they heard the noises. This was a fresh crime, and the detectives believed that the unknown shooter probably knew his way around campus and was probably someone that the female victim knew. This was not, they theorized, a stranger homicide.

Even before eight that morning, police suspicions that the assailant knew his victim were strengthened when Hilscher's girlfriend showed up at the dorm to walk Hilscher to her chem class. The girlfriend told detectives that on Monday mornings, Hilscher's boyfriend, a gun enthusiast who owned weapons, usually dropped her off at the dorm. The police, working on the assumption that the killer and his victim had some relationship, now had a possible suspect, or at least a "person of interest" in the case. It was time to talk to the boyfriend.

Just before eight, when the day's classes on campus were scheduled to begin, the Virginia Tech police chief arrived at the crime scene for an assessment of the crime and an update on what the police had found. He then called the Blacksburg police department and requested that an evidence technician be dispatched to the crime scene so that the now-combined crime scene investigation team could conduct a full-scale forensic analysis. The police had decided to pick up Hilscher's boyfriend, who had possibly returned to nearby Radford University. Meanwhile, because of the magnitude of the crime, the police committee at Virginia Tech and the chief had already notified the Virginia State Police, who officially joined in the investigation.

For approximately an hour and a half, while classes at Virginia Tech were still in session, police set up a search pattern for Hilscher's boyfriend. They checked parking lots on campus for his car, went to his apartment, and, in coordination with the Montgomery County Sheriff's Office, which had joined the investigation along with the state police and the Blacksburg police, put out an all-points bulletin to be on the lookout for their possible prime suspect in the double murders. At the same time, word had begun to spread in the community about the double homicide, a killer possibly at large, and, in response to the police bulletin, the Blacksburg public schools were closed.

There had been a double homicide on campus, and that meant that the administration's emergency protocols would come into play. That morning, while Cho was still carrying out his plan, the campus emergency committee at Virginia Tech met to come up with a plan to announce the double murder in the dorm to the students. Hilscher's boyfriend was still on the loose. And Cho Seung-Hui was at the Blacksburg post office mailing a package to NBC news that would contain not only his confession but his manifesto of rage against the world and his vow to exact revenge, along with videos demonstrating the rage his manifesto described. It would become one of the most infamous mass murder confessions to date. And while Cho was mailing his package, classes began at Norris Hall, the place where Cho would massacre 29 more innocents, few if any of whom even knew who he was.

Norris Hall

Ten minutes after Cho mailed his package—and even as the Blacksburg police emergency response team units were staged in the event that they had to arrest Hilscher's boyfriend, considered armed and dangerous—Cho himself showed up at Norris Hall, the engineering building. He was spotted entering the building at 9:15. Once inside, Cho methodically chained the three main entrance doors from the inside so that no escape would be possible. It was approximately 9:30, and classes were in full session inside the building.

Not far away from where Cho was barricading himself inside Norris Hall, a Montgomery County deputy sheriff, on the lookout for Hilscher's boyfriend, identified his pickup and pulled it over. Very quickly, in response to the deputy's call into dispatch, detectives arrived at the traffic stop to begin their preliminary questioning of the suspect. Within five minutes, a Virginia State Police trooper arrived to help detectives with the questioning.

The trooper performed a gunpowder residue test on Hilscher's boyfriend to see whether burnt powder from the discharge of a weapon remained on the suspect's hands. Unless a person is wearing some kind of protective covering, gunpowder residue from the explosion of the cap inside the nozzle of the gun will drift back over the shooter's hand and adhere to the skin. The failure of the gunpowder residue test, though it did not completely exonerate Hilscher's boyfriend, meant that they could not show that he had fired a weapon before he had a chance to wash his hands.

If the police had been confident that they had located their prime suspect in a traffic stop, their confidence would soon turn to horror as Cho systematically completed his barricades at Norris Hall and made his way along the corridor to room 206, where an engineering class was in session. Professor Loganathan, teaching a graduate course in advanced hydrology, was lecturing when Cho entered the room and began shooting. Professor Loganathan was one of the first to fall to the ground, fatally shot. Cho then killed nine students and wounded three more, leaving only one of the thirteen students in the class unscathed.

The shooting began at approximately 9:40 a.m. and continued right into the classroom 207, across the hall, an elementary German section taught by Christopher James. Cho burst in the classroom, evidently startling the class, and shot James immediately. Then he picked off students in the first row and worked his way back to the door, shooting students still in their seats. It took him only minutes to get back into the corridor where he crossed the hall again to get the next classroom, 205.

When gunshots first echoed through the corridor, students in 205 heard them and, perhaps remembering the shootings at other schools, like Columbine, had the presence of mind to barricade the classroom door. It saved their lives, because even though a frenzied Cho fired into the classroom through the door, no one was hurt in room 205, and Cho moved on.

His next target was room 211, where a French class was in session. However, the students there, just like the students in 205, had also heard gunshots and followed their instructor's advice to jam a desk against the door. The instructor, Jocelyne Couture-Nowak, also asked one of her students to call 911 on her cell phone, which rang through to the Blacksburg Police dispatch.

Cho, however, was already throwing himself against the door, forcing it open just enough for him to force his way through it. Once inside, Cho made his way up and down the rows firing at students. He hit Colin Goddard, who had made the cell phone call to the police, in the leg. As Goddard fell, the phone also fell to the floor, where it was picked up by student Emily Haas, who stayed on the phone with the emergency dispatch, imploring them to get to the scene as quickly as possible. Gunshots rang out in the background.

Cho turned toward the voice of the student on the phone. He aimed at Haas and fired, but, fortunately for her, his round missed and only grazed her. Wisely, Haas, played dead, but left the cell phone connection open while keeping it under her head. Cho looked around at what he thought were his dead victims and then moved out of the room. Haas was one of three students who survived by not moving as Cho passed them.

Goddard's 911 call was picked up by a dispatcher in the Blacksburg police department, who, when she heard Haas say that the shooting was taking place in Norris Hall on the Virginia Tech campus, immediately transferred the information to the Virginia Tech police. They responded within three minutes. However, when the officers from the Virginia Tech Police Department arrived at Norris Hall, they found the entrance doors locked. They could actually hear shots being fired. And at first, they took cover because they thought someone was shooting at them. But when they realized the shots were coming from inside the building, they tried to find a way to open the doors, even by firing their own weapons at the locks to shatter them open. But their attempts failed. Meanwhile, Cho kept on methodically making his way from room to room, pushing himself against the barricaded doors and, even when students on the other side pushed back to deny him entrance, he fired through the opening.

As the sound of gunshots echoed out across the campus, people were able to see police rushing toward Norris Hall to answer the Virginia Tech Police emergency call. Cho, however, undeterred by the students trying to block the classroom doors, went back to room 211, broke into it again, and went up and down the aisle firing at any student who was still moving. He shot Goddard, the student who placed the initial 911 call, two more times before going back out into the hallway, where he reloaded his weapon and did not look to see a school janitor fleeing down the stairway.

His weapon reloaded, Cho turned his attention to Professor Liviu Librescu's Mechanics class in room 204. The sound of gunshots had preceded Cho, of course, and Librescu, a Romanian and a survivor of the Holocaust, knew exactly what to do to protect his class. He ordered his students to open the windows and jump down to the ground. While Cho hurled himself against the door to enter, Librescu threw his own body against the door as a barricade. While bracing against the door, Librescu saw his students hang from the ledge so they could land in the soft grass below. Librescu knew that by using his own body as a human shield his students would be saved even if these were his final moments. He had survived the death camps but would die in his classroom.

Cho was now relentless, playing out in reality the psychodrama he had played out in his darkest fantasies hundreds of times before. As he pressed his weight against the unyielding door, Cho began firing through it, ultimately hitting Professor Librescu a number of times. After the faculty member dropped to the floor, Cho smashed through the door and fired at the two students waiting by the windows to jump. He hit both of them. Then he tuned his attention back to room 206, reentered it, and shot even more students.

It took only ten minutes for Cho to rampage through the second floor. At 9:50, he heard the sound of a police shotgun. A team from one of the emergency response units had found the fourth entry to the building, an entry that led into a machine shop. The police blasted through the regular key lock with the shotgun and made their way into the building, where they heard gunshots from the floor above.

When they reached the second floor, the first police unit saw the devastation that the shooter had wreaked. They began immediately to assist the wounded students, while they followed the trail of blood. Then they heard another shot. What they did not know was that Cho, hearing the sound of the shotgun from the floor below, realized that the police had finally gained entry to the building. And in a final act of grandiose defiance, Cho turned the weapon on himself and shot himself in the head. He would not be taken alive.

It took only another minute for the Blacksburg police and Virginia Tech emergency response teams to converge on Norris Hall en masse, each team accompanied by a paramedic. And with the shooting now stopped, the teams swept the hall with the paramedics attending to the wounded students and the police facilitating the rescue of students trapped by the gunfire or still hiding in rooms. They would find that during his ten- to eleven-minute shooting spree, Cho had killed thirty people and wounded seventeen. He also killed himself, bringing the body count to thirty-one.

With Cho dead and with two crime scenes, crime scene investigators, police, and emergency response personnel at Norris Hall continued to help the survivors, provide immediate first aid to the wounded so that they could be transported safely to the hospitals, and identify the fatalities, including Cho himself. Back at Hilscher's dormitory, another group of investigators searched for evidence and tried to locate more witnesses. Also at this point, neither team of investigators could be sure that there were no additional gunmen still lurking out there, either on campus or in Blacksburg. But, even as they searched for additional shooters, hanging over the heads of both emergency response teams was still the question of "why"—what made the shooter go on such a rampage, how did he choose his victims, and what were the causes of this unspeakable tragedy?

Finally, at 10:08 a.m., the investigators and emergency personnel searching room 211 at Norris Hall discovered Cho, dead from what they assumed to be a self-inflicted gunshot wound to the head. Lying in a pile of his victims with a pair of weapons next to him, Cho carried no identification. The fact that the gunshot wound seemed to be self-inflicted was the only clue at first that the police had to enable them to begin figuring out that he was the shooter.

As the news about the mass shooting and the high body count spread across the news wire services and the Internet, virally burning its way across the country during the morning hours, the magnitude of what had happened and the true horror of the event cast a pall over the country. The news networks set up cameras and live feeds on the campus as the police still tried to wrap up the case, searching for more clues and even other conspirators. Was this another Columbine High School shooting or did the shooter, now identified as Cho Seung-Hui, act completely alone? Were the occasional gunshot-like sounds heard on campus through the morning only engine backfires or was somebody else firing a weapon? Virginia Tech police investigated these and found that they were not the sounds of gunfire.

Finally, near the end of the workday, just a little after four in the afternoon, President George Bush went on national television to announce the news of the shootings to the nation, to mark the historic tragedy, to offer solace and condolences to the victims and their families, and to lead the nation in mourning for the dead. The fact that the president of the United States himself had to weigh in on that afternoon's events only reinforced the magnitude of the crime and the extent to which Cho Seung-Hui had captured the attention of an entire nation. But for those people who thought that with Cho's death the horror of the events would simply begin to fade away on the following day, they were sadly mistaken, because the killer's voice would resonate from the grave only two days later.

The Manifesto

On April 18, 2007, NBC announced that it had received a package from Cho Seung-Hui that contained his manifesto and his video confessing to the killings and setting forth, in his own words and images, his fury at the world. As NBC News anchorman Brian Williams explained to the television audience, the network had agonized over whether to air this video, whether to bring to the victims and their families the face of the person who had killed and wounded their loved ones, and whether to reignite the feelings of helplessness, sorrow, and desolation with which the victims and their families were trying to cope. But in the end, the network said, they chose to air the piece because, the sorrow notwithstanding, it was, nevertheless, newsworthy as an after-account of America's most infamous mass murder.

In this era of handheld video cameras, the Internet, and YouTube, each of us is his or her own director of photography, videographer, broadcaster, and television network of one. And in an age hungry for reality, for any version of what can be called a personal truth, anyone's self-described statement of the truth can stand. So it was that Cho's last statement, a statement made in contemplation of imminent death, was a riveting apocalyptic testament to the psychopathology that drove him to mass murder and suicide and a vivid depiction of what he was about to do, all of it for broadcast on national television.

In a way, Cho's video manifesto, albeit horrific, was vaguely reminiscent of the depiction of the future in the Paddy Chayefsky motion picture, *Network*, in which a news television producer predicts that news will evolve into a horrific reality show with the perpetrators of violence setting forth their own manifestos before committing their crimes. It is as if in a world where one's own private hell can be inflicted upon an unwary public with the swiping of a credit card to purchase a gun, one's manifesto, by the simple fact of its existence, is one's self-justification for the crimes.

In the NBC broadcast of his video manifesto, Cho railed against a world that, he said, turned him into a subject of abuse and humiliation. His existence, he said, was a nightmare of victimization in a society that not only rejected and marginalized him but actually tortured him emotionally. Who was he railing against? Was it Emily Hilscher, who had rejected his advances and who was herself a target of Cho's deviant behavior? Was it Cho's parents, Korean immigrants who had sacrificed so that their daughter could attend Princeton? Cho's manifesto simply blames the world for persecuting him.

In Cho's manifesto, he represented himself as the victim. But beyond that, Cho compared himself and his actions to Jesus Christ, invoking Him as an example of someone who by His sacrifice saved those who followed Him. Who was Cho saving? Who are his children that he refers to or his brothers and sisters? Are they the ones whom Cho believed were or will be similarly persecuted? Or is Cho portraying himself as a Jesus figure out of delusions of grandiose omnipotence, a vision of himself so distorted that there actually is no reality that breaks through the veneer that Cho created for himself—that empty face masked by sunglasses and a ball cap.

Equally telling, law enforcement analysts who were interviewed by NBC said, was the way in which Cho began his manifesto as a mild victim of persecution and ended it with images of him dressed as a killer, the last face his victims would see. He began by explaining that had only those who had persecuted him reached out to him, none of what was about to happen would happen. He was the victim of the world, driven into a corner from which there was no escape.

And like Marlon Brando as Kurtz in *Apocalypse Now*, whose projective identification as the West Point Warrior failed amidst the horrors of atrocities in Vietnam, Cho identified with the ultimate Aggressor—a God of power seeking revenge. So by the end of the video, Cho, wielding handguns and posing with a hammer about to strike, had become the avenger, wreaking upon society what society itself had asked for. It was his message of rage—rambling and disjointed but evidencing the deviant logic of a disintegrated narcissism in which the killer bears no blame because he is really the victim. It is his victims who must bear the blame not just for what they did to him but for what they did not do, which was to care for him perpetually in the manner the omnipotent narcissistic self demands.

To comprehend Cho's logic would in itself be illogical. The world is a stage, and Cho, the ultimate madman, as his video demonstrates, was even more chilling than the Internet postings of Kliebold and Harris in their run up to the Columbine massacre. It revealed, in its gradual escalation from victim to avenger, while still portraying the avenger as a victim, a deeper and more disturbing pathology.

Though only a few years older than Kiebold and Harris, Cho's portrayal of himself, from meek to violently manic, showed how he had escalated his ideations of violence, working himself up like a restless volcano to a full explosion right on the camera that he was using. Of significance was Cho's expressed interest in these apocalyptic suicide mass murderers during childhood.

The video showed, in almost a time-fractal representation, Cho's evolution from the imagined victim of persecution to avenger, always omnipotently filtering every piece of empirical data through a prism of a fractured self. Only through his own damaged defensive projection onto "the others" could he perceive his boiling rage and reconstitute it with an omnipotent identification with the Aggressor about to shock the whole world. This was a horrific identity, fully displayed on video for a national television audience. It was an exercise in fury, to be sure—a manifesto of sorts—but also a kind of insane psychodrama, not unlike the psychological calling cards left by the creation of crime scenes by serial killers or other episodic offenders. In this case, Cho was apocalyptic in his self-destruction and destruction of others in a single act of spree/mass murder.

In the case of a serial killer, the psychodrama is represented secretively in the creation of the crime scene for police to discover and interpret. The serial killer reenacts his psychodrama in episodes as he works out his homicidal pathology on each victim. In the case of the apocalyptic mass killer, it is the killer who is the ultimate victim, taking those he hates with him in an explosion of public violence, which is also his revenge against the society that drove him to suicide.

Because Cho-as-victim perceived himself as ultimately powerless, at the core of his self, there was no self there. He exercised at first a form of passive control by using his victim personality and weakness to exert control. After defining himself as a victim, he cast the blame on those who made him the victim. This is the projective identification justifying violent rage of paranoia. But this projective identification failed, as it did for the ultimate warrior, Marlon Brando in *Apocalypse Now*, incapable of adapting to the horrors of atrocities. And, as in *Apocalypse Now*, Cho, through his own distorted logic, was justified to ascend over his own perceived horrors with omnipotent brutality seldom seen by the world in real time.

Although his actions were horrific, they were still, within context of his psychotic state of mind, defensive. He was no longer a mortal suffering the horrors of extinction of his own self. He was transcendent in this final apocalyptic act of suicide/mass murder with a god-like brutality few had ever witnessed on such a scale. Displaying his psyche on video, Cho demonstrated dramatic conversion from passive and brutally intolerable victimization of his tormented self-image to the omnipotent one, avenging by wielding his hammer of Thor against those whom he perceived were his abusers. He wielded this hammer not just for himself, he raged on camera, but for all those who, like him, had become the victims of a hostile world.

He was not just defending himself, he was avenging others, giving himself his own justification for acts of incredible violence perpetrated upon people who did not even know him. It did not matter, however, because he was the Christ figure who must suffer for the abuses of others and the victimization of others. And, for the rational mind, he showed the most feared peak of insanity, because, unlike Marlon Brando's character's conversion to the God of all Brutality in the face of overwhelming external "horrors," Cho's were all generated from within. If Brando's was the dramatization of posttraumatic wounding of the self, Cho's was that of insanity and the ravages to the self of schizophrenic illness.

For the national television audience and the very perplexed NBC news anchor Brian Williams, Cho was as mysterious as he was violent. But for professionals in the mental health and psychiatric communities, Cho was of a type, a point on a continuum of violence and potential violence, who turns up in local justice and community public heath systems all across the country. The world hears about a

Cho type when that person—usually a male, although women, like Laurie Dann in Winnetka, Illinois, and Susan Secrest in King of Prussia, Pennsylvania, could certainly fall into this category—breaks the surface tension of the news media and commits a horrendous crime.

We are inured, by now, to the stories of workplace shootings, including the recent shooting in Silicon Valley, postal workers who go on killing rampages, violent young adults who are recruited into gangs or into terrorist organizations, but what most people do not know is that a Cho type with a potential for dangerousness or some form of aggressive antisocial behavior exists all along a continuum that ranges from forms of brooding passivity to unexpected eruptions of violence.

What is this continuum? Where is it located among the vast research of psychological disorders? How is it identified? What can we do about it? And, just as a starting point, who was Cho Seung-Hui?

Chapter 2

Who Was Cho Seung-Hui?*

The most commonly detected childhood behavioral abnormalities of patients with chronic psychosis include

1. Speech and language problems
2. Poor coordination
3. Poorer academic achievement
4. Poorer social functioning and fewer friends
5. Delayed developmental milestones

Of significance, all these were observed by astute and trained observers of Cho throughout his entire life. Some children have all these factors and are never psychotic and some who are psychotic have none. But most chronically psychotic patients have at least some of them. We will see the evolution of actual signs of Cho's chronic psychosis, his prodrome of adult schizophrenia, or at least risk factors noted to be red flags of evolving serious mental illness documented by the state investigative commission.

After the smoke had cleared from the Blacksburg campus of Virginia Tech, and the investigation of Emily Hilscher's boyfriend had been concluded, the primary suspect was the lone gunman identified as Cho Seung-Hui, the Korean American student who had largely kept to himself except for his fascination with Emily Hilscher, his first shooting victim and a young woman he had previously stalked. When Cho's video had been aired on television, however, and he became a postmortem national representative of homicidal rage and suicide. Much as with

* Unless otherwise noted, all citations of fact with respect to Cho's childhood are quoted directly from the Virginia Governor's Panel Report.

Kliebold and Harris, people wanted to know, first, who Cho Seung-Hui was, and, next, why he had done this. With the exception of grief over the victims, everything else was secondary to the "who and the why" of such senseless violence on such mass scale. The how, Cho explained in his video, but the why, even though a part of his video manifesto, was still not enough to answer the questions.

Within days after the mass homicide and the release of the Cho video, records began to leak out to the news organizations that had already descended upon the Virginia Tech campus. At first, the various offices that kept relevant records about Virginia Tech students and their problems, including campus security, were overwhelmed. They were overwhelmed not just by the amount of requests and the speed at which they came in but by legal issues that immediately arose. Were there privacy issues? What was campus and public policy with respect to such records, including medical records? Would the release of records violate any state policy? And, not the least, how much liability would the university incur by the release of potentially damaging records? Would it show a degree of negligence in its handling of what might have been a potentially dangerous individual to others as well as himself? Nevertheless, records slowly began dribbling out from various offices until a rough composite picture emerged of a very troubled young man who was on what seemed like an inevitable, catastrophic collision with destiny.

Cho's Childhood

Early records of Cho Seung-Hui describe him as weak and sickly, reluctant to be touched, and withdrawn. His family lived in Korea, where, according to the official governor's report of the shooting, Cho's paternal uncle committed suicide and Cho himself suffered from a heart murmur, discovered, at nine months of age, when he entered a hospital in Korea for treatment of whooping cough that turned into pneumonia. When he was three, he was again admitted to the Korean hospital, this time for an echocardiogram, which, according to the medical reports, so traumatized him that he no longer wanted to be touched by anyone, withdrew into himself, cried a lot, and was constantly sick.

For the next six years, Cho was very introverted and shy, personality attributes, the official report noted, that are appreciated as abnormal in Korea, just as in America. However, when the Cho family moved to the United States in 1992, Cho Seung-Hui's personality issues changed for the worse. All of Cho's personality changes upon being released from the hospital, even though they might have been attributes in the Korean community, meet the criteria of early vulnerability to schizophrenia. This means that most patients who break—for example, develop schizophrenia—as did Cho—have one or more of these changes.

However, some who break have none, whereas some who have all of these personality changes are never diagnosed with schizophrenia. Most likely, those children having nearly all these early personality changes, as did Cho—with the apparent exception of physical awkwardness, leading to nonparticipation in sports—are at high risk.

Thus, Cho was at leasr at high risk, if not in the 2 percent epidemiological category of actually having childhood-onset schizophrenia. In retrospect, it is highly possible that Cho was psychotic before his admission to Virginia Tech, but this presentation in children is more difficult to diagnose than during adulthood. One would expect a child psychiatrist to pick it up. However, because the family was Korean, speaking no English, the patient could not express anything—like hearing voices or delusional thinking—and the South American foreign medical graduate child psychiatrist, interning at George Washington, may not have been familiar with childhood schizophrenia as it presented transculturally in recently immigrant Korean American families.

At home in the United States, the family spoke only Korean. His parents worked in a laundry, hard labor demanding that both mother and father work outside the home. The family struggled hard to make ends meet, a struggle all the more difficult because the father, in a success-driven culture, was simply not succeeding. The Chos were not considered lower socioeconomic in Korea. Cho's older sister managed to integrate well with the school system, but Cho himself did not. As withdrawn as he was in Korea, he became even more so in the United States. He was sickly and shy and had become the butt of jokes in school because, in addition to his inability to socialize, he simply could not speak English the way the other children did. This must have been a major environmental stressor for Cho, at least in part, an associated causative factor in his psychosis. Certainly it was for his duration of untreated psychosis (DUP), known to be a major factor for severity of ultimate disease. It was extreme in case of Cho, although reliable sources deny any traumatic discrimination beyond the expectable for Asian immigrants. Although the choice of medications was not wrong and seemed to help at that time, paroxetine is contraindicated in children at risk for psychosis. Had he been treated early on with antipsychotic medications, such as Risperdal® or Abilify®, the course of the illness could have been dramatically different. All of this is conjecture, given clarity of retrospective evolution of the natural history of his disease.

Statistically, Cho had a 25 percent chance of recovery at the time of his hospitalization as a young adult. But, he likely would have had a far higher chance of recovery or significant reduction in impairment were he to have been treated for psychosis when presenting selectively mute in childhood. In retrospect, most child psychiatrists would now agree that the diagnosis of selective mutism was a minimization of his obviously evolving schizophrenic prodrome or childhood schizophrenia.

By the time he was nine, Seung-Hui had developed at least one friendship with a neighborhood child in Virginia. The family had moved there, likely upwardly mobile, after living in Maryland. Cho seemed to be coming out of his shell after the family moved to Virginia. He was taking Tae Kwon Do lessons, playing nonviolent video games, listening to music, and taking an interest in baseball and basketball. In other words, except for one worrisome problem of selective mutism for which he was being treated, Cho seemed to be turning into a typical American kid. But, that worrisome problem would turn out to be a major problem over the next four years. Cho evidenced ideations of suicide and was demonstrating the other childhood risk factors known to be associated with adult-onset schizophrenia.

Cho's mother told investigators that as her son grew older, he became more noncommunicative, avoiding eye contact with his parents and retreating into a silence that unnerved his mother. She reported to the investigatory panel that sometimes she would become so frustrated that she would shake him to get him to respond. One has to wonder, was he hallucinating? It was not documented whether anyone ever asked him.

It was determined that he was not autistic, but childhood schizophrenia was never specifically entertained, according to reports of his child psychiatry treatment history. And, being true to medical differential diagnostics, one cannot diagnose selective mutism without specifically ruling out childhood-onset schizophrenia. The child psychiatrist intern at George Washington University who saw him would likely agree, although he may recall intuitively ruling out schizophrenia during Cho's childhood without clearly documenting his decision making in reports made available to those working with the child.

When visitors came to the Cho residence, the report continued, Cho would become so nervous when called upon to speak that he would become sweaty and pale and even start to cry. When asked questions, rather than speak, he would simply nod or shake his head. His father, according to reports, even though he, too, was a quiet person, saw Cho's refusal to speak as a sign of disrespect and often scolded him for it. But that only made Cho retreat further.

In elementary school, the report says, Cho was sometimes the victim of taunts from other students, who would also make fun of him. He would not complain about it though, perhaps confiding only in his older sister, and only answered "okay" to questions about his days at school or simply responded nonverbally. His family, according to his sister in the official report, tried to be supportive and reassuring, but Cho seemed to reject all attempts to get close to him and treated himself as if he were an outsider in the family. But there was only so much his family could do, because both of his parents were struggling financially from the time they came to the United States. They had less time for Cho, because they were both working long hours. And they were not fluent in English.

Had it not been for his sister, Sun, who communicated with him and was a kind of link to the rest of the world, Cho might have had an acute psychotic break much earlier in life. The transcultural psychiatric issues emerge in the content of his delusions and presentation in his video manifesto to NBC news. Was there something in the Korean culture that is evident in Cho's ultimate presentation on TV? This is a proud, aggressive, and competitive culture, evidenced by the fear they instilled in their North Vietnamese enemies during the war. Everyone in Vietnam wanted to be near the Republic of Korea Tiger Division defending Nha Trang because the Viet Cong were absolutely terrified of them. And his native land is one still in a smoldering war—if not a totally hot war—with a Communist North Korean neighbor that is terrifying the entire world. Military service would have been compulsory for Cho had he either stayed in Korea or returned.

From his first years in elementary school in Virginia, Cho's teachers were concerned that, even though he was in an English-as-a-second-language program—limiting his ability to interact with native English-speaking students—Cho was largely uncommunicative to the point where he was almost completely unsocial. He did not play with other students during recess. His elementary school teacher was concerned about a child who would only nod or grunt rather than engage in any playtime or projects with other students. Simply stated, Cho had no friends and made no moves to associate himself with any of his classmates. These are two of the major known childhood antecedents of schizophrenia.

Cho's Problems Worsen

Subsequent to his early years in elementary school, Cho's problems caused increasing concern on the part of his teachers. His teachers soon came to the belief that Cho's inability to communicate was more an unwillingness to communicate and that this was an emotional rather than a language barrier and, thus, far more ominous than they could have possibly imagined. The problem worsened to the point where Cho would not even respond to teachers' questions and became unresponsive in class. This severe introversion, in retrospect, was likely childhood-onset schizophrenia, requiring antipsychotic medication to enable Cho to associate with reality and leave his shell. As the problem refused to go away, the school guidance personnel urged Mrs. Cho to seek out some kind of community for her son within which he could make friends and be drawn out. But Mrs. Cho's attempts to integrate Seung-Hui into a church group failed, and she finally gave up and let him be the person she believed he apparently wanted to be. Sometimes, just leaving a child alone to cope is a serious misstep, as it might have been with Cho.

The Middle School Years

When Cho reached middle school, Mr. and Mrs. Cho decided to follow up on one of the recommendations from his elementary school and sought psychological counseling for their son. However, if counseling of this nature is to succeed for a child Cho's age, there usually has to be active parental support. In this instance, though, the Cho family might have agreed to take their son to counseling, but in Korean culture, especially for a Korean family that had been in the United States for only about five years, the social stigma of having a child in mental health counseling was very great. It may have run counter to the Chos' belief system that a member of their family suffered from any kind of mental condition. Therefore, whatever positive benefits Cho Seung-Hui might have gained from his counseling sessions, the family's embarrassment of their son's need for counseling might have been counterproductive. Throughout his later years, too, the governor's panel reported, the Chos decided to let Seung-Hui be what he was, not knowing that the underlying causes of his inability to communicate might be an incipient and dangerous psychotic illness.

The governor's report states that, after initial difficulties in therapy, Cho seemed to respond to art therapy and clay modeling sessions. In particular, it states, Cho's therapist noticed that he would fashion clay houses that had no windows or doors. Did these houses reflect Cho's world as he saw it? Was he locked in? When the counselor questioned Cho about the windowless houses, she noticed that Cho reacted emotionally. And slowly he began to make eye contact. His psychiatrist said that Cho suffered from a personal anxiety disorder, partly the result of becoming acculturated to American society as well as the trauma caused by treatment of Cho's early medical problems. Although his IQ was above normal, Cho was diagnosed as being immature for his real age. He acted and behaved as if he were a younger child.

In reality, Cho was evidencing symptoms of a severe mental illness. Cho was behaving like prodromal patients ultimately diagnosed with schizophrenia and even, perhaps, actual childhood-onset schizophrenia. Had he been intensively worked up by child psychiatry and child psychology specialists with a bilingual clinical social worker, who could obtain a valid childhood history, then intensively treated in child psychiatry, Cho's family would have become aware of the seriousness of his illness and, by history, accepted it. However, his untreated schizophrenia or prodrome was allowed to fester.

When he reached the eighth grade, Cho seemed to withdraw even further into himself. At the same time, his drawings changed, and he began depicting tunnels and caves in his artwork. Cho's therapist saw these as indicators of suicidal ideations, an extremely ominous red flag in child psychiatry, and got Cho to contract with her that he would verbalize any ideations of suicide to his parents or to his therapist. Similarly, she asked him that if he had any urgings to strike out at fellow students at school or to hurt himself, he would take no action outside of telling her about them. And then, about a month later, the entire nation was stunned into a state of absolute shock by the Columbine murders and suicides perpetrated by Kliebold and Harris, the news of which would have a profound effect on an evolving fragmentation of childhood identity deep inside Cho.

The Columbine murders dominated the news as they played themselves out on television. The images of emergency vehicles lined up at the high school, of deputies standing helplessly by as they waited for the emergency response and special weapons teams to deploy, and the images of students, hands in the air, as they were led out of the building by law enforcement personnel while anxious parents waited for their children outside a police perimeter. For children in Cho's situation, children who felt isolated and without any ability to exercise any control over their lives, might the images from Columbine have shown them an alternate reality, an exit from the daily internal terror of being unable to adapt at school?

They certainly did for Cho Seung-Hui, who wrote a paper embracing suicide and saying that he wanted to "repeat Columbine." This was a red flag that Cho's English teacher immediately brought to his parents' attention. His essay was a cause for concern, especially because even though the Chos admitted that their son had had ideas about suicide, this paper was the first time he had ever alluded to homicide. Thus, Mr. and Mrs. Cho were put on notice.

Cho's English teacher and his therapist urged Mr. and Mrs. Cho to contact a psychiatric facility to have their son evaluated. According to the governor's report, Cho was evaluated by a child psychiatrist who diagnosed him with "selective mutism," an inability to speak when speech was expected of him, and "major depression: single episode." Mutism is more than simple shyness. It is accompanied by an almost clinical shyness and an "obsessive fear" to listen to the patient's own voice. Therefore, it goes well beyond just a personality quirk of shyness and reticence; it is, even at its mildest, manifest of severe childhood anxiety that is well beyond the norm for adjustment problems of immigrant children from any country. And the depression that the psychiatrist diagnosed was serious because it presented over long periods and was accompanied by suicidal ideation, requiring his therapist to make a suicide contract with him! It is not clear why more aggressive steps were not taken when threats of violence and suicide became so eminent and externally visible in art therapy. Certainly, in retrospect, based on his presentation and ensuing history, emergency hospitalization for serious childhood psychiatric illness was justifiable and likely available, regardless of financial means. When he was in middle school, therefore, Cho was likely suffering from childhood-onset schizophrenia—or at least the prodromes of adult schizophrenia, requiring professional aggressive psychiatric treatment.

Cho's child psychiatrist prescribed an antidepressant for him called paroxetine (Paxil), which Cho stayed on for thirteen months. During this period, Cho's life seemed to brighten. His depressive moods were less severe, he seemed to be more communicative, and his glowering demeanor even broke into smiles. Such a therapeutic response to antidepressant medication is reported in the prodromes of schizophrenia, but psychiatrists will always wonder how Cho would have then responded to an antipsychotic medication such as risperidone or aripiprazole.

Following this brief course of psychopharmacotherapy on paroxetine, Cho's communication skills continued to deteriorate, especially after he entered high school. The issue of medicating children this young, even adolescents, however, is highly controversial and relatively new as best practice in child psychiatry. Most medications known to be effective and safe for adults must be prescribed off-label for children for lack of a solid research base. Ironically, the very drug that helped Cho was the signature for extreme caution in medicating children. It was discovered in a study that four percent of children treated with paroxetine (Paxil) expressed suicidal ideation. Although he was one of those likely at most risk, it did not for him (Aursnes, Tuete, Gaasemyr, and Natvig, 2005). In fact, it brightened his mood and seemed to improve his behavior.

High School

It was in Westfield High School that a teacher reported Cho's problems to guidance personnel. He barely spoke in class; was very shy, "shut down," and withdrawn; and even when he spoke, his speech was barely audible. This was clearly a student with severe problems, the teacher would advise the guidance department. These were no longer signs of antecedents to schizophrenia. These were more likely manifestations of incipient childhood-onset schizophrenia. However, none of Cho's problems seemed to affect his work, which he submitted diligently to his teachers and which showed that he understood the material being taught.

In fact, despite his communication problems, Cho was a good student. When his teacher asked him whether he would like to be helped with his communication problems, he nodded yes. In other words, even though Cho was sliding toward a psychological abyss, before he reached the point of inevitability, Cho was affirmative in seeking a solution to his problem. He was, however, untruthful, according to the governor's panel, when he told his teacher that he had never before received psychological help with his problem at his previous schools. On the other hand, would Seung-Hui have even known or should he have been expected to know whether he had received psychological help? His parents, of course, would have acknowledged it, but the panel's statement implied a moralistic judgmental level to what was in reality a psychotic child who was likely very scared of everything inside him, that is, the tunnels, the terror and chaos outside the tunnels projected from his sick mind onto the clay.

Under federal law, the governor's report states, schools receiving federal funds must provide for special services for impaired students if, according to the Americans with Disabilities Act, providing those services does not impede or damage the actual educational services offered by the institution. In the case of students with some form of emotional disability, federal law requires that students be placed in the least restrictive environment and be mainstreamed if at all practical. Also, federal law requires that the subject school provide an individualized educational plan for students with mental impairments, assessing the student within various domains. Cho was evaluated in terms of underlying psychological problems, speech and language problems, sociocultural issues, hearing disabilities, vision problems, and any underlying medical/physical issues.

The school ruled out autism as a problem but did not reportedly consider childhood-onset schizophrenia. Two percent of all cases of the full-blown disease of schizophrenia develop in childhood; so, given an incidence (occurrence of new cases) of nearly 1/100 persons, this not an insignificant number. Accordingly, with Mr. and Mrs. Cho's permission, the school guidance department was put in touch with Cho's child psychiatrist, who, in turn, was very pleased that the school would now track Cho's progress.

Another problem Cho had, upon his entrance into high school, was that his elder sister, Sun, was now attending Princeton University and was no longer living at home. Cho communicated with his sister more than with any other person, and the loss of her as a member of the household presented a problem for him. Sun was also an interpreter for the family, who still had difficulty with English. She continued to serve as an interpreter while she was attending college.

In January 2001, Cho began his individualized education program, which included, but was not limited to, special therapy sessions in language. Even though Cho was not pulled out of classes for more speech therapy sessions—the mechanics of speaking were not his problem—he was granted private sessions with teachers where he could verbalize, because Cho's public speaking sessions in front of his class were sometimes met with derisive reactions from the other students in his class. This intimidation was likely not racially based, but it would be impossible to disentangle the transcultural stress on the young Cho from common taunts of children toward the mentally disabled. Cho was very sensitive to that—whether racially based or not—and, as it turned out, this probably played a role in Cho's characterization of himself as victim in his manifesto.

The individualized education plan worked to the extent that his grades improved markedly to the point where he was doing advanced placement and honors work in some of his classes. Because his English was poor, he would only whisper responses to questions in class. He could not write fluent answers on essay exams because he appeared to lack a grounding in English grammar. His manifest language problems, in retrospect, were likely more evident of increasing deterioration of his cognition than that of English as a Second Language (ESL). Although he had English language problems in high school, once Cho reached Virginia Tech years later, he would dramatically demonstrate that on paper he could be very fluent at times.

It was likely that Cho was psychotically preoccupied, presumably more in step with internal experiences, such as voices, disconnected thoughts, and emotionally driven fantasies, than with the reality of the world expected. The Virginia governor's report cites Cho's teacher's surprise at Cho's ultimate choice of an English major at Virginia Tech because Cho excelled in science and math but not at all in English.

The governor's report also raises the issue of bullying that Cho might have received in high school. Although there were no official reports of bullying in Cho's records, the report cites the possibility that Cho might still have been a victim because these incidents might not have taken place within classes or in places where teachers would have seen and reported it. His sister, a reliable observer of Cho's environmental stress, minimized the bullying factor. But, it also might have taken place online in either MySpace or Facebook. These are common forums where bullying and intimidation do take place, as attested to by a recent case in which a teenager subjected to bullying by other teens and an adult online committed suicide. This is not to say that the primary cause of Cho's downward spiral was caused by his sister's leaving the home.

The governor's panel report makes it clear that Sun, because she acted as the family interpreter and could always communicate with her younger brother, might have minimized Cho's isolation to an extent. However, Cho's illness was not the result of that, even though it could have been exacerbated by transcultural issues from which she may have buffered him. In other words, Cho did not spiral down to the point of mass murder and suicide because he was a Korean in America, thrown into a suburban environment as a child. Cho's problems were a severe onset of psychosis. Though it may be true that transcultural issues played a political correctness role in Virginia Tech's treatment of Cho, concealing the need for treatment for his schizophrenia due to fear that an immigrant family might take it amiss that their son's cultural background and ethnicity resulted in his being diagnosed with a dangerous mental illness, Cho's illness far superseded any transcultural issues. In fact, given the severity of Cho's illness, he likely would have committed the murders and suicide had his name been Smith, Jones, Pellegrino, or Stein.

Though it does seem that every administration from elementary school through high school seemed to have bent over backwards to avoid even the appearance of prejudice, this may have simply made matters worse. After a year in the special education program, and as Cho reached eighteen, he decided to discontinue the therapy. He said there was nothing wrong with him, and his family said they could do nothing to keep him in the program.

Had Cho been accurately diagnosed, however, a psychiatrist might have recognized that Cho had developed anosognosia, or a loss of insight into being sick. Certainly Mr. and Mrs. Cho were in no position to recognize that, because they were not psychiatrists. Moreover, as he completed his junior and senior years, Cho achieved an academic grade point average of 3.52, putting him in the honors program. He also scored a 620 in math on his SAT, which became the basis for his admission to Virginia Tech. Virginia Tech, however, had no knowledge of Cho's special education therapy or the problems he had in school with communication and integrating with other students. Moreover, his high school grade point average, the governor's report states, was higher than it should have been because it reflected—although Virginia Tech did not know this—the special accommodations Cho received as part of his individualized education program. In other words, Cho did not compete on the same basis as the other students, because the playing field was modified for him, as was required by federal law.

Cho's high school guidance counselor was concerned that Cho had made his decision to go to Virginia Tech because it was a large campus far away from his home. The counselor suggested that his transition to college life would be harsher than if he attended a smaller school closer to home and that the mix of students at Virginia Tech might make it very difficult for him to succeed there. It would be a great challenge for him, and he would not have the family support he would have closer to home. Cho was adamant in his decision to go to Virginia Tech, however, and his parents were in no position to prevent him from doing so.

The guidance counselor had correctly predicted that Cho needed to be closer to home because, although she did not know it, Cho at the time was already presenting a DUP. Three of the major reasons for DUP are

1. Lack of family support
2. Not being in a structured work environment
3. Denial of illness

Cho, by saying he did not need therapy, denied his illness; his family declared that they could not force him to continue therapy, and leaving his home meant that he would no longer be in a structured work environment. Hence, he fit the profile for DUP exactly and went off to college in Blacksburg, quite literally, a ticking time bomb.

What did the guidance counselor see and know? Was she able to see that Cho was psychotic? She probably saw that Cho was living in a private world and rapidly deteriorating. Thus, living away from home in a relatively unstructured environment would likely be harmful to him and to others. And, she proved to be right in her prediction, although likely as shocked—yet not as surprised—as the rest of us. We can understand, though, that their son's admission to Virginia Tech was a source of pride for the Chos, because having a daughter at Princeton and a son at Virginia Tech was a great measure of success to the family. It was alleged that they had immigrated to the United States for educational, rather than economic, reasons. Thus, the sacrifices and risks taken were bearing the fruit for which they had wished so much for their children in Korea.

College

Entrance to Virginia Tech would become a watershed event for Cho Seung-Hui. He had never been away from his parents and was going to a large institution where he had no family or friends. He would be in an environment where he knew no one. Worse, Cho would no longer be in counseling or have any access to a psychiatrist who had knowledge of him. Cho would be on his own, with no safety net around him for the very first time in his life. He would be in the very situation guaranteeing his excessively long and malignant DUP.

By the time Cho reached Virginia Tech, he was simply unnoticed, processed into the system, and left untreated. Cho's admission to Virginia Tech was all the more problematic because the student records form, the permanent record of all of Cho's elementary, middle, and high school performance and activity, included only a notation in the special services section citing that Cho had been in an ESL program. It did not note any of Cho's special education records, any reference to his individualized education program, or any reference to his special counseling and therapy. Thus, critical records that would have alerted any student health services officer to Cho's special needs and problems prior to entering college were omitted from Cho's permanent record.

The university probably could have obtained the relevant records, but absent any red flag notation, Cho's, amidst the thousands of student records Virginia Tech was processing, would not have stood out. Moreover, it would be politically incorrect for the university to intrude into the past of an Asian student just on the basis of his ESL notation. Some would have called that racist, even though it might have prevented the disaster that would overtake Cho and the university four years later.

In effect, as a person who had manifested recurrent ideation of suicide and mass homicide, Cho was a potential menace, entering a large institution that was unaware of any problems he had had. With good cause, panel members conducting the investigation for the governor's report were clearly surprised at the lack of communication and linkage blindness among institutions that Cho had attended.

When they investigated this, they found that the Americans with Disabilities Act prevents universities from making any pre-admission inquiries about a person's disabilities as one of the prerequisites for admission. However, had Cho requested any accommodation based on his disability, then—and only then—would the university have had the authority to obtain, on a completely confidential basis, records of Cho's disability, including any and all records of his psychiatric treatment and special counseling. Because Cho made no such request for accommodation, those records, under federal law, were unavailable to the university.

In this way, the specific prohibitions of the Americans with Disabilities Act provided a kind of cloaking device for someone with ideations of suicide and mass murder—someone who had professed admiration for the acts that Kliebold and Harris perpetrated at Columbine High School—to enter a large university campus, where he took up residence as a student, completely invisible to the institution he would later victimize.

Given Cho's problems and the lack of a safety net around him, it was remarkable that Cho not only did not crash during his freshman year at Virginia Tech but actually succeeded in getting his room assignment changed in his dorm when he found himself with a roommate whose personal hygiene offended him. Mrs. Cho urged her son to change his room, because she noticed he was unhappy as a result of his roommate's habits. There were beer cans strewn around, garbage cans overflowing, and other indications that the roommate was far less meticulous than Cho when it came to cleanliness. But Cho succeeded in speaking up for his own needs, and he was happier in his second semester. During the first half of the year, his parents visited him every Sunday to make sure he was doing okay.

In his second semester, however, the visits became less frequent, and Cho seemed to be holding his own. He spoke to his parents every Sunday evening, told them that he was getting by on the money he had, and urged them not to send him any more money. His coursework also indicated that he was succeeding during his first year. He took math and science courses, as well as business information and communications. He completed the year with a straight 3.0 grade point average.

In his sophomore year, Cho moved out of the dorm and into an apartment with a senior, who, because he worked most of the time at an outside job, was not at home that much. This allowed Cho more time alone in his residence. However, his grades slipped during his second year and he decided on a new major: English.

The governor's report noted that Cho's choice of an English major seemed odd at first because of the trouble he had with English and his problems with both speech and communication as well as writing in English. However, it seems that Cho's decision was made, in part, because of his experience in an entry-level introduction to poetry class he took in his freshman year. This course was taught by the chairman of the English Department, Professor Lucinda Roy.

He wrote Dr. Roy in November 2004, introducing himself as one of her former students, asking her, because she had mentioned books she had published, whether she could recommend publishers or agents to whom he could submit his novel—which he called a "silly" and "pathetic" version of *Tom Sawyer*. His note was affable, self-deprecatory, but, given Cho's problems with written communication, surprisingly fluent.

He changed his major to English and followed Professor Roy's advice to study creative writing and submit his own writing to publishers. However, in the fall of 2005, what seemed like a promising change in Cho's life turned out to be a change for the worse. Prior to that time, Cho seemed to be engrossed in his writing. He was more expressive, and his family noticed he was hard at work on his manuscript. However, in the fall semester of 2005, now that he was a full-time English major, he was running into difficulties. He discovered that life for an aspiring writer is not easy and is filled with rejection. Just because one writes a manuscript does not mean that he can get it published professionally. And this is what Cho learned when he received his first rejection letter from a publisher. But, his sister, Sun, who discovered the letter in Cho's room, encouraged him to keep on writing and learn the craft.

Cho routinely spent all of his breaks from school at home, oftentimes writing and reading or riding his bike. He had no friends, and, even when he shot baskets, he would play alone. But, perhaps because there were no incidents at school or medical needs that had to be attended to by his parents, Mr. and Mrs. Cho let matters be.

When Cho told his parents that he was infested with mites in his apartment and that they had bitten him, he sought medical help on his own and applied prescription medicine to the skin lesions. However, Cho's concern over mites might well have been an early indicator of his emerging thought disorder in the form of a somatic delusion.

His delusion would be a first clinical indicator that the neurocircuitry of his brain—that of an enormously complicate computing system—was getting scrambled with consequent inability to filter internal and external stimuli. His body sensation and thinking were likely becoming overtly disrupted. In other words, his skin was itching, his scratching inflamed it and broke it into sores, and then he called it mites and got an ointment for it. But it actually might have nothing to do with mites at all. More likely, within the context of his clinical history, it was breakthrough delusional thinking. Up until now, the severity of this thinking disorder and disrupted neurocircuitry was adequately concealed to guard him from major clinical intervention. That guardedness, however, would eventually fail to conceal the convergence of his mental disintegration—fertile ground for the coalescence of a grandiose delusion to replace his progressively fragmented identity.

His doctor in Blacksburg, however—who did not review any of Cho's records from school or his psychological records—said that the young man was suffering from acute acne and prescribed treatment. By fall 2005, the first semester of his junior year, Cho began to slip into worsening behavior again. By the end of that semester, he had turned downright hostile and threatening to others to the point where the university had to intervene.

Cho had already switched his major to English and was pursuing a program in creative writing, probably largely upon Professor Roy's recommendation. But his old behavior was catching up to him. His sister noticed that he seemed to have lost interest in writing, that he was even more withdrawn than he had been, and he seemed to not have any interest in his own future.

Although his father was urging him to go to graduate school, Cho said that he would be finished with college when he graduated. When his father offered to help him find a job, he seemed to reject that too. Life for Cho was most likely coming to an end in despair of losing sense of both self and external reality. In the chaos of unfiltered brain signals, despair sets in; this is the most dangerous time for the schizophrenic patient, the time when the patient, probably with diminishing insight, recognizes the despair of a seemingly hopeless and incurable illness. And it is the time when the schizophrenic patient is at highest risk for suicide.

On campus after break, Cho had moved back into the dormitory, this time into a suite with a number of suitemates with whom he had little social contact. His DUP was getting longer and more dangerous. For example, his roommate and suitemates told the governor's panel a chilling story about how they tried to draw Cho out. They had described him in much the same terms that others had characterized him from the time he was a child. He would hardly speak, but when he did it was almost inaudible. He would respond with gestures or one-word answers. Whatever activities he engaged in, he did alone. And he had no friends and no social life whatsoever. When his suitemates invited him to parties, he would sit in corners alone and speak to no one. Had any professional counselor or therapist witnessed this behavior, he or she would have spotted this as a red flag. Cho at this point was likely psychotic.

On one evening in particular, for example, a group was gathering in one of the women's rooms. His suitemates brought Cho along in an effort to include him, but all he did was sit in a corner. At one point, his roommate looked over and saw that Cho had taken out a lock knife, (what the Governor's Panel refers to as a lock knife, a form of folding knife in which the blade locks into place) and had begun stabbing it into the carpet. That was the last time they took him out with them, leaving him to his own devices.

As the semester wore on, Cho's behavior became even stranger. His roommates remembered that Cho would download movies onto his laptop and watch them privately. They described these movies, according to the governor's report, as "dark." They were describing the probable replacement of his shattered self with a false one, one both grandiose and with monstrous delusions of self.

Cho also listened to heavy metal music and began writing some of the lyrics on the walls of the suite, thus displaying his progressing mental disorganization. Normal kids, regardless of how rebellious they are, simply do not go that far unless there is a severe underlying psychological problem or drug intoxication. There never were allegations of drug usage.

By the following spring, Cho was more regularly writing the lyrics on the walls in the hall. He did not identify himself as the person who defaced the walls, but the lyrics were the exact ones Cho was listening to at the time. And these were the same types of lyrics that Cho was posting on Facebook.

Another unnerving behavior that Cho's suitemates reported was Cho's calling his roommate, asking for himself, and saying that he was Seung's twin brother named "Question Mark." He also posted messages to himself on his Facebook page, again referring to himself as his twin brother. He likely did not know his identity and was trying to get some boundaries for what he could tell was his own mite-infested body and experience. He was rapidly losing it and could conceal it no longer. Was he crying for help?

He was grossly psychotic at this point. His symptoms were getting worse with each semester. For example, Cho also began burning paper in the suite and placing the burnt pages under the couch cushions. Here was the second sign of imminent dangerousness, the first being his stabbing the carpet with a lock knife. Now he was fire-starting and saving the burnt remains as trophies, concealing them from is suitemates.

During the fall semester of 2005, Cho was a student in an advanced creative writing poetry class taught by one of America's most respected modern poets, Professor Nikki Giovanni. Professor Giovanni is an award-winning poet, widely taught in upper-level modern literature classes at colleges and universities around the country. She was a distinguished professor at Virginia Tech.

In her class, Cho began demonstrating antisocial behavior from the earliest sessions. He would come to class wearing a hat pulled down over his face and reflector sunglasses, building a wall of hostile isolation around himself as if he were overwhelmed by stimuli and fearful of being seen. Such fear can be picked up in projective psychological testing wherein the patient, a paranoid schizophrenic, draws eyes that are usually exaggerated.

For her part, Professor Giovanni was so adamant that he comport himself as a member of the class that she demanded he remove his sunglasses and his hat. When he refused to comply, she stopped the class and stood by his desk until he did. After the first part of the semester, Cho began wearing a scarf wrapped around his head, "Bedouin style," Professor Giovanni called it, as if he were trying to bully her into standing down.

Cho was also very resistant to criticism of his writing and, many times, after being given notes on how to rewrite a piece, he showed up in class with the exact same work with none of the rewrites in place. It was a challenge to Professor Giovanni. Had Cho been on drugs, particularly meth, he might have behaved like this. Aggressively challenging behavior is one of the results of meth use, which is why it is constantly revived as a yuppie drug. But Cho was not on drugs to the best of anyone's knowledge. His behavior was the actively and grossly psychotic behavior of worsening schizophrenia.

In another incident, Cho read aloud a paper he had written entitled, "So-Called Advanced Creative Writing—Poetry." He vented anger because the class, according to the official governor's report, had, in his opinion, spent "too much time talking about eating animals instead of about poetry." His essay talked about "animal massacre butcher shop," where he attacked his fellow students, in particularly harsh language, by saying, "I don't know which uncouth low-life planet you come from but you disgust me. In fact, you all disgust me."

The official report is quoting Cho's own paper. He continued, writing, "You low-life barbarians make me sick to my stomach that I want to barf over my new shoes. If you despicable human beings who are all a disgrace to [the] human race keep this up, before you know it you will turn into cannibals—eating little babies, your friends. I hope y'all burn in hell for mass murdering and eating all those little animals."

Cho characterized this essay as a "satire." The Virginia Tech administration had the authority at that moment to both obtain all of Cho's past records, including any records of his psychological counseling, and to send him home. As a result of Cho's antagonistic and antisocial behavior, Professor Giovanni later learned, by asking one of her students, why fewer and fewer of her students attended her class. This was a first for her, and she became unnerved when one student told her that the class was afraid of Cho. Here was another opportunity demanding intervention from Virginia Tech administration.

She confronted Cho, telling him that she did not think she was the right teacher for him and offered to get him into another class. Dr. Giovanni should never have been placed in this position by Virginia Tech administration. Compounding her dilemma, Cho refused. She would have to take steps by herself to get him out of her class; this action should certainly not have been her responsibility in the case of an obviously mentally ill student. Following her chain of command, she could only turn to her department chairman, Professor Roy, whose freshman poetry class had influenced Cho to change his major to English.

Professor Roy offered Professor Giovanni security. Dr. Giovanni refused, saying that she simply did not want Cho back in class and that she would resign if her requests were not granted! Nikki Giovanni was probably one of the wisest people to have encountered Cho. She knew he was seriously mentally ill and knew also that she need not be one of his victims, even though the Virginia Tech administration was throwing her to the lions. Everyone else in the faculty and administration was dependent upon Virginia Tech to take action. Professor Giovanni knew that she was dealing with something so serious that she could not rely on Virginia Tech—only her instinctive sense of fear for herself and others for whom she was responsible as a professor. She had the right to maintain an effective and safe teaching environment; it was the responsibility of administration to assure her of such. They did not and never showed any effort to get involved in the Cho case from beginning to tragic end.

Professor Roy acceded to Professor Giovanni's request and removed Cho. However, Dr. Roy, who remembered Cho from his freshman year, also put other gears into motion by bringing up the Cho situation to the university administration, specifically Dean of Student Affairs Tom Brown, the Cook Counseling

Center, and the College of Liberal Arts. Professor Roy specifically pointed to Cho's objectionable writing and to the cell phone pictures he was taking—suggesting inappropriate lewdness in the classroom setting.

She asked to have Cho psychologically evaluated and questioned whether his taking pictures in class was a violation of anything in the code of student behavior. The dean advised her that, if Cho's picture-taking disturbed the integrity of the class, then it did violate a campus policy for which Cho could be found liable. Of course, based upon Professor Giovanni's students' statements, her students were leaving class because they were afraid of him. This, in itself, defines *disruptive*, demanding swift intervention from administration.

In terms of the paper, however, counselors to whom the Dean referred the matter said they could find no specific threat in the paper. However, they did agree that Cho should be told that he would be referred to counseling for any similar disruptive behavior. There was no formal request from the English Department for any Judicial Affairs intervention and the campus care team—composed of the dean of student affairs, director of residence life, director of student health, and the school's legal affairs office—astonishingly stated that the Cho matter had been adequately addressed with his class change!

Absent any formal request for any type of further intervention, the care team did not pursue the matter any further. With the onus now on Professor Roy to remove Cho from Professor Giovanni's poetry class, she was left hung out to dry, or worse. Most inappropriately for an institution of higher learning, she was placed in the position of having to come up with some alternative study or work plan for Cho to receive the credits he would have received had he passed Professor Giovanni's poetry class.

Dr. Roy emailed Cho to come in for a conference. Cho's response was harsh, a two-page letter that criticized Professor Giovanni's teaching methods and expressed Cho's fear that he was going to get "yelled at" by the department chairman. If Cho had formed some sort of psychological attachment to her, vested some trust in her during his freshman year when he took her poetry class, Professor Roy's email invitation might have been especially deranging for him. Perhaps he felt he needed to cloak himself as a protective device, so he showed up for the meeting wearing his dark glasses inside her office, again obviously overvaluing his sense of sight, very likely overwhelmed with threatening external cues. His senses were picking up a threatening world—one emanating from his interior and not the common experience of anyone else. This was, therefore, extremely paranoid behavior; Cho believed—and at this point, rightly so—that people were looking at him. He was likely perceiving intense eyes staring at him—eyes needing to be blocked out. Cho obviously was suffering with ideas of reference, a classical sign of paranoid schizophrenia, wherein external stimuli, whether relevant or trivial, are all referring to him.

Wisely, and certainly to make sure that there was an accurate record of this meeting, Professor Roy asked department member Cheryl Ruggiero to attend the meeting and to take notes. Whatever the outcome of this meeting, it is apparent that Professor Roy understood that the Cho case presented more than what might appear on the surface and wanted whatever administrative panel, whether ad hoc or otherwise, to have a record of what she said and how Cho Seung-Hui responded.

Both Ms. Ruggiero and Professor Roy noted that when Cho showed up at the meeting, in addition to wearing his glasses, he seemed depressed and withdrawn and appeared to be lonely. He also seemed agitated, as if he were fearing the worst and ready to defend himself from any sort of attack. At the outset of the meeting, Professor Roy sought to set at least one of his concerns aside by assuring him that no one was going to yell at him. Cho's fear of being yelled at was his ideation of a "reference," actually a sign of paranoid delusional thinking, a construct in his own mind that he was the object of an attack. He had never been given any reason to expect such response from the teaching staff. Yet, he had to be assured that there would be no form of retribution—certainly reassurance that was far, far outside both of their job descriptions.

All but literally abandoned by administration to handle the situation as if she were dealing with simply an odd student—not a seriously ill one—she did explain why his essay was taken so seriously by Professor Giovanni and why she, too, thought it presented a serious problem. Cho responded that he was only joking. In fact, the whole thing was really a satire, he said, but possibly a bad joke because no one got it. Whether Cho meant that or not is another issue, but we can conjecture that, even in his state of detachment from reality, he was still in a state of fear that he would face consequences for what he said.

It can certainly be argued that the class and the professor got it all right. They completely understood that Cho meant what he said. Students having to be in his presence for their legitimately chosen education were all rightly terrified. Cho did not get it, because he simply no longer had insight into his impact on other people. He was in another world, a psychotic one, within which his fragmented self-image was slipping to tracks on a final common pathway to the end of his life—a monstrous identity to be witnessed by the world in the video that he mailed to NBC News.

In his meeting with Lucinda Roy, Cho conceded that his essay well might have been "perceived differently" by the class and therefore could be characterized as inappropriate. He told Professor Roy that he was not offended by the class discussion of animals, that it was not a religious issue, and that he was not a vegetarian. He tried to shrug off the incident and seemed upset when Roy suggested that he replace Professor Giovanni's class with an independent study in which Lucinda Roy would be involved. Cho seemed upset that he, in his own words, was being "kicked out" and wanted to stay in the class if he were going to lose credits as a result of this.

Ms. Ruggiero's transcript of the meeting noted that Cho seemed angry and resentful at the thought that he was being kicked out. His being excluded from something against his will had touched a raw nerve, and his reaction to the rejection was not something he could mask. Lucinda Roy also asked Cho to remove his sunglasses. He did not respond; he took a long time but eventually removed them. If the sunglasses were part of his cloaking mechanism, a protective device from perceived prying eyes, and a weapon that enabled him to feel that he was exerting some sort of control in a menacing way, his removing his mask made him seem almost naked to Ruggiero and Roy. Ruggiero seemed to be stunned at first when she saw Cho's face, because she wrote that, after Cho removed his glasses, "It is a very distressing sight, since his face seems very naked and blank without them. It's a great relief to be able to read his face, though there isn't much there."

There was plenty there, but it was not the visible persona of simply a troubled student. She was looking into the abyss of schizophrenic mental decompensation. And, when Professor Roy asked him whether taking off his sunglasses had been terrible for him, she remarked that "He doesn't seem like himself, like the student I knew in the Intro to Poetry class." She was looking at what is known as the negative signs of schizophrenia—the loss of persona—the emptiness. And, soon he would be sleeping a lot, too—as if dead.

Cho's DUP was extending to dangerous lengths, years away now from its onset in early childhood. Roy asked whether anything terrible or bad had happened to him. Cho took a long time to answer, but he eventually said, "No." Dr. Roy, abandoned by administration to be both psychiatrist and professor, encouraged Cho to talk about himself. She also asked whether he wanted to talk to someone professionally—specifically, a counselor—about how he felt. She said she had the name of someone he could talk to and Cho, after remaining quiet and not answering, finally said, "Sure," he would agree to go to a counselor. Contrary to public perception of this massacre, Cho remained, as always, amenable to treatment. It simply was never made available to him at Virginia Tech.

Placed in an untenable situation, Professor Roy also had to take administrative responsibility for Cho's progressive sickness. She said that, in order to receive credit for the course he was taking with Professor Giovanni, she would tutor him for the rest of the semester. They would have to meet at least four more times, and he would have to produce some writing. She gave him one of her books for him to take and noticed that, after he reluctantly agreed and was leaving the meeting, he "appeared to be crying."

At this point, although Cho's emotional state was concretizing like a stone, it still had cracks in it. Reality and remorse could still filter through just a little but, through the cracks, rage and despair would ultimately gush and erupt. It is likely that Cho did see some light. His agreeing to go to counseling was a great opportunity to salvage his life by getting him actively involved in his own treatment. It was far better for a psychotic patient like Cho than waiting for the police to get involved, restraining him with handcuffs, transporting him to treatment with guns at their sides. Guns, batons, handcuffs—none of this would be good for a guy like Cho.

Throughout the course of her subsequent tutoring sessions—she referred to them as an *independent study*—Professor Roy kept in contact with various members of the administration, including the office of the dean of student life. She noted Cho's progress from a "deliberately inarticulate" person to someone who had begun to open up to critical thinking about poetry. Professor Roy used poetry, choosing poets such as Emily Dickinson and William Butler Yeats, to, in her words, "focus Cho's thoughts away from violence" and to open him up to human empathy. Dickinson, in particular, she thought, was a reclusive and introspective person who expressed herself in terms of plain imagery and irony.

Professor Roy, in using poetry to work Cho out of his violent writing—shooting and harming people, "because he's angered by their authority and their behavior"—actually had by default become Cho's therapist. This was poetry therapy, perhaps effective in treating the disconnected language of thought and emotional chaos in schizophrenia, to open Cho up to empathize with human emotion. And in this process, Professor Roy wrote to members of the administration, she kept on encouraging him to see a counselor, even offering to take him to counseling herself. There appeared to be no need to communicate with anyone else, because—clearly—nobody else wanted anything to do with this hot potato—serious mental illness erupting right on campus, amidst thousands of young adults needing both security and peace in order to do their jobs: to grow up and learn.

In some ways, Lucinda Roy knew she was flying blind because she was not a professional counselor or therapist. But she had an instinct about Cho that might have been seeded when she encountered him in his freshman year. Cho clearly needed something, some kind of outlet for his writing. Although Cho might have believed that he wanted to be a published author, it well might have been simply to work with someone about his writing. Breaking mentally, a remaining healthy part of Cho might have perceived Professor Roy's tutoring as a lifeline. This lifeline perhaps held out hope to Cho that he could rejoin the human race from which he was alienated and isolated by illness his entire life.

If Lucinda Roy saw that, and it is apparent that she did, then the course of independent study she laid out for Cho, constrained as it was by the time limitations of the semester and her job, nevertheless could have been the best hope for Cho. Although those responsible for Cho's life on campus might have been approaching negligence in their administrative delegation to a member of the academic faculty with no certification in psychological counseling, they actually might have helped her stave off mass murder at least for a while. But that is something we can only guess at now in the aftermath of that tragedy.

Toward the end of the semester, Professor Roy noted that Cho had opened up and was writing well. He had not taken her up on her offer to take him to counseling and was still very sad and difficult to talk to. But, he was writing well, was working through the poetry, and was making strides. He had advanced during the semester, and Professor Roy wound up giving him an A for the independent study. But, if Lucinda Roy believed that Cho had set forward on the right path, it was a belief not borne out by facts, even though it clearly demonstrated, once again, Cho's treatability, neglected over and over again.

Cho's Psychosis Worsens

Cho's first serious encounter with the campus judicial system came on November 27, 2005, over Thanksgiving break. According to a complaint filed by a student in West Ambler Johnston residence hall, Cho showed up at her door wearing his cap pulled down and his reflective glasses. He told her that he was "Question Mark," the identity Cho used to message himself on Facebook. Cho told the campus police, who paid him a visit on November 27, that he had been text messaging the girl and thought she understood that this was all part of an Internet game. Cho's victim, however, correctly saw it as stalking and harassment. She called the police, who advised Cho that this entire incident would be turned over to campus judicial affairs.

The complainant student's resident advisor also showed up. He later told the governor's investigative panel that Cho had acted "very strange and got stranger" as the interaction between him and the female student continued.

In classical emergency medicine triage protocols, Cho fit perfectly into the presenting problem of "behaving strangely," a triage classification demanding immediate and thorough medical investigation. Ignoring such altered mental state was likely also the cause for delay in effective triage to direct definitive treatment on time for actress Natasha Richardson; she died of a cerebral hemorrhage. How could administration be certain that Cho's specifically cited strange behavior did not signal a catastrophic medical and/or psychological event? But, once again, Cho's DUP was treacherously extended—like a frayed rubber band about to snap.

Just three days after this incident, Cho himself called the Cook Counseling Center, following Professor Roy's advice, and spoke with licensed professional counselor Maisha Smith. In his conversations with the center, Cho asked specifically for Dr. Cathye Betzel, the professional that Dr. Roy suggested he call. His mental state, obvious on campus as strange behavior, was treated as routine, when, in fact, it was a medical emergency demanding immediate clinical investigation.

The center made an appointment for him for December 12, at 2:00 in the afternoon, but Cho failed to keep the appointment. He called in at 4:00 and was scheduled for a telephone appointment, called a "triage appointment," this time conducted by Dr. Betzel at 4:45 p.m. Cathy Betzel told the governor's investigative panel that she did not recall the substance of her conversation with Cho and there are no records that summarize the nature of their conversation. Once again, such official response on a campus of higher education is somewhat astonishing.

Cook Counseling Center did not make a diagnosis of Cho because diagnoses are only made after a clinical in-person appointment. Cho had not appeared for his earlier appointment that afternoon. How such emergency triage is justified without any diagnosis remains a total mystery. But, Betzel did remember that Cho was the person she had talked about in a referral from Professor Lucinda Roy. And, apparently there was recollection of her being disturbed over the violence in Cho's writing, a conversation Roy and Betzel had prior to Dr. Roy's meeting with Cho on December 12.

It is difficult to ignore this clinical encounter, which, in retrospect, could have been a key step for clinical intervention. Apparently the guidance center psychiatrist was not available to assess Cho for antipsychotic medication or facilitate emergency hospitalization. Some in the legal profession might even say that the Cook Counseling Center's statements to the governor's panel bordered on negligence or medical malpractice. To call this triage without documenting both presenting problems and clinical decision making is misstep.

Triage is oftentimes abused as a term to mean nonspecifically "routed" when, in fact, it has very specific meaning and rules, knowledge base, and protocols. Had triage actually been performed by somebody who should have known what it was—rather than simply using the name for routing purposes—the massacre at Virginia Tech might have been prevented because it was still not too late for Cho to be in that 25 percent of complete recovery for schizophrenia. He was young. This clinical encounter is extremely distressing for anyone who specializes in emergency medicine and neuropsychiatric protocols.

It was on that same day of Cho's appointment with Dr. Betzel and his subsequent telephone conversation with her that the Virginia Tech police received a complaint about Cho from a female student living in the East Campbell residence hall. This student had known Cho through one of his roommates. She was the young woman, a sophomore, in whose room Cho had pulled out a knife and begun stabbing her carpet. She told this to the police and said further that throughout the semester she had received instant messages and postings to her Facebook page that were not threatening but unnerving in that they were, in the words of the report, "self-deprecating."

When she made inquiries to the poster as to his identity, suggesting it was from Cho—whom she knew from the party in her room—the poster said, "I do not know who I am." But what really concerned her was that she found a scrawled message outside her room on the white message eraser board that was a quote from *Romeo and Juliet*. It read:

> By a name I know not how to tell thee who I am. My name, dear Saint, is hateful to myself. Because it is an enemy to thee. Had I it written, I would tear the word.

Cho's delusion here sounds suspiciously like de'Clerembault syndrome or erotmania, a delusion often associated with paranoid schizophrenia in which the victim, in this case, Cho, believes that the object of his romantic fascination is in love with him. Thus, stalking this woman, and, perhaps, other women, was as much part of his presentation of psychotic symptoms as was his wearing of reflector sunglasses and a ball cap pulled down over his head. Who was he?

Certainly Cho's use of "Question Mark" to literally announce the meltdown of his self-identity was a presentation of that same psychosis. The young woman who was the object of Cho's delusions had shared the note with her father and explained that she thought it was from Cho. Her father talked to a police chief friend of his, who advised him to have his daughter inform the campus police about this matter. Her communication with the police was the basis for the police action. Campus police contacted Cho on December 13, telling him not to have any further contact with this woman. The woman did not file a criminal complaint with judicial affairs, even though her residence counselor and other members of the residence administration knew of the incident. The incident was not reported to the care team. She was likely terrified, as she correctly should have been—as should have been campus administration and Cook Counseling Center.

The visit from the campus police had unnerved Cho. If he had tried to operate in stealth, camouflaging himself by not using his name, it had failed. Cho sent an instant message to his suitemate saying, "I might as well kill myself." The suitemate reported that communication to the campus police. The police responded that same evening, returning to Cho's room at 7:00. This time they spoke with Cho's roommate without Cho present and subsequently took Cho to the police department for an assessment.

At 8:15 a licensed clinical social worker from the New River Valley Community Services Board conducted a prescreening evaluation. She interviewed Cho, the responding police officer, Cho's suitemate who had reported the instant message from Cho, and Cho's other suitemate. On a pre-admission screening form, she checked the boxes that said that Cho was mentally ill and was an imminent danger to himself and to others and was not willing to be treated voluntarily. She recommended involuntary hospitalization.

As a result, Cho would have to be detained upon the order of a local magistrate once a bed could be found at an acceptable facility. The social worker then found a psychiatric bed for him at the St. Albans Behavioral Health Center of the Carilion New River Valley Medical Center. She then contacted the magistrate to issue a temporary detention order. The magistrate issued the order and the police transported Cho without incident to the medical center.

During his transport to the psychiatric facility, Cho did not speak to the police officer. Once at the hospital, he cooperated with the admissions personnel and was diagnosed with a nonspecific mood disorder, depressive disorder, NOS—or not otherwise specified. Cho did not admit to any prehistory of violence, but he did acknowledge, according to the prescreening paperwork, that he had access to a firearm. That nursing assessment notation, however, may have been a mistake by the admissions personnel, as reported by the investigative panel. Why it was considered a mistake by the panel is unclear, because Cho did acquire firearms—or perhaps already did have them.

Cho apparently reported that he was not taking any medication. He did receive a dose of one milligram of Ativan, almost always reserved for severe agitation. Cho was now in the system, and his evaluation and a subsequent hearing for involuntary commitment would fall under the law of the Commonwealth of Virginia.

Early in the morning of December 14, the clinical support representative for the facility met with Cho to provide him with necessary information regarding the involuntary commitment hearing he would have. The representative then took Cho into a screening/evaluation interview with a licensed clinical psychologist who, as required by law, would conduct an independent evaluation of Cho.

This independent evaluator did not have records to review and, because Cho had not met with the psychiatrist, there were no psychiatric records to review either. The entire evaluation process took only fifteen minutes to complete. He apparently had three more to do that morning.

Done thoroughly, the evaluation could have been completed in twenty minutes and might have obtained the correct diagnosis. But, looking at Cho's behavior, one has to ask, how could a person like Cho, whose emotional state was described by this psychologist as *flat affect*—an emotional state like stone—quite paradoxically have the normal insight concurrently attributed to him. It would be unlikely for Cho to have had normal insight, and the fact that the box on the evaluation form was marked "normal" would demonstrate to an objective clinical evaluator that this documentation was somehow likely in error. To support evidence of this likely error, the evaluator wrote that Cho was "mentally ill." But the doctor could not find any indication that Cho was an imminent danger to himself or to others. Moreover, the doctor said that Cho was not "substantially unable to care for himself as a result of his mental illness" and furthermore did not require involuntary hospitalization.

A special counsel appointed for Cho and a special magistrate—required under law for an involuntary commitment to a hospital absent advocates to protect Cho's constitutional rights under the due process clause of the Fifth and Fourteenth Amendments—both certified the evaluator's report that Cho did not require involuntary hospitalization. That report went to a formal commitment hearing along with a report by the attending psychiatrist at the medical center. The attending psychiatrist also interviewed Cho and said that he did not find imminent dangerousness in the patient and so agreed with the evaluator that Cho did not require involuntary commitment.

Cho's attending psychiatrist recommended that Cho be treated on an outpatient basis with counseling. He prescribed no medication and did not provide any primary diagnosis to direct any clinical intervention—using the catchall term, depression NOS, which is too nonspecific to direct any intervention yet specific enough to prohibit any further detention.

To critique this medical work-up, one would have to ask why the professionals who interviewed Cho did not align Cho's presentation with a valid diagnosis directing treatment. Granted, Cho was probably inaudible at best, silent at worst, and barely responsive. But, these behaviors, within the context of Cho's history, indicate gross psychosis with significant potential for danger to self and to others. More likely than not, the reason Cho was not talking was that he was absorbed in a world of his own, perhaps a hallucinatory one of voices audible only to him. Even the magistrate who first interviewed Cho could tell that something was horribly wrong. As a layman, he disregarded clinical assessment and found him to indeed be imminently dangerous to self and/or others and had detained Cho against medical advice!

The psychiatrist who saw Cho conceded that he had no access to any collateral information about him, other than the evaluator's report. Cho denied having any previous history with either drugs or alcohol or any prior psychological problems. This denial appeared valid to the attending psychiatrist, so he reduced his concern for violence. Substance abuse is a contributing, if not necessary or sufficient, factor for violence in the seriously mentally ill. Cho had previously been diagnosed as seriously mentally ill by the clinical psychologist, who found a most malignant sign of "flat"—or stone-like—"affect."

Because of issues of privacy, none of Cho's elementary, middle, or high school records were available, and the university did not have those records either. Therefore, despite Cho's long history of problems and his experiences with the psychologist at the Virginia Tech guidance center, he appeared before the magistrate at a subsequent commitment hearing with only his own statements, the evaluator's report, and the psychiatrist's recommendation. It was alleged that Cho refused to talk about his past medical history and his previous visits to counselors and therapists, but this refusal was not specifically differentiated from mutism, for which he had both a long history and significant current presentation at point of encounter with campus police; Cho had been silent with police on the way to the hospital.

If Cho had been detained initially because of a complaint filed by a female student alleging that she had been stalked by him, and if Cho's own suitemates contacted the police to report Cho's suicide threat, this was enough for a preliminary evaluation of dangerousness. With that evaluation, St. Albans hospital had every right to keep Cho for a full seventy-two hours of working days. This was adequate time to retrieve all of his medical records and, at the least, contact his parents for more information.

At the very least, they could have tried to reach Cho's sister to throw some light onto this apparently very mysterious case. In emergency presentations—which this was by legal definition—wherein the patient either cannot provide an adequate history or his history is insufficient or inappropriate, it is incumbent upon emergency clinical staff—in this case the psychiatric staff at St. Albans—to contact any collateral source of information necessary to get an accurate history.

This is the "school rule" of medicine, enabling doctors in emergency circumstances to speak with anyone and everyone necessary to obtain adequate information for effective clinical decision making to assure the safety of the patient and all others potentially affected. In other words, emergency detention of Cho wiped out all of the alleged barriers to obtaining information about him. Of course, discretion must be used, and all interventions must document the attending physician's intention and justification. In this case it would have simply been the determination of diagnosis and safety for self and others.

The system failed. Cho was simply pushed through to the next phase of the commitment process, where he was let out the back door. No more was learned about Cho in this most significant clinical opportunity for definitive diagnosis.

In fact, the legalistic spider web of conflicting laws and regulations entrapping patient Cho with a court evaluator and hospital psychiatric staff could not be better designed to facilitate violence and suicide.

This system, as do all court-controlled psychiatric systems, has been retroengineered into clinical dysfuncationality. Remember when Cho submitted his piece addressing classmates as low-life barbarians? He later retracted his diatribe. He was only joking. In fact, the whole thing was really a satire, he said. Ironically, this hospitalization reads like satire as well, because so many laws have been passed to render emergency psychiatry dysfunctional that this staff seemed to have become as anosognosic as its schizophrenic patients. Just a snapshot of that evaluation is very revealing. Cho was a patient on emergency detention and literally deteriorating before the eyes of professionals. However, the court and hospital mission seemed designed at that point not to see and not to understand. To understand would have been to diagnose. No diagnosis or understanding took place, and this failure, sadly, is symptomatic of systemic failure nationally.

Cho was a person who had articulated ideations of suicide and had openly expressed admiration for Kliebold and Harris and what they had perpetrated at Columbine High School. He had been acting out on campus by stalking women via the Internet and appearing at their rooms. He had brandished a knife at a party, which he stabbed into the carpet, and kept a knife in his desk. Actually, in fact, he had arguably also committed attempted arson in the dormitory by burning paper and then stashing it under the couch cushions. Finally, as he appeared before the only system that could have prevented him from doing any violence to others or to himself, he was simply shot right through the cracks of that system.

Following the psychiatric assessment, Cho, along with other detained patients, were escorted into a hearing before a special Montgomery County justice who would provide due process on behalf of the detainees either to commit or to release on condition of instructions set forth by the medical center. First, Cho met with his attorney and then appeared before the special justice. After the recommendations were read into the record, and absent any testimony from either Cho's suitemates or the officer who detained and transported him, the special justice ruled that Cho presented an imminent danger to himself as a result of his mental illness and ordered that he submit himself for treatment on an outpatient basis. Assumably, this was an attorney making this decision, and he made it against medical advice and the advice of the independent evaluator. How could he have done this? We do not know what a lay person saw, heard, or could not hear that clinical professionals were blind—or, agnosonomic—to recognizing.

Cho was released under court-ordered treatment. It was to begin that afternoon. However, the Cook Guidance Center on campus told the governor's panel that it did not receive any hospital records from St. Albans until the following month, January 2006. However, the Cook Counseling Center had been called by the court after judgment and they required Cho to make his own counseling appointment. He did that, according to the panel, from the hospital. Cho kept his 3 p.m. appointment at the Cook Counseling Center, although no records exist of that counseling session or of follow-up triages. Again, no diagnosis was generated from any of these sessions. All that remained was an attending psychiatrist's diagnosis of nonspecific mood disorder, a diagnosis that flew in the face of the whole purpose of emergency triage procedures designed to follow evidence-based practice guidelines.

What was Cho presenting? What was his past history? Were there gaps in that history? If so, it was the responsibility of counselors to fill those gaps by looking for any evidence of past psychiatric problems. If records were unavailable, who were the emergency contacts that Cho would have been required to provide upon his admission to Virginia Tech? Were his parents those emergency contacts? Was it his sister? When the patient, alleged to be violent to self and others, cannot give a reliable history, the finding of "inappropriate history" kicks in the school rule. No judge is going to find fault with clinical staff for doing whatever is necessary to get to the bottom of Cho's peculiar presentation, both on campus and in the hospital. To argue otherwise is either clinical blindness caused by bureaucratic dumbing of clinical decision making or a lack of forensic knowledge of standards of practice in emergency medicine. Emergency detention is emergency psychiatry; psychiatry is the practice of medicine.

When, as in the case of Cho, clinical history from the patient is either inappropriate or impossible to obtain because of mutism, the entire court-directed clinical decision process must stop to get the facts. For at least seventy-two hours, best medical practices trump laws and regulations that entrap patient and psychiatric staff together in a spider web made for the process of law. Imagine assessing chest pain with shortness of breath within such a clinical environment. Every patient with cardiopulmonary disease would die. With schizophrenia, however, it would not be long before lots of people would die, including the patient.

The known clinical presentation here demanded contacts be made to get critical information, especially from the parents. Such information was necessary to direct the next stage of court-determined treatment options: involuntary treatment or leaving Cho to his own devices as his parents did during his childhood. But, his parents could not have known any better and were helpless; St. Albans Hospital was not. Cho was in fact committed, and he was way too sick to either leave or engage in outpatient treatment—even if it were court ordered, which it was, or court supervised, which it was not.

Reportedly, the Cook Guidance Center psychiatrist was not available, so that disposition was inevitably designed to fail too. There was nobody to prescribe medications necessary to start the reintegration process in Cho's disrupted neurocircuitry. This is what is required in emergency psychiatry, and following these practices could likely, we now know, have prevented the disaster at Virginia Tech.

Cho did not make follow-up appointments for counseling because he was not in a supervised involuntary treatment program, although he was under court-ordered involuntary commitment. If that sounds strange, it is because the system is strange. It is designed, as if a bad joke, to lead the psychotic patient, blinded by anosognosia, through a system blinded within a spider web designed for defensive medicine: immunity from litigation rather than the practice of medicine.

Cook Counseling Center on campus knew that Cho had made an appointment under a court order, because the court had contacted them. Why did they not pursue him for not making follow-up appointments? Something was missing in the management of this case that let Cho withdraw from the very treatment that might have prevented him from festering within his paranoid delusions and kept him from the precipice of dangerousness from which he eventually jumped.

At some point, the psychologist at Cook Center would have referred him back to the hospital for readmission or referred him for a psychopharmacotherapy evaluation to clear his obvious psychosis. At some point, someone would have asked for his medical records, and that request would have gone to his parents, who were completely in the dark.

For a variety of reasons, including the fact that Cho told his parents nothing about the trouble he was in and the fact that no one at the university contacted them, Mr. and Mrs. Cho had no knowledge of the events that took place at the end of 2005. They did not know about their son's stalking, the contacts with the Virginia Tech police, his detention, his being remanded to the custody of the psychiatric facility at the medical center, the involuntary commitment hearing, and the court ordering a treatment program as a condition of his release. The university did not contact them or refer Cho to the care of his hometown physician. None of this was relayed to the parents. As a result, they were again powerless to intervene because, in this case, they simply did not know what had transpired.

According to the official governor's report, when the investigative panel spoke to them about these events, they were saddened, because, had they known, they said, they would have kept their son back at home for the ensuing semester and placed him under the care of his doctor. In other words, had the parents been informed, Cho would not have been on campus the following spring, and he would not have fallen into the abyss while away from home and the vigilance of his parents, committed the murders, and then killed himself.

All of this murder and mayhem could likely have been prevented had there been adequate communication and effective psychiatric intervention—rather than a useless medicalized dance behind all the overlapping court rituals. It was a dance, merely to backstop a system for the seriously mentally ill that had totally collapsed and was in ruins. Yet doctors still were present—they were just so tangled up in the web, and their training and capabilities were too bound up in bureaucracy.

So, to extend the DUP some more, Cho took a course in fiction writing with Professor Robert Hicok during the Spring of 2006. This was what the governor's report referred to as a "mid-level" writing course. Professor Hicok told the investigative panel that Cho's writing was violent and lacked much creativity. To make matters worse, Cho was unresponsive and uncommunicative, resistant, and very withdrawn. He made some changes—"edits," Professor Hicok called them—but the violent content of his writing, combined with Cho's silence and inability to keep office appointments, were real signals for the professor. Dr. Hicok consulted with Dr. Roy, but he kept Cho in his class, despite his very deep concerns over the violence he might have believed was brewing in Cho's mind and making its way into Cho's writing.

At times, Cho's fiction was his delusion—his own private venting of the fury that was about to erupt. He was signaling whoever would listen that his delusion, likely with command hallucinations, was soon to be acted upon. And, likely those command hallucinations were presented with graphic clarity in a story that Professor Hicok shared with the governor's investigative panel. It was about a character named Bud.

In the story, Bud, enmeshed in his own self-hatred, gets up one morning with devastating violence on his mind. He, as quoted by the governor's report, "gets out of bed unusually early … puts on his black jeans, a strappy black vest with many pockets, a black hat, a large dark sunglasses [sic] and a flimsy jacket." He observes students at school, "strut inside, smiling, laughing, embracing each other. … A few eyes glance at Bud but without the glint of recognition. I hate this! I hate all these frauds! I hate my life. … This is it. … This is when you damn people die with me. …" Bud enters the building's empty halls and walks into an "arbitrary classroom, where inside everyone is smiling and laughing as if they're in heaven-on-earth, something magical and enchanting about all the people's intrinsic nature that Bud will never experience." Bud "breaks away and runs to the bathroom." "I can't do this. … I have no moral right. …"

Bud is approached by a "Gothic girl"—Goths are counterculture characters out of the world of video games who dress in dark or all-black clothing, paint themselves in very pale makeup to make themselves look vampire-like, and usually wear longish or shoulder-length hair. They represent themselves to be very grim and sullen and usually hold very dark views of society. Both Kliebold and Harris at Columbine might have been described as Goths by those who knew them, outsiders whose views ran counter to the culture of the school. This is the character of the Gothic girl who meets Bud in Cho's story. Bud tells the Gothic girl, "I'm nothing. I'm a loser. I can't do anything. I was going to kill every god damned person in this damn school, swear to god I was, but I … couldn't. I just couldn't. Damn it I hate myself!"

Bud and the Gothic girl drive to her home in a stolen car. "If I get stopped by a cop my life will be over. A stolen car, two handguns, and a sawed off shotgun." At the Gothic girl's house she gets an ".8 caliber automatic rifle and an M16 machine gun." The governor's report says that the story ends with the line, "You and me. We can fight to claim our deserving throne."

The piece Cho wrote, as disturbing as it was, was his grandiose delusion of omnipotent power as he approached what he believed would be his defining moment of revenge upon a world that he believed he could not enter or a world that excluded him. Of course, it was not the world that had excluded him; the world, in fact, bent over backwards to make accommodations for him. His mind was disintegrating, and his recognition that he could no longer fit with such delusional logic was likely the last ray of insight into his fate sealed by schizophrenic illness—first clinically known as *dementia praecox* for the very reason of its early, and progressive, destruction of the human mind. His writings were those of the delusional patient, an extremely dangerous one.

Hopelessly ill, and with the awareness of his failing faculties, Cho-as-author could not even bring himself to do the deed he envisions. In his writing, he fails even at creating his own apocalypse. It is only the figure of the Gothic girl, a figure more powerful than he, an avatar of himself, that brings him to his moment of violence. The amalgamation of Cho and his avatar will form the critical mass that turns these literary ideations of apocalyptic homicide and suicide into a reality. That amalgamation, represented on video in Cho's manifesto, is only a year away.

In another class that spring, Technical Writing, Cho also experienced a run-in with a teacher, Professor Bean, who told the panel that he believed Cho's entire demeanor, his wearing his cap "pulled down," was his method of control, establishing his power over people by making them come to him. Far from the damaged and depressed individual that Professor Roy saw in the freshman and sophomore, Professor Bean saw a manipulative and passively controlling person, a kind of tyrant who exercised his power through a contrived demeanor of weakness. This was, possibly, another aspect of the mental illness called *narcissism*, another very dangerous disease, and one from which Cho suffered.

Bean would have none of it. He challenged Cho on his writing topics, challenged Cho on his use of the English language, even challenged Cho on the fact that he was majoring in the usage of a language that he could not use in writing. Finally, when Cho said that he wanted to write a "real-time" experience of *Macbeth* as it might relate to serial killings, Professor Bean had had enough. He asked Cho to talk to him after class and told him that his topic was unacceptable and that he was doing badly in his class. He suggested that Cho drop the class immediately. Cho said nothing but followed the professor back to his office, refused to sit down when invited to, and then argued with Professor Bean aggressively in an uncharacteristically loud voice. Professor Bean asked Cho to leave his office and to come back when he was in better control of himself. Cho left, saying nothing, but sent Professor Bean an email saying that he had dropped his class. This was almost a year to the day before Cho's rampage.

After the rampage, however, a letter from Cho was discovered in which he said that Bean had "gone holocaust" on him. Bean later said that it appeared clear to him that after Cho had dropped his class, Cho had researched Bean and found that Bean had a great interest in the Holocaust. Professor Bean was lucky to have survived Cho. What Professor Bean described was increasing grandiosity, aggressiveness, and failure in modulating emotional state—from mute to uncharacteristically loud voice. By challenging Cho, Professor Bean had pushed a trip wire that could have set Cho off early.

But, there would be more when Cho returned to campus in fall 2006 for his senior year. He continued pursuing his major in English with writing classes—one of them a playwrighting workshop. Another was a course called "Contemporary Horror." In the playwrighting workshop, Cho's teacher, Professor Falco, told the investigating panel that Cho appeared to be a problem from the very first day when students were asked to introduce themselves. Rather than introduce himself, Cho simply got up and left. Professor Falco said that, although Cho returned to class for the next session and completed the course, his writing was "juvenile" and some of his pieces "vented anger."

Cho at this point was showing signs of extreme deterioration in language and commensurate thinking abilities. His DUP had gone on far too long, and he was near the breaking point. Even Cho's classmates were quoted after the April 2007 massacre as saying that they had joked among themselves about Cho. Remarks were actually made that they were just waiting for him to do something. In fact, the governor's report says, one person told a friend that he was the "kind of guy who might go on a rampage killing." Clearly, someone had picked up and reported a sign that many professionals trained and experienced to see and administrators empowered to act also saw but simply ignored, apparently hoping it would simply go away—at least from them.

In his course in Contemporary Horror, Cho's writing was good enough to earn him a B. Like poetry, Cho's language in contemporary horror was tuned to primary processes, like dreaming. This course probably drew more on his inner turmoil of horror. And, like poetry, it allowed him to express that inner turmoil of horror in a place where the structure did not make him withdraw, allowing his loosening thought associations to acceptably wander. He could exercise his delusions of power in a safe place where expressions of horror were actually welcomed. It was, in its own way, a possible form of reactive therapy that encouraged him to spew forth his brewing insanity.

Throughout that fall of 2006, Cho, still living in a residence hall, seemed to go through an uneventful semester. His roommates said that he was very quiet, kept to himself, and spent his time studying, downloading music, and sleeping. Was his sleep so excessive that even his roommates noticed it? If so, it was probably hypersomnia, a more advanced sign with advancing DUP, predicting a worse outcome for Cho as well as for those with whom he would come into contact.

His residence advisor had been warned by the previous residence advisor that there were "issues" with Cho, the governor's report said. Cho, they were told, had been known to have made untoward advances to some of the female residents and had written strange messages on the eraser boards outside their rooms and on his website. Cho was now, at least to those in the residence community, a blinking red light, someone to watch, someone to be concerned about. Had the university been aware of the student concerns at the care team level the way resident students and some faculty members were concerned, perhaps they would have contacted Cho's parents to report what was happening.

Then Cho took an advanced fiction writing workshop in the fall 2006 semester with a professor he had had the previous spring. She knew, therefore, that Cho was essentially noncommunicative and would have a problem in the class discussions. Cho also wore his baseball cap pulled down low and his dark glasses. His teacher, Professor Norris, checked with the dean's office to see whether Cho was "okay"—perhaps meaning: was he dangerous? The English Department had received no notices from the administration about Cho's stalking, the campus police intervention, or his detention and commitment to a psychiatric facility.

Again, a failure to follow up and communicate had left another professor to fend for herself with a student who was only months away from committing the largest mass school shooting in American history. However, even though Professor Norris offered to help Cho with language, to set him up with student disability services, and to take him for counseling, Cho refused to respond. Did he believe that he was not even good enough to accept help or that accepting help would be a kind of weakness? Most likely not. Rather, he might have been too far gone, his fractured persona already coalescing in the grandiose delusion he would soon present to the entire world.

Whatever it was, he still managed to show up in class, except for the final two weeks, and turn in his writing assignments. Cho had managed to make it through three and a half years at Virginia Tech, despite hitting speed bumps along the way and earning himself the reputation of someone who would do a lot of damage some day. Informally, he had been tracked by the residence hall advisors, his professors in the English Department, and the students in his classes. Officially he had been brought to the attention of the State Superior Court, Virginia Tech police, various deans, the counseling center, and the campus care team. Yet none of these groups, severally, considered themselves in a position to do anything—even after Cho was taken into custody on campus by campus security and transported, still in custody, for involuntary commitment to a psychiatric facility. His case was reviewed the following morning by a special justice, who issued conditions for his release to involuntary outpatient treatment. He had been evaluated, screened, and even cited by the magistrate as imminently dangerous but, still, no one from the hospital or university communicated any of this to Cho's parents or checked with the police about what had transpired on the night he was taken into custody. All that would change as Cho began his spring semester by purchasing guns and ammunition.

The Fatal Spring Semester, 2007

As Cho amassed weapons during the early spring semester, his class attendance began to drop off. He was even less communicative with his roommates—as if that were possible—and retreated deeper into himself. Had his delusions taken over completely? Was the only voice he heard a command voice to kill himself and others?

Legally, were Cho not living in the delusional world of the paranoid schizophrenic, his purchasing of guns and ammunition, after having written violent pieces describing what his character, Bud, wanted to do, would have amounted to premeditation. His use of chains on the buildings to keep first responders out while he was killing, his bringing multiple clips of ammunition to the killing site to allow him to reload, his preparation of the manifesto and mailing it to NBC after the Hilscher murder but before the ensuing rampage—all amounted to his premeditation. But paranoid schizophrenic patients can stay on track like this because their more fixed delusions can keep their behavior better organized than other psychotic patients. We remember Unibomber Ted Kaczynski's rambling and clearly psychotic ranting in his manifesto, which was in stark contrast to his ability to mail bombs from his remote Montana residence. Similarly, Cho was so organized that on April 15—the very night before his rampage—he called his parents, as he did every week, and spoke to them as if he were, in their words, his "regular" self, according to their statements to the investigative panel. His parents asked him if he needed any money, and he said that he did not.

As he was about to hang up, his parents said, "We love you." That was the last time they spoke to their son, having no inkling of what he was about to do early the next morning, when he arose very early, dressed in his ball cap and reflective glasses, gathered his gear, and set out to Emily Hilscher's residence hall for a fateful encounter.

Chapter 3

What We Have Learned from the Virginia Tech Massacre*

The American College of Emergency Psychiatrists (ACEP) has recommended that emergency physicians trained in psychiatric evaluation be given more authority in the involuntary hold process. Since emergency departments are 24-hour facilities, resources are already in place. Because the CSB serves an independent "gatekeeper" role under the Virginia TDO process, emergency physicians and CSB staff are generally expected to work collaboratively in determining whether a TDO is needed for those patients screened in emergency departments. However, where CSB pre-screens are not immediately available, properly trained emergency physicians can effectively screen patients under an emergency custody order and communicate with the magistrate to obtain the TDO when needed. If such a gate-keeping responsibility were to be conferred on emergency physicians, further questions would have to be addressed regarding the respective roles of the emergency

* The Commonwealth of Virginia's Special Report on Cho's mental health and his mass shooting at Virginia Tech can be found at http://www.governor.virginia.gov/TempContent/techPanelReport-docs/FullReport.pdf

> physicians and the CSB staff in exploring alternatives to hospitalization and in participating in the commitment hearing.
>
> **Report of The Commonwealth of Virginia's Special Panel on Mental Health History of Seung Hui Cho**

In order to better understand and prevent such man-made disasters, it is necessary to examine this panel's conclusions and statements. To do this it is necessary to examine them within the contexts of both current conditions within our national healthcare delivery system and the relevant clinical literature.

We also must remember that it was within the context of this very emergency medical care psychiatric system that Cho was first detained, evaluated, given a hearing, and then released. Therefore, the governor's panel focused on the emergency mental healthcare system as part of its investigation of the entire Cho Seung-Hui shooting. Assessment of emergency mental healthcare in this country, however, goes well beyond the Cho case. Therefore, beginning with this panel's suggestion to reduce the risk of future man-made disasters of this sort, we believe it is necessary to reframe this statement to reflect the current state of emergency medicine in America.

Emergency Medicine in America

Although behavioral emergencies were specifically mandated equally with other medical emergencies in the Medic One Law, they were never funded. As Dr. Boyd has written,

> While it was acknowledged that there are numerous and varied emergent medical conditions, it was established that seven critical patient groups were to be identified for regional emergency medical services (EMS) planning:
>
> Major Trauma
> Burns
> Spinal Cord Injuries (SCI)
> Acute Cardiac
> Poisonings
> High Risk Infants and Mothers
> Behavioral Emergencies
>
> An in-depth knowledge of the incidence, demography, epidemiology, and clinical aspects associated with these critical patient categories was mandatory for a systems approach that could be addressed in relation to EMS regional planning and operations. General as well as specific planning for regional EMS response to the routine overall and

> particularly critical target patient groups provided a system of care for critical medical conditions and other emergencies so that all would receive better care and benefit from sound regional EMS system planning and operations. Responsive system plans and operations in the general and critical care areas provided a basis and an opportunity for evaluating these goals and impact with an aim toward prevention. (Boyd, 1982)

Although Dr. Boyd remains saddened by the failure of his multiple efforts to include behavioral emergencies within the funding of our Medic One emergency medical system, he is now attempting to address the needs of troubled Native American youth. Similar to Virginia Tech, the epidemic of youth suicide and violence on reservations was brought to our attention by the horrors of the Red Lake, Minnesota, suicide and mass murder. His scholarly report of the founding of our emergency medical system, however, should be included in any effort to reduce the risk of rampage murders and mass killings of innocents, whether on campus or in shopping centers, nursing homes, or post offices. The recommendations of The Commonwealth Panel, therefore, are not new, and, in fact, ironically, they are already obsolete.

All emergency medicine specialists are trained in emergency psychiatry, just as all psychiatrists are trained in emergency medicine as conditions of receiving their M.D. degrees. Like all specialty-training recruits, graduates, and specialty practitioners, some are more skilled and interested in the psychiatric patient than others. There are rare birds, who are actually dual-boarded in emergency medicine and psychiatry, but, the fact that only 1 percent of questions for board certification in emergency medicine even remotely pertain to emergency psychiatry is telling.

Most emergency medical specialists select the field for saving lives of the seriously medically ill and victims of serious trauma. Whether they are interested in or compassionate toward the emergency psychiatric patient is rapidly becoming a moot point. They simply do not have the time to be dealing with them in any fashion remotely resembling the panel's recommendation. Some of them, bogged down with critical care cases of intentional self-harm or reckless victimization by violence—for example, bar fights and shootings—become resentful of the very population from which Cho emerges within the system.

Histories of stalking behaviors, reports that (Cho) "doesn't answer questions," and extremely complex diagnostics needing specialized outpatient services generally turn off the staff of emergency rooms. After all, they are best trained and experienced in saving lives of automobile and industrial accidents—they did not sign up to be taking care of another specialty's routine business.

Of course, almost all of them know and are prepared for the occasional emergency psychiatric presentation that could not be diverted in any way, for example, the guy who was normal until tonight and then started hallucinating for no reason. And, they also have to take care of mangled hands and injured eyes, until hand surgeons and ophthalmologists can take over care of these patients.

Emergency medicine specialists are generally well trained and prepared for all this, because it goes with their turf. And, they usually are attracted by the variety of multispecialty problems to which they are exposed, including the occasional psychiatric emergency. Except in large medical school training centers that have house staff filling all specialties, however, they are increasingly burdened with having to take care of all specialty cases after hours, along with the most routine chronic and acute care problems, better treated outside emergence rooms (ERs).

Many ER doctors believe that psychiatrists are lazy, because they will not come to the ER when on call and take care of the psychiatric patients. But, now, psychiatrists are no more a problem than orthopedic surgeons, hand surgeons, and cardiologists. As one medical director of a large urban hospital system put it, "I just don't want to be the last American hospital with a call roster." He meant that he was sick and tired of answering complaints every morning about on-call specialists refusing to come into the ER off hours and take care of their specialty patients.

Funding is a big reason for this. Third-party payers either do not cover emergency psychiatry or do not pay enough so that a psychiatrist can afford to even drive to and from the hospital while at the same time incurring substantial malpractice risks. These risks are unmitigated by the Good Samaritan nature of their work when on duty. Orthopedic surgeons, for example—so much in demand in emergency medicine—now charge $1000 per night just to take call, whether or not they have to answer the phone. Complicating the shrinking ER system today is the increasing numbers of primary psychiatric patients coming for primary care there. Oftentimes, as in Las Vegas, where there is minimal outpatient support for the seriously mentally ill patient, upwards of 50 percent of ER patients are seriously mentally ill patients without access to specialized outpatient psychiatric care.

As an example of the abuses in the emergency healthcare system, consider the following from a newspaper in Austin, where it was reported that 9 patients made nearly 2,700 ER visits to only one local hospital in Texas.

April 01, 2009 9:19 PM EDT

> AUSTIN, Texas—Just nine people accounted for nearly 2,700 of the emergency room visits in the Austin area during the past six years at a cost of $3 million to taxpayers and others, according to a report. The patients went to hospital emergency rooms 2,678 times from 2003 through 2008, said the report from the nonprofit Integrated Care Collaboration, a group of healthcare providers who care for low-income and uninsured patients. "What we're really trying to do is find out who's using our emergency rooms ... and find solutions," said Ann Kitchen, executive director of the group, which presented the report last week to the Travis County Healthcare District board. The average emergency room visit costs $1,000.

> Hospitals and taxpayers paid the bill through government programs such as Medicare and Medicaid, Kitchen said. Eight of the nine patients have drug abuse problems, seven were diagnosed with mental health issues and three were homeless. Five are women whose average age is 40, and four are men whose average age is 50, the report said, according to the *Austin American-Statesman*. "It's a pretty significant issue," said Dr. Christopher Ziebell, chief of the emergency department at University Medical Center at Brackenridge, which has the busiest ERs in the area. Solutions include referring some frequent users to mental health programs or primary care doctors for future care, Ziebell said. "They have a variety of complaints," he said. With mental illness, "a lot of anxiety manifests as chest pain." (*Austin American-Statesman*, 2009)

ER doctors lack neither training nor authority to take as much charge of evaluating and making appropriate dispositions of patients like Cho as they either wish or have time to do. It is not unusual, for example, for emergency room doctors to refuse to discharge psychiatric patients, regardless of what their on-call psychiatrist advises over the phone to do. The panel's recommendations for more psychiatric training of emergency medicine specialists, although meritorious, is unlikely, therefore, to get very much traction today in the real world of healthcare service delivery. Furthermore, it ignores the public health context of emergency psychiatry, in both its historical and epidemiological contexts. We have noted the early failure to include emergency psychiatry within the emergency medical system developed under the Medic One legislation back in the 1970s.

Cho's hospitalization vividly displayed inpatient and emergency psychiatry strangled in a web of conflicting law and regulations constructed for trial attorneys, rather than the practice of medicine. Clinicians merely danced in a ritual of assessing very valid allegations of imminent dangerousness and serious mental illness in Cho. How did that come to be? Such assessment is a main responsibility for the cop on the beat when encountering a threatening person resisting arrest.

Even under the ideal circumstances of training a core of emergency medicine specialists in psychiatry, practical treatment dispositions for patients so properly evaluated are diminishing faster than the resultant demand created by such best practices in emergency medicine. The best emergency medicine specialist can do little for patients like Cho Seung-Hui if, as is increasingly the case, inpatient psychiatric units are being shut down for lack of adequate reimbursement by third-party payers.

There are times in Arizona—and likely other states too—when the limited number of acute psychiatric inpatient beds are filled throughout the state and a patient must be sent to New Mexico or Utah. While the hunt for increasingly rare disposition is going on, there is the inevitable hunt for a medical specialist or acute medical/surgical bed for the cardiac and orthopedic patient too. As stated, the on-call roster for all specialties in non-university-affiliated general hospitals today is either dying or dead, whether orthopedics, cardiology, or psychiatry. Additionally, well over 100,000 acute care inpatient medical/surgical beds have been closed. The panel alluded to deadlines in involuntary commitment proceedings, citing potentially wasteful extensions of police time awaiting disposition to a receiving hospital. Nothing, however, was concluded in regard to healthcare infrastructure resources, particularly during those busy emergency psychiatry times at nights and during weekends and holidays.

In northwestern Wisconsin, which is one of the worst areas for preventive detention nationally, there is seemingly not a public or official healthcare concern. The police simply drop off the patient in a receiving hospital's ER, regardless of whether a secure inpatient psychiatric bed is known to be available. If the patient cannot be admitted from that receiving hospital's ER, the police may not return to pick the patient up until the next day. In other words, the police and public safety officials seem to ignore the problem of what to do with patients the community mental health system can't treat.

Idealistic as it may seem to have emergency room doctors taking responsibility for assessing patients like Cho in the middle of the night and then becoming entangled in the chaotic tentacles of superior court testimony on imminent dangerousness during the working day, it is totally impractical. Whatever recommendations ER doctors were alleged to have acquired from the American College of Emergency Physicians regarding this solution, the specialty of emergency medicine in today's world of overcrowded ERs is going to place this commonwealth recommendation from the Virginia Tech massacre close to the bottom of its priorities. Its leaders are trying to find a way to just survive in America's current healthcare delivery crisis—not taking on the burdens of the Chos in our society; they do not belong in emergency rooms to begin with. In fact, their presence in ERs has been determined by lawyers—not doctors. And, such patients are most active at night, the time when lawyers both creating and controlling the court-ordered treatment system are quietly resting up for litigation the next morning. As we will see, there will be plenty for them to do.

In the end, it was not just the irony of coincidence that a lawyer had to act as a layman and commit Cho against both medical and the court's own independent clinical psychological advice. It is hopeful, however, that the American Association of Child and Adolescent Psychiatry and American Association of Emergency Psychiatry, both affiliates of the American Psychiatric Association, have each recognized the needs expressed in the Virginia panel report. This recognition results from the epidemic of youth violence and suicide—Columbine and Virginia Tech simply having been extreme cases and the tips of an ominous iceberg we are rapidly approaching.

Although a hopeful sign that a unique liaison is being developed to explore the possibilities for improving emergency care of children and adolescents, such intraspecialty consultation demonstrates how very far behind the curve of public health needs we really are today. Similar liaison between the American Association of Emergency Psychiatry and the American College of Emergency Physicians has existed for years, yet few emergency medical specialists even know of the American Association of Emergency Psychiatry. Still, the actual volume of patients entering ERs nationally is estimated to be between 7 and 50 percent. Nobody is keeping count, but Dr. Jon Berlin, a national authority on utilization of ERs by patients for their primary psychiatric problems, simply concludes, "It's a lot!"

Board certification for emergency medicine does not have 1 percent of its certification test questions addressing psychiatric knowledge and problems because its leaders believe they do not want emergency medicine to be emergency psychiatry. Despite the idealistic advocacy of the Virginia panel for emergency medicine physicians to be subspecialized in emergency psychiatry, such an expectation is unrealistic. Emergency medicine has too many other enormous problems on its plate right now to even be considering such an additional responsibility on American healthcare's frontline.

The fact that we do not even know the rate of utilization of ERs by psychiatric patients demonstrates the failure to date of this liaison between the powerful medical specialties of psychiatry and emergency medicine. Until public health officials have a clearer idea of this utilization, little is going to be done. But, the liaison to date has probably resulted in preventing the emergency psychiatry crisis from being even worse than it already is. Its critical failings were well documented by the Virginia panel on the Cho case. More importantly, as Dr. Boyd stated decades ago, there was then—and remains now—little prospect for funding of emergency psychiatry to even begin to deserve any sense of consolation from the commonwealth panel's recommendations. The panel's focus on emergency medical services as a viable solution for preventing violence among the at-risk seriously mentally ill patient population, as embodied in the disaster of the Virginia Tech massacre, although meritorious, is impractical and futuristic, at best.

If anything, the damage to the emergency psychiatry system is far worse now than it was when Dr. Boyd's valiant lobbying fell on deaf ears in Congress in 1982. There were far more psychiatric inpatient, crisis, and community mental health center outpatient services available per capita for the seriously mentally ill when Medic One failed to fund behavioral emergencies decades ago than there are now. And, compounding this scarcity of resources impacting emergency services today is the concurrent closure of 25 percent of emergency rooms since 9/11, leaving leaner ER staffs to find dispositions in our current healthcare universe of rapidly dwindling medical/surgical beds, as well as urgent and acute care outpatient resources. To be realistic, we must face the fact that the seriously mentally ill patient, such as Cho, is simply not welcome in the vast majority of ERs today. The process of solving this cross-specialty crisis in medical communications and coordination is just beginning, its solutions just germinating and years from implementation, if ever.

The current state of emergency services is terrible. Most states even flunked tests for standards expected of first responders several years after 9/11. In 2006, teams from the National Institutes of Health, Bethesda Naval Hospital, and the Consortium of District of Columbia Suburban Hospitals celebrated a successful joint hospital disaster drill! It was reported that the multiple layers of radio frequencies currently operating in the area continue to hamper seamless medical communications and coordination. This was several years after the events of 9/11, including a direct hit on the nearby Pentagon.

With billions spent on homeland security to date, one would expect that healthcare facilities in the nation's capital would have been well beyond disaster drills, having accomplished the Standard for Computerized Ambulance Dispatch (CAD) with Diversion, so appallingly absent during Katrina in 2005. Instead, "mid level interagency professional teams planned and effected a first successful Disaster Medicine drill for the DC metropolitan hospitals—with the approval and cooperation of upper level management from all hospitals involved" (Scottsdale Healthcare Center Conference on Trauma Care, Phoenix, AZ, 2007).

This spirited presentation of a "successful drill" in the nation's capitol could have been interpreted, in other words, as being somewhat serendipitous an event. Had some mid-level clinicians from neighboring hospitals, therefore, not made the effort to do something about medical communications and coordination of census and resources for government employees and military alike in the nation's capitol, most likely this drill would still be just an idea floating around! And, had these mid-level clinicians not pulled this off "with cooperation of their upper managements," what would have happened to our nation's leaders had there been another mass casualty incident? Next time, as repeatedly predicted by the Department of Homeland Security, we should expect far more casualties from unconventional weapons.

Aerospace companies with access to necessary satellite communications have developed highly promising medical communications and coordination (C2) platforms that have been relegated to low priority by the departments of Defense, Health and Human Services, and Homeland Security. The tragic consequences of this neglect were visible for the whole world to see in the wake of Hurricane Katrina.

Fortunately, DC, along with California, Massachusetts, and Connecticut, is the only area recently to have received B and B– grades for statewide emergency medical services. The rest of the 47 states examined received either C or D grades, most of them, probably, because they had large populations not served by teaching hospitals staffed with 24-hour/day in-house residents from all medical specialties. California, Massachusetts, Connecticut, and Washington, DC, are relatively rich in teaching hospitals within a range of rapid transport of casualties. But, this examination of ER capabilities was not even performed with risk of disaster factored in—only routine emergency medical services.

Overloading of emergency rooms with the uninsured is relatively well known, although the associated causative factors from closure of 25 percent of ERs and over 100,000 acute care med/surg beds since the events of 9/11 are less well known.

Impaired access into the healthcare system for many millions of citizens is on the political front burner with the current administration, but root causes are far more complex than those addressed in any campaign, that is, quick fix via imposing modern information systems on an information technology that, compared to other industries, is believed archaic. Or, reducing the number of payers, even having one payer, as is falsely alleged and believed to be the case in Canada. The one-payer system in Canada has essentially ended with private clinics that accept alternative payments sprouting up and operational. These "illegal" outlyers fly unprosecuted under the government radar screen in British Columbia, because the rich and privileged Canadian no longer wishes to wait months for surgery or travel across the border for an MRI. Other Canadian provinces will inevitably follow, as new transparency reveals the glaring failures, as well as the better known successes, of the Canadian healthcare system. Few citizens believe the intellectual foundation used to eliminate the legal standard of "care taking" of the mentally ill from our state involuntary commitment statutes. But, they, as the State of Virginia Panel appears to suggest, probably do not know how this legal revolution actually occurred during the latter half of the last century. All they see is the increasing number of homeless they have to step over or around on their way to work every morning in downtown USA. As with the panel reporting on failures of the involuntary commitment for Cho Seung-Hui that could have prevented the Virginia Tech massacre, they are poorly informed of the "why" of this mess. It threatens to turn into disastrous violence, both on an isolated basis everyday and in headline rampage murders like the Santa Claus mass murder and suicide case in California in 2008. Does a week go by now without at least one high-profile apocryphal mass murder and suicide reported by national news syndicates?

Young trial attorneys, aggressively asserting what they called *constitutional rights to the self-determination of individuals displaying aberrant behavior*, successfully moved the courts to abolish all clinical validity for the disease model causing aberrant behavior. This was the disease model that would ultimately explode into the headlines as rampage murders. Thus, it was, for the attorneys well versed in Thomas Szacz's *The Myth of Mental Illness* (1960), that psychiatrists simply shoehorned the person into the categories of their concepts of psychiatric disease. Therefore, Szacz argued, mental illness is a myth, a projection of the concepts of the psychiatrists themselves and not at all an illness. Ironically, Dr. Szacz was practicing psychoanalysis at the time of his writings and never treated the seriously mentally ill even though he claimed treatment of the seriously mentally ill to be his primary clinical expertise. And, through his charisma and writings, he actually did successfully become just that, the self-described expert on serious mental illness, convincing many of the nation's decision makers that the diagnosis of schizophrenia is a myth. One would wonder whether he could have imagined the disaster being unwoven by the Virginia Tech Review Panel on Cho's mental health history emanating from the springs of his wisdom.

Concurrently with Szcaz's anarchy over disease models for mental illness, psychologist John Monahan provided a scientific foundation to the "myth of mental illness." He spent his career demonstrating that there is no evidence for the seriously mentally ill being at more risk of both causing and being the victim of his or her own violence than any other group of people. He wrote:

> The conclusion to emerge most strikingly from these studies is the great degree to which violence is over-predicted. Of those predicted to be dangerous, between 65 percent and 99 percent are false positives—that is people who will not, in fact, commit a dangerous act [but were

> committed anyway]. Indeed, the literature has been consistent on this point ever since Pinel took the chains off the supposedly dangerous mental patients at La Bicetre in 1792, and the resulting lack of violence gave lie to the psychiatric predictions that had justified their restraint [in the first place]. … The population used by each of the research studies reviewed … was highly selective and biased toward positive results—primarily convicted offenders, sexual psychopaths and adjudicated [juvenile] delinquents. (Monahan, 1925)

> … The Desire to predict Events in the world around us and thereby to gain some feeling of control over them may be intrinsic to the nature of man. few events in life have greater physical and psychological impact than violence done to one human being by another. It is not surprising, therefore, that society should devote a great deal of resources to attempt identifying today the person who tomorrow will be violent. (Kelly, 1955, quoted in Monahan, 1975)

It was too late for him to acknowledge more recently, with "deep disappointment," that he was wrong. Yet his opinions were invited for the commonwealth panel to hear. The opinions of Virginia's medical societies, representing the professionals having to make the decisions on cases like Cho, however, were not.

Whether studying those who are violent or those diagnosed seriously mentally ill, Monahan now acknowledges, "the association between violence and seriously mental illness is undeniable."

His retraction of his earlier research, along with the contemporary neuropsychiatric debunking of *The Myth of Mental Illness*, literally dissolves the revolutionary legal foundation beneath state involuntary commitment statutes. A commission was already studying Virginia's commitment laws when Cho struck. The focus in Richmond quickly diverted after the massacre in Blacksburg because of the chaotic web of laws, standards, and procedures that created the deadly web strangling emergency psychiatry at St. Albans Hospital.

The decriminalization of mental illness, however, is not going to be pulled back easily. It is poorly understood by the public, which is miffed by the homeless and the daily acts of senseless violence among them, senseless human destruction supported now by constituencies knowingly gaining from it. Certainly contractors building prisons for the largest incarcerated population in the world are not going to demonstrate for decriminalization of the mentally ill. Special offenders clog our prisons and require more expensive and specialized buildings. And for-profit corrections management companies gain too from the needs of what are now called *special offenders* but who are really the mentally ill offenders. Currently, state hospitals are all but extensions of state departments of corrections, detaining mainly those few adjudicated criminally insane. General hospitals are closing their inpatient psychiatry units as fast as they can, due to discriminatory discounting of reimbursement that forces hospitals to subsidized what once was the state's responsibility, the seriously mentally ill, as well as poorly reimbursed emergency medical services. These services may or may not seem economically feasible to hospital boards of trustees responsible for making certain that their hospitals run in the black. They close services, however, faster than they can possibly be replaced.

The budgetary crises for community hospitals, now incapable of subsidizing either emergency medical or inpatient psychiatric services, and the concomitant rise in imperial for-profit prisons have converged. Metropolitan jails are now among the largest inpatient psychiatric facilities in any state, and prisons are the ultimate long-term detention for the dangerous mentally ill patient—now, labeled *special offenders* in obedience to the legacy of the once popularized—yet, now debunked—myth of mental illness.

These special offenders, with all their hallucinatory, delusional, and behavioral abnormalities, are considered to have had free will in committing their bizarre felonies. They supposedly "learned" everything demonstrated in their offensive behavior resulting in incarceration, whether from the millions annually jailed and awaiting any kind of safe disposition, or in prison, where neither guards nor inmates wish to be in their unpredictable presence.

The majority of Americans would not believe that those people lying on the streets, abandoned by their families and wrapped with dirty blankets in freezing temperatures as they finally give up their hold on reality, learned their offensive behaviors anywhere, whether school, church, or family. But the small number of young attorneys leading the assault on traditional commitment laws convinced a thin judicial bench that exactly that was the case—all behavior, whether offensive or benign, is learned—and, thus, can be unlearned. And so, many attorneys trained in their arguments by the already retracted tenets of the myth of mental illness, were ultimately able to convince judges to put in place a reverse Draconian procedure to handcuff the very institutions that could protect both the mentally ill from themselves and society from the mentally ill. There, now, as we saw in Blacksburg, a mentally ill patient like Cho could be released without known means of transportation to his college following determination by a magistrate that he was imminently dangerous. Months later he pulled the trigger on one of the deadliest man-made disasters in American history, because his mental illness was considered not a factor in his choice of behaviors. Once the judge followed, knowingly or simply instinctively, the ultimate and powerful intent of Wisconsin's revolutionary least restrictive standards for involuntary commitment, he put into motion the final actions of a killer/time bomb whose fuse was already lit. What was so astounding was that Cho was found imminently dangerous and nothing was made to happen to restrict him, other than mandating some elusively and undefined outpatient therapy at a college counseling center that denied providing such services. It had no psychiatrist at the time either and certainly was not set up to provide one. Yet, despite the lack of key services, Cho was allowed to make an appointment at this guidance center, thus meeting criteria for discharge from less than one day of detention at St. Albans Hospital. Not even his family was informed. It was up to Cho to either stop being imminently dangerous or face the consequences of his free will choice in the matter.

How could any disposition have been less restrictive? He apparently was not even transported back to campus via any official vehicle. More damning is the fact that nothing was done either to follow up with examination of the magistrate's extraordinary finding of imminent dangerousness—dramatically overriding the expert clinical opinions of both a clinical psychologist and psychiatrist—or to attempt neutralization of it, perhaps with such anti-Szaczian modalities as psychotropic medication that Cho had voluntarily and reliably taken before with good response.

A further intellectual underpinning to this procedural debacle and disaster at Virginia Tech was the popularized philosopher of the antipsychiatry movement, Ronald Laings. A victim himself of mainly random occurrences of schizophrenia—his daughter having been hospitalized multiple times—he concluded, in apparent desperation, that she and her cohort of seriously mentally ill patients really were normal. Seeking solace from his own despair, Laings founded Kinsley Hall in England for patients diagnosed as psychotic. He allowed them to interact freely, providing medication only when requested by the patient. This was the philosophical basis for setting Cho up to manage his own care under involuntary commitment. If not, then it was simply legal overzealousness and medical cowardice in the face of that legal overzealousness. But, like Monahan, Laings also had to capitulate later, acknowledging total disillusionment with his philosophy, abandoning a thesis that was the basis for government policy for the mentally ill. But his abandonment was too late, coming after, not before, his therapeutic nihilistic anarchy had already spread like wildfire among the constituency most anxious to eliminate schizophrenia from the vocabulary of forensic medicine. A significant portion of this constituency was composed of young trial attorneys who were armed with a few books based on Laings' theory of psychosis being a normal adaptation to life.

As a result of the opinions of Laings and Szacz, a body of legal literature came into being providing insights into how people learned both to become homeless on icy inner-city streets and to behave so bizarrely; they could find their own way to allegedly desired special offender units of prison to spend the best years of their lives behind bars. Their families, as oftentimes proclaimed by talk-show easy-cure pop family therapists, were really the psychotic entities. Even psychiatric residents were required to learn from such charismatic pop psychology lecturers how psychosis moved around within these families like a basketball in a Harlem Globetrotter warm-up. And, voilà, the ball was only to be held by the "identified patient" just as the sheriff arrived for the disturbance call. Then there were the pseudomutuality and schizogenic mother concepts of crazy families. What these Laingsian clinicians preaching their gospels back then were observing is unknown, but few practitioners today believe that any of these family dysfunctions—if they actually exist at all—are the cause of deviant behavior of the seriously mentally ill; even psychiatrists who were heavily exposed to these teachings in the 1960s and 1970s.

There is solid evidence that family dysfunction can contribute to relapse of the mentally ill following hospital discharge, but nobody purports these findings to relate in any way to causation. The crazy family theory of schizophrenia is dead, but its legacy lives on in the shrinking number of psychiatric hospitals still accepting patients like Cho on temporary detention orders in exchange for guaranteed cash flow, no longer a guarantee of third-party payers for voluntary admissions to psychiatric hospitals.

Of interest in reviewing the mental health report of the Virginia Tech Review Panel was the complete avoidance of any reference to what the most competent forensic psychiatrists and researchers in the field of serious mental illness diagnose as schizophrenia or any type of psychosis, whether due to underlying mood disorder or medical illness such as AIDS or brain tumor. Although deference is paid to the obvious mental health problems, still, the panel veers away at the very end from attribution of Cho's behavior to disease, over which he had lost all control. They said,

> Notwithstanding the system failures and errors in judgment that contributed to Cho's worsening depression, Cho himself was the biggest impediment to stabilizing his mental health. He denied having previously received mental health services when he was evaluated in the fall of 2005, so medical personnel believe that their interaction with him on that occasion was the first time he had showed signs of mental illness. While Cho's emotional and psychological disabilities undoubtedly clouded his ability to evaluate his own situation; he, ultimately, is the primary person responsible for April 16, 2007; to imply otherwise would be wrong. (conclusion of the Virginia Tech Review Panel on the Virginia Tech massacre)

This is an astonishingly absolute and self-serving conclusion, disingenuously, but falsely, dispositive. It removes, as many investigative panels do, responsibility from the state for not doing its job competently. It does so by placing the blame on the very person who was incapable of knowing that he was sick. He suffered anosognosia, a condition in which a person who suffers disability seems unaware of or denies the existence of his or her disability. And this is in the face of the fact that there was absolutely no real physical examination of Cho by a competent neuropsychiatrist. Were there no radiologists in Blacksburg? Why is it wrong to imply that brain imaging may have demonstrated a disease of the brain that either destroyed or compromised his ego autonomy or his ability to know and control his own behavior?

Radiology and ultrasound imaging compose the standard of practice in the workup of all psychotic patients before any definitive diagnosis is made. But, the fact of the matter is that Cho, after a total of several alleged psychological and/or psychiatric triages and evaluations, had never even been thoroughly worked up, whether neurologically, as required in the first schizophrenic break; psychiatrically, just assumed; and, in the case of St. Albans, psychologically, oftentimes a luxury in hospitals.

At St. Albans, Cho was actually seen by a clinical psychologist with no time set aside to review clinical reports already generated on Cho or check collaterals for psychosocial information; that is, why was he considered imminently dangerous? It is a very serious matter for policemen and crisis workers to be running around at night trying to simply justify their existence. It should have been assumed that there was something seriously amiss with Cho, and clinical psychologists can test people! Why did he not do so? Would the court, after imposing such Draconian standards of practice on clinicians to do the impossible, actually refuse to pay him to perform psychological testing on such an admission? Likely not, but, if so, then all clinicians should quit this place.

No psychiatrist would expect, in a cursory first interview of a "mute" patient detained by competent authority of court as imminently dangerous, that such patient would admit to anything voluntarily. That is why psychiatrists in acute inpatient facilities interview collateral sources, such as family, police, friends, and others, during such an emergency workup. Yet no one even called Cho's parents or his sister. Did they not have access to Cho's college records, which would have provided at least one emergency contact? Were emergency contacts not mandatory at Virginia Tech? This issue alone boggles the mind.

Essentially, this panel ruled, by somewhat questionable psychological autopsy, that Cho had the capacity to form the specific intent to do what he did; that he knew the difference between right and wrong, knew the nature of his mass violent act, and had the capacity to control his behavior in every felony action. In other words, in legal terms, because Cho was able to form the mental intent, *mens rea*, and because he acted criminally upon that intent, *actus reus*, he is therefore a murderer. Moreover, because he was lying in wait for his first victim and brought many weapons to his second crime scene, reloaded, and kept on firing, he is guilty of murder in the first degree.

What the panel does not address is the fact that Cho, possibly because of a mental disease, could not tell right from wrong. Even if he could tell right from wrong, he did not have the capacity, because of a mental disease, to comport his actions to do right instead of wrong: the modern definition of an insanity defense. Such a conclusion of criminal intent by a committee of laymen is a gigantic leap of faith upon which the panel provided little supportive evidence. In fact, to the contrary, the facts of their own presentation of Cho's psychiatric history argue quite the opposite: that of preventable criminal insanity. Otherwise, why would so much attention be paid to both the failures of the system and questions regarding the impotence of mental health law in preventing what few experts now believe? That is what Monahan now concludes. Identified and adjudicated seriously mentally ill patients are, in fact, at higher risk for violence if untreated than controls who are not identified as seriously mentally ill.

Accordingly, like most official investigative panels, the panel spends time in its conclusions avoiding the uncomfortable facts of their own investigation to remove any blame from the entity that authorized the investigation and empaneled the investigators in the first place. In short, the governor's panel was self-serving and disingenuous at best and blatantly dishonest at worst. Of even more concern to this case, but apparently not to the investigators, was the long history of Cho's loss of touch with reality. This was the loss of reality as so many around him—whether students, faculty, or police—knew reality to be. Also neglected in the panel report was Cho's recurrent and long-standing strange behavior. The latter was so alienating and frightening to so many students, counselors, and educators that class attendance dropped off and professors cried for help—left in vain to improvise mini-therapeutic communities for a grossly schizophrenic patient.

There was simply too much evidence from past and recent history to say that Cho was simply suffering depression, not otherwise specified (NOS). This is such a useless, wastepaper-basket diagnosis that it informs nothing, and nothing is what Cho received. Anyone attending college knows that on any given Sunday, depression not otherwise specified can be identified in the majority of students.

Instead, Cho remained without diagnosable serious mental illness of psychotic nature. Research only shows worse outcomes associated with DUP—extremely long, perhaps nearly lifelong in Cho's case—and the capability today to improve outcomes with early treatment intervention. The same research also shows that today there is a capability to improve outcomes with early treatment and intervention. Although Cho demonstrated remarkable voluntary adherence to evaluation and treatment, even into the year of his rampage murder, clinical evidence shows minimal, if any, efforts while in college to actively engage him in any treatment. His teachers were forced by default, abandoned from Cook Guidance Center to the deans' offices, to improvise therapy for him; that is simply impossible and wantonly dangerous in this new millennium. We cannot say that Cho had even a total of sixty minutes of clinical assessment through several outpatient clinical psychological triages and inpatient psychiatric evaluation encounters. Other than the evaluator, who said he spent only fifteen minutes with Cho, we really do not know anything about his several clinical encounters. In the case of Virginia Tech's counseling center, where he was known to have been formally triaged three times, no records of his triage and evaluation even exist.

There should be strong questions about all of these clinical encounters and how Cho was worked up, if in fact he ever was. We cannot tell from the panel report, but we will try to disentangle what are really legal impediments to treating Cho during his entire career at Virginia Tech from what was merely avoidance of engaging him in the thorough psychiatric, psychological, and social service assessment. All three professional duties were both forensically and clinically indicated with his involuntary hospitalization.

The panel report analyzes Cho's history of encounters on campus in order to make recommendations for administrative healthcare system delivery in college communities and possible changes to the commitment law. The last was, for the most part, delegated to the The Commonwealth of Virginia Commission on Mental Health Law Reform already actively working in Richmond at the time of the massacre in Blacksburg. In the wake of the Virginia Tech massacre, this commission was charged with conducting "a comprehensive examination of the Virginia's mental health laws and services and studying ways to use the law more effectively to serve the needs of people with mental illness, while respecting the interests of their families and communities."

At the time of this writing, a Task Force on Civil Commitment was addressing criteria for inpatient and outpatient commitment, transportation, and the emergency evaluation process, procedures for hearings, training, and—of course, not to be overlooked—compensation for participants in the process and oversight.

The panel report does lay out some critical facts, dramatic testimony from witnesses, and a nightmarish web of overlapping rules, statutes, and regulations bound to stifle any clinical and administrative initiative aimed at future prevention of such disasters on American campuses or, for that matter, improved clinical involvement with the seriously mentally ill at all. Although there may have been issues unique to Virginia Tech—its location in an area underserved by medical specialists, particularly well known as underserved by psychiatry—the panel report serves as a landmark public document for laying out the needs, solutions, and benefits of college healthcare and security services nationwide.

Like a bikini, however, it may be more attractive for what it reveals than conceals. It successfully documents the chronology of significant events in Cho's entire lifetime and those of official entities involved in his health problems on campus. Though the panel appears to have deliberately, unintentionally or by necessity, omitted critical information, questions, and interviews, the text is rich in biography for the perpetrator of this disaster, Cho Seung-Hui.

In a section subtitled "Constraints for Evaluation and Hearing," the panel laid out deadlines for formal clinical assessment and documentation. First of all, these are only realistic within a public health system for the prevention of mental illness that was essentially abolished decades before with the dumping of the seriously mentally ill into the poorest areas of cities. This epidemiology by Leighton et al. at Yale is now known as the *social drift theory of schizophrenia* (Sherman, 1960). Again, this social drift theory assumes that the psychologically and financially impoverished psychotic patients have a choice of where they wish to live—thus selecting our inner-city parks and alleys for their shopping carts and tattered blankets they know as home—"their own bush" as they say to answer questions of their ability to be safe.

This dumping of the seriously mentally ill patient, euphemistically known as *deinstitutionalization of the mentally ill*, was caused by a confluence of factors including but not limited to the closure of state hospital beds, with likely permanent cost shifting for the care of the seriously mentally ill from state to federal Medicaid and Medicare. These federal programs are likewise being gutted, particularly in the area of caring for the seriously mentally ill. They were originally constructed in the spirit of the community mental health movement, made possible by modern antipsychotic medications that reduced much of the most bizarre behavior, delusions, and hallucinations of psychotic patients—that is, if they took them reliably as prescribed, which they oftentimes did not.

This public health disaster of the seriously mentally ill patient going untreated is euphemistically known as *nonadherence*, having been politically corrected from the more sinister clinical nosology of *noncompliance*, caused for the most part by anosognosia, or the denial of disability commonly associated with serious mental illness. But, within the historical context of Laings' antipsychiatry, Szacz's *Myth of Mental Illness*, and Monahan's legal foundation for identifying the seriously mentally ill with the civil rights of disenfranchised blacks in the South, treatment of the seriously mentally ill remains contentious at best and downright nasty at worse. Patients, incapable of either comprehending or rationally asserting their stake in this social chaos of conflicting interests, for the most part simply perish as humans, whether prematurely from horrible disease and suicide, by loss of any persona recognizable to family and former friends, or, occasionally, like Cho, in rampage murders, taking any one of us with them anytime, any place.

The shadowy figure of the treating psychiatrist in this case becomes a near nonsequitor, subordinated to an FBI agent's analysis—"in separate appendix"—for understanding the inner workings of the killer's mind. Would the Virginia panel not be interested in the attending psychiatrist's opinion of the inner workings of Cho's mind? After all, the attending psychiatrist is the expert. Yet, nowhere in the panel report is the alarming absence of meaningful psychiatric diagnosis necessary to inform and direct effective treatment even mentioned. The inadequacy of Cho's evaluation is cited, but that only references lack of knowledge regarding imminent dangerousness, which, as it turned out, was not, in fact, missed by the clinical evaluators. Cho was not imminently dangerous in a strict legal sense. He did not physically harm anyone until the next year, which does not fit the definition of *imminent*. The results of Cho's involuntary detention achieved exactly what the architects of these involuntary detention statutes intended. The emergency psychiatry of Cho's presentation at a medical facility was immediately converted into a legal contest between legal counsel and the patient's treating physician, in this case Cho's St. Albans attending psychiatrist. It turned out to be no contest. The magistrate ruled without following medical advice.

Certainly, a silent and sullen young man like Cho can be aroused on a hospital ward, either with benign intention or coincidental evocation of violence, thus proving imminent violence. In other words, if a psychiatrist believes that a patient is near violent but does not fit the legal definition of imminent, he or she can trigger violence to find a way to commit the person under the requisite legal procedures. Even though that might be tantamount to illegal entrapment, it is the legal game of emergency forensic psychiatry today. But the assumption the panel seems to be making in its report by shifting the blame away from the state's inadequate procedures to assess dangerousness and place it squarely on the back of an individual too sick to know he was sick is that medical students might wish to game the system as a career move to generate as much revenue as possible. As a result, the reasoning seems to go, caution must be taken to keep psychiatric inpatient units starved for cash to keep them from benefiting from liberalization of commitment laws. However, despite disingenuous arguments that Cho is to blame because he lied about his prior encounters with psychologists, the state's treating psychiatrist in this case could be held liable for medical negligence in not taking charge of Cho's long-term treatment. This holds true in spite of his findings that Cho did not present imminent dangerousness.

The treating psychiatrist, under applicable California case law, could be held liable for failure to competently and legally perform his peculiar abilities vested in him through over a decade of specialized education and training, licensure, and board certification as a medical specialist. The Supreme Court of California ruled in the *Tarasoff* case that licensed clinical professionals treating the mentally ill have both special knowledge and ability identical to any physician examining a patient presenting with potentially contagious infection. That is, he or she has the competence to diagnose the illness and the legal obligation to report it in order to prevent the public from being harmed.

Under California's *Tarasoff* ruling, a ruling that courts in other states increasingly cite in "peculiar abilities" arguments with respect to a clinician's special duty of care to the public to prevent them from being harmed by the clinician's patient, a clinician is liable in tort for his or her breach of special duty in not reporting the likelihood of a patient's harming others. This ruling came in the face of the California psychiatrist's argument that as a doctor, he was protected under physician–patient confidentiality. However, the *Tarasoff* court ruled, physician–patient confidentiality is trumped by the physician's special duty of care to protect the public from being harmed by one of his or her patients.

Accordingly, as it might apply to the Cho case, an inpatient psychiatrist with the authority to invoke a director's hold on any patient pending legal review would be considered by applicable state law to have control of Cho. The treating psychiatrist in the Cho case was as much doubly bound by contradictions in mental health law as were Laings' patients whom he alleged not to be really sick—just identified as such within families. Laings, however, gave up on this theory and took to the bottle, acknowledging profound disillusionment with his own pragmatic efforts to treat the identified patient as essentially normal in the same way that Cho was left to take medication if he wished to do so. In other words, for Cho to be released on his own recognizance to take medication without supervision presumed that Cho was capable of making that decision. He clearly was not competent to make any decisions regarding his health because he was violently delusional, seething with rage, and probably under the control of command voices and ideations of suicide and was, therefore, a public menace who should not have been released back into society pending further review of his condition and notification to his next of kin.

Treating psychiatrists in the United States, however, cannot simply turn their backs when finding themselves in the position of Cho's attending psychiatrist. They are responsible, under *Tarasoff*, to control their patients to prevent them from harming others. The *Tarassof* peculiar ability test assumes that the attending psychiatrist for Cho diligently accumulated available data predictive of the massacre, that is, threats, writings, prior treatment, and developmental history. The double bind, however, was the other side of the same coin. The psychiatrist could have been criminally culpable or civilly liable for detaining Cho beyond 48 hours and then riding his patient's back to enforced treatment without a finding of imminent dangerousness. The attending, therefore, is usually damned if he does or damned if he doesn't.

It is impossible to judge the motivations of Cho's attending psychiatrist, but certainly, less can be considered best when in a double bind, the most effective way to practice defensive medicine. In a double bind, the attending psychiatrist is trapped within two mutually exclusive protocols. The first is *Tarasoff*, which requires that under the psychiatrist's special duty of care, the patient must not be released if there is a likelihood—usually court determined, called *constructive*—that the patient will cause harm to others. The second is a type of false imprisonment, a tort, in which a patient is held in a treatment center against his will. If the detaining of the patient is somehow court ordered, then the court must make sure that he or she has access to the court to exercise his Fifth Amendment rights to due process, which may also include a patient's Sixth Amendment right to be represented by counsel. Accordingly, an attending can either be sued under *Tarasoff* for releasing a dangerous person back into the world or be sued for false imprisonment for detaining an individual absent a court-approved due process procedure. But because preparing for such a procedure usually requires significant involvement from either an attending or staff psychiatrist and there is usually no third-party payer, the entire process is beyond the means of underfunded psychiatric care facilities. Hence, they do a walk-through assessment to cover all bases and let the patient go. And this is what happened in the Cho involuntary commitment case. The state's panel exonerated itself by playing the blame game and accusing a psychotic, delusional, and hallucinatory patient of lying about his prior treatment.

Ironically, according to the very antipsychiatric literature spawned by Laings' disastrous Kingsley Home experiment, the then-popularized theory of double-bind causation of what is diagnosed as schizophrenia may have determined his attending psychiatrist's all-but-meaningless assessment of Cho. According to the antipsychiatric school of Laings' double-bind theory of causation in schizophrenia, the threatened victim of the double bind must become inconspicuous to avoid actual nervous breakdown. As a result, the identified patient's response to a crazy situation is incomprehensible to those on the outside even if that response is irrational. Therefore, even trained psychiatrists are supposed to be incapable of making a diagnosis of schizophrenia and, because they are working within the current medico-legal system of involuntary commitment, they are essentially required to submit to a double bind. If the attending were prosecuted for overcontrolling Cho—felony restraint—he had an equal chance of being sued, under *Tarasoff*, by simply minimizing Cho's emergency presentation and letting him walk out of the hospital.

It was theorized within Laings' antipsychiatry movement that the identified patient's psychosocial unit, to which he must adapt, is really crazy. Within this context, Cho's attending psychiatrist's performance could be considered adaptive even if also negligent. Therefore, we know little about the attending psychiatrist's clinical encounter with Cho other than how it ultimately failed as one of the very last chances for preventing this disaster.

Its failure was attributed to suffocating rules and regulations, as well as scarce specialized healthcare resources in the community. In other words, the worst of both worlds: Virginia's mental health law all but predicted this state as the scene for such a massacre, due to prediction of imminent dangerousness being the sole clinical criterion of high risk of violence in the seriously mentally ill. But, imminent dangerousness is not a term of medical science. It is, as Monahan now acknowledges, a law enforcement criterion used by policemen to jail people who resist arrest. There is not a medical student entering school today who would ever expect to be in such a position of making a judgment of imminent dangerousness because it is at the same time nonsensical and paradoxically dangerous for a clinician to be expected to make.

Here is an anecdotal example of the impossible situation criminalization of the seriously mentally ill has imposed upon treating clinicians today.

Sandra was diagnosed with bipolar disorder and stabbed her husband in the neck. She was declared mentally incompetent to stand trial in California and therefore detained in a state hospital for the criminally insane, pending her achieving legal competency to stand trial. Being incompetent to stand trial means that a defendant cannot assist or make decisions in his or her own defense because of a mental illness. Under the Murphy Law in California, a patient considered mentally incompetent but intractably dangerous can be detained indeterminately. Such indeterminate detention in the state hospital, however, requires psychiatric assessment of dangerousness and mental competency to stand trial. For some reason, this determination cannot—or could not—be performed at the state hospital, so Sandra was transported hundreds of miles for psychiatric examination under the Murphy Law in a former county hospital with the capacity to safely detain and treat her, as necessary, while hospitalized for this examination.

The attending psychiatrist found Sandra to be mentally competent to stand trial, and her husband visited her while hospitalized. Even though his scar from her assault was visible across his neck, Sandra denied, right in front of him and staff together, having caused it. The husband was a reliable informant, however, and there was little doubt that she was either amnestic of the assault or in a profound state of psychological denial. There was no animosity or fear observed between patient and her husband.

This was a difficult ethical call for the psychiatrist to make, because the patient was clearly seriously mentally ill, likely criminally insane, yet, in his professional estimation, mentally competent to stand trial because she could make decisions with respect to her own defense. It was only when she was escorted off ward and tried to assault a security guard on the elevator that the attending psychiatrist was ethically enabled to deem Sandra dangerous, and by association, incapable of assisting in her own defense—thus fulfilling the criteria necessary for indeterminate confinement in the state hospital. Curiously, there was no advocacy for her being allowed to stand trial. Like John Hinckley, she had already done enough damage that nobody wanted her back in the community.

I believe that such an end stage of the process of deterioration in the seriously mentally ill is the only forensic psychiatry default now for indeterminate confinement. This is largely socioeconomically, rather than clinically, determined. Sandra was upper middle class. Patients like Sandra, yet poor or minority, are released on a regular basis into the inner city, where random violence such as hers is more normative and acceptable to the majority of Americans. One such patient just randomly crushed the skulls of two children in a Phoenix park following discharge from an overcrowded psychiatric facility. The outcry was loud, yet only momentary, in the big-city news cycle. Other than a few psychiatrists who like to be involved in such a complex legalistic determination, the take-home point from this case is that doctors should be required to think like lawyers when practicing medicine.

Of course, there are psychiatrists who have done this, but they are mostly in academic positions. To expect an already scarce resource of professional psychiatric time to be devoted to such hair-splitting determinations that have such enormous implications for medical negligence on the attending is preposterous. According to malpractice records of successful plaintiff suits and settlements, the attending had as much chance of being sued for letting her stand trial as he had in being instrumental in her lifetime in detention.

As with Cho, Sandra should not have been transferred to a community hospital. But once again, the state had transferred the costs and liability for what was its responsibility to a community hospital incapable of clinical decision making under the Murphy Law. The Murphy Law was passed by the State of California and should be 100 percent adjudicated by the State of California, by state salaried forensic psychiatrists, who, in the wake of mass closure of state hospitals and resultant cost shifting to the federal budget, are now an endangered species, if not totally extinct.

In northwestern Wisconsin, for example, a rural area with universities similar to Virginia Tech, the Catholic hospitals have totally absorbed the state responsibilities for care and temporary detention orders. The burden this places on attending psychiatrists is enormous because of the legal requirements for detention and very few psychiatrists willing to work the on-call hours of an attending. When Cho's treating psychiatrist complained of shortage of psychiatrists, it was never asked: was he the only one at St. Albans, thus on call every night and weekend? There are rural hospitals with a single psychiatrist pulling call 24/7.

Under this pressure, how can an attending psychiatrist respond to the necessary legalities of determining whether a patient meets the requirements for involuntary commitment? And how can that attending's decision stand up to a legal test?

The answer lies largely in the *Lessard* case (*Lessard v Schmidt*, 1972; Brooks, 1978).

Alberta Lessard, a former schoolteacher in a suburb of Milwaukee, was found by police running up and down the apartment aisle on the second floor banging on doors and shouting that the Communists were taking over the country that night. She was also alleged to have jumped from her second-story window and said that she no longer had the will to live, and that she might, if returned to the apartment, jump again (Torrey, 2008).

As Torrey discovered in his on-site research in Wisconsin, a preliminary psychiatric evaluation found that Ms. Lessard was suffering from paranoid schizophrenia and was in need of treatment. She retained counsel through the Milwaukee Legal Services to assert her civil rights during this legal confrontation over her status and was represented by Robert Blondis and Thomas Dixon.

For any lawyers like Robert Blondis and Thomas Dixon, filing a class action was consistent with the civil rights milieu of that era. In a later interview, Blondis frankly admitted that, at the time, he "knew nothing about mental health law," adding, "I had read a few things, including Thomas Szacz's *The Myth of Mental Illness*, and that is where I was coming from." Szacz's 1961 book explicitly denied that mental illness exists in any scientific sense but was instead merely arbitrarily defined categories of behavior.

In researching their class action suit, Blondis recalls "sitting around one evening in the basement law library drinking beer," when they came across the phrase *least restrictive alternative* in a totally unrelated legal case involving state employees in Arkansas; the phrase usually relates to what limitations courts tend to place on defendant state actors in dealing with the constitutional rights of plaintiffs. Lessard's attorneys inserted the phrase in their class action suit, insofar as it dealt with the limitations on plaintiffs' Fifth Amendment rights to due process, and it subsequently became widely used to justify the release of psychiatric patients from hospitals. Its most infamous legacy is the case of Cho Seung-Hui and the Virginia Tech massacre.

Subsequently, in October 1972, one year after Lessard's class action suit had been filed, a three-judge panel of the U.S. District Court—incorrectly, in our opinion—declared Wisconsin's existing civil commitment statute unconstitutional. The *Lessard* decision was called the "first landmark case dealing with the concept of dangerousness ... a high-water mark in dangerousness law" (Torrey, 2008).

The *Lessard* decision was strongly influenced by the theories of the psychiatrist Thomas Szacz, just as the Landis–Lanterman–Petris–Short Act in California had been five years earlier. In their decision, the three judges noted, "Obviously, the definition of mental illness is left largely to the user and is dependent upon the norms of adjustment that he employs ... the diagnostician has the ability to shoehorn into the mentally diseased class almost any person he wished, for whatever reasons, to put there (Szacz, 1960)." With this arbitrary and capricious judicial extermination of psychiatric and clinical psychological credibility, the Virginia panel said this about the forensic psychiatry in Cho's case: "Many of those interviewed expressed serious concerns regarding the paucity of psychiatric information available to the independent evaluator and judge/special justice."

As noted above, the independent evaluator of Cho had only the report from the local designated mental health professional at the student health service and no collateral information or medical records. The independent evaluator plays a key role in the commitment process in many jurisdictions. In Cho's case, notwithstanding the finding from the independent evaluator that Cho did not pose an imminent threat, the special justice nevertheless convened the hearing and actually made a finding that differed from that of the independent evaluator. He did, however, agree with the independent evaluator that inpatient treatment was not required, thus adhering to the powerful intent of the *Lessard* case for least restrictive alternative. Here, once again, the decision making for such matters was primarily legal to guarantee the civil rights of the seriously mentally ill and thus remove culpability from the state for infringing upon those rights. The rights, of course, of those terrified of Cho and later gunned down, might seem distant at this point. The identities of Cho's victims were indeterminate because he had only been detained for stalking and for expressions of suicidal intent.

The problem is that it is not an issue of rights, per se. It is an issue of plaintiff standing under black letter tort law as derived from Judge Learned Hand's minority decision in the *Palsgraff v. LIRR* case, wherein he argued that a defendant owes a duty of responsibility to all those who might be damaged by defendant's breach of that duty, which breach is both the actual and legal cause of plaintiff's damages. Essentially, under the law of torts, one owes a duty of care to anyone who might be harmed by the person's breach of that duty of care if that breach was the actual and proximate cause of those damages. The issue then becomes whether clinicians who released Cho back into the public owed a duty of care to anyone who might be harmed by Cho's subsequent actions.

Thus, within this legalistic conceptualization, there was a balancing test between Cho's Fifth Amendment rights to due process—for example, he could not be denied his freedom absent due process of law—and the rights of an indeterminate and unidentifiable class of plaintiffs who might be harmed by Cho were Cho to have been dangerous to others. If a ministerial or discretionary decision by the state, sovereign immunity attaches just as it would to any decision by a public safety agency to protect X before it protects Y. The Sovereign Immunity clause of the U.S. Constitution protects the state from lawsuits by individuals when the state is acting out of its ministerial or discretionary government powers. However, if pure negligence, wherein the state is acting not out of its discretionary or ministerial function, but as if it were a participant in the medical services marketplace, then sovereign immunity does not attach. A state loses its sovereign immunity if it inserts itself into the marketplace because it then takes upon itself a form of enterprise liability just like any other business. So in that instance, sovereign immunity would not protect the state, and a court should hold that the state would incur liability.

Within the perverse logic of the psychiatric evaluations that bent over backwards to extend due process rights to an absurd point, Cho was never in danger of being deprived of his rights because he was mentally incompetent to care for himself and should have been remanded to the custody of his parents. This raises another issue: because of his mental illness, which was undiagnosed at the time, was Cho competent enough to understand and exercise his constitutional rights or was his mental incapacity such that he was constructively not capable of consent and therefore in need of a guardian to protect his rights?

This raises the corollary issue: because Cho was detained for posing a danger to another person—stalking—and because he manifested a danger to himself—his profession to his roommate of contemplating suicide—was it incumbent upon the evaluators at St. Albans to hold Cho until they could have made a determination with respect to his capacity to understand and protect is own constitutional rights? We believe the answer is yes, that it was incumbent upon his evaluators to hold him to make just such a determination because holding him would not have violated any of his rights insofar as they were making a determination as to whether he should have had a guardian on the grounds of his mental incompetency. At the very least, evaluators at St. Albans or officials from the dean's office should have notified Cho's next of kin. Cho's parents should have been notified by both the school and St. Albans. However, no notification was given.

According to the logic of the evaluators, Cho was not really at risk for losing his ego autonomy and being controlled by delusions and, very likely, command hallucinations. They said Cho was autistically preoccupied; thus his silence. For the psychiatric practitioner, such silence is of paramount importance and not simply the lay observations of the Cho family throughout the boy's life. Even the evaluating psychologist at St. Albans determined him to be seriously mentally ill, presumably because of his autistic mutism during initial emergency inpatient presentation. Was he even asked about his internal psychological experiences, such as command auditory hallucinations? We do not know. Cho implied their existence in a class-assigned short story.

In fact, the final summary made it quite clear that a sick brain was not the determining factor of the Virginia Tech massacre; Cho himself was. Thus, the governor's panel argued the blame away from the state and put it onto a person who, competently evaluated, should have never been released from detention or, as the least restrictive alternative, been turned over to his parents. This argument is convoluted, disingenuous, and ultimately self-serving.

Many law schools have little or no input from psychiatry, as might have been the case when Blondis and Dixon attended law school at the University of Wisconsin in Madison. Even though medical and law schools may, as in the case of University of Washington, Seattle, be essentially across the street from each other, more often than not, faculty have little interaction over the issues involved here.

The public is led to assume that psychiatrists would have been hungry for Cho's detention. In fact, psychiatrists will receive little or no training in the policies of involuntary detention as it pertains to the convergence of a patient's legal rights versus the public's constitutional guarantee of domestic tranquility, if *domestic tranquility* can be defined within the perspective of protection from harm. A maximum of two hours at the University of Washington School of Medicine, which overtly advocated avoidance of forensic psychiatry within the core curriculum, is the type of overview training that prospective psychiatrists will receive. Cases such as *Lessard* and Cho were too legally risky, according to the faculty. So, what the public is led to believe is false.

Similarly with legal education, many major law schools have little teaching in mental health law. Supposedly trained experts making these decisions, therefore, are essentially laypersons. Law students seeking advocacy experience with malleable, easily controlled clients, who are not even competent in most cases to assist in their own defense, and clinicians with little or no training in what they are actually doing are thrown into this lion's den created by activist judges who sometimes misapply their constitutional zeal. Here many young and inexperienced attorneys and mental health professionals of varying educational credentials wrestle, protected as is a hospital ward from the light of public scrutiny, with the impossible balancing acts of a patient's constitutional rights versus the public's right to be protected from harm. All these arguments take place while their patients' and clients' durations of untreated psychosis freely, like a malignant melanoma, take over their personas, and ultimately their bodies, killing both. But at least the arguments survive as legal footnotes, even if the patients do not.

For the student body of Virginia Tech, and parents and their college kids all over the country, this situation is as bad as taking off in an airplane with a pilot having minimal if any flight training. Worse yet, the panel learned that those in the pilot seat evaluating Cho frankly confessed to flying by the seat of their pants, making up what they had to do as they went along. Such apparently negligent procedures and policies were at best barely touched upon by the panel, which reported, "The panel was advised that in many jurisdictions, absent a finding by the independent evaluator that an individual poses an imminent danger or is substantially unable to care for himself, (Grave Disability) many special justices will decline to hold a hearing … Cho, in that case would simply have been allowed to leave on his own without any requirements for followup assessment or treatment" (Virginia Tech Review Panel, 2007).

For some reason that is dramatically avoided in the report, Cho was not simply allowed to leave in this matter. Why was an exception, therefore, made for him? Previous problems with procedures at this facility? No confidence by the judge in clinical assessment—understandable, given the time spent with Cho, likely less than a total of 45 minutes to an hour at most by both doctors together, who said they were rushed and that Cho did not communicate? What were the reasons that Cho was an exception to the rule that the panel states? The report gives no answer.

"It is unclear under existing law whether the independent evaluator is intended to serve as gate keeper" (Virginia Tech Review Panel, 2007). Why should that be unclear? The hospital has policy and procedures covering this matter, or it would not be certified for assessing and managing such highly complex cases as Cho.

"If the opinion of the independent evaluator is to be given great weight, then it is critical that sufficient psychiatric information be available upon which an informed judgment may be made" (Virginia Tech Review Panel, 2007). What is the panel saying here? That such an inpatient psychiatric failure must be brought before a state panel following a massacre? Was this hospital certified by the Joint Commission on Accreditation of Hospitals? It is unclear what the panel is trying to suggest, especially in light of the failure of the psychiatric evaluation procedures to prevent Cho from harming others and himself. Moreover, in acknowledged "drive-by" forensic psychiatry and psychology assessments of a nonverbal patient behaving strangely without any collateral information, the evaluation should be taken as only one component. The magistrate in Cho's case certainly did not place much stock in any of the clinical evaluation. In fact, he ignored it.

What was lacking in the decision-making process is exactly what the panel was missing but might have been available if Cho had been kept for an additional twenty-four to forty-eight hours. Such extension of detention would not have been a threatened infringement upon his due process rights especially in light of (a) Cho's documented threatening behavior to another student and to himself and (b) the dearth of any background information concerning Cho's medical history.

"Background information including records from the current hospitalization must be assembled for review. The Cho case calls attention to the need to assure that the independent evaluator has both sufficient time and information to conduct an adequate evaluation" (Virginia Tech Review Panel, 2007). All of this is so obvious that it almost goes without saying because it is standard of practice in any acute inpatient psychiatric unit, particularly one where such complex clinical and forensic decisions are made. The fact that this was not done at the time Cho was evaluated, after having been taken into custody in his own dorm room at the college, means that, instead of calling for new policy, the panel would have been better off trying to figure out why neither the Virginia Tech police nor the college administration did their jobs properly.

> At Cho's hearing, the only documents available to the special justice were the uniform preadmission screening form, a partially completed proceedings for certification form recording the findings of the independent evaluator and a physician's examination form containing the findings of the treating psychiatrist. No prior patient history was presented; no toxicology, lab results, or physical evaluation from the treating psychiatrist were available. (Virginia Tech Review Panel, 2007)

Critically absent from this evaluation were brain imaging studies, which are indicated in assessment of a first psychotic illness. But Cho was not considered psychotic, at least in the present state of assumed mutism, absent any collateral clinical information.

"The admitting form indicating that Cho had access to a firearm was not presented" (Virginia Tech Review Panel, 2007). Why was this not presented? Did he actually have such access? It is known that he certainly managed to acquire firearms just months later, indicating that if he had access then, he could have had access at the time of his arrest. Yet no determination was made. Indicating firearm access would prove to be a crucial consideration just months later and is standard documentation when there is a finding. It seemed as though the state was so solicitous of not seeming racist when faced with an aggressively hostile Asian student that they threw due caution to the winds. Was this actually a civil-rights-based determination?

Although a small coterie of young trial attorneys and naïve judges in a few states such as California and Wisconsin combined to strike down laws that allowed for the involuntary institutionalizing of the mentally ill by decrying the abridgement of their rights to due process, one wonders how they might testify before a state panel regarding the intellectual and scientific foundations of their cases and rulings forging the template for Cho's clinical and forensic psychiatry treatment. How would they justify the cost of this massacre on campus and other rampage murders within context of *Lessard* and its legacy? Would they say that *Lessard* provided adequate protection for society had the assessment procedures at St. Albans and public safety procedures at Virginia Tech only followed standard practices for gathering medical records and notifying next of kin that a family member had been involuntarily kept overnight in a mental institution? *Lessard* notwithstanding, it was Virginia Tech's interpretation of cases such as *Lessard* that was the problem and not the *Lessard* court's holding.

Whatever the young University of Wisconsin Law School graduates might have thought as they prepared their pleadings in the *Lessard* case, they might agree now that there is a human legacy of destruction that resulted from the way institutions interpreted the holding in *Lessard*. And perhaps even they would agree that it is time for a congressional investigation of what happened at both Red Lake and Virginia Tech. Although it is the states, and not the federal government, whose general police powers govern the treatment of the mentally ill in their jurisdictions, the patchwork quilt pattern of involuntary commitment laws requires some remedy, possibly in the form of a model penal code approach, upon which states can build their own commitment statutes for confining the dangerously mentally ill.

Is there a political reason for such a need? Certainly there is. It would be disaster of national scope with no solution for future prevention in sight. Moreover, changes in institutionalized mental healthcare policy in the wake of *Lessard* fostered a shift in the financial responsibility for care of the seriously mentally ill from states to federal government, essentially bankrupting the system. Who supports St. Albans, California, and Wisconsin hospitals now responsible for the complex forensic and clinical management of the potential dangerous and suicidal mentally ill? Medicaid and Medicare support them, and that revenue source is the responsibility of the federal taxpayers everywhere in this country, not just in Eau Claire, Wisconsin; Bakersfield, California; or Blacksburg, Virginia, the clinical sites herein noted.

Hospitals are complaining that budget cuts in Medicaid and Medicare paralyzed their emergency medical services preparedness with Homeland Security.

According to their Congressional testimony the secretaries of both Health and Human Services and Homeland Security said that "preparedness of local hospital emergency services was the responsibility of neither Cabinet Official" (*USA Today,* 2008). So, how can we expect them to take any responsibility for another Virginia Tech massacre, itself as serious and as likely a threat as a terrorist attack?

According to a study from the University of Evansville in Indiana, at least sixteen mass murders—the deaths of at least five people in a single incident—were committed in the United States since 2005. And according to an ABC news story that appeared on the Internet there were ten dead in Alabama; eight dead in North Carolina; ten dead in California, including two police officers; and twelve dead in a Binghamton shooting. Peter Hamm, a spokesman for the Brady Campaign to Prevent Gun Violence, argued that although the politicians said local municipalities should simply enforce the laws that are on the books, it was clear that those laws were simply not working in the first place.

Were the Cho investigation a congressional, rather than State of Virginia, panel report, more facts would be extracted from witnesses and participants. After all, the State of Virginia had cause to dampen down their findings, if not absolutely whitewash the institutional and professional failures in this massacre. The state would later be paying out the maximum awards to surviving victims and families of victims in tort actions against them. One could certainly say, despite the stated-for-the-record good intentions of the panel, that it had a serious conflict of interest in determining fault and responsibility, which conflict they may have resolved by placing the blame on the one person who had no concept of his own illness. In fact, Cho's parents, limited as they might have been in the English language, said it best when they revealed that had the school only informed them what was happening, they would have kept their son back from his spring semester and there would have been no massacre.

> Panel members have been advised by mental health providers and special justice from other locales in Virginia that it is not unusual for the evidence presented at commitment hearings to be minimal. Due to the time constraints and limitations of resource personnel, the information available to the judge/special justice is often very limited. Witnesses cannot be located quickly and hospital records have often not been transcribed. Additionally, conflicting interpretations of the constraints of the Health Insurance Portability and Accountability Act (HIPAA) and Virginia Code 32.1-127. 1:03 Heatlh Records Privacy (Va HRP) often make it difficult to acquire background medical/psychiatric information on a patient previously treated elsewhere. Legal experts from a research advisory group for the Commission on Mental Health Law Reform participated in the development of a questionnaire for judges and special justices to complete following civil commitment

> hearings in the month of May 2007. More than 1400 questionnaires were returned. They reflected that approximately 60 percent of the May hearings lasted no more than 15 minutes and only 4 percent required more than 30 minutes. (Virginia Tech Review Panel, 2007)

However, if serious mental illness, as defined by psychiatrists and clinical psychologists, is simply an artifact, as alleged by R. D. Laings, or part of medicalized mythology, as alleged by Thomas Szacz, why should it last any longer? In fact, why should it even be held at all, perhaps to hedge the judiciary bet? In other words, as judges and class action trial lawyers, the panel is not asking whether there is not some role for clinical expertise that is at higher level than that acquired at the police academy. What other reason would there be for involving clinical decision making in cases such as that of either Lessard or Cho Seung-Hui, until they actually committed crimes and met the preferred standard in Wisconsin, dangerous, beyond reasonable doubt?

Of course, what rational person would ever expect a person to learn to be as deviant as Cho, taking his own life in the process? According to the legal foundation of current mental health law, he simply learned it somewhere. Where? Other than downloading "dark movies" from the Internet, not a word is mentioned by the panel regarding how Cho learned to do what he did. Nor, in fact, is there one word regarding Cho's loss of ego autonomy. Quite the opposite. It was concluded that, despite numerous encounters with clinical facilities, all of which were either voluntary or, in case of St. Albans admission, "unresisted and uncontested," Cho was the sole person responsible for the massacre at Virginia Tech.

Obviously, this assertion did not hold up later in court, when victims and families received settlements that were maximum within the legal liability of Commonwealth of Virginia. Was the massacre at Virginia Tech simply too horrible a collapse of administrative, legal, and clinical failure to commission away? The answer, unfortunately, is yes, but the panel's findings remain unchallenged.

"Cho was the only person to testify at this commitment hearing, and he was not very communicative" (Virginia Tech Review Panel, 2007). Why was he not very communicative? He presented to a hospital on an emergency basis with the problems of strange behavior, nonverbal; threats of self-harm; and inappropriate history. Such presentation requires emergency psychiatric intervention until either cleared or judged nondestructive to self or others. These are not from rules taught in law school. These are the classical, evidence-based rules of emergency medicine and emergency psychiatry. It is astonishing to see their absence, along with the lexicology of psychosis and schizophrenia, from this report. The question remains just what role should psychiatry and clinical psychology have in such cases when the rules have already been set by lawyers, who by their own admission in the *Lessard* case, are rarely qualified in either abnormal psychology or psychiatry?

As Fuller Torrey wrote to the *New York Times* (April 27, 2007):

> On Sunday, the series "Rampage Killers" pointed out that nearly half of your sample (one-hundred high profile cases) "had some sort of formal diagnosis, often Schizophrenia." The second article showed that 14 of the 24 multiple-murderers' prescribed psychiatric drugs were not taking them. Next came a dissection of our failure to keep weapons from people with mental illness. On the last day, you profile a man who acted on a "divine message to Kill." You inextricably weave multiple tragedies with mental illness; but offer not a word of how our laws stop the treatment of those whose minds are overcome by these sicknesses. In most states, even those transparently incapacitated by severe mental illness cannot be placed in treatment until they are dangerous either to themselves or to others. For no reasons, this prohibition against treatment ensures thousands are left to suffer. And, as your series evidences, waiting for people with mental illness to be dangerous before helping them, also guarantees that some will become just that.

While Dr. Torrey was writing this letter in 2000, a young Korean-American boy was getting sick, and seven years later Americans woke up to the consequences as stated by one of the world's leading recognized experts on schizophrenia. This event is evidentiary support of Dr. Torrey's ominous warnings about neglect of the deinstitutionalized and seriously mentally ill (SMI) within our society.

Fuller Torrey later wrote in a personal communication with the author:

> All previous rampage murders, however, pale to that carried out by Cho Seung-Hui in April 2007. A 23-year-old senior at Virginia Tech, Cho killed 32 students and teachers in a carefully planned attack. He had previously told his roommate that he had an imaginary girlfriend who "was a supermodel and traveled through space." That he had an imaginary twin brother and that he had "vacationed in North Carolina with Vladimir Putin, the Russian President." His behavior and writings were so bizarre that both students and faculty were afraid of him. Following his harassment of two female students in 2005, Cho was court-mandated to be psychiatrically evaluated; he was held overnight in a local hospital but apparently not treated. He was ordered to get treated as an outpatient but did not do so. The counseling center at Virgina Tech University received a copy of his court order mandating treatment, but they apparently did nothing. According to an official investigation, the center did not accept "involuntary or ordered referrals from any source," and even students with schizophrenia were treated only if they request it. The Virginia state law for involuntary psychiatric commitment and treatment requires that the person be an

> "imminent danger" to himself or others or to be "substantially unable to care for himself." This is one of the most stringent state commitment statutes in the United States and another example of how changes in Mental Illness laws in the 1970s and 1980s continue to have real consequences. (Torrey, 2008)

> Lack of insight is so frequently present in schizophrenia (and some other psychoses as well) that it is unreasonable to expect patients to always recognize or accept their need for treatment on a voluntary basis. If we can agree with the premise that the liberty to be psychotic is no freedom at all, then we can begin to examine some of the current plights of the mentally ill patients. (Rachlin, 1974)

Postmortem, one of America's leading forensic psychiatrists, Dr. Michael Welner, stated in an interview with ABC News:

> Therefore, when a 23-year-old shows an impaired capacity to stifle a fantasy before it develops into a complex mass shooting plan, as a forensic psychiatrist, I wonder about the sources of his developmental limitations. As previously documented, Cho had all of the known antecedent risk factors predictive of schizophrenia, thus the developmental core of this disorder presenting in nearly 1 percent of young people during a narrow window age—that most likely to place them on college campuses. Paranoia, in my professional experience, is the most important element to understand in the possible motives of mass shootings. Virtually all mass shooters are paranoid to some pathological degree. Some of them have suspicious personalities but otherwise maintain a connection to reality. Others have paranoid delusional disorder and have irrational and fixed false ideas about a particular theme. The most extreme of those with paranoia have schizophrenia, a condition that may be associated with intense hostility and different degrees of emotional and mental limitations and—particularly important to mass shooting—progressive and humiliating decline and alienation. … How he related to his roommate was just too bizarre to be depression.

Yet, that was his only diagnosis at time of discharge from St. Albans Hospital, and it was considered so mild that no psychiatric treatment was recommended. Nor is that the intensity of mood disorder to which Welner is referring. Welner is likely alluding to major depression with significant disability for which antidepressants and psychotherapy—not counseling—are indicated and can itself lead to violence against self and others. This enhances the questions of whether a psychiatrist even evaluated Cho. There is no clear evidence that he did. From the disparity of alignment between Cho's presentation and the documentation of the attending psychiatrist's brief encounter with him, it is not certain that comprehensive admission evaluation was performed at St. Albans Hospital.

Cho was diagnosed with mood disorder, not otherwise specified. On any given day, thousands of Cho's peers could have fit the criteria for that all-but-meaningless diagnosis that informs and directs, at most, follow-up evaluation, if persistently troublesome. But, not even that is documented to have occurred, despite court-ordered outpatient treatment.

> The bizarre content of his plays—mashing a 'half eaten' banana in someone's mouth, the hypersexual, nihilistic (death obsessed) obsessions in the absence of depressive guilt or tearfulness are another clue. The progressive decline of a period of years. Those with schizophrenia, especially in their earliest years, are not readily recognizable as such—their condition evolving. (Welner, interview with ABC News)

Hence, the first childhood diagnosis of the anxiety disorder, selective mutism, that responded to antidepressant and antianxiety medication, Paxil (paroxetine). This proved not to be a valid diagnosis, because it did not prove the test of stability over time; Cho was much sicker but may not have appeared as such as a child and did, like early schizophrenia sometimes does, respond to antidepressant medication.

> But here was someone who, as early as 2005, was carrying himself so strangely that he was a spectacle. The depressed withdraw and disappear. Those who are so peculiar in their manner so as to be inappropriate [taking cell phone pictures of his teacher, speaking inaudibly, pulling a cap low over his eyes] exhibit signs and symptoms more indicative of schizophrenia. He was communicating in a rambling manner reflective of what we appreciate as autistic thinking characteristic of schizophrenia. (Welner, interview with ABC News)

He is not diagnosing autism here—rather, language driven more by internal emotional processes than the realities demanded of the paucity of interpersonal communication seen in autism. Immediately after the incident, reports carried speculation by family members in Korea that Cho was autistic (*Time Magazine*, 2007). However, no known record exists of Cho ever being diagnosed with autism (*Time Magazine*, 2007; McLean & Shankar, 2007), nor could an autism diagnosis be verified by Cho's parents. The Virginia Tech Review Panel report dismissed an autism diagnosis (Virginia Tech Review Panel, 2008; Associated Press, 2007) and experts later doubted the autism claim (Schulte, B., & Craig, 2007).

"In a similar vein, Mr. Cho's stilted communication in his homicidal note (deceitful charlatans—not language of a 23-year-old college kid) is also the manner of a schizophrenic's communications, as is his pronounced delay in responding to questions" (Welner, interview with ABC News).

This latter element to which Welner is referring demonstrated interference in the reality mode of interpersonal communications. Such interference is the overwhelming and autonomous inhibition from internally driven emotion and associated disorganization of thought. This is called *thought blocking*, likely documented in Cho as early as middle school.

> The most obvious reason for a college-age man acting with the maturity level of a self-absorbed high school or middle school student is a major mental illness such as schizophrenia, which arrests psychological development from the point of its dominance in a person's life. A person who develops full-blown schizophrenia at 15 or 16, for example, will mature at a far more arrested pace than a person without such an affliction … [In addition to paranoia] … despair contributes to the person's recognition in that his lot will not improve. (Welner, interview with ABC News)

That is when the schizophrenic patients are at their statistically highest risk for suicide, common during their youthful first full acute, untreated episode and first psychiatric inpatient discharge. The greater the DUP, as cited here, the higher the risk of such a lethal outcome.

> While many mass shooters have depression, many do not. And depression is not what sparks the mass shooting, hopelessness is. We also are left, as forensic psychiatrists, with having to understand why something happened on that particular day. There may be a clear conflict. In my experience, there is also an unconscious trigger as well. That trigger may be all the more lethal because mass shooters may be less likely to introspectively reveal that they are wrestling with other conflicts as well. As, in postmortem assessment or as was obviously the cases with Cho's repeatedly reported "quietness, non-communicativeness and mutism." The unconscious trigger, inspiring a sense of life failure and hopelessness, is always elusive and especially so because the killer takes the secret with him when he dies. (Welner, interview with ABC News)

Within the context of this postmortem expert testimony, we can continue with the panel report.

> The prescreener was not present, nor was any representative from the CSB (the agency originating the Temporary Detention Order based on robust evidence of Serious Mental Illness and Dangerousness). The independent evaluator was not present. The officer who detained Cho was not present. Cho's roommate, suitemates, and Cho's family were all absent. This apparently is not an unusual scenario for commitment hearings in Virginia. (Virginia Tech Review Panel, 2007)

This conclusion should not be misinterpreted as standard of practice. The routine cited in this standard of practice is not equivalent to the standards of practice in either Virginia or Hawaii.

> Often the prescreener is off duty by the time of the hearing. CSBs with limited staff frequently do not send a substitute. The commission's survey reflected that the CSB representatives attended only half of the hearings held in May 2007. Independent evaluators, paid $75 per commitment evaluation, often feel compelled to return to their private practice rather than waiting for hearings that may be held hours after the evaluation is complete. The responses to the questionnaires indicated that the independent evaluators were present at approximately two-thirds of May's hearings. (Virginia Tech Review Panel, 2007)

That is within a public safety and public health system in which the prescreener is the one who accesses collateral information from police and witnesses to determine probable cause for detention with psychiatric examination! That would not have made a difference here, in that Dr. Crouse, the independent evaluator, did not find Cho to be imminently dangerous. And to avoid duplicity, lawyers should not be concerned about this. The basis of Virginia's preventive detention legislation is the mythology of diagnosis.

With this intellectual foundation of involuntary commitment law, decisions for preventive detention should be left to the police. They are best able to predict imminent dangerousness because they are best prepared to get slugged, stabbed, or bludgeoned by a stranger. One has to ask whether those who were responsible for arguing the case that got us into this mess were ever exposed to imminent violence from a stranger. They had not been away from Madison very long when setting up their legal memorandum in the basement of the Milwaukee Law Library. Although the streets of Milwaukee are not that safe, those of Madison are very safe.

And one answer might be that it did not matter whether the lawyers were exposed to imminent violence at all because what mattered was the law, not the patient, not the indeterminate victims, and not the institution where the patient was taken. As difficult as that may be for a psychiatrist to accept, lawyers who believe that a principle of law is at stake will argue that principle no matter what the social or political consequences. It is just a different mindset, even though it seems oblivious to some potentially dangerous consequences.

> Officers took Cho to Virginia Tech PD for assessment, and a pre-screen evaluation was conducted there at 8:15 PM by a licensed clinical social worker for New River Valley Community Service Board (CSB). The pre-screener interviewed Cho and the police officer and then spoke with both Cho's roommate and suite mate by phone. She recorded her findings on a five-page uniform pre-admission

> screening form checking the findings boxes indicating that Cho was mentally ill, was an imminent danger to self or others and was not willing to be treated voluntarily. She recommended involuntary hospitalization and indicated that the CSB could assist with treatment and discharge planning. She located a psychiatric bed, as required by state law at St Albans Behavioral Health Center of the Carilion New River Valley Medical Center and contacted the magistrate by phone to request that temporary detention order (TDO) be issued. (Virginia Tech Review Panel)

This social worker's forensic assessment and documentation, followed procedurally by necessary administrative disposition to a hospital that admitted patients on probable cause detentions, would prove to be both the first and last effective clinical intervention in both Cho's and his murdered victims' lives.

"Cho was admitted at 11:00pm. Cho did not speak at all with the officer. The diagnosis on admission orders was Mood Disorder NOS" (Virginia Tech Review Panel, 2007). On what basis of clinical decision making was that preliminary diagnosis made? What efforts went into determining whether this preliminary diagnosis was either reliable or valid or, as so often is the case, was it simply anchored with documentation of preliminary diagnosis.

Clinical psychologists, after all, have powerful tools for eliciting psychological data via validated psychological tests. Psychiatrists are both trained and experienced in detailed neurological and neuropsychiatric examinations. Cho was not saying anything. His presentation, therefore, was that of strange behavior, nonverbal—thus unlikely to be mood disorder. At least mood disorder should not have topped the priority list for rule-outs for purposes of both public safety and the patient's best treatment; no mention was made of psychomotor retardation, the main accompanying sign of mutism with depression. Cho was not retarded in his activity level; he appeared to be active—so active, in fact, that he required emergency tranquilization with one milligram of Ativan on the night of admission.

It is assumed that public safety as well as Cho's well being were paramount issues causing all of this on the night of admission. Ordinarily, these professionals do not run around at night screening patients for severe psychological disorders unless there is significant threat to public safety. "On the Carilion health screening form for potential violence, it was marked that Cho denied any prior history of violent behavior but he did have access to a firearm" (Virginia Tech Review Panel, 2007).

The panel believed this may have been checked off in error. Why did they believe that? It is very possible that this is one of the few things he told anyone, whether he did or did not have access. Maybe he was delusional in believing he did. That had to be asked. "What access do you have?" Instead, the night nurse's affirmative answer to the question is simply negated in an arbitrary and capricious way. Too explosive a documentation to explore further? What if his blood pressure had been 240/140? Would that have been arbitrarily considered an error, because it was not treated and he did not have a stroke?

Cho was treated for severe anxiety and agitation with 1 mg of Ativan and was put to bed. "The following morning the clinical support representative for St. Albans met with Cho to give him information about the mental health law" (Virginia Tech Review Panel, 2007). Amidst the wreckage that is our modern community mental health system, this, of course, takes priority over any clinical workup. Emergency inpatient psychiatry is heavily dependent on court funding, which, in turn, guarantees heavy administrative influence of local attorneys. They are usually immediately on-site, preempting such medical traditions as rounds on new patients by doctors. They, of course, are there to protect people identified as patients from any healthcare, such as antipsychotic medications, under the assumption that they are as likely to be "fake" patients, as theorized by Laings—literally sculpted by psychiatrists into "artifacts" labeled mental illness.

Cops control people for a living. So, why not become a doctor and do that, too, while potentially facing a physical beating as well? If this sounds exaggerated, it is part of the foundation behind the rulings leading to the debacle at St. Albans Hospital. In effect, what began in a Wisconsin courtroom as an argument over an involuntarily committed patient's right to due process became, decades later, a legally protected, potentially lethal extended duration of untreated psychosis.

At St. Albans the night that Cho was admitted, the local healthcare emergency treatment system was tested and failed when, according to the report, "Around 7:00 a.m. the representative escorted Cho to meet with a licensed clinical psychologist who conducted an independent evaluation of Cho pursuant to Virginia law" (Virginia Tech Review Panel, 2007). How could one design a less therapeutic alliance in this hospital? A paranoid patient is encouraged in this way to be even more paranoid and distrustful of anyone trying to help. Such procedural correctness would ultimately kindle one of the worst man-made disasters in U.S. history.

Whether Virginia's procedures represented their best attempts at standards of care or legally sufficient routine procedures, it turned out to be a 15-minute examination limited by exigencies of the psychologist's economics. Dr. Roy Crouse was on contract to receive a per evaluation fee regardless of how long that evaluation took. He told the panel that he had to leave promptly for financial reasons. What might that have been, his private practice?

"The independent evaluator (Dr. Roy Crouse) reported to the panel that he reviewed the prescreening report but that due to the early hour there were no hospital records available for his review" (Virginia Tech Review Panel, 2007). That is extremely unlikely because any competent nursing staff would have filled in a rather extensive and informative health assessment. That is one of the priorities of the night nursing staff with a new admission. Where was that assessment? It had to be in the chart by the time Dr. Crouse arrived. Who documented Cho's access to a firearm? That was the previously cited hospital health form, essential information to review prior to seeing any new patient, or any patient on rounds, for that matter.

"He did not speak with Cho's attending psychiatrist who had not arrived yet. The evaluator has no specific recollection, but believes that the independent evaluation took about 15 minutes" (Virginia Tech Review Panel, 2007).

For somebody alleged to be mute, any clinical decision making leading to a diagnosis would have to be tentative at best with a patient so tough to interview and from whom it would be so difficult also to extract information. Yet, despite this enormous communications barrier, along with introduction placing his interview already within an adversarial mode with a paranoid patient on emergency detention, Dr. Crouse was able to determine Cho's mood to be incongruent—a bright red flag for psychosis!—"mood depressed, affect flat." That incongruency immediately placed this patient's presentation out of the domain of mood disorder, NOS, for emergency inpatient assessment.

From its very origins, schizophrenia has been known for the schism within emotional state—that is, appearing to feel one way—depressed—while expressing it differently—here, with flat affect. Dr. Krouse was actually documenting the "rule-in" for schizophrenia in its most classically defined paradigm—that of the schism between emotional state felt versus that expressed. Such schism between emotional state expressed and that assessed by "experience-near" examination is termed *affect incongruent with mood.*

Although not specific for psychosis—particularly schizophrenia—it is a rule-in for both, along with other potentially lethal neuropsychiatric syndromes, and thus required a differential diagnosis. To rule these out takes a psychologist more than 15 minutes without any consultation with other examining professionals or supplementary medical and psychological testing. But, then he had to rush off before further examination for what he said were "financial reasons." What reasons prevented him from spending more time with Cho? We will never know. All we do know is that a more comprehensive diagnosis and examination might have kept Cho at the hospital long enough for his parents to be called to pick him up, take him home to a doctor's care, and spare the lives of his future victims.

Dr. Krouse went on to essentially contradict what is known about patients showing such a schism in their emotional state by saying that Cho's insight was normal. It would be impossible to determine that with a selectively mute patient in 15 minutes. That box likely was checked in error, but the access to firearms very possibly was accurately checked. That did not mean that Cho had access to firearms. We know that his history was inappropriate, because of incongruent affect and total absence of patient history supporting benign behavior—in fact, absence, most likely, of any history from Cho himself.

Cho was more likely than not preoccupied. Was he, in fact, preoccupied with hallucinations commanding him to kill? This question was literally begging to be asked, but there is no evidence that it was. Imminent dangerousness cannot be ruled out in such a presentation as Cho's without specifically inquiring about auditory command hallucinations to kill one's self and others. The panel never addressed this inquiry.

"The evaluator completed the evaluation form certifying his findings that Cho is mentally ill; that he does not present an imminent danger to himself or others. or is not substantially unable to care for himself, as a result of mental illness; and that he does not require involuntary hospitalization" (Virginia Tech Review Panel, 2007).

It is deliberately unclear, as a result of twisting and obfuscation of the involuntary commitment law, as to what is meant by "does not present an imminent danger to himself or others." Cho really did not communicate or did at least minimally within 15 minutes. But, this could mean that he did not threaten or assault anyone overnight and therefore, more likely than not, would not threaten or assault anyone on the way out of the hospital, which proved to be correct. But how short-sighted was that judgment? As a prediction of potential behavior, it is worthless. Such judgment, although the law, is essentially of no value above the judgment of the police officer arresting him to make certain that Cho did not have to be forcefully subdued or shot to protect the police or other victims.

Police can be the best judges of imminent dangerousness for many reasons. Some they can explain, and some they cannot. In fact, a stranger flapping his lips on the street is oftentimes considered less dangerous than Cho, who did not talk. There is an emergency medicine literature on the "fuckshouter" to support this anecdotal legend from beat cops. The fuckshouting patient in the ER is not the threat. The strangely behaving, nonverbal one, however, is. And that is what Cho was. But, there is no indication that his muteness projected anything of substance clinically to this evaluator within his 15-minute evaluation—known in such inpatient circles as a *drive-by*—rather than a clinical workup. And, what did Dr. Crouse think Cho's mental illness was? We do not know. He obviously could tell that Cho was seriously mentally ill, but what was the diagnosis?

"The independent evaluator did not attend the commitment hearing; however, both counsel for Cho and the special justice signed off on the form certifying his findings" (Virginia Tech Review Panel, 2007).

Thankfully, counsel was there to protect Cho from any clinical professionals at the hospital inclined, as the Wisconsin Judge asserted, to shoving a person into the shoe that best fits the clinician's diagnosis. Dr. Crouse cannot be accused of doing that. And, thankfully for the commonwealth, the special justice looked at Cho and, all but alone in that barren room with no other way out of this debacle, was forced to communicate with him. The justice put no credence in the psychologist's evaluation or in the psychiatrist's alleged agreement with the psychologist.

This magistrate judged Cho to actually be imminently dangerous. This is most unusual but perhaps a sign of our times that the legal profession has totally coopted emergency inpatient psychiatry. They show here that they are probably by now better judges of future behavior based on present state exams than the clinicians they employ. Is this the type of judgment Szcaz proposed? It certainly is contrary to what the Supreme Court of California held in *Tarasoff*!

We know that an attempt was made to speed the dictation of the psychiatrist's special examination of Cho, documenting his clinical decision making for diagnosing a walking wounded person's condition most everyone has every Sunday night on campus: "mood disorder, not otherwise specified." Everyone cannot be on antidepressants starting the new week in school. Thus, only counseling was recommended and not medication.

Why the chasm between the magistrate's findings and the CSB social worker's findings the previous night and the clinical psychologist's documentation of serious mental illness with flat and inappropriate affect? One milligram of Ativan for severe agitation would not explain that difference, but perhaps in today's world of revolving door emergency nonpsychiatry, it really does not matter either what he did or what he thought. Cho only received popularized court-ordered least restrictive alternative testing and disposition unsubstantiated for either humaneness or clinical effectiveness. Everybody's backs were covered.

But, no one in the practice of forensic psychiatry—whether lawyer or clinician—can ever be certain when snake eyes comes up on the table. Despite all the covering up and the defensive medicine, the patient blows up in your face. And that is what happened just months later.

"Shortly before the commitment hearing, the attending psychiatrist at St. Albans evaluated Cho. When he was interviewed by the panel, the psychiatrist did not recall anything remarkable about Cho, other than that he was extremely quiet" (Virginia Tech Review Panel, 2007).

As noted above, Cho's silence was, in fact, an obvious sign of severe psychopathology in a patient detained for imminent dangerousness caused by mental illness and previously diagnosed as mutism, a most serious psychiatric disorder.

"The Psychiatrist did not discern dangerousness in Cho, and, as noted, his assessment did not differ from that of the independent evaluator—that Cho was not a danger to himself or others. He suggested that Cho be treated on an outpatient basis with counseling. No medications were prescribed, and no primary diagnosis was made" (Virginia Tech Review Panel, 2007).

Here was a psychiatrist who finally learned his true role within society and healthcare: a marginal functionary. What was the process of his decision making, or was he also in a rush for personal reasons that morning? Or had he been awake for nights on end due to an excessive and dangerous on-call schedule, for some reason seemingly tolerated by boards of Catholic hospitals—perhaps with the rationale of their mission. Was his evaluation, like that of the clinical psychologist, another drive-by, because the patient was noncommunicative?

> The psychiatrist's conclusion was based in part on Cho's denying any drug or alcohol problems or any previous mental health treatment. [Was there a urine drug toxicology screen performed to support Cho's inappropriate history? He also said he had guns.] The psychiatrist acknowledged that he did not gather any collateral information or information to refute the data obtained by the pre-screener on the basis of which the commitment was obtained. He indicated that this is standard practice and

> that privacy laws impede the gathering of collateral information. The psychiatrist also said that the time it takes to gather collateral information is prohibitive in terms of existing resources. (Virginia Tech Review Panel, 2007)

Caveat: What he said was routine practice at this hospital should in no way be interpreted as meaning standard of practice. This statement is astonishing in the United States of America. This was an emergency psychiatric detention of a patient unknown within this hospital. The assumption here that Cho was capable and competent enough to enable him to provide psychological evaluators with an accurate medical and psychiatric history of himself was patently absurd given the fact that Cho was introduced into the system as an involuntarily committed patient and, hence, should have been treated as an adversarial party rather than a cooperative one. To rely on an unresponsive patient to provide an accurate medical history is a mistake.

It appears that Cho was unable to provide much of a history, which means that his clinical history is automatically, under classical rules of triage, a medical emergency in itself. Nothing can be taken as reliable from this patient, already deemed a serious threat by a competent clinical social worker's evaluation the previous night and a campus police report.

Privacy obstacles in such a case are merely smoke and mirrors. Inappropriate history in emergency inpatient psychiatry, particularly with history of either threats or actual harm to self and or others, less than 24 hours prior to this assessment is a serious red flag. Prior to this assessment Cho's psychiatric presentation demanded further investigation, including gathering information from collaterals. The school rule protects clinical staff in such a situation from breaching what ordinarily would be privileged communications to obtain information to protect both the patient and potential victims' safety.

Again, the lack of time to do this is likewise simply obfuscation of what had to be the facts, if St. Albans was a duly licensed psychiatric facility. It must have been, to be receiving court-detained patients. In such a licensed facility, it is the responsibility of nursing and/or social service to gather collateral information. If the attending psychiatrist was saying that such investigative assets were not available at St. Albans Hospital, then St. Albans Hospital should have been closed long ago.

One would wonder whether any of the clinical staff directly involved in the case of Cho Seung-Hui continue to work on the St. Albans Hospital inpatient psychiatric unit after this debacle, foretelling one of the worst man-made disasters in American history.

Chapter 4

Prediction of Violence: Who Is Dangerous to Whom, Why, and What Can Be Done about It?

Any professional searching for predictive clues to what Cho ultimately perpetrated can easily see in hindsight, of course, a roadmap to violence. Where were the switch-track monitors who were supposed to predict Cho's potential violence along a continuum of likely possibilities? Were they asleep at the switch? Where were the watchers protecting the community and protecting Cho from himself?

Only a special magistrate could see that there was trouble on the horizon. The governor's panel ultimately found a way to exonerate the state and lay the blame upon someone who lied about his previous psychiatric treatment. But this was someone so delusional he was barely communicative. The governor's report, however, does set forth the question for everyone charged with maintaining safety in our educational systems: how can we predict dangerousness? And that is the question we must answer.

Predicting Future Behavior

The work of John Monahan has humbled the mental health professions by casting grave doubts and concerns over our special abilities and knowledge to predict future behavior. His career spearheaded research on the detention of mentally ill offenders, criminals, and people among us generally considered at risk of committing violence—that is, the bad and the mad. John Monahan's consultations are included in the final Commonwealth Commission's report that laid out mental health law reform in the wake of the Virginia Tech massacre.

In study after study, Monahan has argued, with a preponderance of evidence, that clinical interventions to protect the public by predicting who is too violent to be free are at best Orwellian. And, at worst, such clinical authority to predict who is too violent to be free unjustifiably, he asserts, crowns mental health professions with tyrannical authority.

Monahan then highlighted the broad reach of using prediction of violence for determining crucial adjudications of persons to be detained or freed and through what means and where, that is, monitored bracelet in halfway house or solitary confinement. These transactions affect millions of Americans every day and include the following:

- Civil commitment of the seriously mentally ill patient
- Mental health evaluations forced upon apprehended violent felons
- Incarceration of mentally ill offenders deemed dangerous
- Presentence reports determining suitability of convicted felons for probation
- Setting bail at preliminary and bail hearings
- Trying juvenile suspects as adults for serious crimes
- Deciding when an indeterminate sentence will end
- Determining suitability for placement, whether type of security setting within prison or local jail system
- Parole, for either determinate or indeterminate sentences.

Thus, professional prediction of future violent behavior, whether by a mental health professional or judge, is ubiquitous. It involves thousands of critical decisions every day about whether to deprive millions of people of freedom and, if so, how much. These actions are routine in criminal justice settings.

Monahan reviewed most of the existing studies setting standards for public policy in protecting the public by use of predictive powers of professionals with peculiar ability. *Peculiar ability* defines the basis for legal authority of physicians reporting contagious disease. It attributes to the doctor examining a patient special knowledge to diagnose measles, both predicting that the patient will likely spread it to others and reporting it for control.

This medical model has rightly or wrongly been applied to violence. This attribute of peculiar ability to know better than anyone else that a given person will be violent thereby empowers the credentialed professional to invoke controls over the person. Monahan is essentially saying that this medical paradigm for reportable contagious diseases does not have equivalent validity—that violence and contagiousness of infectious diseases are not equally predictable by clinicians. It cannot be shown by any research that anyone has special knowledge about violence. Therefore, he has argued, clinicians should not be depended upon for the second element of their peculiar ability—that is, controlling the subject.

But, the public wants the doctor to do this—and believes that failure to do so causes unnecessary violence. Thus, most students and faculty at the University of Wyoming believed that psychiatrists were responsible for increasing violence in the state. Their opinions were based on the belief in state psychiatrists' success in freeing criminals on insanity pleas. Up to the time of this survey in the late twentieth century, however, there had only been one NGI case tried in Wyoming!

And, the court's holding in *Tarasoff v Regents of the University of California* now sets the standard for all clinicians evaluating or treating potentially dangerous patients. The Supreme Court of California ruled that all clinicians have the duty to warn and do everything practically possible to protect potential victims from their patients making threats. The intent of this ruling was to put clinicians on notice that, in the event of a heinous crime committed by their patient, they could not simply hide behind either Monahan's research findings or privileged communications. In fact, any of the mishmash of obfuscating rules and regulations unearthed and quoted from the Virginia Governor's Panel could cover the debacle that was Cho's apocalyptic mass murder suicide. No time limits were written into this decision. Reasonable expectations of sensible clinicians was the message the justices were trying to communicate to mental health professionals in the wake of Tatania Tarasoff's murder. The basis of the decision? Psychiatrists and psychologists, the California justices maintained over considerable challenges, have peculiar ability, just like doctors responsible for diagnosing and reporting communicable disease.

So, despite overwhelming evidence to the contrary, society stubbornly holds to the thesis that crazy people are so often in the control of psychiatrists that, as doctors, they, more than any other party to that "mad" subject, can stop violence by diagnosing and controlling them just as the bespectacled family doctor thumps a child's chest and diagnoses a contagious disease in his office. Forever, madness has scared people exposed to it. And, they are right in some cases. They may, however, be as good at predicting the strange or "alien" person's future violence as any professional. At least that is what Monahan asserted decades ago.

Monahan made it clear that clinical management of violence cannot be supported by the definition of evidence-based medicine attributed to the unambiguous reporting of contagious disease. At the Massachusetts Center for Diagnosis and Treatment of Dangerous Persons in 1972, for instance, an opportunity presented to get some metrics for clinical predictions of violence. Nearly 600 "violent" inpatients were carefully examined by two psychiatrists, two psychologists, and a social worker, all having extensive forensic experience. They then made determinations of likelihood for future violence, were the patient set free.

Approximately three quarters of the patients were set free. About 10 percent of these patients had been diagnosed as high risk for future violence, whereas about 90 percent were predicted to be at low risk for future violence. Furthermore, the court released about 50 patients against the advice of clinical staff, and one third of them did commit violence again.

The latter robust statistic did vindicate the predictive powers of this interdisciplinary team's intensive and sophisticated prerelease assessments. And, further supporting their predictive powers was the low rate of false-negative predictions; less than 10 percent of those released as nonviolent actually committed violence again.

The good news from this study, supporting the public policy of pervasive prediction of violence by professionals when done right, is the low level of false negatives. Clinicians proved that their predictive powers and techniques had validity.

The bad news is that nearly two thirds of inmates would have been deprived of their civil liberties had the judge not overruled the clinical staff and kept all 50 patients locked up based on clinical predictions of future violence.

Of course, clinical knowledge is better now, but, in the realities of our current clinical forensic capabilities, these assessments were more likely than not as good as we could do today. Could we take the techniques and follow-up studies of this classic case and improve upon the results? I believe that we could, given all the necessary manpower resources available in this study and complementing them with currently advanced knowledge.

But, clinical manpower resources for forensic evaluations are not even close today to what was available to the State of Massachusetts in the 1970s. Could we do so now without having a false-negative error rate that deprived nearly two thirds of inpatients of their civil liberties based solely on best practices informing solid clinical judgment? It is unlikely that we will ever have the opportunity to find out, because the state mental hospital system studied in Massachusetts no longer exists and likely never will again.

To justify the authority to control people throughout the broad spectrum of transactions now dependent upon prediction of violence, we would have to do considerably better to protect the public from violent insanity than reducing false negatives to 10 percent at the cost of depriving one third of the seriously mentally ill of their civil liberties. Unfortunately, we would do well to duplicate the accuracy of this staff's predictive power. That would even be true, in my opinion, were we to have experienced, quality forensic psychiatry and psychology clinical staffs in house to do so—which we no longer have.

Dr. Arnold Hutschnecker, a psychiatric consultant to the National Commission on the Causes and Prevention of Violence, advocated that the Rorschach test be administered to all six-year-olds in the United States to determine their potential for criminal behavior. The tests were to be followed by massive psychological and psychiatric treatments for those children found to be criminally inclined. Such a program, Hutschnecker said, was a better short-term solution to the crime problem than urban reconstruction. Teenage boys later found to be persisting in incorrigible behavior would be remanded to camps.

It is astonishing today that such a recommendation could have made it so high within the levels of a presidential administration. But this was 1970, a new decade after both American society and government had been, many believed, fleeced for billions in the war on poverty and Lyndon Johnson's Great Society programs. This was a new era under a Richard Nixon redux, who had promised to end the war in Vietnam and turn around the guns-and-butter spending of the Johnson years. Americans were now threatened by the violent revolutions of both campus youth and blacks, perceived to be both united and armed by Vietnam Veterans against the war in their campaign to destroy existing structures of government "of the people." But, of what people and for what people? Whoever they were, President Nixon promised law and order and a solution to the violence caused by what he called "those bums" who threatened domestic tranquility.

Of course, the vast majority of psychiatrists would consider Dr. Hutschnecker to be a nut with as dangerous a faulty ego as the kids whose madness he was attempting to identify early. Very likely he was stacking the cards, presumably with the unintended risk of shipping a disproportionate number of minority youths off to camp. This is reminiscent of enforced boarding schools for Native American children just decades before. We know that did not work very well, and most likely we are now reaping the rewards of that racist, dehumanizing, and megalomaniacal debacle. But Hutschnecker's recommendation came at a critical time in the antiwar movement and the Counter Intelligence Program (COINTELPRO) operation and drew immediate and intense condemnation from the press. It gave the whole field of preventive criminal justice a bad name.

So, within the spectrum of solutions, where do we go as professionals whose current responsibilities still include documentation of future destructive behavior, whether suicide or violence to others? Do we simply challenge the Supreme Court with professional nihilism and stand down from claiming, as well as allowing claims to be made upon, our peculiar abilities of knowing more about violence? In this way we abrogate society's apparent expectation that we exert control over those clinical encounters we believe to be at high risk of future harm to self or others.

First of all, we need to define violence at least as well as we can define the syndrome of mood disorder. Unfortunately, however, we run into more problems, because only in a perfect world can we come close to defining violence within the context of a psychiatric syndrome, whether antisocial personality, intermittent explosive, or conduct disorder.

It was not until after the breakup of the Soviet Union, for example, that we knew that serial lust murder had been committed within a Communist society. And we know that Citizen X, Andrei Chikatilo, had been trolling train stations for years, literally feeding his lust before the very eyes of the local police. When finally put on trial, it was clear that he was criminally insane, as diseased as many of our own serial killers and episodic offenders. Why did the Soviet's complex psychiatric system not identify him? We know now that the Soviet psychiatric system was not designed to catch those who were mentally ill. It never was. It was a system of asylums for those whose political views needed correction or for those *refusniks* who needed sequestration.

Psychiatry in the Soviet system was for those expressing opposition to the Communist government. They were judged mentally ill and committed to psychiatric hospitals and treated against their will. We know now that the judgment of who was dangerous to whom within the Soviet Union was primarily determined through an extremely corrupted and ideologically distorted lens. In a perfect society generating a pure government, there could be no mental illness, except in those seriously criticizing governmental authority. In such a society, it was not necessary for the KGB to diagnose dissidents as insane. Psychiatrists simply knew what to do and supported each other in doing it—that is, the involuntary commitment of perfectly rational political dissidents to psychiatric institutions, where they were forced to take powerful antipsychotic medications with extreme side effects. Psychiatrists simply belonged to that species, *Homo Sovieticus*.

The reverse of this ideological political catastrophe was seen in the Society Islands in the South Pacific before recent contamination by Western tourism. Discovered and named by Captain Cook in the 1760s, visited and made famous by Captain Bligh and his frigate HMS *Bounty*, depicted by the beautiful paintings of Paul Gauguin, and fought over by the United States and the Japanese in World War II, these islands, such as Bora Bora and Tahiti, have evidenced the near absence of anything we know as violence. Described by the novelist James Michener as the must beautiful place on earth, sociologists and anthropologists have written that these islands debunk the theory that man is inherently violent. The Society Islands were noted to have low competitiveness, low intensity of interpersonal relationships, and low population asynergies—that is, economic and racial asymmetries and conflicts. What we are so careful to judge in a court of law as violent crime simply did not occur at significant enough frequency and severity to be a problem in the Society Islands.

The paradise of the Society Islands and the romance of Gauguin and Michener's *South Pacific* notwithstanding, Western civilization is besought with aggression, competitiveness, and violence. All governments have tried to cope with the challenges of violence from the philosophies of Locke, Hobbes, and Hume to the Draconian order of the USSR. However, we are not the Soviet Union, and even that government, knowing firsthand the insanity of Hitler, would probably have just made President Nixon's Dr. Arnold Hutschneker a staff psychiatrist. Hutschneker could have functioned well, assessing dissident mental patients considered too dangerous for hospitalization and needing transfer to a Siberian Gulag for protection of the State. And, the USSR already had youth camps over which ordinary parents had little control for their children's required attendance. Unfortunately, America is highly competitive with emphasis on high-intensity interpersonal bonding, again, challenged by revolutionaries of the 1960s through communal sex and now by polygamist cults in Texas.

We know that our society is not highly synergistic in the aftermath of the Civil Rights movement and race riots. A major race riot just exploded nationally after the Rodney King incident in Los Angeles. And, waves of Third-World immigration into traditionally minority neighborhoods in Los Angeles, New York City's outer boroughs, Chicago, and Detroit are creating new asynergies. These asynergies resulting from African and Middle Eastern immigration are also cropping up in Europe, especially in the suburbs of Paris. If we, as professionals working with violent people, want to work in the United States, we must take America as it is. The alternative is to convert to political radicalism or revolution. And to take America as it is, rather than overthrow the government and start over, we must start with at least a reliable, if not truly valid, definition of violence.

The National Commission on the Causes and Prevention of Violence (1968) operationally defined *violence* as "overtly threatened or overtly accomplished application of force which results in the injury or destruction of persons or property or reputation, or the illegal appropriation of property."

A majority of interested experts could agree—and likely did agree—with this definition, but an entire book could be devoted to simply demonstrating the problems of validity in this definition. For example, would Nazi and Japanese war crimes be covered by this? That is, can governments be violent within this definition or only individuals? And, if a reporter damages the reputation of a crook, is that reporter violent?

Is the Taliban government violent in stoning a woman judged immoral according to their interpretation of the Koran? Are the fundamentalist Hezbollah and Hamas violent in enforcing the social mores of seventh-century Islam? Is the Bible violent for punishments meted out to incorrigible sons, homosexuals, and sexual partners committing incest? And, the report says nothing of capacity to form specific intent to commit a violent act, thus negating the role of altered consciousness in violence. This is a major expertise claimed by and expected of psychiatrists and psychologists in our courts of law.

Finally, suicidality must be included in any definition. Had apocraphyl mass murder/suicides been attenuated or prevented, thousands of people would be alive today particularly in light of 9/11. Likewise, their loved ones would have been spared the indirect injuries of the inevitable complicating posttraumatic syndromes with profound intergenerational consequences. The separate determination of harm to self and harm to others is a legal construct created by courts to enable involuntary commitment and release of patients; clinically, however, the dichotomy is both fraught with error in reality and quite dangerous. Those determined at risk for self-harm, as Cho was by the CSB evaluator, are frequently dangerous to others too. (EMPsych)

Standards of evidence also define violence, because violent felons have the right to be tried before a jury of their peers. It is they, and not one person or arbitrary panel, who judges beyond reasonable doubt whether their fellow citizen, for whom they are expected to be impartial, was violent. We now know that this standard, although likely more valid than predicting violence in specialized hospitals, is not perfect either. Innocent people are convicted and imprisoned but certainly not to the extent that they risk detention based solely on professionals predicting their potential for future violence. And, from the Simpson case, we now know that violent people are found innocent and released, for reasons having little to do with the facts of what they were purported to have done.

Accordingly, we need a better concept of any violent act that fits the definition above. Until our knowledge base improves, a multidimensional concept could help. It appeared to work in the Massachusetts project, just with too many false positives that appeared to detain an unacceptable number of apparently nonviolent patients. Using a multidimensional concept approach, there could be a way in which we do not throw the individual's own history and clinical status out with the prediction bath water. Even Monahan agreed to some extent in his most cynical years, simply asserting that more attention needed to be paid to the situation of violence. He properly questioned why those predicted to be violent and released anyway did not commit violence.

Monahan even raised doubts over the basis of his own opinions. Violence is underreported compared to, say, cardiovascular disease or even psychosis. Perhaps those predicted to be violent and released against medical advice could have committed violence without detection or reporting, but at the two-thirds level? Most likely the situations they experienced after discharge, for the most part, did not elicit violence as it had in their pasts. Or, perhaps their treatment was better than staff credited themselves for providing in their hospital. Or, maybe, they were living under less stressful circumstances—that is, in treatment with a guaranteed monthly disability stipend and supervised housing, altered family situation, or different vocation.

All professionals in clinical and criminal justice vocations can dodge the dilemma of predicting violence. They can do research on it or simply teach. But, most clinicians, like Dr. Crouse at St. Albans, will have to both make and document assessments of violence, whether self-harm or harm to others, in order to make a living encountering potentially violent people. As forensic psychiatric expert Seymour Halleck states:

> Many individuals now argue that the dangers done by depriving the so-called dangerous mentally ill of liberty may outweigh the advantages that involuntary confinement and treatment brings to either the individual or the society. Noting that psychiatrists have no special expertise in predicting violence … states are now restricting the power of medical commitment except in instances where mental disorganization is blatant and the individual either makes strong threats of violence or has a history of violent behavior. In dealing with the problem of civil commitment of the mentally ill, society is obviously confronted with a complex choice. By opting for the value of liberty over the values of stability, health or control, we may be risking a slight increase in the amount of violence some disturbed individuals direct against themselves or others. On the other hand, if we continue to commit large

> numbers of mentally disturbed individuals, it is probably that many will be unnecessarily deprived of liberty. My own feelings with regard to this ethical conflict are that involuntary confinement of some emotionally disturbed individuals is justified if they have a treatable mental illness and if their threats of violence or previous violent behavior has been well documented. (Halleck, 1977)

So, within the context of Halleck's conceptualization, we learn more about the positive correlations in the multidimensional universe of moving parts that determine any act of violence. This is the toolbox that we use for evidence-based assessment and management of either the violent person or one at risk to be violent. First of all, at what point is clinical intervention aimed at preventing future violence most likely to reap rewards of controlling people to obtain valid diagnoses driving evidence-based treatment?

Wolfgang studied a birth cohort of 10,000 young males born in 1945 and residing in Philadelphia (cited in Chappell & Monahan, 1975). He followed them to age 18. Ten percent of his cohort was followed to age 26. Because of the serious epidemiological problem of underreporting crime, he said that he assessed the number "caught in the network of the juvenile justice system." The subjects of such events were termed "delinquent." He found one third to be delinquent. This was startling for him, because it was previously believed that only 2 percent of juveniles are delinquent and, perhaps, 5 percent in the black ghetto.

Also, he found, that if one waits until age 26, another 10 percent will get caught in the "net." He then theorized that over the life cycle, 50 percent of males will be adjudicated for a crime. There was a differential favoring ghetto blacks offending in this study, and, as now known, mostly intraracially. He found that black youth in Philadelphia had a 50 percent chance of being delinquent before age 18.

Only 6 percent of the entire cohort and 20 percent of the delinquent subgroup were adjudicated delinquent more than five times in their adolescence; he defined these young males as "chronic offenders." They were, however, responsible for half of all documented cases of juvenile crimes within the 10,000 male cohort. Furthermore, they were disproportionately represented in the violent offenses. More than half of violent offenses were committed by this small, easily identified subgroup, including most robberies and 100 percent of homicides. And, when following each boy's offenses out to fifteen index crimes, many stopped after the first offense. The vast majority of these boys' offenses were trivial. Another subgroup of the delinquent group, equaling one third of his cohort, stopped after their second offense. Finally, statistical progression stabilized, and he found that one third stopped after each succeeding offense.

When comparing this small and progressively diminishing subgroup with the entire group of delinquents, the gap between crimes committed by this small and shrinking group and all the others was like the difference between all those living on top of the Grand Canyon and the small population at the bottom. This robust evidence from such a large prospective study, therefore, both isolates and clearly illuminates a huge default and chasm dividing people. One small group likely commits most serious and violent crimes and others either do nothing illegal or are caught for trivial and petty infractions loaded with little predictive power for future violence.

Wolfgang argued that concentrating society's resources on this subgroup at the time of their third offense maximizes impact in reducing crime. His opinion empirically supports evidence-based interventions in a well-defined subgroup of males providing high enough likelihood of reoffending to warrant aggressive intervention. Most likely, such interventions broadly invoked would reduce the mortality and morbidity of violence in our society.

Contrast this to Dr. Hutschneker's policy of performing Rorschachs on all six-year-olds, which, by the way, aroused the interest of President Nixon until it was reported in the press and soundly denounced by policymakers and lawmakers alike. Not only is there a paucity of evidence to support findings of such a test at that age, but there is no more to support the indiscriminate sentencing of delinquent adolescents to camps. Here, therefore, we differentiate a profound example of where to draw the line in the sand to begin assessing and treating a well-defined at-risk subgroup of youth likely to be violence prone into early adulthood. It is not coincidental that this is also the highest risk group for violence demographically—young males between ages 16 and 26.

The Neuropsychiatric Assessment of Violence

Physicians have been classifying the physical and emotional distress of their patients since Hippocrates. The historical evolution of this taxonomy—or hierarchical organization of patient presentations—has resulted in clinical nosology of the World Health Organizations disease classifier, the International Classification of Diseases (ICD9). *Nosology* is the naming and definition of syndromes such as major depression or, in Cho's case, mutism. Diseases can be identified by their causes and by their symptoms. For example, again in Cho's case, his mutism was identified by his clinical therapist at George Washington on the basis of Cho's failure to respond verbally and interact verbally. Major depression is defined by a constellation of symptoms that include depressed mood or loss of interest and at least a minimum of four other symptoms of depression that could include insomnia, guilt, suicidal ideation, agitation or loss of weight.

ICD9 classifies problems necessitating encounters with clinicians for diagnosis and treatment. These classifications are more or less based on fact, dependent upon known causation and clarity of presentation. The cause of burns is based on hard fact and the appearance of burns is apparent because burns have a high degree of clarity. In other words, you almost always know what can cause a burn and most burns are very easy to see. Juxtaposing the cause and appearance of delinquency in a 16-year-old boy to that of a visible burn, we find both the unknown causation and lack of clarity to be striking.

The multiaxial diagnostic template known as the *Diagonstic and Statistical Manual of Mental Disorders,* 4th Edition (*DSM IV*) refines the taxonomy of ICD9 through a comprehensive nosology designed to capture all clinical encounters of mental disorganization and emotional distress. As such, it needs to meet the demands of diagnostic sensitivity to avoid missing symptoms or signs signaling significant psychopathology, for example, all the nuances of insomnia.

Conversely, its taxonomy must generate a clinical nosology that creates meaningful borders between the normal and abnormal. Thus, within the abnormal, discriminators must serve as tags for meaningful mapping of clinical presentations. Presentations signaling either mental disorganization or strange behavior need to be separated from dysphoria of emotional distress. The mentally disorganized person, like Cho, may neither solicit clinical help nor even have a chief complaint, whereas the patient suffering from emotional distress will do both due to emotional pain and knowledge that it is not healthy. The latter was more true of his surviving victims than Cho himself.

In this example of delineating taxons that are discriminators of presentations—or, syndromes—the clinician is informed in the former to take caution in an encounter with the person behaving strangely. In the latter, the emotionally pained—dysphoric—presentation most likely signals insight with capacity to communicate for purposes of a therapeutic alliance promising safety for patient and society. Cho undoubtedly suffered the classical anosognosia of denying his own schizophrenic illness. Thus, it made communicating with him on the basis of developing a therapeutic alliance very difficult because Cho was in denial that he needed therapy for anything. We can see this denial at work throughout Cho's medical history, especially during his years at Virginia Tech. Therefore, because he was in real denial—anosognosia—with respect to his having a mental illness, his denial that he had sought and received prior psychological counseling for a disease is part of that illness, belying the Virginia governor's panel's laying the blame on Cho for lying to the clinicians at St. Albans.

The current upgrading to *DSM V* is a further work in progress. Because we rarely know the causation of people presenting clinically with emotional distress or mental disorganization, it is necessary to categorize presentations into constructs that first of all have interrater reliability. Most experienced clinicians agree with the criteria for major depression. Such interrater reliability is necessary both for researchers having to isolate and delineate problems for meaningful multicenter studies and for third-party payers to translate a code into monetary value.

Interrator reliability, however, does not ensure diagnostic validity. This latter requirement for a meaningful and functional diagnostic system demands both informing selection of treatments from a standard menu to predict effectiveness of outcomes and ensuring stability of naming a condition over time. In the case of Cho, for example, neither the diagnoses of selective mutism nor depression, not otherwise specified (NOS), stood the test of time. Thus, these diagnoses proved in the end to lack stability. And they did not predict either successful treatment or outcome; in fact, unfortunately, they did the opposite. Cho was left on his own to seek counseling with unsupervised court-ordered treatment that both was totally undefined and omitted his need for psychotropic medication. Although outpatient counseling may be appropriate in the case of depression NOS, Cho proved to be neither simply mood disordered nor not otherwise specified. He was flat-out psychotic, suffering from classical schizophrenia.

Let us take the example of a patient seeking help for depressed mood who meets all the criteria for major depression, with insomnia, loss of appetite, lack of interest, and thoughts of suicide. She meets the criteria for major depression. This is the third time such depression has occurred in her life, and there are no other diseases, such as depressed thyroid function, or psychiatric disorders, such as alcoholism, to either cause or correlate with her clinical presentation. Furthermore, she is well organized mentally without disordered thinking or abnormal perceptions—that is, delusions or hallucinations, respectively. Most clinicians will agree that the patient fits the criteria for major depression, recurrent and severe, without psychosis.

Most researchers now can begin to screen this patient for inclusion in studies of mood disorders. But, how does this inform best practices for treatment? If suicidal ideation affects proper assessment and a plan to keep the patient safe, and insomnia with lack of interest leads to a prescription for paroxetine (Paxil), then the diagnosis most likely has high validity, too. Paroxetine will likely be an effective first choice medication for both antidepressant action and nighttime sedation. Its slight adrenergic action could also help improve interest, believed to be dependent on adequate brain adrenalin.

If, however, the patient develops panic attacks and total wakefulness over time, the validity of the diagnosis is poor, because it is not stable over time. The patient has likely become manic and thus more likely has bipolar affective disorder. And, the patient could lose insight during cycling mood disorder and convert primarily into self-harm and kill herself and others in a manic state.

In this case, the diagnosis was sensitive enough to pick up a lethal psychiatric disorder, and it was reliable enough for a multicenter research study where everyone has to agree on what is wrong with all subjects. It was not valid, however, because it did not predict treatment for effective outcome, nor was it stable over time. The diagnostic name had to be changed, totally altering operational demands of clinical management. In fact, it was so unstable over time that the patient lost insight in a manic state, cycled, and killed herself. The diagnosis of bipolar affective disorder would have been a more valid—even if not more reliable—diagnosis from the beginning, because it would more likely have prevented premature death and remained stable over time. Lithium is FDA approved to reduce suicide risk in bipolar affective disorder, so the invalidity of her diagnosis, although reliably diagnosed by other evaluators, deprived her of life-saving treatment.

All clinical disciplines seek diagnostic specificity, and modern genetics and imaging promise improvements in this requirement for a meaningful and effective nosology. For example, we know that delinquency is associated with attention deficit hyperactivity disorder (ADHD) in up to one third of cases. There is also considerable evidence supporting the theory that ADHD manifests as the phenotype of an abnormal neuropsychiatric genotype. When we identify the DNA marker—perhaps in an abnormal enzyme assay of serum—and consistent patterns of abnormal regional metabolism on PET scans, we can segregate a large cohort of delinquent young males whose behavioral problems are more biologically driven and hence may lend themselves to more traditional medical intervention.

Right now, however, the critically important nosology of conduct disorder, whether that of childhood or adult, is so nonspecific to defy standards of practice for its management. From the multidimensional perspective of violent behavior, the lack of standard best practices for a reliably diagnosed delinquent boy as conduct disorder can be due to many factors. These include socialized violence in a gang or an underlying manic depressive illness masquerading as impulsive violence. Fulfilling the criteria for conduct disorder in childhood could simply be the harbinger of an evolving career criminality without any psychiatric signals to inform treatment. But, with more specificity to classify individuals within this nosological syndromic diagnosis, more discipline will come for early identification, diagnosis, and treatment.

Taxanomy of Syndromes Manifesting as Violence

Here is a taxonomy of syndromes manifesting primarily as violence. It is not our purpose to argue the human propensity toward violence nor, as previously discussed, the distorted lexicology of behavioral scientists struggling over human perception and ambiguity without hard evidence of blood tests or x-rays to make highly specific diagnoses, such as tuberculosis. The diagnostic system proposed here is to support both identification and effective selection of menu options for clinical intervention.

I. Psychosis
- A. Organic brain disorders
  - 1. Drug and/or alcohol induced
  - 2. Organic delusional disorder
- B. Paranoia
- C. Schizophrenia
- D. Brief reactive psychosis
- E. Bipolar affective disorder
- F. Atypical psychosis

II. Complex partial seizure disorder

III. Impulse disorders
   A. Intermittent explosive disorder
   B. Isolated explosive disorder

IV. Paraphilias
   A. Pedophilia
   B. Sexual sadism
   C. Atypical paraphilia, e.g., lust murder

V. Adjustment disorder with disturbance of conduct
   A. With Axis II personality disorder
      1. Borderline personality disorder
      2. Narcissistic personality disorder
      3. Compulsive personality disorder
      4. Antisocial personality disorder
      5. Paranoid personality disorder
      6. Mixed personality disorder
   B. Without Axis II diagnosis
   C. With dysthymic (chronic depressed mood) disorder

VI. Conduct disorder
   A. Socialized aggression
      1. Gang violence
      2. Fraternity initiations
      3. Cult violence
      4. Police violence (excessive force)
      5. Gang rape
      6. War crimes
   B. Undersocialized aggression

VII. Personality disorders
   A. Antisocial personality disorder
   B. Personality disorder, mixed type, with borderline, narcissistic and/or antisocial features

VIII. Dissociative disorders
   A. Multiple personality disorder with violent alters (very rare)

IX. Anxiety disorders
   A. Posttraumatic stress disorder, chronic and delayed type

This system draws upon the nosology of *DSM*, attempting to favor more modern *DSM IV* nomenclature and criteria whenever possible. And, where necessary, for purposes of enhancing sensitivity to diagnosing violence within the clinical setting, we have named subcategories otherwise termed xyz disorder, NOS—or not otherwise specified. This will be most helpful within the classical—yet markedly reduced—nosology of conduct disorder, one of the most two-dimensional diagnoses in psychiatry.

By *two-dimensional*, we mean that the diagnosis is more likely to be unstable over time than most others. How can we, for example, meaningfully apply conduct disorder to Wolfgang's delinquent males, problem police officers, military atrocities, and juvenile gangs? Within this context, therefore, we think that naming individuals at high risk for conduct disorder occurring mainly with "the pack" as socialized could still be valid, even though it is no longer included in *DSM*. Also, actually naming some not otherwise specified conduct-disordered variants aids in communication and standardization of behavioral science investigations into violence within the contexts of war, cults, or other areas.

Within the *DSM* taxonomy, the clinician is directed to think multidimensionally to remain flexible with respect to the fluidity of psychiatric diagnosis, depending on symptom complexes influenced by both medical/surgical diseases and psychosocial stress. Likely, there will be more of this in the future, as better understanding of causes and effects for acts of violence emerges. Axis I disorders are psychiatry's equivalent of medical/surgical diseases; that is, major depression needs to be considered when diagnosing coronary artery insufficiency, because they are associated frequently enough to be considered interactive risk factors. Perhaps, in fact, they are embraced in a syndrome when occurring together. When two diseases and/or disorders frequently occur together, this phenomenon is called *comorbidity*. Attention deficit hyperactivity disorder occurs frequently enough with conduct disorder in children and adolescents that their comorbidity is a significant signal and perhaps even a risk factor for violence.

Axis II disorders are enduring sets of specific traits that concentrate in dysfunctional people enough of the time to warrant diagnostic identification as "personality disorder." How childhood developmental problems diagnosed on Axis I affect abnormal development known as adult personality disorder is critically important for both understanding violence and finding effective interventions. Similarly, the interaction of substance abuse and dependence problems on both Axis I and Axis II frequently creates abnormal psychobiological dynamics that result in heightened irritability, loss of impulse control, and violence. Such dynamic interaction, therefore, is the purpose for multiaxial diagnosis, thus avoiding the error of reducing our understanding of a violent act as an isolated and static factor such as antisocial personality. Sociopaths do not spend every day of their lives committing violence. Why, then, sometimes and not others?

Axis III requires a complete differential diagnosis of known and suspected medical/surgical diseases. Again, hundreds of known diseases can, in and of themselves, cause depressed mood, severe anxiety, and psychosis, all of which can tip the vulnerable person from nonviolent to violent. An example would be the undiscovered abdominal tumor growing in a silent area without physical symptoms such as pain or indigestion. Such a tumor, for unknown reasons, most likely either causes or unmasks depression. Subsequent irritability can convert a nonviolent person to violent. This is an example in which everything can be within normal limits on all other multiaxial dimensions except the medical/surgical Axis III. Thus, a single medical/surgical disease on Axis III can uncommonly be the necessary, if not sufficient, cause for a violent attack or suicide.

Axis IV requires the clinician to assess stress level associated with both onset and perpetuation of disorders on Axis I, as well as diseases on Axis III and emergence of abnormal traits—such as impulsivity—on Axis II personality disorders. Stress can be the enduring oppression of racism and poverty in the ghetto or a concentration camp or a recent life change, such as death of a spouse, or extreme trauma like rape, whether the assault was remote or recent. Axis IV provides the discipline for behavioral scientists and physicians alike to assess environmental currents and countercurrents impacting an individual's behavior at any point in time, including the future. It is, of course, our understanding of both the past, present, and expected future on Axis IV that, with few exceptions, will determine the extreme expressions of behavior such as violence.

Finally, Axis V directs the clinician to assess seriousness of physiological and psychological dysfunction based on calibrated metrics termed Global Assessment of Function (GAF) Scale. Zero means totally nonfunctional, as in retarded depression causing inability to move or eat. A 100 rating means normal function. Once again, these metrics and their calibration are not specific. So when seeing a 70 GAF on Axis V, do not take this for fact that the patient is not badly off. There is both wide fluctuation in GAF scores and vast differentials between clinician calibration on the same patient over a short period of time.

A patient can be transferred from a psychiatric crisis center at one hospital with a GAF of 15 because of high risk of harm to others or self and be judged GAF of 50 by the admissions staff one mile away within a few hours. Very little ever changes, other than what is in the eyes of the clinical beholder and documentation needs. Unfortunately, financial and legal demands such as antidumping laws protecting patients do influence the numbers in diagnostic coding. The shipping entity needs to justify emergency transfer, whereas the receiving entity may or may not be committed to keeping the patient for many reasons. It would be suicidal legally to discharge a patient with a 15 GAF and hard to justify keeping that same patient with a 70 rating.

In the case of Axis V, interrater reliability must be the worst of any axis of assessment in multidimensional assessment in any clinical encounter. Experience indicates that most metrics used to judge point of care impairment are driven by experience, rather than covert administrative agendas. It is hard to put a number on the person who clearly intends to kill himself when he otherwise appears highly functional. Nonetheless, it is uncommon to admit patients from the ER with recent GAF scales under 20. Still, a GAF over 20 communicates that the patient is not imminently suicidal.

Again, as with all we have discussed in the lexicology and taxonomy of violence, perceptual distortion is constantly in operation. Nonetheless, diligent attention to accurately determining every factor of the multiaxial DSM system can construct an accurate portrait of what is wrong. One needs to ask what in the environment is tipping and turning all the moving parts and, finally, how badly off this person is.

In the case of impairment, again a somewhat arbitrary calibration metric is used that is unreliable, because it is not stressed in clinical practice. But in the investigation of an act of violence, accurate assessment of all the factors involved in human functioning and how they have both changed and could be changed has validity in improving prediction of behavior and clinical outcomes. For example, if a person is acting strangely, determining how long and in what areas of life he is impaired will be more predictive than not knowing that he has been this way for years or was just fired after being divorced and faces felony charges. In the former scenario most would sensibly consider him less violent in the future than in the latter case.

The problem with all diagnostic templates and clinical nosologies of disease is that they can dominate clinical practice and behavioral science investigation. With the advent of promised deliverance from all the woes of current healthcare through clinical computing, the demands for consistency and simplicity in language become even more important. It is amazing to work within large institutions and, over and over again, see patients carrying multiple diagnoses for the same presenting problems.

Current military medical standards, for example, demand solid proof of extreme trauma in order to diagnose posttraumatic stress disorder. More often than not, it is tough to get this hard proof because in the heat of combat, medics are not thinking about how documentation of Axis IV factors is going to affect whether a soldier gets a pension when he is out of the army. So, this returning combatant will frequently have a string of diagnoses on his electronic health record. They will usually span everything from occupational problem, essentially meaning trouble fighting; depression, not otherwise specified, even though his best friends were killed; adjustment disorder, because he can't sleep before the 10th straight combat mission that month; or acute stress reaction, which is really a factor for Axis IV.

Occasionally somebody will diagnose posttraumatic stress disorder, and then the playing field gets tipped. Can he fight again? If so, should he be discharged with a pension and full benefits? Should he be disciplined for showing up late for formation and simply discharged without any Axis I diagnosis to inhibit later tracking for compensable disability? Unfortunately, this is the real world of diagnostics. It is increasingly driven by documentation, rather than sound clinical practice. In other words, documentation drives clinical practice rather than clinical practice driving documentation.

Oftentimes what gets missed in such an institutionalized diagnostic system controlled by documentation is a critical clinical element. For example, panic attacks with agoraphobia could be muted by a soldier during combat in a Baghdad marketplace but not in the local shopping center or daily formation on garrison duty. Such panic attacks with agoraphobia could be adaptive in Operation Iraqi Freedom and lead to the brig during garrison duty upon returning home.

Similar problems exist for nurses in intensive care units trying to communicate critical nursing problems. They are captive of a medical documentation language imposed upon them by programmers only minimally experienced—if at all—with actual clinical practice. The nursing profession is now trying to develop a language that works for them. "Falling" is not a recognized diagnostic entity, but it is lethal and critically important for nursing assessment. So, to simplify diagnostics for all parties encountering a patient, including first responders, medics, or crisis counselors in correctional settings, we should supplement the lexicology of multiaxial diagnosis with that of best practices from evidence-based triage.

Both insurance adjustors and the now ubiquitous insurance doctors have an insatiable appetite for diagnostic and assessment terms that are rounded off enough to fit into their round holes. They have their needs, but their needs are more often than not distracting from the task at hand, which is spending time face to face with a patient to translate symptoms and signs into valid diagnostics. Symptomatic occupational problem following combat is an oxymoron! Personality disorder, for people who simply do not respond to treatment and whose impulsivity and bad judgment frustrates the overwhelmed clinician short on time and heavy on documentation demands, anchors such a person forever. By that, we mean that expectations for patients carrying such a diagnosis will always be relatively diminished and treatment resources covertly, or even intentionally, rationed.

Principles of Triage

Classical triage is the best practices of both time-determined and epidemiologically informed clinical decision making. The Cho case demonstrates, as does the emergency medicine data backlighting his case, the need today for enhanced point-of-entry diagnostic validity caused by increasingly accelerating patient flows of pre-9/11 rationing, particularly that of resource destruction in psychiatry, compounded by new contingencies of post-9/11 disaster medicine. *Time-determined decision making* is the clinical discipline of prioritizing presentations for selection of who is seen first and for how much time to minimize morbidity, mortality, and cost—or service optimization—for either a single patient, like Cho at Cook Guidance Center, or an entire gateway into the healthcare system, like the community service boards and emergency rooms of western Virginia.

The language of triage emerges operationally from the actual practices of clinicians effectively managing patients through the inductive reasoning process of

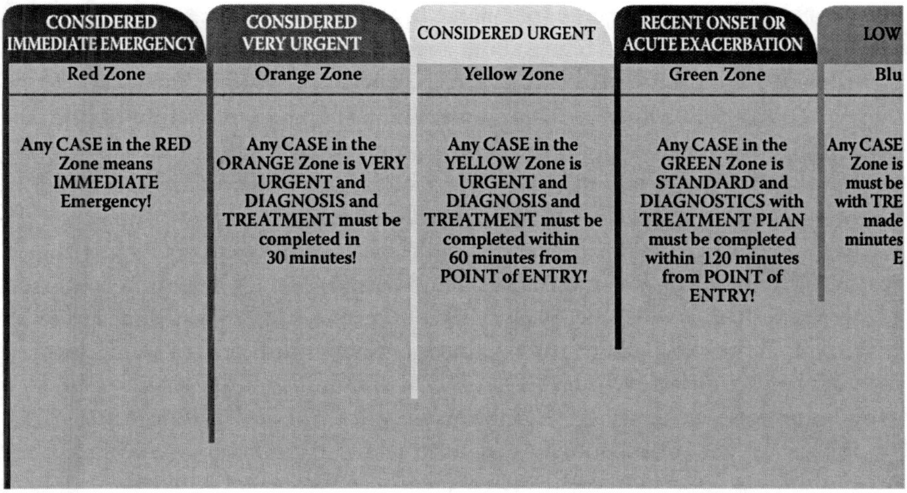

Figure 4.1 Begin diagnostics. The amount of time you have to complete treatment depends on the zone.

time-determined clinical decision making (see Figure 4.1). By that is meant the process of working from the most isolated symptom or sign having pathognomonic value, for example, "red eye." If this specific discriminating sign of red eye is unassociated with either pain or other specific or general discriminating symptoms and signs, the default for time-determined clinical decision making is set at the lowest acuity and severity triage category. This person, John Doe, is now triaged as patient, John Doe to triage category "blue."

The addition of the general discriminator, pain, to the presentation, however, increases the default of acuity and severity for time-determined diagnostics to category "green." Addition of that specific discriminator requires definitive diagnostic assessment with treatment within a minimum of two hours. The additional complaint of decreased visual acuity raises the default for time-determined clinical decision making to one hour; John Doe is now triage category "yellow," requiring definitive diagnostic assessment for clinical intervention within one hour. Severe pain, a general discriminator, raises the default level for John Doe to "very urgent status," triage category "orange"; patient John Doe must be seen for definitive diagnosis and treatment intervention within thirty minutes.

If through any prehospital or ER assessment times, it is discovered that John Doe's presentation was caused by chemical eye injury, he is now an emergency; failure to follow specific procedures for emergency eye wash will likely result in permanent blindness. Conversely, if via phone or intake triage, the presenting eye problem is known to be caused by chemical eye injury, this person immediately becomes patient John Doe, category "red," chemical eye injury. Such an evidence-based clinical default trumps every other discriminator that is not emergency medical immediate emergency; there is zero time to wait to spare vision in both affected and unaffected eyes.

Thus, as we move from the single specific discriminator of red eye that sets the default at the lowest acuity level, we can see how addition of certain other specific or general discriminators raises the default progressively higher. John Doe rapidly becomes either a low-acuity patient in triage category blue, "Eye Problem, Red Eye, Category Blue," or high-acuity patient: "Eye Problem, Red Eye with Pain, Category Green." Progressing to higher defaults, John Doe becomes high acuity and higher severity: "Eye Problem, Red Eye with Pain and Loss of Vision, Category Yellow." And higher yet to high acuity and severity of very urgent, "Eye Problem, Red Eye with Severe Pain, Category Orange." At any time causation is suspected of being chemical eye injury, the clinician overrides all categorical discriminators designating John Doe as an immediate emergency: "Eye Problem, Chemical Eye Injury, Category Red."

In this last documentation, no specific or additional general discriminators are necessary to tag John Doe as emergency medical. Of course, I only build this case scenario for John Doe from the lowest level of acuity and severity to highest in order to explain how the inductive reasoning process of differential diagnosis provides a lexicology for clean diagnostic defaults.

In reality, clinicians working smart under constraints of high patient volumes caused by the demand rationing of managed care—or in ERs and crisis clinics—start the inductive reasoning process at the top of the hierarchy of each presentation; most presentations today are either unknown or unremembered patients and require the ruling out of general and specific discriminators. Via this process of inductive reasoning, the clinician first diagnoses a patient for one of the five prioritizing triage categories, the platform for time-determined clinical decision making.

Having studied how clinicians actually work, particularly in busy settings where time is of the essence, I have found that, to survive and practice effectively, they must work smart. Such clinical intelligence will have little to do with the deductive reasoning process taught them in training; nor will the foundation for documentation generating codes demanded medico-legally and for reimbursement make any point of entry smart.

Clinicians also work within the standards of medical certainty—that is, on a more likely than not basis. That means they judge what will or will not happen were this to be done or not done to this patient. If they do first encounter a person and accumulate all the data necessary to predict everything ultimately to be discovered on autopsy, that is the necessary, but insufficient, foundation, for best clinical practices known as the *clinical pathological conference*, or CPC. CPCs are educational and usually make a lot of professors of medicine appear as smart as they should be or embarrassed. This is done in search of the valid diagnosis that would have predicted an already known outcome—namely, death; time is, therefore, not of the essence. If a stopwatch graded this academic exercise, they would have to switch the mode of their differential diagnostics to that of time-determined clinical decision making.

The active and effective clinician must work inductively based on the evidence-based rules of time-determined clinical decision making exemplified previously. Additionally, they must be epidemiologically informed, because every population within which a clinician is immersed has a different mix and concentration of genetic vulnerabilies, demographics, and environmental stress. Thus, to work smart, that same clinician works off the platform of likelihood too, guided by time-determined general and specific discriminators of triage.

Epidemiologically informed decision making is the clinical discipline of reducing invalid diagnoses within time constraints utilizing knowledge of the likelihood for certain presentations within a particular gateway at a particular time. As in the case of Cho Seung-Hui, this requires the heightened awareness of newly psychotic students presenting as emergencies within college community health facilities of all types. Currently, time-determined and epidemioligially informed clinical decision makings are learned via clinical practice rather than formal clinical training. The exception to this is EMS health professional education and emergency medicine residency training for "the red zone"—or immediate emergency care.

Triage skills for most frontline clinicians, therefore, are built almost exclusively upon intuitive capabilities of practitioner experience. Effective ER triage nurses and point-of-entry primary care physicians serve as operational examples of these highly developed intuitive skills. They are rare these days and have short career expectancies, caused for the most part by combined ignorance and political denial of increasing scarcity of healthcare resources in primary and urgent care.

The Gathering Storm

Our healthcare system is broken. And everyone acknowledges that there are two sides across the great divide between the medical profession and a government that always tries, but fails, to fix it. In a lawyer-driven, not a doctor-driven, system of delivering heath care to a mass population, gradually getting grayer and more in need of gerontological care, of highly stratified income groups, the healthcare service is simply not reaching the clients efficiently or scrupulously. It is worse now than it has been for decades, and it is still getting worse.

The services, and the money to pay for them, are being chewed up in an overadministered system of defensive delivery more geared to protecting the insurance companies than the actual patients. As a result, patients in real need of immediate care are not getting that care and are dying right before our very eyes. In the case of Cho Seung-Hui, the death was very public and took many other lives. But other children are dying, too, and their deaths go largely unnoticed, whether their families live in rural areas, in the forgotten sections of rusting suburbs, or deep in hidden parts of inner cities. In Arizona, for example, the case of one such child illustrates the larger point behind the Cho case: emergency healthcare services simply fail to meet patients' needs.

The headline in a local Mesa, Arizona, newspaper read, "Child Denied Care and Dies." The story concerned a 13-year-old girl named Gricelda Zamora Gonzalez, who was crying out in panicked anguish from severe pains in her stomach. Her parents took her to an emergency room and to a local doctor for help, but she received no help and died hours later at another hospital. Why?

The little girl's family had no medical insurance and, thus, the newspaper said, without the actual cash to pay for medical services, the family was denied care at the doctor's office and directed to another facility. The doctor claimed that he would see the child for no fee, but that he did not consider her critical. The parents say he gave no indication of when he would treat her, and the girl was in agonizing pain. Who was right?

Stories abound from all over the country about clients who are turned away from emergency rooms and doctors' offices because they are uninsured and have no cash to pay the fees. Worse, according to some, they are being treated rudely, as if they were freeloaders, simply because they are among the vast number of Americans who have no health insurance. And we are including in this category the increasing numbers of Americans who can't qualify for health insurance or who can't pay the staggering premiums, because they are diabetic, one of the most treatable and preventable diseases on the planet. And when this group reaches the age for Medicare, not to mention the state plans, in just a few years, the costs of public healthcare may well collapse whatever system is left, assuming, of course, that lawmakers make good on their promises to provide a healthcare solution.

No Exit, Not Even for Doctors

The balancing act among delivering quality healthcare to patients—saving lives—playing defense medicine against the legal establishment, and getting paid by insurers or other payers to sustain their practice has become so exasperating to many physicians that they allegedly are seeking disability to get out of the business. And it is only getting worse at an increasing pace. But physicians cannot just close up shop if they are not retiring. They also need to provide for their families, and so an increasing number are alleged to be seeking disability payments as a path out. But a major disability carrier has, in fact, stopped writing disability policies for doctors unless they are part of a large group.

"Own occupation" disability contracts written in a much more innocent family doctor world of the 1950s are now an issue for insurance carriers because they are traditionally structured to provide income protection insurance for sick doctors. But doctors are trying to get under the umbrella to avoid being entrapped in a world of managed care. Managed care both restricts physicians' abilities to provide the healthcare for patients they want to provide and requires them to take steps they would not normally take simply to lawyer-proof themselves against the pro forma malpractice suit that any storefront lawyer can file, secure in the knowledge that he or she will reap at least some benefit from the almost automatic insurance settlement. Apply this to the moments that Cho came onto the radar screens of St. Albans and the Virginia Tech health services, and one can see the problem that Cho presented.

Medical Receptionists as Gatekeepers

In too many cases, the decision to admit a patient, either to a doctor's office or to an emergency room, falls upon the shoulders of a medically inexperienced receptionist, a gatekeeper whose job it is to make sure the facility can recoup the cost of patient care. Thus, the first questioning concerns the ability to pay, the search for the insurance card, or the authorization of a credit card. And in the case of the uninsured and unemployed, the child, unless convulsing or bleeding out, is simply shunted off to a county or municipal facility where he or she may be left in a waiting room for hours because the case is not deemed critical or life-threatening. And the case with Cho—although insurance wasn't a factor, Cho was deemed not critical and shunted off to fend for himself despite a court order to follow up on his counseling.

Clearly something is missing in this modern-day paradigm for point-of-entry assessment, the assumption that most people who come through points of entry either do not think they need to see a doctor or, as implied by the doctors, probably are not that sick to need attention, at least not that day. How is that decision made in this managed care and underfinanced patient care system? And to make matters worse, many patients do not even have the ability to show a "co-pay" identification.

The U.S. Census Bureau reports that the proportion of Americans without health insurance is the highest in a decade. As of the end of 2009, with over 10% unemployment, the number of Americans without any health coverage was the highest in a decade. However, with the passage of President Obama's new mandatory health insurance program, over the next four years most Americans will be covered by some form of health insurance.

To make matters even worse, those medical offices whose revenues are restricted by managed care providers and contracts cannot afford the luxury of charity patients and those patients who can barely pay but not all at once. It is a situation where the health insurers and managed care providers are actually squeezing the uninsured and underinsured out of the healthcare system. Although this may seem tangential to the Cho case, it is actually on point because students like Cho who are dragged into emergency rooms because someone complained about them but who do not openly or vociferously present obvious symptoms such as raving lunacy about the end of the world are handed cursory treatment in overburdened

ERs and sent on their way. And this is exactly what happened at Virginia Tech. But, according to the panel, it was Cho's fault because he lied about his own condition.

Validity of Diagnosis for Service Optimization

It may seem strange to talk about bringing digital technology to the art and practice of medical diagnoses, but this is very germane to the Cho case because of the lack of coherent diagnoses Cho received. Had there been an organized, objectively optimized diagnostic system in place, Cho might not have slipped through the gaping seams in the emergency room system.

We suggest that what was lacking in the Virginia Tech case was a methodology or series of computer-based protocols to evaluate Cho Seung-Hui. For example, computerized clinical decision support could advance the current art and practice of clinical medicine by supporting selection of both diagnostic and therapeutic technologies in a significantly more objective and effective manner than what is the current state of practice. Service optimization, particularly for the constant diagnostic screening in both triage and continuous tracking along clinical pathways, is key to operational success for both cost and quality control in managed care.

And it is not just diagnosis, it is differential diagnosis, one of the most important discriminators in medical practice. "For what purpose is differential diagnosis, if not at least partly, to predict clinical course and treatment response?" asks Donald Klein, M.D. He further emphasizes the importance of validity in diagnosis along neuropsychiatric clinical pathways, accounting for nearly one half of all "high utilizers" and nearly one half of all utilization of primary healthcare.

> The advent of psychotropic drugs has enormously improved psychiatric care. … It has been repeatedly shown that the majority of patients with psychiatric illness go undiagnosed, and even if diagnosed, they are inappropriately or ineffectively treated, both by psychiatrists and primary care practitioners. … The DSM process improved clinicians' ability to communicate with each other by explicit inclusion and exclusion criteria. Nonetheless, our eventual goal is diagnostic validity, which means that diagnoses have practical value. In this context, the use of one diagnostic criteria set rather than another should lead to a superior ability to prescribe, treat, and render a secure prognosis. Here there has been only moderate progress. A clinician's problem is deciding what treatments to select for a particular patient and how to do it. Diagnosis alone is not sufficient, although usually necessary. (Klein, 1993)

It was, in part, the failure to make a differential diagnosis that was primarily the fault of the system into which Cho fell after he was taken into custody by the Virginia Tech police. Had it not been for that failure and had Cho been at least partially diagnosed as a danger to himself, or at the very least remanded into the custody of his parents, it is likely that he would not have been on campus the following semester to cause the deaths of Emily Hilscher and the other unfortunate students.

The opportunity to zero in on the systemic failures of the healthcare system was missed in the wake of the Cho case. The Texas ER study dramatically proves the need to target the high utilizers of healthcare services to make available specialized resources necessary when the Chos of this world present at any point of entry, whether voluntarily in a guidance counseling center on campus or involuntarily via a police hold and crisis evaluation in Blacksburg, Virginia, or emergency forensic inpatient psychiatry evaluation at St. Albans Hospital in New River. Innovative diagnostics for both triaging at points of entry, then managing clinical pathways, could be applied to the high-utilizing population of sick Americans with savings of up to 0.7 percent of the total GNP now devoted to healthcare.

As demonstrated in the Texas study, ERs could then be freed up for real emergencies like those of Cho; major trauma, for which they were developed under the EMS Act; and post-9/11 disasters. Other less studied, high-utilizing populations, such as the seriously mentally ill patients dumped through deinstitutionalization into broken community care centers could also benefit, generating enormous savings in both direct and indirect healthcare costs through better medicine.

Efficient clinical screening with both diagnostic sensitivity and specificity, so obviously lacking in the case of Cho, has successfully met operational tests of diverse and meticulous scrutiny in both clinical and forensic medicine settings. Of the 10 percent of Americans, previously labeled as high utilizers, who consume nearly 50 percent of all primary care services, major psychopharmacotherapy and psychotherapeutic interventions are required in 50 percent of them, or 5 percent of the total population of the United States. In addition, therapeutic interventions, when performed effectively, can reduce excessive utilization to a more equitable and cost-effective rate of utilization, but, of this 50 percent of high utilizers of primary medical care needing psychiatric treatment today, 50 percent are misdiagnosed, and 25 percent are inadequately medicated.

Conversely, inadequate treatment may account for nearly 20 percent of all utilization—for the most part unnecessary—along primary care clinical pathways.

Improved diagnostics at points of entry, such as St. Albans, along with effective consultation-liaison psychiatry within specialized populations like school campuses, could reduce the primary healthcare expenditure for this group of high utilizers by 15 percent. Implementation of this managed care innovation could save $20 billion for a 0.5 percent reduction in our GNP devoted to healthcare.

The cost of unlimited access to and provision of unlimited quality psychiatric care, assuming triage by the gatekeeping physician with concurrent internal control of clinical pathways, can be accomplished with universal coverage for less than $500 per citizen annually.

Pilot projects have shown that the other half of high utilizers, the seriously and chronically ill—mainly geriatric and chronically seriously mentally ill patients—can be cared for in nontraditional ways with vast improvements in quality of both life and care. A 15 percent cost savings compared with traditional modes of chronic care alternating with acute hospital care can be achieved. Expensive modes of care could be rendered medically unnecessary or even contraindicated for up to 30 percent of the severely disabled population through innovative utilization of home-care nursing supported by geriatricians, geriatric psychiatrists, and specialized day care programs for chronically impaired psychiatric and substance-abusing patients. Such deinstitutionalization of this population of high utilizers could reduce healthcare expenditures by another $30 billion, for a 0.2 percent reduction in our total GNP now devoted to healthcare.

Targeting only these two small groups of high-utilizing patients through enhanced triage and internal control of clinical pathways could reduce the percentage of healthcare expenditure in our GNP from 14 percent to 13.3 percent—or $52 billion—along with marked enhancement of quality of both life and care. Little has been done on a major scale to impact cost and quality of care, however, for either of these two patient groups—the overinstitutionalized disabled nursing home and the inadequately treated psychiatric patient—currently absorbing upwards of 35 percent of all primary healthcare services. The Commonwealth of Virginia vetted a special commission even before Cho struck; diverted by the real problem presented here, it could have focused on the real issues of systemic failures and practical remedies. We will see, however, how it failed to do so.

Innovation for Service Optimization via Progressive Computer-Assisted Screening

Geographically distant case managers, supported by programmed algorithms, already determine clinical choices, but doctors in special settings such as military, corporate, and school campuses and working with clinically reliable algorithms protocols for triage can take the lead. Patients still want and need their doctors to control their care, but for this to happen, their case managers and clinicians must communicate from reliably standardized protocols and semantic mapping. Now, however, their case managers track their care via telehealth, a computer-based distance diagnostic system that optimizes the resources of any healthcare facility. The electronic medical record in ambulatory care is in its infancy and rarely clinician driven. More consensus needs to occur between managed care case managers and frontline clinicians, or patients will inevitably be stuffed into cookie cutter protocols and managed clinical pathways—or, as in the case of Cho, find no pathway and literally derail and go berserk.

A patient- and clinician-friendly diagnostic screen can efficiently and uniformly assist triage of patients entering the healthcare system at all points of entry, including the corrections system, as with Virginia Tech campus police or St. Albans Hospital. The incredible costs of underdiagnosing, with attendant denial of treatment for the complex medical, mentally disorganized, and psychic impaired patients, will eventually demand revolutionary approaches at the points of entry to health services. Whether that point of entry has the form of clinical office, public health services, emergency rooms, or jails can ultimately make no difference, because that is where the at-risk people present for the infrequent opportunity of comprehensive, computer-enhanced diagnostic assessment.

Computer Software Can Model the Clinician's Triage Decision Process

We already have a sufficiently comprehensive knowledge basis to apply artificial intelligence algorithms to patient solutions. Simple artificial intelligence can be a doctor's companion for expanding diagnostic sensitivity while enhancing both the art of medicine with diagnostic specificity that promotes evidence-based pharmacotherapy, as well as selection of diagnostic and invasive procedures. Such modeling must be adaptable to clinicians' needs for making frequent changes in time- and cost-determined clinical decisions to avoid dangerous and destructive cookie cutter stuffing between patient presentation and rigid, superimposed algorithmic pathways.

Diagnostic Specificity Necessary for Documentation and Service Optimization

In the practice of medicine, specificity is only necessary for validity if it improves service optimization or medico-legal documentation. It can be seen in the life line of Paul Keller—convicted for the worst solved arson case in American history—how interventions throughout his life may have prevented catastrophic psychobiological collapse.

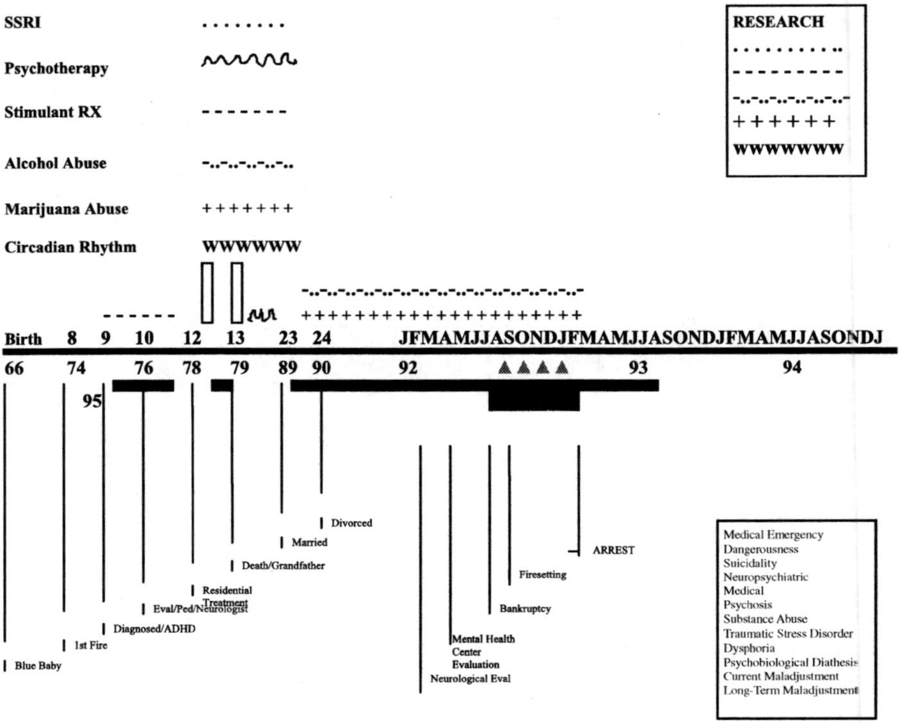

In retracing his insidious deterioration—then acute collapse—we devised the JAL triage algorithm.

Time-determined clinical decision making is a process of organizing differential diagnosis and resultant patient management decisions into time-determined bundles. In Figure 4.1, you can see an example of evidence-based choices for encountering an unknown or unremembered patient—that is most of our patients today in acute care and certainly nearly all in emergency and disaster medicine. Begin diagnostics. The amount of time you have to complete treatment depends on the zone.

In this evidence-based model for acute care, you first decide how long any patient can safely wait before definitive clinical intervention. Of course, first of all the patient's life must be saved, and that is the red zone of emergency medicine—the ABCDE of conventional triage. If you decide that the emergency is immediate and there is no time to wait, your clinical state of awareness is represented by the red zone. You would, therefore, select the red tab, a process demonstrated here to rather crudely replicate the way we think. We have some forms of these tabs in our brains that organize information, and we refile, refile, and refile constantly based on experience and formal education.

Pros in emergency services work off some variation of the rules and embedded protocols when they are in their clinical state of awareness replicated within this red zone.

Unresponsive Child

I) Tap infant to elicit response.

II) If infant cannot breathe or is UNRESPONSIVE:

A. DO NOT hyperextend neck!
B. Open airway.
C. If not breathing, ventilate w/TWO puffs of air - NOT FULL BREATHS!
D. Reposition head & chin and ventilate again with TWO puffs.
E. If UNSUCCESSFUL - Invert infant on arm by supporting, cupping face in hand.
F. Perform 5 blows between shoulder blades.
G. If nothing comes out, roll infant supine on arm and perform 5 chest thrusts.
H. Look in mouth and remove object if visible.
I. If nothing visible, ventilate.
J. If UNSUCCESSFUL, repeat back blows, then chest thrusts, and mouth inspection. Ventilate until object removed or breathing begins.

Intubate endotracheally if possible when necessary and connect ALS.

Figure 4.2 Protocol for the unresponsive child.

But, once that is quickly accomplished—and all emergency professionals do that so quickly and well that we can move to the next indicator lights, dangerousness to others and suicidality. For those in trauma care it is of interest to know that dangerousness has one sixth the mortality of accidental death and suicidality has one third the accidental death rate. Let us not jump over the emergency medical too fast, therefore, and take anyone's word at face value for that ("D") unresponsive child or ("E") severely bruised senior, both allegedly having fallen down the stairs (Figure 4.2).

After you have cleared the red zone, you may quickly change your clinical state of awareness to code orange. We are becoming used to these color-coded states of awareness periodically broadcast from Department of Homeland Security—we recently went from yellow to orange and then back to yellow in order to train our senses for vigilance, where "every American is a soldier." Generally speaking, I think that we understand that means we need right now—in the yellow state of Homeland Security alert status—to be more vigilant for suspicious and unusual activities than we were on September 10, 2001. But, when we are told that the nation is going on orange alert, what are we to do that is different? Well, be more vigilant. And, when they say we are in red alert, something is happening; that means you act as if you are as close to being a citizen soldier without being in the military and an attack is in progress or definitely imminent—not just anticipated within next few days. It is now. It is in progress and represents imminent threat to you; you must be ready to survive on your own and protect friends and family with minimal or no government support. In emergency psychiatry, action and brain chemistry are deteriorating so fast that you have no alternative in your red zone other than for immediate clinical intervention, whether with physical restraint or emergency medications.

Let's start with neuropscyhiatric indicator lights from the JAL triage algorithm by first taking the lead of a neurological mnemonic, "Throw Out the

Table 4.1 Emergency Red Zone!

Diagnosis and treatment must be immediate.		
• Use mask and gloves if patient appears febrile with rash. • Use mask, gloves, and gown if patient appears grossly contaminated or disheveled until contagiousness is ruled out.		
Triage is as easy as ABCDE		
Airway compromised		
Breathing inadequate		
Circulation inadequate		
Disability severe		
Exposing body shows severe		
If I throw out the GUNS	**Act myself**	**Clearances**
Guns and weapons	Agitation severe	NOT immediate emergency
Using drugs	Combative	Major incidents NEW patient
Need to protect	Threatening	Immediate emergency OVER
Situation of imminent violence outside	Male, young, and sociopath	Orange
	Empathy lacking	Yellow
	Limits disregarded	
	Fighting wounds	

Note: The Triage Algorithm, ABCDE.

WWHHHIMPS" (withdrawal, Wernickes, hypoglycemia, hypoxia, hypersensitive encephalopathy, intracerebral bleed, meningitis, poisoning, encephalitis, status epilepticus). By following the lead of this mnemonic at this time, you will immediately clear the very urgent disturbances of consciousness; these are the ones that will kill your patient upon presentation, unless your intervention is on automatic (Table 4.2).

Controversial as it is, I think that I can show you the importance of having the discipline to always assess central nervous system syndromes presenting without acute or gross lateralizing neuro signs—i.e., neurologically symmetrical

Table 4.2 Throw out the WWHHHIMPES!

Barbituate **w**ithdrawal
Wernickes
Hypoglycemia
Hypoxia
Hypertensive encephalopathy
Intracerebral bleed
Meningitis
Poisoning
Encephalitis
Status epilepticus
Clear emergency altered conciousness

presentations caused by irritated cortex of high-acuity chronic and acute brain syndromes. What was the neurologist thinking of, for example, when he ordered an MRI on Paul Keller early in the acute and unremitting clinical destructive process that resulted in the most destructive solved arson case in American history?

One could correctly say that auditory, olfactory, and visual hallucinations are psychotic; I have heard that argument, driven by emergency room personnel, when the only beds open are psych beds. Rarely, however, are olfactory and visual hallucinations an indication for psychiatric admission; they are most often acute medically or surgically treated (med/surg) diseases manifesting with perceptual abnormalities. The next crisis almost certainly will be recognition of such on the inpatient psychiatry unit and complex, high-risk transfer process to med/surg unit or a fatality cloaked in the *DSM* jargon of psychosis NOS. True, encephalitis may technically present as psychosis, and if you also enjoy having your fingernails bisected with a scalpel, admit the patient to inpatient psychiatry with "Dx: Psychosis, NOS."

Sometimes diagnostic specificity is thrown out for diagnostic hypersensitivity based on administrative exigencies; that is not what Donald Klein meant by diagnostic validity that more effectively informs treatment.

Follow down the left side of the JAL triage algorithm and clear the "medical" indicator lights; you have a statistical chance of well over 50 percent for admitting a patient to a psychiatric unit whose underlying disease process is medical rather than

Table 4.3 Exposed Med-Surg Problems

Burns and scalds	Foreign body	Focal inflammation	Rashes
Chest/abdomen wound	GI bleed	Major trauma	Sore throat
Diarrhea	Head injury	Nasal problems	Vomiting
Eye problem	Limb problems	Pelvic/vaginal bleeding	Wounds

Note: GI = gastrointestintal.

Table 4.4 Emergency Medicine Protocol for Eye Injury

Eye injury
Is this a chemical injury?

psychiatric. Statistically, your chance of the same invalid diagnosis influencing your decision to have this patient worked up in outpatient psychiatry is about 10 percent.

Table 4.3 demonstrates presentation-based triaging of emergencies threatening life and limb. For clinicians on the fly, a template such as this must simply be remembered, because there is no time to go to the book for long lists of differential diagnosis. The purpose of presentation-based diagnostics in emergency medicine is to spare the Golden Hour. The Golden Hour is that critical time between initial contact with a patient and definitive clinical intervention that spares life and limb.

For purposes of demonstrating the importance of this Golden Hour, rapid scanning of the patient's body must clear injury or disease of exposed tissue. One example can be seen in Table 4.4, where an eye injury is observed or reported. Chemical injury to the eye is the only ophthalmology emergency wherein there is no time to wait before specific clinical intervention—that is eye wash that carefully spares the chemical from running into the unaffected eye, causing total blindness.

Similar protocols are demonstrated for other exposed body parts, such as burns that require immediate treatment. This is the Red Zone of emergency medical triage that spares the Golden Hour from first point of contact with the patient, prehospital care and transport, and, ultimately, definitive emergency clinical intervention—as in following procedures for washing eye with chemical injured by chemical. The details of the emergency medicine diagnostics and interventions are beyond the scope of this book, but these diagrams demonstrate the medical necessity for time-determined clinical decision-making—or, emergency triage.

After all emergency medical problems are immediately addressed, the frontline clinician must then screen for very urgent problems that must be identified and

Table 4.5 You Are Entering the Yellow Zone. You Have One Hour to Identify and Treat Presenting Problems!

Identify precautions if contagiousness suspected	
Reassess	
T A C O S A L A D	
Reason for Entry Here	**Brought By**
Emergency	Police
Urgent medical	Medics
Strange behavior	Self
Appears drunk	Other
Self-harm	Psyche problem

Table 4.6 Eye Problem

Ocular burns	Sudden, recent, and complete loss of vision
Globe rupture	Severe ocular pain
Moderate pain	Loss of vision

treated within ten minutes—or the time it takes to move a patient from stretcher to bed. After clearing medical emergencies and very urgent presentations, the front-line clinician now has one hour to clear the remaining problems to spare life and limb. Thus there is another menu of protocols for urgent care shown in Table 4.5. Urgent eye problems that must be treated within one hour to spare vision can be seen in Table 4.6; of course, the protocols for each of these very urgent problems will be more complex and time-consuming than that of emergency eye-wash for chemical injury of the eye.

Such protocols may or may not be available to you at your work site; so for purposes of demonstration, this is what you need to know—and all you need to know—until the ophthalmologist arrives. This, of course, is my testimonial. Obviously, for very urgent ophthalmology presentations shown in the orange zone of clinical states of awareness, you do not have time to use clinical decision support; these are, therefore, rudimentary replications of your clinical states of awareness. In the yellow zone representing your clinical state of awareness for "urgent," however, you do have some time for utilizing clinical decision support.

Table 4.7 Reassess

Red Zone	*Orange Zone*	*Yellow Zone*	*Green Zone*	*Blue Zone*
Any case in the red zone means immediate emergency!	Any case in the orange zone is very urgent and diagnosis and treatment must be completed in 30 minutes!	Any case in the yellow zone is urgent and diagnosis and treatment must be completed within 60 minutes from point of entry!	Any case in the green zone is standard and diagnostics with treatment plan must be completed within 120 minutes from point of entry!	Any case in the blue zone is chronic but must be diagnosed with treatment plan made within 240 minutes from point of entry!

Such support may be embedded in your electronic medical record, telehealth communications and coordination system, or Web sites such as Medscape. Instead of detailed protocols burned into the hard drive of your frontal cortex, you need a seamless file that is presentation based to guide you to diagnostically valid protocols that are, therefore, most effective. The more safe time you have before definitive clinical intervention, the more you need to know; the more you need to know, the less you will remember and the more dependent you are on outside support to put flesh of clinical knowledge on the skeleton of your mental constructs for rapid clinical decision making.

And simulations of triaging decisions such as this cannot be frozen in time, because either the patient's status oftentimes changes or your clinical judgment does. Simulation of the need for fluidity in your clinical assessment and judgment is seen in Table 4.7.

Think of how many times you change your mind, particularly when working the ER. I have never researched the "reassess" simulation in actual ER practice, but ghost documentation in an actual clinical decision support system would likely show that the majority of documentation tracks would be replicated in this "reassess" function.

When you judge the patient you are encountering to be either nonemergent acute or the acute exacerbation of a chronic condition, you make the judgment that you have two hours for workup and safe clinical intervention (Table 4.8).

In acute care, we are technically limited in talking about a clinical course that is six weeks or less in duration. In this green zone of acute care, it is our determination that a clinical presentation is either the first manifestation or an aggravation of a chronic process. When you judge that you are encountering a chronic illness without acute exacerbation, your clinical state of awareness is represented by the same history form in blue (Figure 4.3).

Table 4.8

You are in the green zone. You have 120 minutes to diagnose and treat presenting problems.			
The following Digital Clinician® evaluations are based on the copyrighted materials from the JAL Health Questionnaire-Driven Structured Interview.			
Due to the in-depth triage involved at this level many treatments and procedures have been disabled for this demo. However, we encourage you to continue the demo in order to experience the fast and accurate decision-making properties that have been embedded in the Digital Clinician.			
The following data would be entered by the clinician or staff member; however, all data entry and risk management modules have been disabled for the demo version.			
Name	Jane Doe	Severity of presenting problem	
Sex	F	Emergency	Reassess
Age	30	Very urgent	
How arrived	Brought in by friend	Urgent	
Who brought patient	Friend	Standard	
[FrontPage Save Results Component]			
Why?	Sudden blindness and pain in right eye		

The replication of clinical states of awareness to frame your decision making into colored zones of decreasing lethality and acuity—red, orange, yellow, green, and blue—is a paradigm for reorganizing differential diagnostics operationally rather than nosologically. This is a concept, therefore, that could embrace all of acute care because of the high volume of patient flows caused by the demand management of third-party payers. Those of us who have survived thus far, in other words, know what to focus on first; then we can either make timely, effective interventions or do no harm by deciding to temporize.

Images that are accompanied by complete ophthalmology protocols both define and simulate best practices for time-determined clinical decision making. They are by coincidence and tradition very similar to independent states of vigilance adopted by Homeland Security to help frame citizens' states of vigilance for a terror attack.

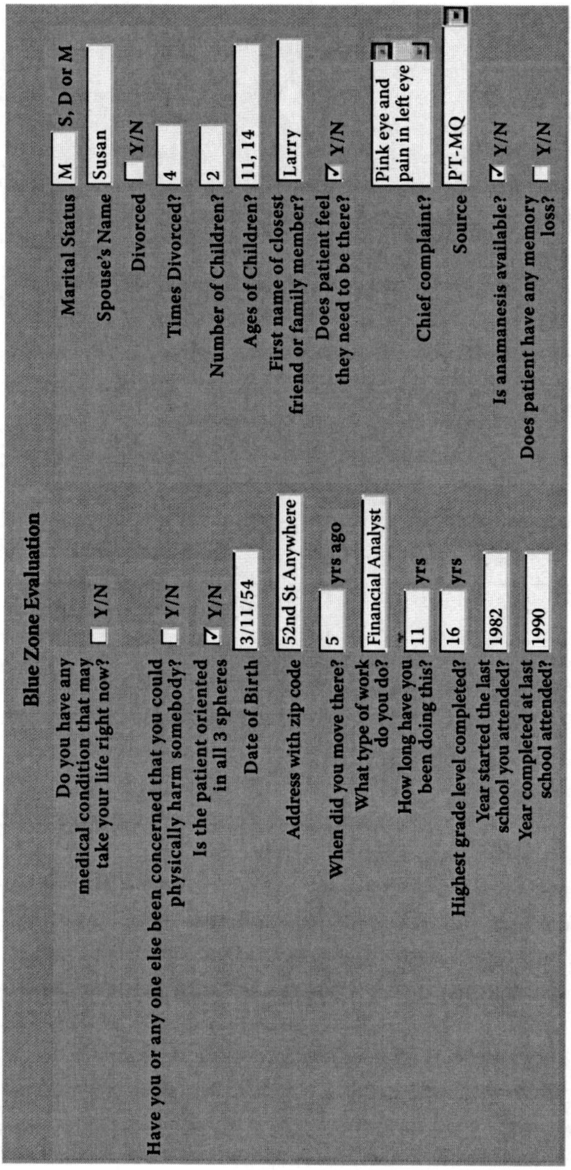
Blue Zone Evaluation

Do you have any medical condition that may take your life right now? ☐ Y/N
Have you or any one else been concerned that you could physically harm somebody? ☐ Y/N
Is the patient oriented in all 3 spheres ☑ Y/N
Date of Birth 3/11/54
Address with zip code 52nd St Anywhere
When did you move there? 5 yrs ago
What type of work do you do? Financial Analyst
How long have you been doing this? 11 yrs
Highest grade level completed? 16 yrs
Year started the last school you attended? 1982
Year completed at last school attended? 1990

Marital Status M S, D or M
Spouse's Name Susan
Divorced ☐ Y/N
Times Divorced? 4
Number of Children? 2
Ages of Children? 11, 14
First name of closest friend or family member? Larry
Does patient feel they need to be there? ☑ Y/N
Chief complaint? Pink eye and pain in left eye
Source PT-MQ
Is anamanesis available? ☑ Y/N
Does patient have any memory loss? ☐ Y/N

Figure 4.3 Blue zone evaluation.

I adapted them from police science "shoot–no-shoot" replications; the red zone would represent a police officer's state of mind when a citizen's face is in his gun sight. The blue zone would represent his state of mind when rubbernecking with another patrol car and sharing information. The orange, yellow, and green zones escalate in "hype" as violence and lethality become imminent, just as it does for you in emergency psychiatry.

When the neuropsychiatric and medical clearance indicator lights are not blinking, you have cleared medical on the JAL triage algorithm. Proceeding to states of mental disorganization you first determine whether the patient has functional psychosis—most commonly decompensated schizophrenia, a psychosis associated with affective disorder or, more and more frequently, substance abuse–induced psychotic disorder secondary to polysubstance abuse, usually including cocaine.

So, is the patient psychotic while also being neurologically cleared? Then, what about substance abuse? It is epidemic and exacerbates all psychiatric illness; in fact, the lethality of comorbid substance abuse is not additive but synergistic. You have a far greater chance, for example, of taking a punch from the intoxicated patient who is threatening you than the sober one saying the same words.

From the investigation of this case, and from this investigation, JAL triage algorithm, we can see demonstrated how user-friendly algorithms can model triage decisions to reduce the errors so devastating in the Cho case—as well as others highlighted in this book. We organized time-determined clinical presentations into four categories as follows.

Emergency

In progressively screening from highest to lowest levels of lethality, the emergency screen prevents patients from leaving the point of entry when screening of a presentation predicts severe morbidity or mortality, violence, or deliberate self-harm for follow-up outpatient disposition.

This was not done during clinical encounters with Cho that could have utilized the commonsense invocation from the California Supreme Court case in *Tarasoff*; Cho had been certifiably dangerous for a long time.

Medical/Surgical

Misidentification of the medical-surgical, particularly the neurological, patient as functional is a legendary albatross for all clinicians at the point of entry, leading to dispositions that are dangerous, not only for the patient but for case managers and providers' risk management. In the case of Cho, we will never know whether a medical-surgical illness, such as a slow-growing brain tumor in the frontal lobe, was the cause of his catastrophic decompensation. Of course, this does not appear likely, but the standard of practice for his first serious psychotic break—identified by Dr. Crouse at St. Albans—makes such screening mandatory; it was not, however, done, because Cho's presentation simply was not taken seriously. For some reason, never addressed, Cho flew under the radar screen, even when detained in a specialty neuropsychiatric center! Mutism, for example, could have been a seizure disorder, but, for some reason—perhaps limitations of medical insurance or court reimbursement—Cho was not thoroughly worked up—if he was worked up at all.

States of Mental Disorganization

With the modern public awareness and newly effective treatment modalities of psychological medicine, both diagnostic sensitivity and specificity can initiate clinical pathways that have tremendous leverage in reducing morbidity, mortality, and overall healthcare costs. This, as has been seen, was totally ignored in the case of Cho, even though valid diagnostic information from numerous collaterals was available; clinical staff at St. Albans had both access and time to gather and assess all of it and the clinical psychologist came very close to actually documenting schizophrenia. He documented serious mental illness, described the signs of schizophrenia, but stopped short of naming it. As the saying goes, if it walks like a duck, quacks—then, well, is it not likely a duck? Or, if not, then what kind of serious mental disorganization did Cho present at St. Albans? He was taken there by the police for a very sound reason—not as a show of force; it was, however, an exercise in futility, as the tragedy later proved.

Impairment

Screens for impairment emphasize acuity rather than severity or lethality and enable the sophisticated diagnostic tools, now available for selecting effective clinical pathways with frequently misdiagnosed patients—particularly high utilizers. Dissecting presentations of unknown and complex, unremembered patients for subtle comorbidity at all points of entry improves long-term morbidity and mortality as well as the direct and indirect costs of healthcare. Again, this was avoided or simply missed out of prejudice or inadequate professional examination time. In Cho's case, the CSB crisis counselor documented severe impairment, although the attending psychiatrist did not. What kind of impairment? Why the extreme divergence in diagnoses? There is a giant gap between conclusions of serious mental illness with imminent dangerousness at night; serious mental illness with no imminent dangerousness the next morning—and, later that same morning, minor depression requiring nonspecific follow-up! More admission discipline must be directed toward alignment between clinical evaluation and diagnostics of the same patient by multiple qualified examiners over a short period of time. Such misalignment, according to Miller, is too common to simply ignore again after this disaster.

Paul Miller, MD, is a professor of psychiatry at UCLA, whose course, Computer Assisted Diagnostic Interview, which I attended at the annual meeting of the

Psychiatric Institute, American Psychiatric Association in Los Angeles in October 1998, is the basis for the information from him detailed below.

Epidemiologically informed clinical decision making disciplines clinicians encountering the unknown patient, such as Cho and those around the events of 9/11, to work smart by knowing the likelihood of presentation at the sites of certain points of entry to the healthcare system. Venomous bites are rare in Seattle but not in Arizona. Blast injuries are rare in North America but common in Afghanistan and Iraq. Acute states of mental disorganization are more common on college campuses than in factories because of median age of the population. Domestic violence is a very common presentation in ERs, as is drug and alcohol intoxication and their complications. These epidemiological facts must be known; thus, ERs within college communities must be on heightened alert during the academic year for psychotic breaks in students, whether their first or a recurrence, and every ER today must know what cutaneous anthrax looks like to pick up early alert to attacks by unconventional weapons.

Within the time-determined screening process, the clinician can quickly rule in common presentations based on their likelihood; ideally, this should be accomplished in prehospital transport before arrival at the ER. Thus, the ER doctor at St. Albans should have already had a differential diagnosis from the first responders of the campus police and community service board examiner completed and handed to him by the transporting police. In Cho's case, the ER was pretty much a pass through, because he had been detained by the court and accepted for admission. Nonetheless, it was incumbent upon the ER on the night of his admission to rule out acute medical disease causing his emergency detention. We do not know who performed a medical evaluation along with lab tests and imaging studies or even whether they were performed.

But, the methodical process of ruling out begins with the initial nursing assessment, which has a variety of templates to assure thoroughness. Many of these templates, however, do not reflect the way clinicians actually think and are more books of lists. Experienced clinicians, whether nurses or doctors, think in terms of prioritizing based on time for safe intervention; and they work smart, knowing likelihood of presentations. Large animal bites are less likely to occur, therefore, in Chicago than in the Arctic, where polar bears roam the streets with humans and frequently attack. This, of course, is an extreme example of the defaults for working smart, but there are many nuances that simply have to be either known or available on electronic medical or health records to support clinical decision making. It has been proven that clinicians need more information than they know during the course of practice every day. How to make that additional information available has vexed the experts in medical informatics for decades. But, we can have some basic rules embedded in our clinical consciousness, as well as our record keeping, whether still paper or electronic.

Thus, before ruling out emergencies to leave the patient unattended, even briefly, all emergencies, whether medical or psychiatric, must be ruled out, preferably in the emergency room. Thus, it simply must be known that sudden confusional or personality states could be immediately lethal, for example, insulin overdose, commonly ignored at enormous risk, or epidural cerbral hemorrhage, overlooked in the triage of Natasha Richardson following her apparently minor ski injury. Fatalities from such neglect are quite inexcusable and rarely justified; they are simply failure to follow the classical evidence-based rules of triage. These rules follow the laws of nature that simply cannot be broken or ignored by humans, regardless of clinical credentialing. To make it easier to follow and more fail safe, I drill into the time-determined presentations by including critical epidemiology.

Emergency Screens

Following immediate clearance of clinical presentations threatening sudden death or acute and irreversible morbidity via easily remembered triage formulas for both single and multiple patient situations, any new patient should immediately be screened for psychiatric emergencies to protect clinical staff as well as the patient and others in the vicinity from violence. Although it is true that violence and suicide—oftentimes preventable and among the leading causes of death and morbidity in America—cannot always be accurately predicted, neither can the results of bilateral mastectomy or total resection of the prostate. Such maiming surgeries are hardly less risky clinically than humane restraint, whether pharmacological or physical. Prediction of violence can and will be improved—not necessarily through scientific advances but because of current public health demands and medical liability. The case of Cho Seung-Hui proves this.

Federal crime statistics reveal that 6,620,000 Americans were victims of violent crime in 1992. Considering that only 10 percent of violent crimes are recorded through arrest, serious, life-endangering victimization likely afflicts close to 20 to 30 million Americans every year.

The direct treatment costs for gunshot wounds alone has doubled since 1990 and exceeds $20 billion.

In the nation's capital an African American youth has a 10 percent chance of being shot and a select subgroup of aging juvenile offenders (1 percent of any large male cohort in prospective criminal research) commits 98 percent of our very serious crimes. The vast majority of these violent youthful offenders have robust evidence of brain damage (80 percent, including epilepsy in 20 percent), paranoid ideation, (frequently misdiagnosed as callousness), and histories of either witnessing or experiencing extreme child abuse in their families.

These are all diagnosable conditions and, if associated with later-onset conduct disorder, can be effectively treated in more than half of the cases with family therapy—rarely provided to this highest-risk population. The prevalence of conduct disorder is 10 percent in males and 2 percent in females.

Follow-up research on 300 children referred to a child guidance clinic in St. Louis for antisocial behavior (conduct disorder) showed that in 35 years, 71 percent had been arrested and 50 percent, had multiple arrests and incarceration. Nearly one third were diagnosed in adulthood with antisocial personality disorder, and almost all who committed four offenses went on to adult criminal careers. Only 16 percent were ultimately found to be free of psychiatric illness.

The severity and number of antisocial behaviors in childhood conduct disorder predict adult behavior better than any other variable, including social class and family background. If it were not for this progression of conduct disorder in comorbidly attention deficit–disordered males to a malignant form of adult sociopathy, defying current corrections efforts, our streets, when curfewed from adolescent reoffenders and drug dealers, should be safe. But, currently nearly 20 million people move in and out of jails in the United States each year, most with past violence-related injuries and high risk of future violent injuries or death; 26 percent had survived prior gunshot wounds. Statistics demonstrate combat strategies to deliberately wound rather than kill; the nonfatal-to-fatal ratio is 12 to 1 in drive-by shootings.

Of more concern is the fact that 90 percent of illegal acts in juveniles are undetected and that nonpsychiatric dispositions in the criminal justice system are now, at best, politically expedient, despite the fact that the metro jails are among the largest psychiatric inpatient facilities in most states. In other words, in large cities our corrections systems are actually de facto in-patient psychiatric clinics where there is little or no psychiatric treatment. Thus, the sick get sicker and return to the same facilities only to get sicker and more proficient in committing violent crimes on the streets.

What is the remedy? Ultimately, presentence investigation will have to once again become an integral point of entry into the healthcare delivery system, unless we are prepared to write off a generation of young males, now mostly low-income minorities, and mortgage our childrens' futures to pay for life and healthcare for millions of men behind bars with three strikes. The corrections industry is booming, with no end in sight, incarcerating many young males who are either mentally ill or who should have been aggressively treated when found delinquent in childhood.

Violence toward Staff

Violence is also a major risk for medical personnel, particularly psychiatrists and emergency room staff, as evidenced by the double homicide at Fairchild Air Force Base psychiatric clinic in Washington State and the increasing targeting of plastic surgeons. Of course, the most recent act of mass homicidal violence took place at Fort Hood on November 4, 2009, when Major Nidal Hassan, an Army psychiatrist about to be deployed to Iraq killed twelve soldiers at a medical facility before being shot by military personnel. Hassan's actions, entangled as they were with the possibility that Hassan was a terrorist and not a psychotic killer, put the Army on notice that violence, even at medical facilities, was a real threat. Although not considered completely preventable—perhaps due to routine destruction of basic training files—the Department of Defense is changing administrative procedures when mentally ill personnel are identified. A racial debate is even occurring over fixed versus portable metal detectors in emergency rooms. Minorities assert that portable metal detectors discriminate against them. Most clinical staff in emergency room and psychiatry settings either will be or have been assaulted at the level of a felony. Signs in emergency departments now boldly warn, "Assaulting a healthcare professional in this state is a felony." Clinical staff is now in the center ring of urban violence every hour of every day they work! This is not workplace violence, as in the case in the recent apocryphal suicide and mass murder at the North Carolina nursing home. Clinical work in emergency medical—particularly acute care psychiatric settings—is dangerous. Self-defense courses are now required for staff before working in many high-acuity hospitals managing the seriously mentally ill patient population.

Assessing Dangerousness

The cycle of violence, perpetuating enormous social dysfunction and disruption, can be broken because child abuse can be detected. The statistics are overwhelming proof that most abuse victims turn out to be abusers when they get into positions of power over others, usually their children. Most will justify it, saying that they learned how to behave from strict parents, which did them well so they pass it along. But it is a self-deception that only recycles abuse from one generation to the next. However, most victims will not abuse if treated before starting their own families. Diagnostic sensitivity with an appropriate index of suspicion and psychosocial intervention can break the cycle of this human destructiveness; 70 percent of all abuse victims will abuse their own children if not treated.

There are over 1 million cases of child abuse presenting for medical treatment annually, and over 4,000 children are murdered every year by their parents, many of whom, because they were abused by their parents, have neither coping skills nor resiliency. With an extremely conservative estimate of gross emotional abuse, over 300,000 cases are reported every year. The toll is clear. The American home is frequently a dangerous place, especially when child abuse is passed on to subsequent generations in a recycling of violence. For example, in a recent *Detroit News* series, "A Hidden Health Epidemic," it was noted that 10 percent of the hospital costs for treating victims of violence, or $22.5 million, was discovered to be the result of violence against children in southeast Michigan during 1998 and 1999. Violence against children, in fact, ranked among the top five causes of death for all children under 14, regardless of race.

Over 75 percent of violent adolescent offenders have a history of extreme child abuse. Morbidity figures are further impacted by the 13 percent of adult women who have been physically abused and male rape victims, representing about 8 percent of male psychiatric inpatients, yet 30 percent of prison inmates are raped. How can that be corrections? Fear of Bubba makes boys stop being bad?

What needs to be done to reduce both direct and indirect healthcare costs, aside from the moral dilemma of perpetuating violence through clinical denial and ignorance, is to intervene early in the cycle of abuse. It is from this cohort of male and female victims of childhood abuse that both malignant character pathology and paraphilias emerge, recycling violence like a perpetual motion machine through institutional processes defying human inventiveness. Our workplaces, school campuses, and military bases are now ground zero for prevention of violence, because they are where the at-risk person, usually a young male, is when awake.

Despite the political wrangling and inadequate epidemiological studies in domestic violence, it is conservatively estimated that spousal abuse victimizes 6 million women per year. Assaults are not usually followed by emergency room visits because of threats of reprisal, but there are still multimillions of emergency room visits per year for domestic violence.

These assaults are preceded by a nonviolent domestic altercation in 90 percent of cases. Diagnostic sensitivity with an appropriate index of suspicion, therefore, may prevent assault and murder when psychosocial interventions are made during the premonitory marital conflagration. Currently, however, intervention rarely occurs until the police are called, and by that time, especially in Los Angeles County, the offender, if not immediately incarcerated, is at risk for well over $50,000 in legal and court costs as well as at risk for losing his or her freedom. For nonspousal abusers such as stalkers, the consequences, if imposed, can be far worse. But, tragically, in the case of Cho Seung-Hui, little credence was even placed on the police encounters with him and so he was, in effect, enabled from one level of serious offense to the next until he committed the ultimate acts of violence upon others and himself.

In fact, political correctness, racism, and sexism contaminate the diagnostic process at the points of entry into the healthcare system. Abuse is discovered by half of female physicians in the first interview, whereas male physicians usually do not discover it until the third interview, if they ever even ask about it. Why was Cho's violence repeatedly missed in clinical triage? There had to be a similar distortion of the diagnostic lens brought to him; unlike the professors, nobody took the time to clinically unmask him and see the emptiness behind the face—or, later, the tears and social isolation with progressive introversion—all signs of suicidality, never to be distinguished clinically from dangerousness to others.

Other Violent Crime Statistics

Robbery and assault victimize 3 percent of Americans every year, and inner-city syndrome, an indirect healthcare cost, is now a psychiatric defense in felony cases. In fact, violence is apparently so prevalent in urban America that researchers studying the impact from terror of the Atlanta child murder case in a multi-city study were unable to differentiate Atlanta's inner-city cohort from control communities.

Yet, these statistics are well below the radar for most average Americans not otherwise in the criminal justice business.

Inner-city high school and middle school teachers are almost inured to some level of violence, but police and juvenile justice officers are probably the most exposed to it. It is an epidemic eating away at our youth, our nation's future, and yet there is very little outreach to the medical community, particularly the psychiatric and emergency psychiatric community where most of the potential help is already available.

Most robberies are drug associated and are, therefore, preventable. The problem goes beyond the loss of property for robbery victims, the associated trauma, and the ancillary violence. The disposition of drug-related robberies through the criminal justice, court, and corrections systems is an internal drain on our economic resources even as we fight legitimate wars in the Middle East. For $5 billion, enough substance abuse slots could be created to absorb the 80,000 convicts now on waiting lists. They will strike again and, if for the third time, will be wards of the departments of corrections for life. Instead, as was demonstrated in the Texas ER study, they overload and drain our emergency medical resources. "Bullet wounds take a big share of bills" for hospital care in southeastern Michigan, and "Fistfights, beatings keep hospitals busy. … Incidents are the most common form of violence treated" (*NY Daily News*, 2000). Has the Cho case simply dramatized to us that, as clinicians, we are simply getting deafened, blinded, and dumbed?

Rape victimizes 200,000 women every year for an incidence of one sexual assault per 1,000 citizens. This is a very conservative statistic from actual reports and arrests. Posttraumatic stress disorder will occur in 80 percent of the victims. This statistic also applies to the Cho case because Cho was obviously a threat as a sexual predator on campus. His stalking and gross voyeurism were simply overlooked, by both administration and guidance center clinicians alike. Cho's menacing demeanor and his threats to female students, especially, were so disturbing that Professor Nikki Giovanni had to give her department chairman an ultimatum: get him out of my class or I will resign. And yet, rather than bring in Cho's parents, he was allowed to remain on campus, essentially untreated, with his condition deteriorating until he became a national headline of homicidal violence.

Had there been real intervention by a medical doctor who, with his family's consent, had administered drugs to ameliorate Cho's worsening condition, all of this might have been avoided. Psychopharmacology is promising for the treatment of sexual violence but, until proven as a preventive tool in sexual violence, presentence diagnostics must be restored within the criminal justice system in order to separate psychopaths from less malignant sexual offenders such as Cho Seung-Hui. He could likely have been effectively treated for the underlying psychosis driving his erotomanic predation.

Certainty of sentencing is of little value without certainty of prosecution and cannot replace diligent presentence investigation. Correctional booking offices are processing clinical cases in numbers approaching any point of entry due to deinstitutionalization of the mentally ill and the criminalization of drug abuse and addiction. The knowledge of predicting dangerousness is advanced, although, like all of medicine, far from perfected. Still, nothing is currently being done to make the diagnostic distinction, crucial for incarceration and probation. Consequently, thousands of sexual assaults occur needlessly. Furthermore, nearly 50 percent of assailants are either well known to or actually dating the victim at the time of offense. And, in the case of Cho Seung-Hui, he was well known by competent observers, the guidance center, and victims alike. Such statistical knowledge about this frequent and destructive offense places rape within the context of relational adjustment, likely presenting, as does domestic violence, with nonviolent manifestations at a point of entry to the healthcare system. Cho appears in retrospect to have had erotomanic delusions about Emily Hilsher, but she was helpless to do anything about it.

The incidence of homicide is conservatively estimated at nine murders per 100,000 Americans, approaching the mortality rate from suicide. More alarming, however, is the fact that an increasing number of young males have been killed, particularly in the inner city, where the killed-in-action rate from gang warfare has approached that of the Vietnam War. Like suicide, homicide could oftentimes be prevented, because many murders are preceded by clinical presentations at points of entry to the healthcare system. This was definitely the case of Cho Seung-Hui.

Despite the highly publicized war on our streets, 50 percent of victims, like Nicole Simpson, are still killed in their own homes or on their property, and over 1,000 homicides occurred in the workplace in 1992. This latter rate has escalated, and, homicide is the second leading cause of death in the workplace today. For females it is the number one cause of death in the workplace.

Witness the apocalyptic suicide and mass murder in L.A. last summer and the nursing home massacre in North Carolina more recently. Today, the workplace is no longer considered a refuge from human violence but, like our streets, could once again be safe. Timothy McVeigh and infamous arsonists, Keller and Pang, both of Washington State, were not undetectable. They were undetected prior to going berserk. And this is the key element of the story of Cho Seung-Hui.

Assessing Suicide Intent

Suicide, now the ninth leading cause of death in America, takes the lives of nearly 100,000 Americans every year for an incidence of 12 per 100,000 annually. In southeastern Michigan, according to the *Detroit News* (2000) investigation of "the hidden epidemic," "Suicide attempts put burden on society and cost $42.3 million to save those who try to kill themselves." This cost for medical treatment of suicide attempts alone, therefore, represents about 40 percent of the $210 million hospital bill to treat violence in southeast Michigan during 1998 and 1999.

Youth suicide is approaching epidemic dimensions. Yet, as in Cho's case, many suicides can be predicted and prevented because 75 percent of those completed suicides are preceded by a visit to a physician. Victims appear to have wished to discuss their intent but were rarely asked anything about suicidal intent.

Untreated depression is a highly lethal disorder. Cho's depression, although not his primary disorder, was picked up at Virginia Tech but was never treated. His guidance counselor in high school could communicate effectively with him, but nobody at Virginia Tech could. There is considerable evidence that Cho, in fact, did wish to see a professional, like 80 percent of completed suicides demonstrate, to talk about his inner, personal descent into hell.

Although there are numerous false positives in the prediction of future behavior, the lethality of the high-risk suicide patient demands emphasis at all points of entry into the healthcare system. We have learned through the Cho case that improved suicide prevention would also eliminate posttraumatic syndromes in the survivors left in their wakes. Millions of dollars in compensation by the commonwealth cannot come close to alleviating the psychological damages, rippling like waves across the pond after a rock is thrown in. Proven posttraumatic sequellae in a majority of these surviving victims will ultimately compound the healthcare utilization problem as well as transmission of familial psychopathology into future generations; this will never be addressed by the commonwealth, other than in testimonials from Richmond in the wake of the massacre in Blacksburg and indefensible legal settlements to survivors.

According to the *Detroit News*,

> The $210 million hospital bill to treat violence in Southeast Michigan during 1998 and 1999 is more than half of what it cost to build the Tigers' new Comerica Park. Still, it is only a sliver of the region's actual medical bill for violence, because the records that area hospitals supplied to the *Detroit News* for this analysis did not uniformly include two of the most expensive healthcare costs, doctors' fees or pharmaceuticals.

"Repeat victims clog health system," but the issue is still not a priority, Detroit newspapers reported. But, the reports revealed that the expense to taxpayers from violence was $210 million at local hospitals. Obviously this not only burdens taxpayers and hospitals financially, but it punishes the nonviolent citizen with higher insurance premiums because of the large number of insured victims.

At the same time, media attention is only now beginning to recognize that the massacre at Virginia Tech was not an endemic anomaly to be expected as a risk for trying to succeed in life. It is, more often than not, preventable, but not when the state has dismantled its mental health system and shifted responsibility for violence prevention to emergency rooms. Conversely, emergency medicine is not in the business of preventing violence, although that is one of its responsibilities. It is in the business of saving lives from unpreventable trauma; most ER staff personnel resent the injuries perpetrated on both themselves and others by violent people. They cannot be expected to prevent the massacres at Virginia Tech, but we will see that they will get the burden of responsibility for doing so—simply because state officials either choose not to see or are blinded to the ravages of untreated mental illness within a supposedly affluent, modern, and civilized society.

Medical Screens

Any implementation of a comprehensive diagnostic tool at multiple points of entry into the healthcare system must, of course, be sensitive to early detection, hence, secondary prevention, of atherosclerotic disease, cancer, and infections, particularly hepatitis, AIDS, and TB. It must also complement a comprehensive review of systems and physical examination with specialized neuropsychiatric and somatoform screens embedding parallel screening for comorbid psychiatric disease that more often than not creates a conundrum of both morbidity and mortality. David R. Boyd, M.D., recently was honored as father of the 911 Emergency Services program nationally, decades after its implementation and national acceptance as a best practice. When entering trauma centers and fire departments, we tend to forget that this uniformly accepted program did not grow out of spontaneously cooperative efforts of healthcare providers and government agencies. It was a hard-fought legislative and administrative battle.

Although Boyd accomplished much against great odds in making Medic One a standard of emergency practice, western Virginia, perhaps suffering from the unique problems of rural healthcare, is more like the rest of American healthcare in the Cho case than different. There was plenty of time for a multidisciplinary and multispecialty evaluation of Cho Seung-Hui; collateral information was abundant re Cho. And St. Albans hospital had adequate resources.

In this case, for some reason demanding explanation, it was blind to the pathology of Cho Seung-Hui. If St. Albans were unique or the Cho case simply an anomalous incident, then the matter would not require forensic examination of a suicide autopsy. Unfortunately, although not the standard of practice, the routine practice cited at St. Albans is more routine than anomalous nationally. To single their failures out would simply be nonproductive scapegoating; St. Albans is the tip of an iceberg toward which universal healthcare is plunging ahead like the *Titanic*.

Neuropsychiatric Screen

There are 8 million head injuries per year in the United States. The cost approximates $10,000 per case on the average—or nearly $80 billion per year. Additionally there are more cases of brain injury, both identified and undiagnosed, than from heart attacks, toxic shock syndrome, and other causes that add to this cost. Special programs for the brain injured, an additional example of innovation in the service component of the healthcare industry, have begun to reduce the total costs of the acute brain-injured patient. Instead, brain-injury patients, both diagnosed and largely undiagnosed, gather in large concentrations within our prisons. And so do adults with attention deficit disorder, afflicting over 20 million children in the United States. More than 60 percent of these children will not fully recover, and residual attention deficit disorder will afflict them in adulthood. Of all adolescents with attention deficit disorder, 50 percent are arrested for a serious offense, and 25 to 45 percent are arrested for multiple serious offenses.

Conduct disorder in childhood, usually associated with comorbid attention deficit disorder, frequently progresses to antisocial personality disorder in adulthood, generating a prevalence of over 6 percent antisocial personality disorders in the population. Research demonstrates that aggression can be reduced in 60 percent of this adolescent population. Chronic depression in the mother, spousal abuse, bad schools, and delayed diagnosis in early childhood—all remedial—predict a bad outcome.

Attention deficit disorder is not a difficult diagnosis with current real-time diagnostics. It is a controversial diagnosis, which, when made in childhood, places demands on our schools but ultimately saves both child and adult lives. Furthermore, when identified in the adult male patient, along with history of childhood conduct disorder, it greatly reduces the risk of imminent violence after release from points of entry to the healthcare system. In the female patient, identification with appropriate treatment can dramatically and effectively reduce the morbidity of chaotic family lives. School violence must be seen through the lens of this epidemiology, unless it is the intent of society and its politicians to simply feather nests of for-profit corrections corporations flying high in the face of societal denial of the epidemiological trends in child psychiatry. When these young males arrive at prison, neuropsychiatric diagnostic workups are either prohibited or by then a moot point.

Medical/Surgical Screen

Accurate medical-surgical diagnosis at the point of entry into the healthcare system is noncontroversial and self-evident. Nonetheless, nearly 50 percent of hospital-admitted psychiatric inpatients and 10 percent of psychiatric outpatients have physical illnesses that caused or aggravated their psychiatric disorders. Most of these patients have been medically screened before referral. The healthcare costs, unnecessary suffering, and risk in the neuropsychiatric, medical, and surgical population alone are enough to justify objective diagnostic screening for all identifiable psychiatric patients at points of entry to the mental health and correction systems. This type of screening was not done in the case of Cho Seung-Hui, against best practices for first diagnosed acute psychotic break, as at least implied by Dr. Crouse at St. Albans in documenting serious mental illness. The lack of screening is evidenced-based best practices for all emergency psychiatric admissions, as well as outpatient referrals, such as repeated official triages at Cook Guidance Center.

It will never be known whether Cho was medically ill and whether such medical illness—such as a brain tumor—caused his rampage murders. From our perspective, it is doubtful, but such conjecture is the same as all other diagnoses with Cho—simply that—conjecture. Actually, Cho deserved better, as did his family, classmates, Virginia Tech community, and survivors. So did citizens exposed to such horror on a supposedly secure island dedicated to socialized maturation and education of the young. Certainly the recent murder/suicide of the minister in Illinois proves the necessity for thorough medical workups of patients whose personalities are known to be altered. We are not saying that Lyme disease caused the murder, but patients with Lyme disease become psychotic and are misdiagnosed; that is why it is known as the great pretender of all illnesses. Most Lyme patients are likely buried with no diagnosis of it.

Screens for States of Mental Disorganization

Psychosis

Psychosis is debilitating for 0.7 percent of Americans either at some point or through most of their lives and, along with brain damage and abuse in childhood, remains a major risk factor in violence, such as, but not exclusive to, hate crimes, as in the recent Binghamton, New York, apocalyptic mass and suicide murder and the events of 9/11. Ignoring robust research findings on family stress and occupational disability as aggravating factors in this population has generated homelessness and other social disruption. Psychosis is treatable with access to and availability of adequate psychiatric resources and modern psychopharmacotherapy. Unfortunately, however, despite its inclusion within the seven critical categories targeted under EMS legislation listed above, it was mandated but never equitably funded or supported, if at all, compared to other categories such as "acute cardiac." Cho Seung-Hui will likely be the tragic poster child for this always uphill climb in preventive and treatment services.

Substance Abuse

Alcoholism afflicts 9 million Americans, impacting one third of all American families. Medical complications fill our hospital beds. Nearly 10,000 babies are born every year in this country with permanently disabling fetal alcohol syndrome. Children who physically survive become victims, now labeled *adult children of alcoholics*.

Most arrested males are inebriated and most deaths in young adults and adolescents are alcohol related. Among alcoholic women, there is a 90 percent incidence of childhood abuse histories with severe physical abuse at 45 percent and sexual abuse at 66 percent. Among combat veterans, the incidence of alcoholism associated with posttraumatic stress disorder is 35 percent (blacks 20 percent).

Drug abuse and dependence afflicts over 6 percent of Americans. Denial at the point of entry to healthcare services must be abolished in order to identify this population, usually youthful, before they become violent felons and/or, med-surg invalids. The majority of arrested criminals undergoing drug testing are under the influence of cocaine.

For $5 billion, the substance abuse treatment slots could be doubled. Much of this could be extracted from taxes on addictive products already designated for education and treatment, if anyone could find their way through the bureaucratic maze and find the consuming taxpayers' money. Substance abuse treatment can reduce the crime rate in America, just as it has in Europe. To this point, the Rand Corporation has demonstrated that if just 13 percent of cocaine abusers reduce their intake, 1 percent of total market demand—estimated at 330 tons per year—will disappear. But, there are 80,000 convicts on waiting lists for treatment. With "three strikes" under the law, they represent violent menaces to society if untreated. Their nominal terms are for political propaganda, and, like Charles Manson, they can be returned to society by departments of corrections anytime—with cause, such as overcrowding of a facility.

Polysubstance abuse among Vietnam Veterans with posttraumatic stress disorder is also common and associated with the imprisonment of over 200,000 combat veterans from the Vietnam War in 1994. It is likely that another 200,000 combat veterans were in jails or homeless because of comorbid substance abuse. An increasing percentage of substance abuse victims are veterans of Gulf War I and Operation Iraqi Freedom.

Most criminal offenses today are associated with substance abuse and or illicit drug trafficking. Consider the costs of treating criminal offenders for substance abuse in ERs to noncriminals insured at higher premiums, taxpayers, and metro hospitals as cited in the *Detroit News* study. To complicate the cost of associated violence, about one third of AIDS victims are drug users or sex partners or children of users. Over 100,000 children will be orphaned by the AIDS epidemic, inseparable from the drug epidemic by the year 2010. Obviously, substance abuse must be ruled out in all diagnostic assessments. It was one of the few pathologies actually alleged to be ruled out in the case of Cho.

The patient's own presentation is frequently inadequate, but inestimable direct and indirect costs of healthcare could be impacted by accurate diagnosis of substance abuse disorders that afflict more than 16 percent of Americans. We can see from the Texas study how they drain emergency medical services put there for emergency care of the medically and surgically ill—and some acute psychotic patients like Cho and a growing number of his at-risk peers on campuses today.

Traumatic Stress Disorders

Because of the escalation in domestic and street violence, concurrent with our legacies of wars, the majority of Americans have been psychologically traumatized with adequate severity to cause illness in any healthy adult. Of this majority, 60 percent of Americans, including the 35 percent of all adult females who are child abuse victims, most will acquire partial posttraumatic syndromes during their lifetimes. Nearly 20 percent of trauma victims—or 10 percent of all Americans—will develop full-blown posttraumatic stress disorder during their lifetimes.

The incidence following rape is 80 percent, dramatizing the unique devastation of this crime. Cho's surviving female victims were not raped, but they were stalked and were traumatized for life. So, according to research studies in Seattle, will be the vast majority of loved ones of those murdered and committing suicide.

With both our delayed diagnosis and neglect of critical incident stress debriefing, a high percentage of these cases will deteriorate into physical illness—unnecessarily taxing medical services—and/or character deformity—unnecessarily taxing social services and society itself. Critical incident stress debriefing (CISD) was never mentioned in the Virginia Commission report, even though its primary foundation is close to Richmond, in Elliott City, Maryland.

Gulf War Syndrome, within the context of posttraumatic stress disorder, may not be delayed like post-Vietnam Syndrome, but after Oklahoma City, military clinicians can no longer be complacent about the long-term social consequences of even military victories. McVeigh was a combat veteran of Desert Storm who later failed an attempt for Special Forces career advancement. So was Mohammed, the trainer and controller of the Beltway Sniper. New cases present every day from old wars, and can Operation Iraqi Freedom be far behind? Suicide rates among Vietnam veterans are suspected of exceeding the rate for their peers by 500 to 1000 percent, spotlighting the potential lethality of this condition. Unfortunately, research on this legacy of war is hampered by selection criteria for cohort study; the sickest survivors are least likely to avail themselves for study due to homelessness, incarceration, "trip wire" style residence in wilderness, and occult or ritualistic suicides. Furthermore, it is from this population of traumatic stress disorders that forensic cases have placed increasing demands on our courts in the form of false memory civil cases, legal defenses for violent felonies, and veterans compensation. Inner-city syndrome from gang warfare has even been introduced as a criminal defense.

These legal highlights emphasize the importance of improving standards of both diagnostics and care for this clinical population, a significant part of the high-utilizing population. If, for example, psychiatric sequellae of wounds are unexamined in the 50 percent of jail detentions that manifest them, how will the terminal posttraumatic process of the wound eventually register as social or health cost? There is a massive body of literature on the psychotherapy and biological treatment of trauma victims, most of it encouraging and optimistic. Immersing this population of patients into generic clinical pathways of mental illness and substance abuse, as is too often the current practice, could be considered malpractice.

With FDA approval of sertraline (Zoloft) for treatment of posttraumatic stress disorder, diagnostic screening in primary care and mental health points of entry will be as imperative, when indicated, for risk management purposes as a CBC (complete blood count). We do not know whether Cho suffered posttraumatic stress disorder; the issue was apparently never raised. But, now, certainly, we know that massive numbers of his survivors and loved ones of survivors will, including his own family, both here and abroad.

Clinicians must be vigilant for false claims and compensation neurosis but should not overrate their role as guardians of the personal injury gates. It is almost impossible to fake posttraumatic stress disorder in a true therapeutic alliance. It is also extremely difficult to fake multiple personality disorder in the hands of a competent psychiatrist today. Posttraumatic syndromes are not difficult diagnoses clinically. They are politically controversial, generate potential claims for compensation, and arouse the passions of clinicians, clouding diagnostic objectivity. Lives can be salvaged when properly diagnosed.

Threats of false memory suits, for example, will reduce clinician sensitivity to the diagnosis, but enhanced diagnostics reduces the shell game of both personal injury recoveries and fiscal exigencies of institutional denial of trauma.

In Washington State, for example, psychiatric illness is not compensable as occupationally induced except in rare and exceptional cases. How will the survivors and their families of apocalyptic suicide and mass murder be handled in the aftermath of disaster? Will the solution, as in many disability settlements, be conditional on sealing the records?

Psychiatric Impairment

After med-surg, neuropsychiatric, and the mental states of disorganization in the psychotic, substance abuse, and traumatic stress disorders are ruled out, the diagnostic screen can safely progress to the second large group of high utilizers of primary healthcare services in a cost-effective manner. This is another screen—the last—where Cho could have been identified. He was notably impaired, and nobody who knew him would deny that.

Triage for psychic pain and suffering can divide this enormous patient population between clinical pathways requiring psychiatric treatment and those requiring various forms of effective, nonmedical psychotherapies. Diagnostic screens can also separate minor depression from major psychiatric disorders. This distinction is crucial in today's managed care environment, because effective, nonmedical psychotherapy can be performed for almost one half the cost of psychiatric treatment. This discrimination is enormously important in the macroeconomics of direct and indirect healthcare costs. It was also critically absent in the clinical management of Cho Seung-Hui from day one of the recognition of his illness to his death.

Dysphoria and DSM IV *Screen*

Nonpsychotic, ambulatory mood and anxiety disorders alone afflict 15 percent of Americans every year—23 percent for varying periods of their lives—at an estimated cost of $60 billion per year. For example, Pacific Bell found that 11 percent of their disability costs were due to nonpsychotic mood disorders. Patients with these disorders utilize over 25 percent of primary care medical services in this country and are usually undiagnosed or almost always denied appropriate psychopharmacotherapy with concurrent psychotherapy. Adequate psychiatric treatment, 80 percent effective for panic disorder and 65 percent effective for depression, can reduce direct healthcare costs by 15 percent for these patients. This compares with 52 percent effectiveness for atherectomy and 41 percent effectiveness for angioplasty, both of which, on the other hand, were rapidly accepted invasive treatments.

Untreated depression is potentially a lethal condition, frequently terminating in suicide. The indirect costs of mood disorders in lost productivity, social dysfunction, and societal disruption exceed $80 billion per year. The magnitude of importance for accuracy of diagnostics for treatment optimization, therefore, is obvious. The masquerade of clinical depression in other clinical dress requires more objective, yet very user-friendly, diagnostic screens, because missing the diagnosis has enormous consequences for morbidity, mortality, and effective utilization of health services. This was where Cho actually was identified: selective mutism and depression NOS. At least he was identified, but he never received any treatment following brief child psychiatry intervention in grade school.

The *Detroit News* investigation of eastern Michigan healthcare costs caused by behavioral emergencies again highlights the importance of such diagnostic sensitivity, and even vigilance, at all points of entry: over $40 million for hospital costs alone to save the lives of suicide victims in one metropolitan locale in two years! Such devastating costs for our hospitals, taxpayers, and health insurance system demand suicide prevention measures on a grand scale.

Such measures are not, once again, restricted by the science of behavioral prediction. They are more matters of moral reassessment, health professional education, and standards of practice. The Commonwealth of Virginia missed the opportunity to truly address the tragedy of its Blacksburg massacre by simply avoiding the gross errors of his management and attributing it, in the end, to his willful badness. Such a conclusion is somewhat unbelievable in this era of modern clinical science.

Psychosocial Maladjustment

It is well established that certain populations are at risk for psychiatric impairment due to psychosocial risk factors. Poor, single-parent families with an adult son at home, for example, are at particularly high risk for having one of the 14 percent of patients who are afflicted with the most serious psychiatric disorders. In fact, in a Kentucky study (Kessler et al., 1994), family analysis predicted future psychopathology in 82 percent of cases. Both causative and aggravating stress from dysfunctional families and employment environments can be identified, further reducing the costs of medical services greatly within the population of high utilizers of primary healthcare services. Although addressed well in public school, Cho's stress was ignored by Virginia Tech administration, left to his professors to ameliorate and hopelessly address.

Pelvic pain syndrome in females, for example, where nonrecognition of sexual violence in patients' histories, with its attendant marital strife, results in expensive medical and surgical, rather than psychiatric, treatments, and escalates both pathology and attendant utilization of primary health services. The popularized syndrome of chronic fatigue is usually associated with antecedent occupational stress. Again, costly medical interventions and disability obstruct clinical intervention into the workplace, where costs of treatment and lost productivity could more effectively be impacted.

Type A behavior and life events are well-documented risk factors for both heart disease and dysfunctional family and occupational life—as well as violence, whether at home or on campus. It is generally ignored in both diagnostics and therapeutics in favor of laboratory tests, not only unproven for their ability to predict cardiac events and violence but costly too. Geriatric patients in Florida are oftentimes tested for cholesterol routinely despite the lack of demonstrated validity in this age group; each test costs almost $10 and is paid by Medicare to the tune of hundreds of millions of dollars of direct medical costs in just one state. Yet, significantly, McDonnell Douglas Corporation found that provision of managed mental health services to employees, including collateral services to dependents, saved even more on dependent medical claims ($3 million over 4 years) than its cost-offset savings in employee claims ($2.1 million).

The high incidence of life-threatening events associated with onset of depression in most Americans afflicted with affective disorders every year is testimony to the need for sensitivity to trauma and patient resiliency at points of entry and along all clinical pathways. Nonetheless, only one half of the sickest psychiatric patients gets any medical treatment; only 1 in 15 enters separate mental health clinical pathways and 1 in 17 enters substance abuse pathways—frequently inappropriately. The main reason for this gross neglect is that psychological distress screens are more discretionary than complex, differential cholesterol screens. Current maladjustment, however, not only predicts serious psychiatric diseases like depression but may predict spousal abuse; suicidality; serious medical illness, particularly heart attack and concurrent illness in families of the seriously ill; as well as relapse in schizophrenia and substance abuse. In the case of Cho Seung-Hui, it could have predicted massive violence. He kept saying what he was going to do. Fellow students picked it up; for reasons important to understand, however, those responsible for this ticking time bomb were blinded.

Any effective diagnostic system, therefore, must be sensitive to current adjustment in order to reduce the patient's risk for malignant psychosocial distress. Psychotherapeutic intervention, including family therapy, marital therapy, and supportive individual and group psychotherapy, is essential to reducing morbidity and mortality in the time- and event-determined processes such as nonendogenous depression, suicidal depression, myocardial infarction, schizophrenic relapse, and situational violence. Research on critical incident stress debriefing shows that supportive group psychotherapy following traumatic events for emergency personnel reduces the incidence of posttraumatic syndromes from 16 to 4 percent in the first four months.

In addition to aforementioned acute maladjustment problems, inestimable social disruption and family dysfunction result from enduring patterns of maladaptive personality traits, which operate regardless of the person's environment. This is known as *character pathology*, and there is evidence that it is increasing in prevalence in today's society. Undetected and untreated character pathology results in countless episodes of violence in the workplace, now the leading cause of death for women at work. Pathological dysfunction in organizations, as well as families, is frequently traceable to character pathology in leadership positions. Police and military organizations are particularly at risk for rewarding character pathology with promotion.

"What Killed Bob Lyon" is the classic occupational psychiatry case of a suicidal employee so hungry for rewards that he was promoted beyond his level of competence. Police scandals, as well as the Rodney King and O.J. Simpson cases, illuminate problems of maladjustment in police forces. Less violent forms of character pathology, such as pathological narcissism, are responsible for inestimable family dysfunction, violence, marked disability, and societal woes. Many, like Paul Keller, a case of pathological narcissism, cannot tolerate stress and break down with lethal episodes of violence, in this case 96 fires with 3 fatalities in just a single 6-month period. Only one professor thought Cho was mainly character disordered, but it was not his responsibility to make that diagnosis. Also, he is lucky to be alive, because Cho wrote about him before his death.

In the workplace, character-deformed individuals cause stress casualties in other employees and can ruin operations before either detection or disciplinary action. The healthcare industry can do little to change social trends so conducive to the pervasive character-disordered behavior that infects our society today. But, clinicians can discreetly identify individuals like arsonist Keller before too much damage is done to either the patient or others, including clinicians themselves.

The treatment literature for character pathology is based on case reports rather than double-blind research, but psychoanalytic, learning theory, and group therapy literature is rich enough in successful outcomes to warrant diagnostic selection of patients for appropriate nonmedical treatment modalities. And, of utmost importance diagnostically is identification and incarceration of the psychopathic individual before he wreaks the havoc of such notorious killers as Bundy, Bianchi, Wayne Williams, Dahmer, and Gacy. They killed hundreds of people in the most brutal ways. The prevalence of antisocial personality disorder in America today is 3.8 percent. Because false negatives for prediction of dangerousness in this population can be significantly reduced by case detection, the importance of diagnostic sensitivity and accuracy in diagnostic screening with such pervasive psychopathology impacting our society in so many destructive ways can no longer be denied with rationalization of constitutional law.

Miss Tarasoff's killer was evaluated and released through official commitment channels. Her murderer's psychotherapist at the University of California Health Center was found liable for not protecting the victim, but he did all the right things "constitutionally." Differential diagnosis within the criminal justice system, where treatable character pathology and reversible neuropsychiatric, posttraumatic, and substance abuse disorders must be differentiated, is currently deemphasized or even devalued. Tragically, that is where many of these people must now be properly assessed through presentence investigation or even at booking.

The corrections business is booming, even though nobody knows how to correct or even what to correct. To make matters worse, most offenders will be released untreated and uncorrected, despite determinate sentences, because many states reserve the authority to release anyone they so choose to release if beds are filled and no corrections disposition is available.

Judicial discretion must become the governor's discretion, because the United States cannot really afford to incarcerate 1,500,000 adults, particularly when incarceration has such a minuscule impact on crime, and now corrections is the end game for serious mental illness too. More than ever, corrections will be rapidly politicizing, dissociated from both judicial discretion and medical diagnostics. With new crime legislation, $100 billion annually will be spent to segregate offenders from society with minimal effect, and future medical care for this aging, dependent population was never factored into legislation. As with immigration and the legacies of wars imported into this country, a massive balloon payment will come due in the next millennium, unless clinical diagnostics is restored within the presentence investigation and prisoner classification of 20 million detentions annually becomes integrated within the healthcare system. With the dismantlement of the state mental health system and resultant criminalization of the seriously mentally ill, corrections, like emergency medicine, will bear the impossible burden of social and political denial of reality. Cho Seung-Hui, and other violent people, have been mentally ill for a long time with no help available to them, until it is too late for them to recognize need for it.

Enhanced diagnostic screens that are both patient and health professions user-friendly can efficiently and uniformly assist triage of patients entering the healthcare system at all points of entry, including the corrections system. Physicians, nurses, and paraprofessionals, in other words, must be on the "same page" or "garbage in will be garbage out"—bad practices.

Such a system must enhance treatment selection and service optimization in disease specific management for emergency, complex medical presentations, disorganized mental states, and psychic impairment at any point of entry to the healthcare delivery system. This could be accomplished with minimum modifications of the multiform gateway system to American healthcare, whether the patient enters on his own to an outpatient clinic, campus health center, or ER; is directed via demand management phone triage or is booked into jail; or, in Cho's case, is detained as seriously mentally ill. Like modern retailing, the brick-and-mortar gateway that leads into the healthcare system is likewise becoming a "wired gateway."

Improved diagnostics have not yet been proven to reduce either excessive or inappropriate healthcare utilization, but it is only a matter of common medical sense that they will inevitably be pressed to do so. The incredible costs of underdiagnosing, with attendant denial of treatment, for the complex medical, mentally disorganized, and psychic impaired patients will eventually demand as revolutionary approaches at the points of entry to health services as AIDS has demanded from our schools. Whether that point of entry has the form of college health center, clinical office, remote medic site, emergency room, demand management phone call, or jail ultimately makes no difference. The point of entry into the system makes no difference because that is where the at-risk people present for the infrequent opportunity of comprehensive diagnostic assessment. It was such infrequent opportunities that were tragically missed in the case of Cho Seung-Hui.

We have seen how certain subgroups within our population are at higher risk for violence, whether to self or others. Halleck (1975) identifies the robustly disorganized mentally ill patient subgroup with documented histories of threats or acts of violence. Within the entire universe of actions documented globally, it may be true that acts of violence appear to be too rare to predict—at least those completely adjudicated in court. Public health statistics, particularly those from cities like Detroit, provide little solace from such mathematical modeling. Were pulmonary anthrax in the top ten or fifteen causes of death annually, we would probably be under martial law because of an "epidemic." Violence is not rare enough to sit on our hands and take a libertarian approach of keeping the intrusive forces of government and public health out of what is an epidemic of injuries, disability, and deaths from violence toward self and others.

This also holds true within the universe of comparative statistics that does not quantitatively differentiate between violence caused by serious mental illness and people not diagnosed as such. One diversion from exploring these statistics in more depth is the frequent response from constituencies dedicated to preserving the rights of the mentally ill: the seriously mentally ill are more often victims than perpetrators of violence. What does that tell us? Black-on-black homicides far exceed black-on-white homicides, too. Should that divert us from emphasizing risk for violence within black society for fear of being racist? Few black leaders today advocate that, but, of course, they do not want violence in America attributed simply to the presence of black people among us. That is a political risk requiring diagnostic caution—as is the traditional intuitive fear of madness, whether based on fact, myth, or subjective response.

There is adequate evidence statistically to support efforts to identify the highest risk subgroups of patients adjudicated as seriously mentally ill to emphasize the necessity of better care of these people. To say that this subgroup is less dangerous, whether to each other or anyone else, conveniently perpetuates the current policy of doing little or nothing for them since deinstitutionalization dumped them into community mental health programs—subsequently robbed of the assets necessary to treat them. "Who cares if they injure each other" perhaps is the public attitude as they drift downward away from more politically powerful suburban neighborhoods.

But, what about a guy like Seung-Hui Cho, going to class and living with our kids on campus? At-risk people such as Cho also go to shopping centers, gyms, churches; they drive cars and even go to work. So, if not properly cared for, they can hurt all of us. A subgroup within this population is at high risk for suicide, substance abuse, impairing controls and judgment, violence toward others, with or without suicide; and, finally, accessing weapons. All this can result from lack of care.

Wolfgang (1975) provides government a legitimate point of entry into carefully assessing child development, without wasting money on useless programs or committing violations of civil liberties by examining minor delinquencies or every child born, as advocated by Hutschnecker. That point signaling clinical and psychosocial intervention is the third time a juvenile is charged with an offense; that triggering event for intensive intervention is also evidence-based medicine. Government and public health authorities have undisputed rights to do just this without violating anyone's rights. How it is done, of course, cannot simply be in clinical darkness and requires significant judicial oversight.

Utilizing the medical diagnostic model of *DSM IV* and time-determined, epidemiologically informed clinical decision making, how can such interventions therefore be made with just these two subgroups at seemingly high risk for both violence and suicide? These tools provide both the multidimensional illumination advocated by Halleck, as well as the critical situational factors advocated by Monahan. Halleck is an M.D.; Monahan an aggressive critic of the medical model as applied to the phenomenon of violence.

To be epidemiologically informed, according to Halleck (1975), is to take better care of a subgroup of the seriously mentally ill. Monahan (1975) asserts that to be epidemiologically informed is to reduce the influence of clinical practices in acts of violence. Although his studies make us necessarily humble and honest, the California Supreme Court in *Tarasoff* runs counter to and supercedes Monahan's scientific authority. Clinicians, these justices determined, do have peculiar ability with special knowledge and capability of control equivalent to any physicians diagnosing and treating contagious disease.

Within this profound ambiguity must be found the most effective and ethical role for clinical interventions to reduce violence while somehow preserving patients' constitutional rights. This was the challenge that faced the evaluators of Cho Seung-Hui. Had they only detained him for one more day to contact his parents, his emergency contact that Virginia Tech had on file, and located the records of his treatments as a child in elementary and middle school, it is likely that Cho would have received help and his rampage would never have happened.

Ultimately, the politics and economics of the next millennium will require both the healthcare provider and insurer to respond with improved diagnostics for treatment selection and service optimization. Unless other major factors are missing from the equation, healthcare costs can be adequately reduced to prevent legislated reform based only on economic necessity and mandated universal coverage. Here could still be the primary lesson taught by the Commonwealth of Virginia to American education.

Chapter 5

The Virginia Panel and Campus Safety

Fuller Torrey (2008), in *The Insanity Offense*, writes:

> Here, then, are the roots of deinstitutionalization's failure. Most laws governing the treatment of mentally ill individuals assume that such individuals are competent to accept or reject treatment, with the sole exception of dementia. Yet, the contemporary research has established that up to half of all individuals with severe psychiatric disorders are not competent to assess their own need for treatment. The consequences of this misunderstanding have led to increasing numbers of mentally ill individuals who are homeless, incarcerated, and victimized, as well as increasing numbers of individual who commit homicide and other violent acts. This misunderstanding underlies one of the great social disasters of late twentieth-century America. ... (Virginia's) is one of the most stringent state commitment statutes in the United States and another example of how changes in mental illness laws in the 1970s and 1980s continue to have real consequences. After the fact, it became abundantly clear that Cho was, and had for some time been, psychotic. ... Thirty-two families were left to mourn and wonder what went wrong. (p. 122)

The Commonwealth of Virginia, in a state of shock and rightfully fearful of extreme liability exposure that was later confirmed in multimillion dollar settlements to survivors, established a special panel to investigate the Virginia

Tech massacre. Months earlier, because of aggressive advocacy from constituencies dedicated to reversing the legacy of deinstitutionalization ravaging the lives of the mentally ill, as well as their families and communities, over 100 separate bills on mental health reform had already been introduced in the Virginia legislature.

As a matter of law, post *Lessard* and according to the Governor's Panel, the legal standard applied for involuntary treatment of Cho at Carilion St. Albans Psychiatric Hospital during this legislative debate was still that of "Predonderance of Evidence for Cho's being imminently dangerous as a result of Serious Mental Illness." The Commonwealth Special Commission working on this legislation was diverted to join the Special Commonwealth Panel in the wake of the massacre in Blacksburg to bring hope out of despair for mental health reform, both for Virginia and institutions of higher education across America.

Tragically, leaders of colleges and universities will get no hope from Richmond, nor will they find guidance for protecting their own campuses from future apocalyptic suicide and mass murders.

After the mass murder at Virginia Tech in 2007 and the ensuing investigation into that crime, Virginia looked into the abyss of what an untreated psychotic could perpetrate on his innocent victims. The state had the opportunity and the ability to improve treatment laws for people who exhibited dangerous psychotic symptoms. Yet the state never took the major steps toward reform. They blinked. They made some improvements, but they did not go nearly as far as they should have and, as a result, the state simply has a bad law. It is better than having one of the worst treatment laws in the country, but it is still bad. The state missed a chance to do something meaningful. And that could be interpreted as a collective slap in the face to the victims' families. The families and friends of the students who died that day deserved more. So do the thousands of commonwealth residents who need treatment for severe mental illnesses but are not aware of their own need for medical attention.

The Virginia legislature made a slight adjustment to the legal standard for placement in treatment, from showing that a person presents an imminent danger to self or others to one allowing involuntary treatment if it can be shown that "the person will, in the near future, cause serious physical harm to himself or others as evidenced by recent behavior causing, attempting, or threatening harm" (Virginia Tech Review Panel, 2007). Did Cho Seung-Hui meet this standard before he opened fire on the campus? It is unclear.

> While Virginia was tinkering around the edges of what needs to be done to prevent tragedies, Illinois, Idaho, and Louisiana all enacted significant reforms to provide treatment to those with severe mental illnesses. They should be commended.
>
> Virginia did leave the door open to consider the measure again next year. The many family members and advocates who want to improve treatment will be knocking. (Entsminger, 2008)

As we learned from the Special Commonwealth Panel, the Community Resource Board Emergency Crisis Evaluator found probable cause for Cho's being imminently dangerous right before involuntary psychiatric admission to St. Albans. The magistrate found a preponderance of evidence for his being imminently dangerous less than 24 hours later. In between these assessments, the independent evaluator, a clinical psychologist, found serious mental illness without imminent dangerousness in a 15-minute interview of Cho. The attending psychiatrist found only depressive symptomatology, failing to meet the criteria of either any significant and specific psychiatric disorder or imminent threat to self or others.

There was no communication between any of at least four clinical evaluators during this 24-hour emergency assessment. Furthermore, there remain questions as to whether any totally noncontroversial internal hospital reports from any reliable resources such as nursing admission assessment were reviewed. Were any medication reports from the evening shift or medical clearance, assumedly performed with physical examination, and laboratory examination in error by any evaluator?

Most likely the ruling magistrate read some, and this magistrate had to act—by default—as both clinical evaluator and final clinical decision maker re Cho's prospective dangerousness. Clearly, the substance of inpatient psychiatric workup had finally met its expected fate in a mental health system that is barely visible in the landscape of disaster that Torrey describes.

Clinical evaluation at St. Albans was merely a shadowy form, both barely visible behind claims of restrictive legal barriers preventing any attempt to acquire critical information from collateral sources and bereft of adequate resources for minimal examination. There could be no peer-review support for this inpatient evaluation, regardless of any perceived legal barriers to assessment, communications, or reporting, because there was little of substance made available to the state panel in the wake of Cho's apocalyptic suicide and mass murder.

Cho actually arrived back on campus after discharge under involuntary commitment to outpatient treatment. He arrived without harming himself or anyone else, although nobody to this day knows how he got there but assumedly with no supervision while supposedly under court supervision. Arguably, in the senseless inpatient environment of today—one created and maintained by courts rather than clinicians—the fact of Cho's apparently safe arrival back on campus after discharge from emergency hospitalization vindicated both the evaluating psychiatrist's and psychologist's opinions that he was not, in fact, imminently dangerous. *Imminent*, though open to some legal interpretation, means imminent, as in, arguably, within an hour or two but not within twenty-four hours.

The magistrate disagreed with these clinical opinions and found Cho to be imminently dangerous to self and/or others and ordered his involuntary commitment. Although only he knows why, we can speculate that the fact that Cho had told his roommates he was contemplating suicide and had a history of stalking made the magistrate wary of simply letting him out to care for himself. In so doing, he overrode the clinicians at St. Albans. Yet, the governor's panel, staring the magistrate's decision in the face, concluded with the strong refutation to loss of ego autonomy in truly serious mental illness by unambiguously holding Cho, and only Cho, responsible for the disaster at Virginia Tech. It was an easy and expedient decision for them to make, albeit disingenuous.

The state commission, already well into discussions about mental health law reform, later joined them, along with the legislature and governor, and effectively dodged the entire issue of causation for Cho's chronic and escalating psychotic illness. So, the primary message for college administration from all of these legal and political man-hours—along with the sacrifices of many other interested parties—is "take care of yourselves. Do not wait for your state government and its courts, the original instruments of deconstruction of our public mental health system, to begin its reconstruction." The resources to create and administer a serious emergency mental health triage system are beyond the scope of governments, under too much control of the courts and aggressive litigators who do not understand the nature of the individuals they are dealing with and the harm they can cause, and at best, critically understaffed. Police and local jails have become the safe haven for the dangerously mentally ill because, at least behind bars, they cannot hurt others except inmates and guards.

Within the strictest legal technicalities of the law, both the magistrate's opinion and community service board's emergency detention decisions to detain, both counter to St. Alban's clinical conclusions, based on findings of imminent danger to self or others were proven wrong. Cho was not imminently violent. Instead, he was just one of the most violent and insane persons ever discharged from a psychiatric hospital in this nation's history. Imminent is a legal standard, which, although one element of the diagnosis, was only a part of a larger picture of the menace that Cho presented. By looking at the one, doctors missed the larger issue entirely.

Accordingly, and perhaps realizing their shortsightedness, in the wake of Cho's rampage murders, the Virginia legislature made one small step for man by expanding the window of predictable time of likely violence from imminent to near future. But, this supposedly major opening of the window for predictive discretion in forensic clinical examinations, along with reams of new legal text to debate again for years, and adding to the pot a sweetener of millions for local evaluator boards to safely detain patients in more special crisis beds in ERs, was touted as one giant leap for mankind, too.

"A positive response to a terrible tragedy; Virginia stakeholders have worked together to craft legislative solutions in the wake of last year's Virginia Tech shootings," announced by the Mary Ann Bergeron report (2008).

Mary Ann Bergeron was registered as a lobbyist for the Virginia Association of Community Service Boards. Her local boards came out with millions of dollars for their budgets; these boards are responsible for determining probable cause of either future violence to self and/or others or grave disability. Such determination can lead to upwards of 72 hours of involuntary hospitalization for psychiatric evaluation in order to either rule in or rule out these three medico-legal problems.

"Within weeks of the tragedy (at Virginia Tech)" she states,

> ... each of Virginia's 40 community services boards (CSBs) had examined in minute detail its own process of emergency services response in coordinating efforts with magistrates, private and state hospitals, law enforcement, and the local court systems of special justices (attorneys appointed by the respective circuit courts to preside over involuntary commitment hearings). CSBs, the local authorities designated by the Code of Virginia, are mandated to ensure, within every Virginia locality, provision of emergency services for psychiatric issues. Among their broad spectrum of services, CSBs can recommend individuals for involuntary temporary examination, detention, diversion, and outpatient treatment. Internal scrutiny by CSBs produced revisions in local practices and additional evidence for necessary changes in the law. (Bergeron, 2008)

Assumably, this internal finding and renewed legal responsiveness refers to requirements that the CSB crisis evaluators have to at least be available to the magistrate for presentation of their probable cause evidence for initial detention. Also, they are to be responsible for both facilitating and monitoring disposition in event of judicial determination to commit. This process was notably absent from the case of Cho following his involuntary commitment to outpatient treatment services that neither he nor anyone in the superficial suicide autopsy of the commonwealth panel could find.

It is not clear what the credentials of these emergency evaluators were at the time of Cho's assessment, currently are, or are intended to be under this new legislation. At least in the Cho case, it is hard to find that they were the critical missing link in the chain of events gone awry, because Cho was formally evaluated by a Viriginia Tech clinical psychologist in conformance with the magistrate's involuntary outpatient treatment order. The college guidance center knew, or should have known, that he was there under involuntary commitment. An appointment was made for him from the hospital before discharge. It was made in conformity with the university guidance center's policies requiring Cho to make the appointment himself. The panel reported that he did this before discharge and that he showed up at the guidance center where he was officially documented as having been triaged and evaluated. The clinical record of his first clinical evaluation after involuntary commitment to outpatient treatment had been lost. Likewise, at least two official triage evaluations prior to commitment were similarly lost. However, in July 2009, Virginia's Governor Timothy Kaine announced that Cho's missing records were discovered in the home of Dr. Robert C. Miller, former director of the university's Cook Counseling Center. Dr. Miller had taken them home when he left the center in 2006, but they surfaced during the discovery phase of the final lawsuits against the university filed by the families of two of the victims. The state gave no explanation for the missing records or why they had been removed from Cook Counseling Center by its director.

At the time, the loss of all of the serial triage reports at the university guidance center was not considered a threat to confidentiality, but other conflicting rules and regulations were. The loss of these clinical triage documents was certainly a critical gap in the chain of custody for Cho. These apparently conflicting laws and regulations were not really a barrier to full and proper clinical assessment of Cho at any time, but the loss of his multiple triage evaluations at the guidance center was, in fact, a huge threat of violation to his privacy. Their loss should have been of concern in view of the vast amount of time and discussion devoted to unique concerns for privacy and confidentiality of students, which never apply anyway under the forensic circumstances of Cho's involuntary commitment. In such cases of emergency psychiatry, wherein the attending clinical staff has an indisputable "need to know" under the school rule of forensic medicine as set forth in eMedicine Psychiatry, the attending physician has the authority to gather information and consult with anyone deemed necessary to solve the problems at hand—that would include Cho's parents, treating psychiatrist back home, campus police, resident counselors, and professors.

The responsibility of the Department of Psychiatry at St. Albans Hospital was the determination of both the diagnosis and causation for Cho's dual presentations of strange behavior (nonverbal) reported by the CSB crisis evaluator the night before, along with that of serious mental illness diagnosed by the clinical psychologist that same morning. Additionally, whether he was in a clinical state of unremitting destructiveness, thus being at imminent risk of harming self or others, was the other criterion supporting need for further involuntary detention. This, in fact, was done, but there is no visible thread of either clinical evidence supportive of the decision or the differential diagnostic and evidence based therapeutic logic to support it.

"True to his word," Virginia Community Service Board Lobbyist Bergeron continues,

> Kaine announced last fall that his biennial budget for 2008–10 would include allocations for a $42 million "down payment" to begin upgrading mental health services. It is significant that funds were designated to CSBs to improve the following community services: emergency, outpatient, case management, and crisis stabilization capability for youths and adults suffering from psychiatric disorders. Kaine specified the need for identifying problems, intervening, and treating them as early as possible, so that individuals with mental illness can engage in services quickly and begin a path to recovery that could avoid psychiatric crisis and the trauma of involuntary detention or commitment. (Bergeron, 2008)

Here, possibly, is the one step forward out of our current national disaster, whose ground zero could be considered the campus of Virginia Tech University in 2007. There is not an interested clinician or college administrator who believes that ground zero could not have been any campus in America. It had been at the University of Montreal, where strict gun control did not prevent a massacre, and it had been earlier in the United States at Northern Illinois University.

The apocalyptic suicide and mass murder perpetrated by Cho Seung-Hui was simply over the top. No longer, as in Northern Illinois University, could it be simply sterilized as random and unpreventable. There simply was too much carnage and bloodshed from too many innocent and decent people. There were also too many bloody tracks in the snow leading up to the massacre this time. And when one realizes that all of this carnage was completely preventable from at least three directions and probably more, one realizes how much this tragedy is compounded.

The campus police should have held Cho for stalking and brandishing a weapon. St. Albans should have held Cho involuntarily until they obtained his complete medical record from Cook Counseling Center, the outgoing director of the center should have never removed Cho's records from the center, and the university should have called his parents. In essence, the Commonwealth of Virginia created the perfect storm for this tragedy to have been perpetrated. And then they simply covered it up by laying the blame on a psychotic person out of touch with reality for not being in touch with reality.

Lobbyist Bergeron saluted Virginia State government's sensitivity at a time of gaps in the state budget:

> This "down payment" proved how serious the governor was in pledging to improve the system. Standing with him as he made the announcement were key legislators of both parties, state officials, family members of Virginia Tech victims, the Virginia Association of Community Services Boards (VACSB) and the Virginia chapters of the National Alliance on Mental Illness and Mental Health America. With the governor's announcement, mental health reform had begun in a nonpartisan and meaningful way. (Bergeron, 2008)

This legislation was undoubtedly political, but it was primarily the presentation, rather than the substance of the deal, that was projected from Richmond. It was nonpartisan, except that the medical societies, in particular, the Psychiatric Association of Virginia, were not invited to participate; nor was the Treatment Advocacy Center, the only effective force in this nation for actually making the meaningful changes necessary to reduce the risk of such violence on campus.

> There were better options. The Virginia senate gave up an opportunity to follow New York's lead and enact something very similar to that state's successful Kendra's Law. That model, rejected in committee, would have made assisted outpatient treatment more widely available to people incapacitated by severe mental illnesses, even if they didn't pose

> an immediate danger to themselves or others. The documented record of success in New York is clear. Of those in New York's program, 74% fewer experienced homelessness, 77% less psychiatric hospitalizations, 83% fewer arrests, and 87% fewer imprisonments as a result of the measure. (Entsminger, 2008)

Also left out were the organizations representing the actual parties—the doctors—ultimately responsible for putting their careers, bodies, reputations, economic security—even their lives—on the line for determination of two critical criteria: diagnosing serious mental illness and assessing future expectations for potentially destructive behavior.

According to President Steve Brasington, M.D., "The Psychiatric Society of Virginia (PSV) allied with other medical organizations and, in an effort led by the Medical Society of Virginia, pushed for expanded access to care for patients, higher standards of care, and patient privacy. They've (State of Virginia) moved from a higher standard to a lower one in this legislation" (Levin, 2008).

A major concern expressed by Brasington in regard to the highly touted new commitment law is the fact that a physician or even a doctoral-level psychologist will no longer be required to evaluate a person for commitment. A designated employee of the local community services board may do so. Brasington believes that doctors were also removed from the commitment process to eliminate the appearance of financial conflict of interest should patients be committed to the doctor's own facility. In the era of increasing costs, liability risks, and the Joint Commission on the Accreditation Healthcare Organization (JCAHO) standards for care, all juxtaposed to concomitant reduction of reimbursement for psychiatric illness, Brasington addressed the lack of understanding of our current public health crisis in inpatient psychiatry. The possibility of conflict of interest is remote, according to Brasington, because facilities often lose money on the care of involuntary patients, and doctors are not reimbursed for the time spent at hearings. Curiously, there has been no mention of how administrative costs within CSB and their salaries, along with billable legal hours, will be affected by this legislation. But because of its textual complexity and substantial change operationally, neither CSB nor mental health lawyers will come out with less than before Cho went berserk.

Richard Bonnie, director of the Institute of Law, Psychiatry, and Public Policy at the University of Virginia School of Law, believes that Brasington's objections are more perception than ones of substance. "The status of who performs assessments reflects reality," Bonnie states in response.

> The problem is that in many parts of the state, there are no psychiatrists or psychologists available, so the law will allow a licensed counselor or social worker to be appointed as an independent examiner. ... Our goal was to promote consistency by trying to give more guidance to judges

> who make commitment decisions. … I do not feel that the psychiatrists' point of view was overlooked. … I believe that this is a case of variance between perceptions (which we need to correct) and reality. (Bonnie, 2008)

It is more than perception. It is a matter of training and professional experience. Psychiatrists who work in hospitals and treat the seriously mentally ill see the constantly deteriorating standards of care caused by unrealistic withdrawal of financial support that causes affiliate hospitals to put their units at the front of the budgetary chopping block—just ahead of emergency rooms. There is no backup any more, because state hospital beds have all but vanished. Florida, as an example, has decreased the ratio of its publicly funded inpatient psychiatric beds from 56 per 100,000 population in 1960 to 8 per 100,000 in 1990. Whatever the number was over 20 years ago, it has certainly decreased over the past 20 years.

The State of Virginia did not address this continued meltdown in resources in the wake of the deinstitutionalization disaster. To correct this alleged spread in perspective, one must also recognize countertrends within psychiatric practice today, complicated by rapidly advancing neuropsychiatric diagnostic technologies, such as imaging and genetic testing for pharmacokinetic aberrations. Ironically, the very pioneering advances of neuroleptic pharmacotherapy of serious mental illness that first justified shutting down of public psychiatric beds—and now serve as justification for protecting patients from their undesirable side effects—have significantly advanced again, promising better patient response without associated side effects and adverse events more commonly caused by first-generation neuroleptics such as Thorazine and Haldol.

This has vastly changed the landscape of school campuses today because students with psychiatric illnesses presenting in childhood could not have matriculated without more modern medications that are both safer and freer of side effects than original neuroleptics and tricyclics—for example, Elavil—or monoamine oxidase inhibiting antidepressants—for example, Nardil. This critical fact was not addressed at all by the commonwealth in delivering signed mental health legislation to the citizens of Virginia and nearly 20 million students plus their families at risk on campuses of higher education nationally.

But, the massacre on the Virginia Tech campus and original impetus for the State Commission for Mental Health Reform merely converged to highlight what Torrey (2008) asserts in *The Insanity Offense* are the consequences of misunderstanding "that have led to increasing numbers of mentally ill individuals who are homeless, incarcerated, and victimized and increasing numbers of individuals who commit homicide and other violent act."

One small step for man: hospital stays are still restricted to a usually ineffectual few days, with third-party payers pushing utilization review nurses to demand discharge planning to coincide contemporaneously with admission evaluation. There seem to be as many doctors calling floor physicians from well-concealed third-party payer offices across state lines, demanding daily status of treatment plans and progress, as there are doctors actually trying to diagnose and treat patients. The money is better with insurance companies, and it is a lot safer in every way behind that large mahogany desk across state lines from frontline medicine, with supporting call centers oftentimes outside the country.

The rush, in other words, is converted to push, euphemistically referred to as *throughput*, the responsibility of directors of nursing, considered more malleable than more "independently minded physicians" (*Lean Management of Healthcare, King County Medical Society Bulletin*). And *throughput* means "start shoving" right from the moment of admission to ever-dwindling inpatient psychiatric beds and almost no functional outpatient services. Discharge is also to be noon or before, oftentimes with no opportunity for ward case managers to even arrange for transport to a safe downstep facility, home, or friend. This is true of all acute care medicine and surgery but, at the current rate of decline, inpatient psychiatry will be all but extinct in a matter of years.

> "The stats are disconcerting," according to Kellerman (2007). "While visits to emergency departments increased by 26 percent from 1993 to 2003, hospital beds plummeted by 198,000, and 425 ERs around the country shut down."

Yet, compared to public psychiatry this extreme downsizing of acute and emergency medicine beds, much of it since 9/11, only causes death rattles for other specialties. Resources are so tight in psychiatry in California that exchanges must be worked out between diminishing community psychiatric units and public state hospitals when the involuntary treatment facility cannot manage the patient and refers to the state hospital. As condition of acceptance of that patient, the local facility usually must take one of theirs, usually an equally dangerous patient from an entirely different area of the state.

So, discussions that emphasize least restrictive alternative, the basis of involuntary treatment reform decades ago, will ultimately be like enhancing the lives of the Condor, now all but extinct. And, most patients, like Cho, are sicker now too, not only in their presenting psychopathology but from cradle-to-grave neglect based on supposition that their behavior is learned and a matter of ego autonomy—or personal choice based on faulty learning and decision making in life. As a result of this neglect, similar in principle to our treatment of Native Americans, whose enforced dependency has ended abruptly with tribal emancipation, leaving them to their own, the seriously mentally ill population has far more medical comorbidities such as diabetes and heart disease.

These medical comorbidities shorten their life spans compared to their protected days of state hospital care, as at the former Northern State Hospital in Sedro Wooley, Washington, a state-of-the-art facility designed for the care of patients who simply cannot be managed yet within the community. This means that cases like Cho may be the harbinger of worse things to come, violent sprees seemingly coming out of nowhere but easily traceable to a source of psychosis once the light of real medical evaluation shines on it.

Increasing scarcity of inpatient treatment beds, both at the state and community level, is all but ignored by the State of Virginia. In fact, the legal spokesman for this legislation, Attorney Bonnie, believes that the problem is more one of maldistribution of inpatient beds rather than statewide scarcity. That may be the case in Virginia, but it certainly is not the case in the rest of America. There is still a certain disconnect between legal opinions of mental illness and the realities of psychiatric practice. "Without inpatient hospital beds allocated to mental health, some patients who are committed could tie up emergency department slots for several nights, controlled with multiple doses of medications, until they are stable enough to go home," said Brasington. "That would defeat the purpose of commitment" (Levin, 2008).

Not only were emergency medicine physicians not prominently represented in the Commonwealth Commission's planning process as part of organized medicine in Virginia, but the commonwealth's investigative panel advised their obtaining additional training in psychiatry to perform the necessary emergency evaluation functions! Although this might fly past the average citizen on the street, it is simply ludicrous. First of all, ER doctors are trained in psychiatry as a condition of graduation from medical school, whether in Richmond or Charlottesville. It is a rare one who wants more to do with escalating demands of psychiatric patients turning to ERs for care due to absence of state care. The vast majority want far fewer psychiatric patients clogging their ERs; few would want more psychiatric emergency services beds on their units either. They cannot simply dissociate themselves from medical responsibilities of these patients, even if the government and legal profession can dissociate the vaguely formulated CSB from emergency medicine by semantic omission on paper.

So, by not involving organized medicine in this piece of legislation, the crisis in emergency medicine, inevitably exacerbated by this law, was simply avoided. For colleges and universities, it will be their local ERs that can help them secure their campuses without undermining the rights and clinical needs of their students. The crisis in emergency psychiatric medicine will not be resolved by college campus health and counseling centers. They are even more under water in today's new era of outpatient treatment for the seriously ill psychiatric patient, a student who is more likely to be living on campus than a student who is living at or near home.

It's a familiar story: America's emergency rooms are in crisis. But it's far worse than you think. How does the ER prepare for a terrorist attack when its medics can barely cope with the routine flow of mayhem on a Saturday night? A worried doctor traveled to Washington to sound the alarms.

A *Newsweek* story covers the experiences of Dr. Arthur Kellerman, who, with the House Committee on Oversight and Government Reform, was invited to attend a briefing on Capitol Hill with Dennis Smith, director of the Center for Medicaid and State Operations. The briefing covered a prospective rule change by the Bush administration. The change effectively cut millions of dollars from hospital funding across the country, virtually severing the federal lifeline for emergency medicine and was the fulfillment of a prophecy for Kellerman, who had watched emergency rooms around the country shut down for lack of funding. This is further evidence that emergency medicine and emergency psychiatry have become financial hot potatoes. States have used mental health reform to shift cost for their responsibilities in treating the mentally ill to federally funded programs, such as Medicaid, and emergency medicine will be next to get the axe.

What does Bonnie think differentiates Virginia from Georgia and New York? How can ERs absorb the crisis intervention beds Bonnie promises as Virginia's only practical answer to its debacle, ultimately erupting in the bloodshed at Virginia Tech. Its change of criteria for predicting violence is of little substantive clinical meaning.

We are still not clear about what serious deficits in mental health were specifically determined to be in need of reform in Cho's going berserk. Was it clarification of laws covering confidentiality, alleged to have paralyzed the definitive hospital workup and chain of custody in Cho Seung-Hui's management for years? Is it more investment statewide in crisis management, particularly provision of discretion for her client's CSBs to determine quality and standards of clinical assessment in areas like Blacksburg, considered short of psychiatric resources? Extending the trajectory for clinical prediction by empowering clinicians with peculiar abilities of special knowledge and control of patients to look out to expected behavior in the near future. It is far better than relying on a definition of "imminent" because one can't predict what a patient will do in the ensuing one or two hours unless that person is actually wielding a weapon. Practically, that means less demand for evidence of violence perpetrated by the patient while actually on the inpatient psychiatry unit, one major operational criterion for imminent violence.

This is important, because most psychiatric clinical staff have been victims of serious assault or can expect to be in their careers. In one study, more than 50 percent of psychiatrists and 75 percent of mental health nurses reported an act or threat of violence from patients within the past year. Units and outpatient facilities caring for the seriously mentally ill are far higher in this prevalence of violence toward staff. Involuntary units managed by nursing staff belonging to the Teamsters Union in California have considerably less violence toward staff than those managed by social services in Washington State; not coincidentally, malpractice damages are also capped in California and not in Washington.

It is curious that the health and safety of psychiatric staff, to say nothing of malpractice risk dealing with seriously disturbed patients, was not specifically addressed, other than, perhaps, in a backhanded way. Eliminating *imminent* could result in fewer serious injuries to the clinical staff. This staff is only vaguely, circumspectly, and indirectly referenced in the legislation as having the duty to assess clinical states of unremitting destructiveness.

It is also assumed that recruiting for such staff, whether medical, psychological, nurses, or mental health technicians, has no barriers in the alleged competition among hospitals to get a piece of this supposedly lucrative new market for care of involuntary commitment patients. In fact, legal spokesmen hailing the legislation specifically stated that concerns over hospitals using this liberalized legislation to solicit committed patients had to be considered in drafting this legislation. Concerns about loading financial rewards in both community service boards and lawyers were not mentioned, however, because these constituent parties dominated the process of drafting the legislation.

How the term *near future* will ultimately be defined by appeal after appeal to supreme courts across the land will have to wait. But unquestionably, it is unlikely that a shiner, whether on the face of a patient or ward staff member, will have to be presented to the magistrate anymore as evidence of imminent dangerousness. That is what I mean as one small step for man.

But, Bergeron (2008) holds up far higher expectations under Virginia's mental health reform.

> [The political declaration of consensus victory] continued as Democratic State Sen. Janet Howell and Republican State Delegate Phillip Hamilton, both members of the Commission on Mental Health Law Reform and leaders in services for behavioral health, agreed to introduce the governor's omnibus bills for mental health reform. The bills would bring the recommendations of the Virginia Tech Review Panel and the commission into a legal framework within the Code of Virginia. The omnibus bills clarified the ability to share vital information while preserving confidentiality and remaining in alignment with federal laws, including HIPAA and FERPA.

Other than the loss of Cho's guidance center triage records, these should never have been an issue in the Cho case from its beginning. Nor are they the problems that either Virginia Tech or any other college and university faces today to improve campus security while attending to students' medical and psychological needs.

Bergeron said, "Major roles and responsibilities for CSBs, the courts, facilities where individuals are detained involuntarily, and for independent examiners who recommend treatments to the courts were clarified in the bills." (Governor's Panel)

In fact, the credentialing process for independent examiners broadened authority for standards and oversight to be either at the discretion of CSB or with the courts. It is not clear which. But clinical experience and training do not appear to be considered more important for preventing man-made disasters on campus since the Virginia Tech massacre. Rather, alleged scarcity of resources in underserved areas of Virginia was, thus giving local CSBs more autonomy to set clinical standards for evaluators.

The medical profession of Virginia was assured that psychiatrists were never, and would not be, prohibited from participating in such emergency evaluative decisions, always requiring both the ruling in and out of medical medical/surgical diseases and psychiatric disorders. Otherwise, how can the primary criteria, "by reason of mental illness," be determined? Obviously, continuing at issue by circumspect omission here is just what mental illness is and who should define it, as well as how and by what standards. This takes us back to Milwaukee circa the late 1970s when the court agreed with the attorneys representing Lessard et al. that mental illness should not be medically determined, because the phenomenon termed *mental illness* had no scientific basis within contemporary medicine. The federal court in Wisconsin set a troublesome and confusing precedent, which legislatures, as in Virginia, and the courts that oversee them will be digging out from under for decades to come. In fact, what looked like a successful ruling for Lessard's attorneys has turned out to be a disaster for the seriously mentally ill and everyone having a stake in their lives and care, particularly about 20 million college students and their parents.

Commentators have praised the Virginia legislation because a section in the bill outlined a very specific mandatory outpatient commitment process. But committed patients are not required to take medications, even though nonadherence to psychotropics is both the single most common cause of emergency detention of the seriously mentally ill and one criterion separating the small minority of the homicidal seriously mentally ill patients from the vast majority who are not. Yet, apparently the State of Virginia believed that such a provision would narrow the legal definition of mental illness to actually requiring a diagnosis informing best practices and evidence-based medicine. It would also alienate some consumers, who are either currently taking psychotropic medications or did so previously. Many patients either cannot tolerate or simply do not like the effects of psychotropic medications, whether because they simply get brought down to reality from manic euphoria or experience side effects, and some side effects are really troublesome, i.e., sexual dysfunction. There are those patients who took older psychotropics who suffer adverse effects from them in the form of involuntary movement disorders. This is known as tardive dyskinesia. But the latter adverse reaction is now rare with the use of modern psychotropics and can be picked up early in treatment and prevented by switching to different medications.

Side effects require working with patients; most side effects can be ameliorated but that takes time and recognition on the part of the prescriber. Unfortunately, many patients drop out of treatment because of side effects, and that is a huge challenge for modern psychiatry. And, paranoid patients are very difficult to medicate because they are intolerant of someone else in control of their mind and feelings. As "consumers" they would probably be against the medical model of treating specific diagnoses with medications. So, right now diagnostic specificity accompanied by court-ordered medications is a very tough sell to the public—particularly consumers or family members active in the politics of treatment of mental illness who have not had good experiences with medications. The constant challenge is finding the balance between tolerability of side effects and risks of disastrous and endangering relapses without medication. Psychiatry is getting better at this; medications are getting much more tolerable without losing their effectiveness.

But the resistance to psychiatrists having court-ordered authority to administer medication to patients will be dependent on a specific diagnosis like schizophrenia remains considerable. Regardless of political reasons, right now, such specificity would stray way too far from *Lessard* and leave the term *diagnose* specifically undefined, if not ultimately undefinable.

Schizophrenia, from which Cho clearly suffered, requires antipsychotic medication, and with suicidal threats, most likely Clozaril for treatment. Bipolar disorder, on the other hand, requires mood stabilization, with addition of lithium to reduce suicide risk. Such specifics of evidence-based medicine for reducing disastrous outcomes in the management of the seriously mentally ill patient are glaringly absent from the commission report, thus losing an opportunity to actually reduce the risk of the massacre at Virginia Tech from occurring again, whether in Virginia or another state's campus.

Immediately following April 16, Governor Timothy Kaine named a panel of experts with broad powers, the Virginia Tech Review Panel, to conduct a thorough investigation of the tragedy. During those hearings, the poignant testimony from parents and families, even in their pain and grief, contained their overwhelming requests to ensure that within the public mental health system people receive the treatment they need. Perhaps, just perhaps, Virginia has begun the task of creating the most significant legacy to the individuals who died: a vital and dynamic system of mental health services.

The Virginia Tech Review Panel's August 2007 report made broad recommendations that included campus and law enforcement security procedures at state universities; mental health practices and procedures relating to emergency services, temporary detention, and civil commitment processes; needed legislative changes in information exchange; and improved coordination among involved agencies and the courts.

Cho Seung-Hui's family made his health and school records available to the panel (not to the public), which allowed for deeper insight and led to recommendations around information sharing and coordination of efforts between and within school systems. Amazingly, Cho did well with special accommodations in school and intensive and consistent counseling outside school hours during his school years in Fairfax County, well enough to be accepted by Virginia Tech.

Governor Kaine, in his initial response to the panel's report, publicly affirmed that community mental health services, when provided appropriately, work well. There was near universal acknowledgement that the public mental health system was severely underfunded. The governor stated that Virginia must be prepared to invest in community services that work and produce results. A legislative response from the Virginia General Assembly echoed the need for investment in such services.

As has been the history of most community mental health systems, Virginia's community system has not only been severely underresourced but, in hard economic times, a target for budget reductions or budget conversions. Such policy actions have been complicated given Virginia's stringent Medicaid eligibility criteria; Virginia has one of the country's least inclusive state systems for people with disabilities. More than twenty legislative studies conducted in Virginia, from the 1950s up to this century, reflect the same systemic issue: scarce and fragmented resources, and varying levels of these scarce resources across the commonwealth, contribute to an uneven and often piecemeal service system, even for mandated services.

> As the panel worked tirelessly on its report to Kaine, the Virginia Inspector General for Mental Health, Mental Retardation, and Substance Abuse Services, as well as the Commission on Mental Health Law Reform, initiated by the Virginia Supreme Court, were formulating reports and recommendations regarding reform. The commission, at work since 2006 through five well-organized task forces, included all stakeholders in its review of the entire process of involuntary civil detention and commitment. It is noteworthy but not surprising that the recommendations in all the reports were similar, if not identical, in terms of the needed legal reforms, services, clarity of roles and responsibilities, and changes in practice by courts, providers, public safety officials, facilities, and evaluators. (Bergeron, 2008)

Mary Ann Bergeron is a registered lobbyist for and executive director of the Virginia Association of Community Services Boards. One can see from their Web site (www.vacsb.org) that they are apparently flourishing financially (www.vacsb.org). But, again, it is not clear what relationship they—the ones vested with real capital—have with primary, secondary, and tertiary prevention of serious mental illness.

"Individuals with mental illness," Bergeron (2008) states,

> proved to be exceptional advocates and successfully convinced the General Assembly that language supporting recovery should be included in the final bills, as well as language that promoted consumer preferences for treatment. These advocates were not in favor of the broadened criteria for involuntary detention and commitment. Even though the new criteria were adopted, these individuals educated legislators and others about the potentially serious and permanent side effects of psychotropic medications and what it takes to engage people in the mental health system in a positive, voluntary way.

Thus, this legislation is popular with consumers of psychiatric services, but what about the large number of patients who are incapable of allying voluntarily with their physicians in either outpatient or inpatient treatment because they do not believe they need treatment? That cohort is where the Chos of this world live.

This legislation was not driven by conflicted and distressed patients who are fully competent mentally to make decisions about their treatment, whether for better or worse, and form therapeutic alliances with clinicians!

"Our shared goal is to intervene, engage, and stabilize individuals early; provide vehicles for adequate follow-up treatment; promote recovery-oriented services; and avoid individuals' cycling in and out of emergency rooms and psychiatric facilities," Bergeron (2008) continues.

These "frequent flyers" are in that revolving door because they simply cannot work within a therapeutic alliance, no matter how competent the therapist is. Recall that that is what turned their most vocal advocate, Laings, to medicate himself with alcohol as he sank into deeper despair. There are no specific statements of how diagnoses will be made, by whom, and for what purpose. Assuredly, regardless of legal, consumer, and bureaucratic interests and successful influences, the nearest emergency room is going to be ground zero for the foreseeable future, particularly now with budgetary deficits.

"Individuals with mental illness will be asked to take some responsibility for their own disease management and recovery" (Bergeron, 2008).

If they are so seriously mentally ill to need these services—yet, all but by definition, deny being in need of treatment—how will this be accomplished in the wake of the massacre at Virginia Tech?

"A massive training effort will be taking place, inclusive of every participant in the involuntary civil commitment process, to help in understanding changes and new parameters in the Code. Training cannot guarantee that interpretation and implementation will be as intended, but training will be of great assistance in achieving the intent of the legislation" (Bergeron, 2008).

This will be costly and financially beneficial to the training industry—already advertised on the Virginia Association of CSBs Web site. But, how, as is implied by Governor Kaine for America's college administrators, will trying to comprehend this legal text help any clinician in an emergency room setting diagnose and design clinical management of the next Cho Seung-Hui? How will such training help keep colleges safe and civil places to learn, instead of—increasingly—security compounds struggling with both students and faculty arming themselves?

> Despite the multiplicity of challenges Virginia faces, the vibrant and positive response to the Virginia Tech tragedy allows us the opportunity to create a lasting legacy to those who were slain, to their families, and to all the citizens of Virginia. We shall never forget what occurred at Virginia Tech on April 16, 2007, but we can be immensely proud of how the Tech family members and citizens demanded an improved public mental health system and how Virginia produced a stunning and positive response. (Bergeron, 2008)

Under Virginia's new mandatory outpatient treatment process CSB employee or designee must be present at each commitment hearing. For mandatory outpatient treatment (MOT) to be ordered, the person must desire to live in the community, must agree to receive treatment and adhere to the treatment plan, and have the ability to understand to what he/she is agreeing. Outpatient treatment, however, does not necessitate taking psychotropic medications. What else, besides long-acting and relatively well-tolerated and safe long-acting Risperdal injections work?

Regardless of the entity(ies) that provide services, the CSB must monitor and ensure that the person is adhering to the treatment plan. If the person under order is not adhering to the plan and the nonadherence is substantial in the CSB's judgment, the CSB must notify the court, and an evaluation can be ordered.

It is not explicitly stated, however, whether nonadherence to psychotropic medications or positive urine toxic drug screens are mandatory or negotiable with the patient in this law. How can anyone negotiate with a delusional patient? As the saying goes, "God does not need medicine." Assuming for the sake of argument that a delusional patient believes that he or she is God, will clinicians then be required to testify in court under cross-examination what he or she believes is God, and why this person—or "entity"—is not God? Of course, this might seem ludicrous when rational people are engaging rational people and even disagree, possibly with passion bordering on violence. But what about the rational person engaging the irrational person diagnosed as seriously mentally ill and dangerous? This latitude cited here, albeit seemingly just a matter of perception, as Bonnie would say, is wide enough to drive a truck through when it comes to mental health courts.

The disaster that is now recognized by states like Virginia, attempting to reform mental health, has many primary sources, one of the most significant elements of which is the neuropsychiatry of anosognosia, or the loss of awareness of one's own state of health and thus denial of obvious impairment. Following a stroke, Supreme Court Justice William Douglas became paralyzed on the left side. It is alleged that he denied his paralysis as a myth and continued to invite reporters on hiking expeditions with him. Of course, there is no attorney viewing this denial of neuropsychiatric reality who would advocate for Justice Douglas's taking up rock climbing against medical advice. What Mr. Bonnie refers to as a "case of variance between perceptions (which we need to correct) and reality" in response to the Virginia Psychiatric Association's lack of input into commission and panel work in the wake of the Virginia Tech massacre, therefore, is really that of diagnostic realities, not social, legal, economic, or political ones.

The neuropsychiatric denial of his own neurological impairment is accepted for stroke patient Douglas. The same denial is harder to accept by attorneys in the seriously mentally ill patient. As in the *Wisconsin v. Lessard* case, such denial can also be both an early source of trial experience and income for trial attorneys who ally with the patient's delusional state and take their mentally incompetent clients to court to spare them treatment, case management, and, in rare cases, longer term inpatient rehabilitative care.

It takes considerable psychiatric residency training, complete with numerous embarrassing failures, to recognize the smart patient's denial of reality in his own mad world. How then can attorneys recognize it without treating patients like this? Most legal advocates know precious little about psychiatric patients other than the popular psychology literature like Laings' *Myth of Mental Illness*. Tragically, as demonstrated in Virginia, does anyone currently in the legal and political system know anything about these psychiatric issues? As long as legislators stand before the TV cameras and make the case to their constituents that they have answers to the problem within the appropriate budgetary constraints, they believe they will have mollified the public. They will only have to answer to the public in the event of another Cho-type case at a public facility. Just as final comment, Bonnie reminds us that the law can always be changed again. Yes, after the next massacre, but, ideally, not to be on another college campus, particularly in Virginia!

Mary Ann Bergeron and Treatment Advocacy Center spokespersons challenge the hype and expected solutions to problems causing the Virginia Tech massacre. "Yet, even in the wake of the Virginia Tech tragedy and this flurry of legislative activity, the Virginia legislature made only incremental changes to Virginia's strict 'imminent danger' treatment standard" (Bergeron, 2008).

Treatment Advocacy

Ten years ago, there was no national organization uniquely dedicated to advocating for improved treatment laws and assisted outpatient treatment. The Treatment Advocacy Center (TAC) was created to fill that void. Initially started as part of the National Alliance for the Mentally Ill, the Treatment Advocacy Center was officially formed as an independent organization in 1998 and quickly grew to become a strong and influential force for changing state treatment laws and practices.

Today, the Treatment Advocacy Center looks back on a strong track record of success. Since the Treatment Advocacy Center was formed, eighteen states have made important changes to their treatment laws. Numerous states have adopted assisted outpatient programs. The Treatment Advocacy Center has assisted local communities in implementing assisted outpatient treatment programs. And thousands of families have received practical guidance from the Treatment Advocacy Center so that they could find needed help and resources for a loved one struggling with severe mental illness.

"A decade ago, there was reluctance—almost fear—to talk about assisted outpatient treatment for people with severe mental illness," says Treatment Advocacy Center founder Dr. E. Fuller Torrey. "That thinking has changed as the Treatment Advocacy Center has changed the terms of the debate" (personal communication, 2008).

The vision for forming the Treatment Advocacy Center was born out of Dr. Torrey's compassionate work with people with severe mental illness and his recognition of the impact of deinstitutionalization. "The policy of the 1950s and 60s to move people out of mental hospitals and into the community began with noble intentions but ultimately produced disastrous results," says Dr. Torrey. Witnessing increasing homelessness, incarcerations, victimization, and incidents of violence among people with untreated severe mental illness, Dr. Torrey became a strong voice for reform long before the Treatment Advocacy Center was formed.

People with untreated severe mental illness are the most obvious victims of our broken mental health system. The magnitude of personal and family tragedies brought about by deinstitutionalization and poor treatment laws is enormous. Today, 200,000 people with severe mental illness live among our homeless. Another 280,000 languish in prisons and jails. Each year, over 5,000 people with severe mental illness lose their lives through suicide.

Sadly, it is the tragedy that makes for headlines and prompts changes in policy. A few months after the Treatment Advocacy Center was established, the paths of two very different lives collided in a subway station in New York City. Andrew Goldstein, a lonely yet once promising student with untreated schizophrenia, had fallen through the cracks of system that did not hear his cries for help. One gloomy January night, he encountered Kendra Webdale, a bright, zestful person just starting to carve out her life in the big city. In a second, these lives were forever altered when Goldstein pushed Kendra Webdale off the platform and onto the tracks, where an incoming train abruptly ended her life.

"The outpouring of support to improve treatment laws in New York was almost instant," recalls Jonathan Stanley, longtime Treatment Advocacy Center attorney and current board member. Stanley was instrumental in spearheading reforms in New York and numerous other states. "Kendra's Law now lives as a tribute to our progress and as an important reminder that there is more work to be done," he said.

Kendra's Law wound its way through the New York State legislature with the strong support of Governor George Pataki and advocates throughout the state. The law makes assisted outpatient treatment much more widely available to people in New York. No longer must a person who is lost to severe mental illness be found to present an imminent danger to self or others in order to receive assisted treatment. It was implemented not only to help the patient but to help the patient's victims from his uncontrollable violent moods. We can only speculate how that program might have helped Cho and saved the lives of Emily Hilscher and his other victims.

"Kendra's Law is a template for change," says Treatment Advocacy Center executive director Kurt Entsminger. "Together with the Treatment Advocacy Center's Model Law for Assisted Treatment, it serves as a logical starting point for a state to reform treatment laws." Treatment Advocacy Center attorneys drafted the Model Law for Assisted Treatment in 2000 to promote standards that would allow for earlier and more effective intervention for the sickest of the sick. The Model Law was composed of provisions from various existing state laws that offered assisted treatment for people lost to severe mental illness who were too sick to recognize or respond to their own need for help.

According to Kurt Entsminger, the extensive work of the commonwealth commission and panel in the wake of the Virginia Tech massacre was almost entirely political, rather than the all-inclusive debate around facts so necessary while the Cho massacre was fresh in the public consciousness. It was, however, a missed opportunity to strengthen treatment laws. He cites the success of Kendra's Law as an example of assisted outpatient treatment for the rather small but highest risk cohort of the seriously mentally ill from which apocalyptic suicide and mass murder are most likely to emerge and the identification of individuals within this cohort. Oftentimes these are patients with anosognosia who cannot see the need for medication and may even convince legislators—certainly attorneys—that it should be their choice as consumers. Kendra's Law has worked spectacularly—the State Office of Mental Health reported this year on those placed under an initial six-month court order under the law: 77 percent fewer were hospitalized in the half year after the treatment mandate than were in the six months before it. And 85 percent fewer experienced homelessness, 83 percent fewer were arrested, and 85 percent fewer were incarcerated.

Patients need diagnoses, so that dilemma was left in perpetual ambiguity with which clinicians will continue to struggle, with little support, every night, every weekend, and holidays, too. Most experienced hospital psychiatrists know how active the seriously mentally ill become when the sun goes down and the structure of city life recedes on Friday afternoon. So, what is the purpose of involuntary outpatient treatment as a condition for students like Cho to remain on campus?

Tragically, we must endure the excruciating wait to find out, but meanwhile Kendra's Law seems to be far more than one step for man and a real leap forward for mankind, if not a giant one.

In a statement issued by Treatment Advocacy Center Executive Director Kurt Entsminger, Esq. comments that Virginia's commitment law raises many questions

> Virginia should instead adopt a more progressive standard, such as the one developed by the Commission's Task Force on Commitment. That standard allows someone to be placed under a treatment order if he or she is "unable to comprehend the nature of his illness," is "substantially affected by his illness" and will, absent treatment, "continue to suffer a substantial deterioration in his previous ability to function in the community."

Virginia Must Adopt Kendra's Law

> Kendra's Law is court-ordered community treatment—a less restrictive, remarkably effective, and far less costly alternative to hospitalization. Current Virginia law requires someone to meet the inpatient hospitalization standard before they

can be court-ordered to outpatient treatment. This makes the current law largely unusable because community treatment is not for those who are imminently dangerous.

A better choice is a law like New York's Kendra's Law. Of those in that program:

- 74% fewer experienced homelessness;
- 77% fewer experienced psychiatric hospitalization;
- 83% fewer experienced arrest; and
- 87% fewer experienced incarceration.

Senate Bill 177 is a version of Kendra's Law. (Entsminger, January 25, 2008)

In the *Insanity Offense*, Fuller Torrey (2008) wrote

> The Treatment Advocacy Center remains poised to spearhead more legal reforms and to promote improved treatment practices over the next decade. The Treatment Advocacy Center will also continue to offer practical assistance to families who seek assisted treatment for loved ones lost to severe mental illness. Operating on a budget of just under one million dollars a year, the Treatment Advocacy Center today employs a professional staff of 9 people and supports a network of thousands of local advocates across the nation.

"Finally," according to Bergeron (2008), "the omnibus bills proposed a major change in the criteria for involuntary detention and inpatient/outpatient commitment. Virginia code prior to July 1, 2008, had required that the person 'presents an imminent danger to himself or others as a result of mental illness or is so seriously mentally ill as to be substantially unable to care for himself.'"

As of July 1, 2008, the language of the code lowers the evidentiary bar for involuntary commitment to "substantial likelihood that, in the near future, he or she will cause serious physical harm to himself or herself or another person or will suffer serious harm due to substantial deterioration of his or her capacity to protect himself or herself from such harm or to provide for his or her basic human needs."

The liability issue for physicians and nurses alike, both of whom must carry personal malpractice insurance to work on these involuntary detention wards, will not be relieved for now. Physicians in Virginia still have an equal liability risk for violating patients' rights by excessive detention beyond the vaguely defined "near future" as they always have had for discharging a dangerous patient who commits an assault or suicide in the near future. Nothing will change on that score, until a body of decisions is accumulated in the common law. But, by that time it will again be time for another commission somewhere, responding to another man-made disaster like the massacre at Virginia Tech.

Clinicians, as in the case of Cho, will continue to be forced to think like lawyers, rather than be encouraged to use their best clinical judgment based on thorough assessment of the patient. Such assessment must follow known best practices, recognizing that they never have enough information about the patient. Less is not best, as was the tragic lesson learned in Blacksburg; most is best, as previously cited from the literature of Lawrence Weed, M.D. The school rule of forensic medicine will almost always trump all other overlying redundancy in rules, laws, and regulations, most of which are contradictory and untested in supreme courts for their validity. Sound and well-documented clinical judgment will always prevail in a court of law, regardless of which professionals spend hours and millions of dollars learning the nuances of Virginia's new commitment law, much of which could be overturned in any major case by any court in the land, including Virginia's.

Thus, when it comes to both the safety and well-being of the obviously sick patient and the public's commensurate safety, good clinical judgment will win out in the end. That is nowhere as true as it is on school campuses, where, as the settlements against the commonwealth clearly establish, administration has a degree of stewardship responsibility for its residents beyond that of the mayor outside the gate for his streets. To what degree, we do not as yet know, because these millions of dollars of Virginia Tech settlements are not open to scrutiny. Furthermore, in today's high-risk malpractice environment, wherein only California and a couple of other states have been able to maintain caps on malpractice awards after recurrent challenges in state supreme courts, nurses and physicians alike have to take responsibility for their own professional fortunes.

"Nobody is going to look out for you in this system," is the most common legendary advice on the floor where veteran clinicians try to take care of the seriously mentally ill patient. While on the fly under pressure of both throughput and the court's schedule, trumping clinical demands, they must both know and respect literally minute-by-minute patient rights—from raising bedrails to prevent their falling out of bed—a form of restraint—to tranquilizing them when escalating to point of being threatening as reported the previous night. They must take courses in self-defense and learn how to block punches to the groin or choking, until the court determines that a consumer who is now confined for 14 days under a California hearing 5250 (Detention of patient on probable cause of harm to self or others) is actually a patient requiring medication. In California, 5250 is essentially a detention order petition after an initial 72-hour involuntary detention in which the psychiatrist must go before a judge and establish with clear and convincing evidence that the patient following involuntary detention for 72 hours on probable cause remains dangerous to others, to self, or both, or is so gravely disabled he cannot meet the needs of sustaining life, namely, necessary nutrition, housing and protection from weather, i.e., clothing if freezing cold.

Oftentimes, these patients, as in California, retain their rights to refuse medications, even when detained. To administer medications on schedule for their own safety and that of others, attending psychiatrists must prove with clear and convincing evidence that, unless medicated, harm will come to themselves or others.

A lawyer, not a trained physician, will make the final decision. In California, this is known as "Riesing" the threatening or agitated patient who refuses scheduled medication. Until then, the detained person remains a consumer rather than a patient. That is, he either buys the medication or refuses to buy it, in effect creating a de facto, if not de juro, consumerism. Riesing is the acronym for filing a petition with the court to get authority to administer medication to a patient determined too dangerous to self or others or gravely disabled; it follows receipt of authority to detain for two weeks under 5250.

Had anyone in decision-making positions during this legislative and political process ever have to take a 5250 case before a magistrate in California to get a detained person Riesed as a patient? Of course, this sounds rather nitpicky, but that is what the world of involuntary emergency inpatient psychiatry has become today. There are very few hospitals and medical staffs, contrary to Mr. Bonnie's concerns, who want anything to do with having such units on their campuses; certainly the Arizona hospital with the consumer who ran away and jumped off the freeway bridge decided that it did not. The injured victims of this consumer, merely driving on the freeway, decided that he was no consumer. He was a patient!

Forensic medical expert Aaron Beck, M.D., informs us that *Tarasoff*, like its converse, imminent risk, can likewise be overvalued in the real world of actual case law. But, the intent of the Supreme Court of California remains paramount. Any physician is expected to have special knowledge and power to control his patient's disease process as in contagious infectious diseases.

Physicians, therefore, above all else, are expected to use good judgment and common sense when exercising such duties as diagnosing serious mental illness, communicating with relevant parties to the case, developing a treatment plan based on best practices, and either further detaining or discharging the patient. Also, how that patient is discharged and to whom and for what are the attending physician's responsibility. To ignore the Supreme Court of California's admonitions and its intent in *Tarasoff* is to fly a plane without either instruments or weather reports.

Dr. Beck would agree that his reassurances about risk of being sued under *Tarasoff* could be a premature announcement of its death as either legal precedent or even creatively extended to progeny. For example, was the consumer who ran out of the hospital's psychiatric emergency service (PES) before being evaluated really a consumer, or was he a patient under the control of a physician; in this case, likely the medical director, who, probably, like most others, read it in the next day in the newspaper.

As Dr. Rea predicted as a result of *Lessard*, courts in Wisconsin have to react to involuntary commitment challenges by the patient as if the mentally ill patient is criminalized and his or her rights are being denied. However, ironically, the law facilitates efficiencies for psychiatrists and county prosecuting attorneys to extend a probable cause chapter for detention beyond 72 hours. The initial 72-hour hold is necessarily initiated by "chaptering," which must be performed within Wisconsin's criminalization paradigm by local police. It is well known by judges in smaller communities just which facilities and psychiatrists can be trusted for their opinions regarding diagnosis and assessment of dangerousness. Thus, it is no longer the law itself, still particularly medieval in Wisconsin, that creates the barrier. The barrier is, as Rea reminds us, healthcare access.

Of considerable concern in northern Wisconsin is the fact that the Catholic hospital system, filling the vacuum left by exiting of community mental health centers and state hospitals alike, frequently shares actual turf with major university campuses. That is the case in Eau Claire, Wisconsin, home to both a Third Order Regular of St. Francis Sisters of Sacred Heart Involuntary Inpatient Psychiatry Unit and the University of Wisconsin-Eau Claire. Although seemingly ideal, the problem is lack of clinical staff for 24/7 psychiatric specialty coverage, adequately staffed beds, and follow-up outpatient resources, already jammed to capacity with appointments strung out with longer and longer intervals between. More patients enter outpatient care, whereas few are officially discharged to make more beds available. Staffing, however, is not funded to keep up with increased patient flow within channels. Credentialing is liberalized, allowing less expensive prescribers to replace psychiatrists, and the health information systems technology is among the best in the world. But no psychiatric clinician in northwestern Wisconsin would dare say that they are staying ahead of the surge in critically ill psychiatric patients within an arena from which the State of Wisconsin has all but totally withdrawn.

Psychiatrists must carry huge loads of seriously mentally ill patients or simply resign and go elsewhere to avoid facing disciplinary action. Not surprisingly, recruitment in such areas, where the state is least visible in caring for its wards of the court, increasingly depends on foreign medical graduates with green cards. They fill the gap silently for fear of immigration and naturalization complaints from the ERs and hospital administration. The Wisconsin State Supreme Court did not help recruiting by eliminating the capping of malpractice awards. The result was that doctors did not want to come to Wisconsin to expose themselves to the possibilities of runaway juries imposing Draconian medical malpractice awards on plaintiffs. The drop in solicitations for recruitment was for internists and surgical specialists. It is now far worse in psychiatry where practitioners are caught between the catch-22 of punitive damages under *Lessard* and multiple damage awards under *Tarrasof.* Child psychiatrists must be given special protection from recruiting by assuring them freedom from the on-call roster of hospitals filling the vacuum in care for the seriously mentally ill by the State of Wisconsin. That leaves 24/7 care to a handful of the willing, who must exceed the hours permitted for resident psychiatrists in training or quietly resign to avoid desecration of their professional credentials. This applies only to U.S. citizens. For foreign medical graduates, it is more dangerous to buck the inhumane call schedules, because there are worse places than northwestern Wisconsin, including deportation home.

But the state is there with prisons. Wisconsin prisons are swollen with the seriously mentally ill. Disgusted cops simply drop off people they believe should be hospitalized, thus paralyzing emergency room services. ERs in turn dictate throughput—administrative bureauspeak for discharging—to psychiatrists just to get patients out of their ER beds. Medical clearance is neglected because psychiatry units are staffed by medical personnel at least on paper. Such internal dumping of the nonmedically cleared confused patient into already crowded 72-hour hold units like that of St. Albans where Cho was admitted simply compounds the problem (*Lean Management of Healthcare, King County Medical Society Bulletin*). Every day is a roll of the dice, as hospitals try to simply survive without a headline catastrophic event to attract the local TV cameras. Northwestern Wisconsin is simply harder hit than most, but most likely it is, like rural Virginia, extremely vulnerable to the man-made disasters of Virginia Tech.

Moreover, emergency service transport, oftentimes burdened by rejection from one hospital ER to another, is known to simply open ambulance doors for chaptered patients demanding their freedom after futile rides of hours, dodging dangerous deer through the Northwoods roads. Who knows where they go, but at night it is hard to see in either dense woods or cornfields, where chaptered patients can easily disappear from sight and hopefully live for another day—and, inevitably, another admission when a bed opens up—that is, if they survive as psychiatric patients and do not convert to DOAs or med-surg lifetime cripples for nursing homes or felons for prison while AWOL from being chaptered.

What this means is that for all the seemingly well-thought-out arguments in the *Lessard* pleadings and the learned opinion of the court, there are, in Norman Mailer's words, invisible "armies of the night" of the mentally ill overflowing onto our streets, living in dumpsters, committing almost casual violent acts to score a few bucks for their next meals, and, in more than a few cases, committing murders with little understanding of the reality of their crimes or the consequences. And who will the court in California hold responsible for violent acts by the mentally ill previously under the custodianship of a special care mental health practitioner? The psychiatrist. Thus, very loosely put, what *Lessard* giveth, *Tarrasof* taketh away.

It was the *Lessard* court that built the atomic bomb wrecking public care of the seriously mentally ill in Wisconsin. The bombs, however, were dropped by state treasuries who rapidly found new sources of revenue for discretionary general funds by transferring responsibility for care of the seriously mentally ill to federally funded Medicaid. Dr. Kellerman reports kneeling and praying in the parking lot at Grady Hospital before starting his ER shift. He now fights for the life of ER, because Medicaid funding is also shriveling up. The Wisconsin Department of Corrections now finds the cost of antipsychotic medications a critical budget item, paying millions for Seroquel in one year alone. Prisoners not needing it now have access to Seroquel and find ways to shoot it up for a high.

In an article in *Current Psychiatry*, Editor-in-Chief Henry Nasrallah, M.D., introduces the March 2008 issue by crying out, "Bring back the asylums? The tragic consequences of deinstitutionalization."

> One of psychiatry's so-called triumphs was the discovery of antipsychotics (starting with chlorpromazine in the 1950's) and the ensuing release of the seriously mentally ill into the community. State hospitals were rapidly evacuated, and patients supplied with the new "miracle drugs" were relabeled as "clients" or "consumers" as if they did not have severe medical illnesses. Asylums that had offered medical care reputably and safely were doomed to the trash heap of psychohistory.
>
> How naïve we were. As we discovered, antipsychotics are so limited in efficacy and tolerability that most patients eventually stop taking them and relapse, leading to recurrent hospitalizations. Little did we know, although Kraeplin had warned us that schizophrenia's disability is caused not by psychosis (as in hallucinations and delusions) but by severe cognitive deficits and negative symptoms that neuroleptics fail to reverse.
>
> They may have regained their civil rights when they left the institutions, but they could not effectively exercise those rights. Left to their own devices, [as in the case of Cho Seung-Hui] they were expected to become independent and autonomous, but many were too cognitively disabled to do so. The results, in my opinion, have been tragic, inhumane, and disastrous for the 3 million Americans who have schizophrenia. Yet I'm perplexed that there is no public outrage about the misery of these seriously mentally ill individuals. Consider deinstitutionalization's unintended consequences. (Nasrallah, 2008)

Dr. Nasrallah cites homelessness, incarceration, poverty, substance abuse, and crime—the five deadly sins of antipsychiatry—all disproportionately as perpetrators and as victims. He cites medical illness, poor access to primary care, early mortality, loss of social relationships and stability, and social disability and stigma as contributors to a mental health crisis in America, a country that has, in all but name, turned its back on its growing mentally ill population. As Dr. Nasrallah states, "Yesterday's state hospitals have morphed into today's jails and prisons. Correctional facilities are bulging with mentally ill inmates, and I don't think they are receiving better care than in the old asylums. Their illness behaviors have been criminalized and deemed illegal, because they live in the community, not in a medical facility" (Nasrallah, 2008).

Yet, despite the acknowledged foolhardiness embodied in the Wisconsin court decision on *Lessard*, attorneys, led by powerful advocates for legal, rather than medical, control of the most serious schizophrenic and bipolar disorders, hang on and continue to institutionalize the criminalization of these clearly neuropsychiatric disorders. Not apparently wishing to return to earth and start over, Virginia's memorial to the victims and survivors of the massacre at Virginia Tech was little more than a face lift to preserve the status quo that Nasrallah cites. Is Dr. Nasrallah simply trying to feather his nest, having devoted his entire career to treatment and research on schizophrenia? Would he be a person worth consulting in the wake of Virginia Tech's man-made disaster, following on the heels of a massacre with fewer killed in action and wounded in action at Northern Illinois University? He would be the last person, it appears, from whom those proclaiming victory in the wake of the Virginia Tech massacre would wish to hear.

Nasrallah continues,

> Deinstitutionalization [took place] because society's good intentions were guided by legalisms and sociologic notions, rather than scientific principles. Serious mental disorders are neurobiologic diseases that severely limit independent function. Until effective treatments are found for schizophrenia's cognitive deficits (like dyfunctioning neurocircuitry of the parietal lobe of the brain in anosognosmia) and negative symptoms (like associated dysfunctional neurocircuitry of the prefrontal cortex), we should seek a more humane model of care. We should be bold enough to restore comprehensive long term health facilities where patients' mental and physical illnesses can be stabilized and then can achieve supervised autonomy through evidence-based biopsychosoical and rehabilitative therapies. (Nasrallah, 2008)

Even though courts of law are driven, as they must be, by legal principles, still one of the most respected models of such care was Northern State Hospital in Washington, whose doors were slammed shut—once again, as recently the case in Virginia—with total disregard for the medical associations of Washington (Liebert, 1982) "And institutional mode of care is rational for at least some persons with schizophrenia who are suffering under a politically correct system of care. Without medically driven care, the misery will continue."

Just tour West Seattle and Harborview Involuntary Treatment Units to witness how Governor Evans's budget cutters in Olympia successfully shifted the cost of care for the seriously mentally ill from the Department of Social and Health Services to the State Department of Corrections and federally subsidized Medicaid. Of interest is the new administration's trial balloon for doing the same for combat veterans. Does nobody recall the riots on the Capitol steps following World War I, which were the impetus for building veterans hospitals? The issue is different, but the political attitude remains the same. Psychiatric care is an expense that can simply be eliminated within the shell game called mental health law and behavioral health administration. The hands of politicians, lawyers, and their accountants, without doubt, are quicker than the eye.

Most significantly and most regressive in mental health reform, as in Virginia's legislative compromise, is its carefully steering clear of and obfuscating any clear and convincing evidence of neuropsychiatric specificity and commensurate demands for valid diagnostics to direct effective treatment. By continuing to promote ambiguity by retaining serious mental illness—what is that?—and achieving a renaming of state institutions devoted to it—behavioral health versus mental health—neuropsychiatric research is shortchanged in favor of psychosocial and legal fixes that are more of the same failed solutions of the past but now dressed up in new garb. This is one of the main issues that the Treatment Advocacy Center has with the final product from Richmond: the failure to identify a tiny percentage of the most seriously mentally ill with anosognosia and robustly demonstrated history of assault, as well as inability to control aggressive impulses, both toward self and others.

For example, is a patient recurrently walking on the freeway because she thinks she is a skin walker—thus transcendant from her body—a danger to self, others, or gravely disabled with grandiose delusions and anosognosia? Or is this person deep within a hallucinatory state after ingesting psilocybin in some form but otherwise not psychotic? Within the paradigm of criminalization of serious mental illness, it is the police officer's responsibility in Milwaukee to take care of this dangerous deviancy. Milwaukee police, as a result of the *Lessard* holding, oftentimes have to intervene with these patients at enormous and unnecessary risk to life and limb, including their own.

There is not a day that goes by in Milwaukee hospitals that one such patient is not in the revolving doors of Wisconsin's involuntary treatment system. There continues, despite these recurrent tragedies and treacherous events, a strong reluctance to acknowledge the grave intellectual error that was the foundation of *Wisconsin-Lessard*. The patient walking on the freeway simply did not learn that from her family, church, or school. She does not do it with free will. She has a delusion that tells her that cars can go through her with no threat of injury to self or others. She is, of course, seriously mentally ill. She is also, more specifically, suffering from the neuropsychiatric disease of schizophrenia and only has a chance of surviving and staying out of the road if required to take antipsychotic medications. Failing that, she must reside in the protected environment of the state hospital. If, however, she fails treatment in Milwaukee, she will more likely end up dead or convicted of negligent homicide and sent to prison.

Where is the Wisconsin Bar Association in all of this? Certainly they can see this failure in administrative law and the failure of the political system to provide a safety net for the seriously mentally ill. Lawyers, as officers of the court, certainly do have a responsibility to protect everyone's rights, including this woman's rights. But what are those rights? Does her constitutional right to due process under the Fifth Amendment trump her constructive right to keep on living? Do her constitutional rights obviate the obligation of the state to provide her protection under the law from anyone who threatens that right, including herself? Should there be a form of a *Miranda* ruling for those too mentally ill to understand and exercise their rights to due process? And who protects the public at large from the mentally ill?

One might argue that at a most basic level what protects the mentally ill from themselves and what protects the public from them is the state's own criminal code. On the surface, it is not hard to figure out. If a mentally ill patient is acting up in a way that endangers others, the court steps in and restrains that person until the person can be released back into the public. If the person cannot understand the criminal proceedings and is incompetent to assist in his or her own defense, the person can be declared incompetent to stand trial and held in an institution until competent. If a person commits a crime and is deemed to be insane—a defense to criminal prosecution in which the person admits the crime but denies that he or she willfully committed it—the person, like would-be presidential assassin John Hinckley, is remanded to a mental institution.

The principle behind this is basic to our entire system of criminal law. In order for a defendant to be found guilty of a crime, the prosecution must prove beyond a reasonable doubt that the defendant is guilty of every element of that crime. The person, at base, must have had an intent to commit the crime, called *mens rea*, a guilty mind, and the person must have actually committed the crime, called *actus reus*, a guilty act. All well and good on the surface. But what about Cho Seung-Hui? What about Lessard? The problem is not in the theory behind the law but in the application of the law to the mentally ill, who cannot have a guilty mind by reason of insanity. Thus, if Cho was acting out a hallucination, an ideation of apocalyptic suicide, as if he were walking through a dream state, and he was brought to trial because his self-inflicted wound was not fatal, he would have to show a jury that he was insane because he could not tell right from wrong or that even if he could tell right from wrong, his mental disease prevented him from doing what was right. But how does all this apply to the Lessards and Chos of the world who rely on their rights to due process before their personal freedom can be taken away? Where does this fit under the *Lessard* ruling?

First of all, and especially at a time when public healthcare is at the top of the political agenda, the state and should protect the rights of the mentally ill to get them treatment, to protect them from themselves, and to protect the public from them. Secondly, a mentally ill patient can always sue in the event that she is in fact treated with excessive restraint, whether physical, as in walls, bars, and leather, or medications, like Thorazine, still used to tranquilize the excited patient in hospitals. Finally, she can sue if she gets the wrong treatment that results in harm to body and psyche not caused by the disease itself. For example, hardly any patient today should acquire tardive dyskinesia, a neurological syndrome caused by the long-term use of neuroleptic drugs to control various psychotic symptoms. Its symptoms include repetitive and purposeless involuntary body movements and facial movements such as overt jaw movements, chewing without food, grimacing, tongue protrusion, lip smacking, and leg jerking. The disease is now a rarity with novel antipsychotics and has become a tragic relic of older days of rougher drugs and worse prescribing practices.

Funding was mandated for research into causation of behavioral emergencies under the original Emergency Medical Services Act in the 1970s, but that element was never funded in favor of circulatory illnesses and major trauma. Similarly, such neglect extends through commitment reform that both acknowledges behavioral emergencies and mandates changes in their management, while continuing to neglect research into causation, as mandated in the EMS Act. Leadership at institutions of higher learning can take the lead to lobby for funding of research into behavioral emergencies mandated in the EMS Act giving us Medic One.

Dr. Kellerman is trying to keep emergency rooms open for life-threatening medical-surgical emergencies and preparedness for attacks with unconventional weapons of mass destruction, all but promised by our federal government to occur in the foreseeable future. But he does not appear to be one of those rare ER docs who is dedicated to alleviating the grossly inappropriate referral and clogging of our ERs with the seriously mentally ill patient. The woman in Milwaukee who walks on the freeway should do it once only, not twice, or even several times. Every time she does it she unwittingly adds to the intolerable stresses to our ERs, in both the time she takes for ER care awaiting scarce disposition of involuntary treatment and injuries caused to self and others by her insanity.

Rebutting both state and national psychiatric experts, Mr. Bonnie states,

> There is a shortage of beds in some parts of the state [of Virginia], but not in most regions. Increasing the number of places for people who need beds would help, but beds in crisis-stabilization facilities may be an alternative to acute hospitalization for some individual who are now being admitted to emergency rooms and hospitals for evaluations. Those services would be enhanced by a "major part" of the additional $42 million budgeted for mental health, so that impatient rates would rise less than some fear. (Bonnie, 2008)

It is unclear what Mr. Bonnie's authority is to make such a statement, never assumably having been on call in such a hospital facility or performing the emergency clinical decision making involved in such cases. The seriously mentally ill are more active at night, placing a lot of strain on the on-call specialists after hours and on weekends and holidays. Orthopedic surgeons in some cities charge $1,000 just to be on call! After all, it may be your hip being replaced in the morning, and one wants a surgeon who has not been working all night. Beds covered 24/7 by resident psychiatrists in training, restricted to 30 consecutive hours of work and supported by second-call attending supervising psychiatrists, are available in Richmond and suburbs of DC and Charlottesville, because those are academic medicine centers. So, this is apples to oranges for communities supporting colleges such as Virginia Tech or its equally vulnerable University of Wisconsin-Eau Claire.

Not being the last hospital in America to have an on-call schedule, as one medical director recently remarked in Phoenix, is the rule rather than the exception these days for all departments of emergency medicine. That is just one reason we have lost over 20 percent of emergency department beds. This is ironic since the surge of interest in disaster medicine following 9/11. More have been shut down since the next surge of interest in the wake of Katrina. It is naïve to simply assume that emergency departments of any hospital are desirous of—or even willing to have—crisis beds. And, if they do, they do not want triaging to occur without medical clearance. That means more demands on already overloaded ERs and their staff, whose increasing load from the seriously mentally ill patients contributes to their financial vulnerability under the axe of hospital CFOs.

Both the naïveté and neglect of valid diagnosis in Bonnie's response to complaints of the Virginia Psychiatric Association must be addressed. No doubt, crisis stabilization beds in ERs will begin the repair caused by concomitant destruction of state inpatient and outpatient care of the seriously mentally ill in the last fifty years. Certainly some ERs or ER docs might be saved with such beds, but Bonnie fails to address the nature of the problem. Validity of diagnosis is not only that nosological entity—that is, acute psychosis with alcohol abuse and schizophrenic disorder, paranoid type—that best predicts outcome and directs effective acute care intervention, it also must have stability over time. Also, the majority of schizophrenic patients deteriorate over time, particularly when diagnosed late. This was Cho's case, which was inadequately treated over the lifetime of the disorder. The lack of a valid diagnosis and appropriate treatment appeared to be the beginning of Cho Seung-Hui and his family's fate with chaotic and sloppy case management in 2006–2007.

Mr. Bonnie may refer to metropolitan regions of Virginia with access to colleges of medicine that have in-house staff available on call for the emergency rooms functioning as initial points of care in emergency detention. This is most important in the apparent first psychotic break, likely with this disease to initially occur for students while they are on campus. The reason for this is the course of the schizophrenic illness, oftentimes showing no behavioral problems until the early twenties, the very time they are on campus without any psychiatric history.

It is not coincidental that emergency medical services were determined to be average or below in all states with the exception of Massachusetts, Connecticut, California, and Washington, DC All of these states received a mid- to low B, and part of the state's region to which Bonnie refers can be considered metro DC. All these regions of our nation are disproportionately rich in medical colleges that have in-house resident on-call specialty staffs, including psychiatry. They make up a tiny area of this nation, even considering California, whose many colleges of medicine are concentrated in metropolitan areas. Virginia Tech is not in such a region, nor is Northern Illinois University, also victim to rampage murder and suicide.

To assume, then, that richly funding CSBs to solve the operational crisis of the seriously mentally ill at the furthest point of intervention downstream—that is literally terminal tertiary prevention—is not well informed regarding the current state of healthcare delivery in this country. Furthermore, for a victory touted to be this enormous for all Americans in the wake of the Virginia Tech tragedy risks further dehumanization of victims of what already is a social disaster affecting millions of patients, their families, and their communities, including school campuses.

Assuming there are considerable monies to be spent on crisis intervention services, just where in Virginia or anywhere in this nation other than big city hospitals or medical teaching centers are these beds to be placed to rescue the terminal bodies before they float out to sea? The last bridge, the ER, as can be seen, is crumbling, too, and about to collapse itself. The last thing ER docs want in hospitals not already swamped by the seriously mentally ill is likely a crisis unit demanding more of their own medical resources. These patients cannot simply be recycled through crisis beds without considerable investment of emergency medicine resources. These patients have to be seen by an ER physician before diversion to crisis beds. So again, back to earth. This legislation is designed, either by intent or inadvertent oversight, to shove further downstream, under broken bridges and jammed locks, instead of courageously heading upstream where the problem began in the first place, which is the criminalization of the seriously mentally ill and resultant closure of psychiatric systems for their care.

It is the unfortunate legacy of sweeping court decisions based on the known falsehoods of Monahan's earliest quantitative modeling of clinical discharge planning, supported by antipsychiatry philosophies of both Szacz and Laings, that treatment of the seriously mentally ill patient is institutionalized within court empowered systems of lawyers and social services rather than medical doctors. Of course, as this legacy repeatedly returns to bite us with rampage murders by the suicidal seriously mentally ill, as it coincidentally did during the process of commitment law reform in Virginia within the wake of Cho's killing spree, nothing really changes at the point of care, other than public perception.

Psychiatrists and clinical psychologists are not going to be more thorough in their workups than they were at St. Albans Hospital with Cho because the law now permits them to predict violence further out into the future than simply, as Cho proved he could do, getting safely off the hospital grounds without killing self or others. How many hours, days, or months are near future? Furthermore, what graduate of doctorate programs in either medicine or psychology is going to pursue such nonsensical gambling with his or her own future and body? Curiously, for a legally driven solution, malpractice risk is not mentioned once in this legislation. MDs, whether psychiatrists or GPs, are successfully sued as often for holding a patient not considered dangerous as they are for releasing one who proves to be dangerous.

In one exemplary case, a woman named Susan was tasered by city police for resisting arrest when threatening fellow shoppers in a strip mall. She was involuntarily administered medications on an emergency basis after detention at a university-affiliated county facility. She was diagnosed and treated by three different psychiatrists, all of whom held university medical college appointments, and all of whom documented the same robust psychopathology of both acute manic psychosis and total denial of illness, or anosognosmia. As an arrestee, she was held in custody during these diagnoses.

After her discharge, she retained counsel, who strongly believed her case and wanted to sue the police, doctors, and hospital. Hospital and police records all aligned and documented the same behavioral emergency: psychosis with dangerousness. Counsel's reviewing psychiatrist advised him not to pursue the case, however, and refunded his professional retainer. Counsel complied with his expert's opinion and did not pursue the case. Although this attorney listened to the advice of his psychiatric expert to not pursue an action that he now believed was either frivolous or would constitute a violation of model rules of the state bar association because he knew that his client was filing false charges against the defendants, other attorneys do pursue these cases. Some of these cases are very likely legitimate, particularly back in the days when there was little judicial oversight or funding problems for involuntary hospitalizations. The obverse of this coin, of course, is the previously discussed *Tarasoff* ruling, wherein a patient was released without a warning to the threatened party.

The point is, contrary to Mr. Bonnie's expressed concerns, psychiatrists have little motivation—certainly not monetary—to hold patients against their will. In fact, they are well advised by risk management of their hospitals not to do so for equal threats of being sued for violating patients' rights as failing professional duty to protect society due to their peculiar ability, as cited by the California Supreme Court. Brasington (2008) alleges that psychiatrists and other medical groups were removed from the legislative process in Virginia, as well as from positions of authority in involuntary commitment to "eliminate the appearance of financial conflict of interest should patients be committed to the doctor's own facility." This possibility is remote, however, because facilities often lose money on the care of involuntary patients, and doctors are not reimbursed for the time spent at hearings.

In addition, doctors are not reimbursed for their time on call, which in some places, like Wisconsin post-*Lessard*, can be up to 4 straight days and nights without relief. Although MDs in training are subject to the restrictions of 30 consecutive hours of duty without guaranteed rest, no such provision applies to psychiatrists on call for hospitals accepting involuntary patients. It is doubtful that more than one or two of the hundreds of parties involved in the decisions made by the legislature, including Mr. Bonnie, have either been on such call or even witnessed what not only promotes medical errors but risks serious health problems, as do violent and unsupervised patients, from serial nights of sleep deprivation without daytime relief on regular duty.

As Kurt Entsminger from the Treatment Advocacy Center stated, the opportunity to return from space to earth with bold reforms was lost, leaving the state only "having one of the worst mental illness mandatory treatment laws in the nation to merely having a bad law" (Entsminger, 2008). This is not a matter of perceptual gaps between social services embodied within CSBs and lawyers versus psychiatrists and other MDs, both personally responsible and professionally liable for this population. It is maximum feasible misunderstanding of urgent demands for primary, secondary, and tertiary prevention of serious mental illness.

Without resources for valid diagnosis of these millions of seriously mentally ill people, how can there be effective clinical intervention, either from the earliest evidence of the illness or way too late, when there is full-blown psychosis that inevitably predicts progressive deterioration without intensive treatment and case management? It appears that Mr. Bonnie believes that Band-Aids are enough, but for what? Band-Aids are enough for a clean cut on a limb that does not damage nerves or vessels or portend infectious wound complications. But is it enough if the femur is broken too? That causes life-threatening hemorrhage. What is the difference? It appears to be the massive involvement of the legal profession in micromanagement of psychiatric illness, court-based maintenance of the system broken by bad judicial decisions, and now its inability to withdraw from the mess created. It must be withdrawal, that is, with legal safeguards of patient rights still protected by proper judicial oversight and continued risk management from massive tort liability, unique to the United States.

What is hailed as a fitting memorializing of those lost and traumatized by the apocalyptic suicide and mass murder of Cho Seung-Hui changes the lexicology of a statistical models. Monahan apparently approves of near future as opposed to imminent predictability of violence even though he has never been in the position to have to do either. The lobbyist for community service boards in Virginia received a rich reward for building her institution. This was certainly needed if for no other reason than saving what remains of our emergency medical system from further dumping of seriously mentally ill patients into the hands of doctors trained to save victims of serious medical-surgical diseases, a bigger Band-Aid for those bleeding to death.

Lawyers now have a lot to do because there is layer upon layer upon layer of clauses determining the fate of anyone making a clinical decision about the schizophrenic patient in crisis. One cloud of obfuscating confusion, almost, but not quite, justifying the tragic negligence in managing Cho's unremitting clinical state of destructiveness is now replaced by another, even larger and more complex, cloud. How many legal cases will there be to determine the difference between *imminent* and *near future*? Nowhere is it mentioned, in all the legislative reports, whether in committee or political victory statements, just what the problem was in making the change. This piece of legislation as any first-year law student knows, will have to be decided in the courts, which will have to construe the intent of the law.

Would we pass legislation to manage serious circulatory illness by funding community outpatient surgery clinics overseen and administered by lawyers and social service personnel without designating whether cardiology was needed for the heart, neurosurgery for the brain, and vascular surgery for the legs? Preposterous? Of course, but that is what we have as memorial to the preventable campus tragedy that is the Virginia Tech massacre.

It is easier for attorneys to manage such cases post hoc than it is for psychiatrists to do so in either immediate inpatient or outpatient settings. The reason is that the neurocircuitry that is disrupted during psychosis more often than not wipes out a patient's ability to know that he or she has experienced a serious loss of health. Of course he or she will agree with counsel not to be forced into receiving an injection of major tranquilizer every two weeks. Who wouldn't? But is the patient mentally competent to refuse treatment? Attorneys are more likely to see the restrictions of civil liberties in the enforced treatment plan that includes such regular injections for an indeterminate time, years to decades. Psychiatrists, however, working with this population in the hospital setting, see the futility of their efforts, because most of their patients keep coming back after stopping treatment, whether inadequately supervised under involuntary commitment to outpatient treatment or discharged to voluntary outpatient care.

Finally, Virginia has done little to ease the concerns of parents, either intending to or currently having their children on campuses today. There has been no initiative in all the flurry of legislative and political actions emanating from Richmond in the wake of the Virginia Tech massacre to identify the underlying neuropsychiatry of Cho's eruption. Parents and school officials, including faculty with their own families, know it can happen again. By now, they simply do not believe that it is simply random violence traceable to man's earliest recorded history, as asserted publicly by Illinois authorities after the Northern Illinois University massacre.

The multimillions in lawsuits settled with the commonwealth defendant strongly make a contrary statement: dangerous suicidality, including apocalyptic suicide and mass murder, although still rare, is not simply random. There is adequate evidence to show that they are now epidemic, requiring executive action from both government and officialdom within higher education itself. All these parties have a stake in higher education. There are nearly 20 million students on campus, and they all have teachers and families at home. The next one cannot be neglected by public authorities as simply random, and, in fact, the commonwealth did not take such a stand by asserting that these things happen and no place can be immunized from their terror and bloodshed. They did acknowledge that something drastically different must be done. They just left what has to be done for another day, a "someday" in the future after the next worst rampage murder in U.S. history, leaving it for the rest of us to confront that future.

Chapter 6

An Epidemic of Campus and Workplace Suicidal Mass Murder

As tragic as the Virginia Tech murders were, if they were the only instance of a campus or school shooting, it would have been a one-time tragedy. If school and campus mass shootings and subsequent shooter suicides were rarities or anomalies, we might say that they were unforeseen tragedies. But, sadly, neither is the case. The Virginia Tech massacre was part of a trend and the trend itself is part of a larger trend in the United States. Individuals who suffer from growing and uncontrollable rage, who are schizophrenic and dissociated from reality, or those who can no longer cope with the deep depression they live in sometimes see a validation for their existence by ending that existence in a very public and bloody way, often taking multiple victims with them. And, all too sadly, each one of these mass murders/suicide was most likely 100 percent preventable.

The American College Health Associations found a significant increase in the percentage of students on campus in 2004 with a diagnosis of depressive disorders compared to 2000. Of 47,202 students surveyed on 74 campuses, 15 percent reported treatment for depression, one third of them newly treated within 1 year of survey, and 10 percent reported history of serious suicide ideation. This was a nearly 50 percent increase in the prevalence of mood disorders at heightened risk for suicide than the general population matched for significant variables of age, sex, race, and ethnic background.

The proportion of students who sought mental health services for depression at the university counseling center increased from 21 percent between 1988 and 1992 to 41 percent between 1996 and 2001. But, compared to the nonstudent cohort of peers, their suicide rate was found to actually be one half the rate for the community at large outside the gates. The rate of depression among students doubled within the past 13 years studied, and the number of suicidal students tripled! More than 40 percent of college students reported feeling so depressed that they had trouble functioning, and 15 percent suffered from clinical depression. About 45 percent reported episodic binge drinking and 10 percent reported that they had seriously considered suicide.

Perhaps 25 percent take some kind of psychiatric medication, 23 percent meet criteria for alcohol or drug dependence, and 44 percent admit to binge drinking (Kitzrow, 2003). With this unique concentration of young adults and their known epidemiology, it is not surprising that suicide is the second highest cause of mortality on college campuses, next to accidental death, more often than not associated with alcohol abuse. There were 1,600 alcohol associated fatalities in 1998 and 1,700 in 2001.

Highlighting the epidemiology of this population, we find that 10 percent of them—or 2 million young adults—experience profound suicidal ideation while on campus, but less than 20 percent of these seriously impaired students were in treatment while on campus. This statistic demonstrates an apparently severe barrier to access for psychiatric care, likely even worse than in the population at large outside the campus gates. Within this latter population at large, less than one in twenty patients impaired by psychiatric illness receive any type of psychiatric or substance abuse treatment, despite obvious impairment and heavy utilization of primary care for psychiatric impairment. The numbers for suicidality are not known but are likely higher than that 5 percent for all primary care patients requiring psychiatric assessment and mental health interventions.

The problem, as we addressed earlier in both the *Lessard* and *Tarasoff* cases, is that this is more than a public health problem, it is a legal problem, both for institutions as well as private practitioners.

The intellectual concept of "harm to self and harm to others" has become so legalistic, as in so much of the management of serious mental illness, that the clinical realities are ignored. To segregate out suicidality from homicidality is dangerous. Cho was committed for suicidality. He killed 32 people before he killed himself. Legalistic constructs of psychiatric emergencies do not accurately model the real clinical world in which the suicidal person is also likely to be dangerous to others.

Consider the case of a patient by the name of Clint, who was admitted to a healthcare facility for threatening to commit suicide by inhaling carbon monoxide exhaust from his car. Healthcare workers making rounds discovered Clint holding a sharpened chair leg to his chest and threatening to stab himself. Clint was over six feet tall and over two hundred pounds, and when approached by hospital workers to drop the chair leg, he attacked the hospital workers. Security had to intervene to protect the hospital workers as well as the patient. Was Clint, then, dangerous to himself or to others? Both, of course, and that is clinical reality—although potentially diversionary medico-legal reality—as it tragically was with Cho Seung-Hui.

Thus, for clinicians working either on campus or within community ERs and clinics serving college students, working smart means knowing the likelihood of certain disease presentations, whether they are those of sexually transmitted diseases, highly contagious meningitis, or debilitating and potentially lethal psychiatric disorders. All of these are uniquely at high likelihood for occurring on campuses due to both the residential realities of higher education and the concentration of young adults more successfully treated as children, thus enabling their matriculation. Decades ago, they would not likely have either made it to or stayed on campus. And this new cohort of diagnosed young adults has less stigma to reporting emotional distress and higher acuity needs for access to treatment at time of matriculation as young adults.

As in Cho's case, the unique stresses of campus can set off an otherwise quiescent psychiatric disorder, at the genetically timed peak onset of symptoms of mental illness. Matriculation of this unique population most at risk for acute episodes of potentially lethal psychiatric disorders during late adolescence and early adulthood encounters numerous unique stresses. Most are living away from home for the first time. They are pressured to succeed after the stress of admission and desire to fit into a uniquely demanding social environment. Oftentimes, as in Cho's case, there is geographic disruption. Sleep deprivation is ubiquitous, and excessive alcohol abuse is widespread. Expectations for autonomous decision making beyond their age-associated cognitive capability—that is, career and gender choice—along with intimate mixing of males and females in residential sites on and off campus are the signature stressors for this young adult population, as combat is for its military peers.

This epidemiology shows in the wake of the Virginia Tech massacre that campus life now is far more fragile than it was decades ago, when psychiatrically impaired kids simply could not matriculate or stay in school. Now they do both; they come to school and they stay. Something needs to be done because this is a huge problem within a huge population nearly the size of Canada. Cho's parents were right; they should have simply brought him home and taken care of him. So was his high school guidance counselor, who expressed grave concern about his attending Virginia Tech, so far away from the fragile support system he actually had as his illness was obviously progressing.

We can see in the case of Cho that career pressures were building with his father's expectations for him to go on in school and make something of his college education. That was certainly reasonable. But Cho's father was never given a clue that his son's life was attenuated by serious mental illness. This was obvious to everyone encountering him except those empowered to do something about it, namely, Cook Guidance Center, the Virginia Tech administration, and St. Albans Hospital. His apparent erotomanic delusions of females were the likely result of converging forces from his own increasing hormonal drives; fractured self-identity, including his sexual identity; and his intimate life among young females freed within a psychosexually complex liberated world that is higher education today.

This epidemiology also supports the recurrent evidence of both increased prescribing of medications called selective serotonin reuptake inhibitors (SSRIs), such as Prozac, and their effectiveness. Their ineffectiveness and even adverse reactions causing impulse dyscontrol are legendary and a matter for debate between scientology and psychiatry and beyond the scope of this chapter. But of interest, the initial question raised in school shootings is about the patient's being on psychotropic medications. There is no doubt that SSRIs can cause serious reduction in impulse control and even suicidal intent, but such adverse reactions are very rare. The studies on increased suicidal ideation on children treated with Paxil (paroxetine) resulted in a black-box warning for use of that drug in child psychiatry, ironically the only medication Cho ever took.

Paroxetine (Paxil) helped him a lot. But there is no way to determine whether that 4 percent increase in suicidal ideation was caused by the drug or was despite the drug. Let's play it safe and assume it was caused by the drug, because, again, no drug is 100 percent safe or without disturbing side effects. The problem evidenced by the epidemiology of this special population is not that they are on medications. The problem is continuity of care once arriving on campus without access to psychiatric services. Paroxetine is contraindicated for patients under the age of 18. Although patients with mood disorders often require careful supervision because of an inherent risk of suicide, any pediatric patient currently taking paroxetine should be screened for suicidal thoughts, suicide attempts or episodes of self-harm. Serious consideration should be given to changing therapies in all pediatric patients except those who have nearly completed successful courses. The drug should not be discontinued abruptly (this can lead to serious SSRI withdrawal symptoms; rather, a gradual tapering of the dose is recommended). The relative safety of other antidepressants and SSRIs in pediatric populations is unclear. The current warnings do not apply to adult users of paroxetine.

The studies are not robust enough to put an accurate risk factor on treating depressed children and adolescents with Paxil, but to be conservative a prescriber should be aware that there is an increase of upward of 4% depressed children taking Paxil versus children taking a placebo experiencing suicidal ideation. I do not prescribe Paxil for children, except after all other medications fail and informed consent is given by the parents regarding the risk of suicidal ideation occurring in their child. Telling them that there is a 4% chance of their child experiencing suicidal ideation is medicolegally necessary. That does not mean that Paxil causes suicide. Even putting these kids on placebo results in about 2% having suicidal ideation. It is just that more kids — probably 4% higher rate — get suicidal ideation.

Is this population overmedicated? Possibly. Is that the main problem? Definitely not. Can psychotropics cause dangerous disinhibition? Rarely with SSRIs. But, as far as intoxication is concerned, we have far more to worry about from those selling kegs, hard liquor, and illegal drugs, including LSD, than from physicians prescribing psychotropic medications.

Nearly half of students reported having been involved in binge drinking. Alcoholism is somewhat higher on campus compared to cohort peers in the working world at home: 18 percent versus 15 percent, male students nearly twice the number versus their female peers. The interaction of substance abuse with underlying psychiatric illness, whether manifest or dormant, is also of major concern. As properly considered at St. Albans Hospital, Cho's history of not being a substance abuser did in fact reduce the risk of his violence. The seriously mentally ill, and even walking wounded with depression, are more at risk to commit impulsive acts of self-harm and violence when intoxicated. But Cho and many other suicidal and homicidal patients are not intoxicated when they kill. There was no evidence that Cho was intoxicated at any time throughout the duration of his untreated psychosis.

Though the Cho case might have been the big headline maker as it concerned school shootings and mass murder, it was by no means the only headline-making case. The roll call of school shootings, including, of course, the infamous Columbine High School shootings perpetrated by Kliebold and Harris, whom Cho said he wanted to emulate, stand out like spray paint on a wall of shame.

In March 2009 in Germany a 17-year-old former student shot and killed 15 students before killing himself. Within a day or so, 28-year-old Michael McClendon killed 10 people, including his parents, before killing himself, in rural Alabama. Just about a year earlier, a former student named Steven Kazmierczak shot and killed 5 students in a lecture hall in Northern Illinois University and wounded 18 others before he killed himself. Six months earlier, in December 2007, teenager Robert Hawkins killed 8 people at an Omaha, Nebraska, shopping mall before killing himself. Back in 2006, in Pennsylvania, 32-year-old Charles Roberts shot and and killed 5 girls at the West Nickel Mines Amish School. And the list goes on, stretching back more than 20 years to school mass shootings, workplace mass shootings, and mass murders in public places, almost all of which resulted in the suicide of the shooter and follow-up discovery that the shooter had for some time exhibited signs of aberrant, extremely deviant, criminal, or downright diagnosable psychotic behavior. As in our research into serial killers, once we looked into the background of these offenders, either episodic or apocalyptic suicidal, the long path of their severe psychological deviance showed up like disappearing ink turning brown over a hot lightbulb.

In the wake of the Virginia Tech and Northern Illinois mass murders, but not to minimize the long history of school and workplace mass murders and suicides, U.S. Senator Dick Durbin (Illinois) introduced the Mental Health on Campus Improvement Act (S 3311) to bolster mental health services at colleges and universities. In essence, the act would funnel federal dollars to colleges and universities via Department of Education grants to institutions to provide mental health services to students, their families, and faculty, as well as to hire mental health staff and expand training programs.

Durbin's bill also would require the Centers for Disease Control and Prevention (CDC) in Atlanta to work with national behavioral health associations along with colleges and universities to create a public awareness campaign addressing the stigma surrounding mental illness among college students. The act also would establish a federal interagency working group to support innovations in mental health services for college students. Durbin's bill is supported by several college/university national associations and mental/behavioral health organizations, including the National Council for Community Behavioral Healthcare.

With expectations created by this well-meaning and popular bill, colleges are expected to beef up psychiatric services. Thus, they find themselves in the untenable position of meeting totally unrealistic expectations for commensurate demands for enhancing security and providing individualized and community psychiatric services on campus. The socioeconomic and political background behind this bill, however, dramatically shows the decrepit state of affairs of our public psychiatric system; it is doubtful, under the best of circumstances, to meet the resource requirements of Durban's bill on any but the most well-endowed campuses in America.

Despite the well-meaning nature of the approach in Durbin's bill, commentators and critics alike fear that removing mentally ill students from campus will simply remove them from the one support system that can actually help. In other words, it is a two-edged sword. What if removing Cho from Virginia Tech might have saved the lives of his victims but not the life of his long-term and ultimate source victim, himself? Would the school have done the right thing politically by saving the lives of the many at the expense of the one? Yes, from a sovereign ministerial perspective on the discretionary behavior of public safety officials in their roles as state actors. But medically, would it not have been better to notify Cho's parents that their son was likely not competent to determine his own fate or exercise his own civil rights and then seek their permission to act as guardians and remand Cho to the temporary custody of a mental health facility for evaluation and diagnosis?

Furthermore, the failure in Durbin's legislation to define the limits of governance officials' public health responsibilities leaves them wide open to liability risk. In the case of *Shin v. Massachusetts Institute of Technology et al.* (2005) (settled out of court), the parents sued MIT after their daughter committed suicide by setting herself on fire. She had sought and received therapy in the student counseling center, but the center's caseload had swelled without commensurate increases in resources.

The inadequacy of such resources was believed to be causative for Ms. Shin's successful suicide and, hence, provided the basis for a cause of action by Shin's parents to sue MIT, the institution that had, first, been a special relationship with Shin in a school–student relationship but also established a special duty of care because they had begun the process of therapy. Under established tort law, which applies to MIT in the Shin case, if a party begins a special care relationship with another party, it has imposed upon itself a duty of care. If the caring party then abandons what it is doing, particularly if it can show no compelling reason for having done so, that party has breached its duty of care and may be liable under tort law for resulting damages. Thus even if MIT had claimed that it was not legally responsible for Shin's loss of life because she was the one who took her own life—hence possibly breaking the chain of causality—and that suicide was unforeseeable, they still might be liable because she was under counseling at the university for mental health issues.

On the other hand, even if we assume that any mandatory counseling or inpatient treatment requirement for student health services is built into various state codes regarding student mental health treatment, it still does not account for students who, out of fear or out of denial, simply refuse to come forward. Such students, those who can keep themselves out of harm's way and under the radar from campus administrators, will turn themselves away from treatment, only get worse, and possibly postpone until they our out of college some form of extreme, if not deadly, act in the workplace instead of in a dormitory. At least the college might be spared liability even if the former student becomes his or her own victim.

Students can also be either characterized unfairly as requiring mental health counseling or characterized as dangers to the campus community and either be suspended or expelled for refusing to comply with school requirements as to their treatment. Two students, one at George Washington University and another at Hunter College, both sought legal remedy from their respective institutions for what they deemed improper behavior with respect to how they were treated for their alleged problems and both ultimately settled with their institutions. Their cases, contrasted with the Cho and the Northern Illinois cases, indicate that although it is difficult for colleges to get it right, there has to be some balance between the respect and protection of a student's rights with the protection of the student body from violence and the protection of the student from himself or herself. The question is, how do institutions navigate, beset as they are by legal constraints on one side, by state policy makers over which they have no control on another side, and by the real and constant threat of mental illness–driven student violence on yet another side, balance the competing obligations.

Failure, therefore, to achieve a proper balance on this issue leaves colleges and universities vulnerable to legal action on both sides of the ledger. Schools can face lawsuits if they choose to expel or take disciplinary action against students with mental health problems. This was the course Virginia Tech deliberately chose, although silently behind the scenes, while teachers, security officers, and students were left to struggle with Cho's obvious insanity and inevitable volcanic eruption. On the other hand, their failure to deal with potential threats from mentally ill students can lead to horrific violence on their campuses that may leave them susceptible to legal action for failing to protect their communities. Cho's murderous rampage was the consequence of the deliberate hands-off policy from the top.

The Virginia law, enacted post-Cho, required a stringent outpatient commitment process. But committed patients are not required to take medications, despite the fact that nonadherence to psychotropic medication is the single most common cause of emergency detention of the seriously mentally ill. It is also one criterion separating the small minority of the homicidal seriously mentally ill patient from the vast majority who are not.

Schizophrenia, from which Cho likely suffered, requires antipsychotic medication and, with suicidal threats, most likely Clozaril. Bipolar disorder, on the other hand, requires mood stabilization, with addition of lithium to reduce suicide risk. Such specifics of evidence-based medicine for reducing disastrous outcomes in the management of the seriously mentally ill patient are glaringly absent from the commission report. It is for this basic reason that an opportunity to actually reduce the risk of the massacre at Virginia Tech from occurring again, whether in Virginia or on another state's campus, was completely lost.

"The life of every Virginian, perhaps every American, changed as a result of the tragedy and loss of life at Virginia Tech on April 16, 2007. Those individuals who were killed and wounded will be remembered with reverence and honor, not only by their families and friends but by all citizens throughout the Commonwealth," the official governor's statement read (Governor's Panel Report).

And that is all they can expect from the Commonweatlh of Virginia after the smoke of the massacre had cleared while the fire burned on. So, as a result, the primary message for college administrations from all of these legal and political man-hours—along with the sacrifices of many other interested parties—is take care of yourselves. Do not wait for your state government and its courts—the original instruments of deconstruction of our public mental health system—to begin its reconstruction.

Chapter 7

The Psychotic

Letter to the Editor, New York Times, *April 12, 2000*

On Sunday, the series "Rampage Killers" pointed out that nearly half of your sample (one-hundred high profile cases) "had some sort of formal diagnosis, often Schizophrenia." The second article showed that 14 of the 24 multiple-murderers' prescribed psychiatric drugs were not taking them. Next came a dissection of our failure to keep weapons from people with mental illness. On the last day, you profile a man who acted on a "divine message to Kill."

You inextricably weave multiple tragedies with mental illness; but offer not a word of how our laws stop the treatment of those whose minds are overcome by these sicknesses.

In most states, even those transparently incapacitated by severe mental illness cannot be placed in treatment until they are dangerous either to themselves or to others. For no reasons, this prohibition against treatment ensures thousands are left to suffer.

And, as your series evidences, waiting for people with mental illness to be dangerous before helping them, also guarantees that some will become just that.

E. Fuller Torrey, M.D. (Psychiatrist)
President, Treatment Advocacy Center, Arlington, Virginia

While Dr. Torrey was writing this letter, a young Korean-American boy was getting sick, and seven years later Americans woke up to the stated consequences of Dr. Torrey's ominous warnings about neglect of the deinstitutionalized and seriously mentally ill (SMI) within our society.

So often, Dr. Torrey writes in his latest book, *The Insanity Offense*, the killer's family was helpless in seeking psychiatric treatment. Their immigrant status and English-language skills were part of the problem, and discrimination was an environmental stressor—no doubt. But cultural issues were merely crosswinds in the ultimate emergence of a rampage murder against which all 100 previous cases reported by the *New York Times* paled. Yet, the answer to why so many killings has been shouted over and over again, only to land on deaf ears: untreated serious mental illness.

In a personal communication about the Cho case, Dr. Torrey wrote: "All previous rampage murders, however, pale to that carried out by Cho Seung-Hui in April 2007." Dr. Torrey stressed that not only was this a "planned and orchestrated attack," Cho, he said, "had previously told his roommate that he had an imaginary girlfriend who was a 'supermodel and traveled through space;' that he had an imaginary twin brother, and that he had 'vacationed in North Carolina with Vladimir Putin, the Russian President.'" Cho's behavior, writings, and menacing demeanor were so bizarre that students were afraid of him and the faculty sought ways not to deal with him.

Dr. Torrey continues with his assessment of the facts:

> Following his harassment of two female students in 2005, Cho was court-mandated to be psychiatrically evaluated. He was held overnight in a local hospital but apparently not treated. He was ordered to get treated as an outpatient but did not do so. The counseling center at Virginia Tech University received a copy of his court order mandating treatment, but they apparently did nothing. According to an official investigation, the center did not accept "involuntary or ordered referrals from any source," and even students with Schizophrenia were treated only if they requested it. The Virginia state law for involuntary psychiatric commitment and treatment requires that the person be an "imminent danger" to himself or others or to be "substantially unable to care for himself." This is one of the most stringent state commitment statutes in the United States and another example of how changes in mental illness laws in the 1970s and 1980s continue to have real consequences. (Torrey, personal communication)

Back in 1974, in his discussion of the quintessential neurological element of the disease that is schizophrenia, anosognosia, Stephen Rachlin wrote that "If we can agree with the premise that the liberty to be psychotic is no freedom at all, then we can begin to examine some of the current plights of the mentally ill patients" (quoted by Torrey in *The Insanity Offense*, 2008). Accordingly, the Cho case, dramatic as it is, should not be viewed as an isolated incident, another violent crime in a history of campus shootings. The Cho case, especially the way it was mishandled by Virginia Tech and St. Albans Hospital, floats on the entire history of modern psychiatry in America and must be viewed within that context.

Modern Psychiatry and the Psychotic

Modern psychiatry is of recent origin, dating back to the middle of the last century, when Largactil, the first major tranquilizer, was introduced into North America by Dr. Heinz Lehman, at McGill University in Montreal, Canada. Back in the 1950s premed students rotating through teaching rounds through the caverns of Verdun Protestant Hospital in Montreal could find themselves in a scene from the classic movie, *Titicut Follies*. One McGill professor was famous in the 1950s for demonstrating the classical presentations of schizophrenia by having four seriously mentally ill patients sit on a small stage. One was catatonic. He lifted the patient's arm in the air where it remained in statuesque form. Another grimaced constantly in response to an internal world, defying the awful reality all about us. That was the hebephrenic type of schizophrenia. And one just seemed unfazed by anything. He was the "simple" type. Finally, the paranoid man continued to demonstrate hypervigilance and reveal his preposterous delusion about the Mounties spying on him. That was then. Now, we are in a different world but, as Cho demonstrated, one possibly even more dangerous because of the hidden dangers in new pharmaceuticals.

Current studies of the brain allow us to reduce what we observed back in the 1950s to what textbooks titled "The Positive Symptoms of Schizophrenia." They are both the perceptual distortions of that patient grimacing at his exclusively private hallucinatory world and the connative behavioral disturbances of a man who could suddenly go from statuesque immobility to an explosion of motion known as *catatonic fury*.

The antipsychotic drug, Largactil, originally developed as an antihistamine, was coincidentally observed to create tranquility and indifference within this horrible inner world while simultaneously reducing the motion of the agitated schizophrenic patient. Tested in animals, Largactil and its descendant major tranquilizers were found to cause extreme motor slowing and behavioral indifference when injected into animals. This biological response in animal research is known as *neurolepsis*. Hence, this first group of major tranquilizers is known as neuroleptics.

Largactil worked—seemingly miraculously—and was obviously more than just the medical straight jacket of a sedative knockout from the previous decade or, worse yet, the real straight jacket. Nor was it the scandalous assembly-line shock treatments of the neighboring St. Jean de Dieu clinic in Montreal.

The neuroleptic revolution in psychiatry had begun. Largactil, now known as Thorazine, made the motor excitement and emotional responses to the inner horrors of schizophrenia more tolerable to the public. It continues with the more recent phenomenon of deinstitutionalization and case management, in other words, the transfer of care for the severely mentally ill from the state hospitals to the community. All of this was made possible by neuroleptic medications.

Modern technology has provided a window into the microworkings of neuroleptics. Their therapeutic effects, along with their side effects, likely result from blocking transmission of the neurochemical dopamine in the brain. The cost of doing business, however, was the nonselective blockade of dopamine nerve cell receptors throughout the brain. The uniquely nonsedating tranquilizing effects came with undesirable side effects, both mimicking Parkinson's disease—uncontrolled facial spasms and chewing motions—and worsening the negative symptoms of schizophrenia, which are the schizophrenic patient's core psychopathology of apathy, emotional flattening, social blunting, and seeming indifference within relationships.

Recent introduction of Clozaril has begun the era of the novel—or atypical—antipsychotics. They are novel and atypical because they tranquilize with significantly less drug-induced indifference and movement disturbance than Thorazine and its neuroleptic derivatives, such as Haldol. Unfortunately, an uncommon adverse reaction with Clozaril is suppression of the bone marrow, leading to reduced white blood cell counts and a resultant lowering of immunity to infection. This adverse reaction can be fatal. Therefore, prescribing of Clozaril requires repeated blood tests that limit its practical use. Especially effective in clearing the mental disorganization of serious mental illness and stabilization of mood, utilization of Clozaril has been limited by the expense of laboratory monitoring for its uncommon adverse reaction.

Other effective antipsychotics that also stabilize mood have therefore replaced Clozaril. Two of particular importance are a long-acting intramuscular preparation of Risperdal®—Consta®—that is effective for 10 to 14 days, and Invega, a once-per-day oral preparation. There is even evidence that Clozaril improves the most debilitating psychopathology of schizophrenia, specifically the negative core signs mentioned above such as apathy and deterioration of socialization. Compared to the older long-acting formats of neuroleptics, such as Haldol and Navane, patients do not have the discomfort of many of the side effects from Consta. In fact, they oftentimes report feeling better, when before they either ignored the need to take the medicine or avoided it because of side effects.

By the time these pharmaceutical breakthroughs occurred late in the last century, many schizophrenics became victims of the success of neuroleptics after state governments found justification for discharging the seriously mentally ill from state hospitals. Because the voiceless and helpless seriously mentally ill patient and family could allegedly be managed on an outpatient basis, an enormous cost shift occurred, saving state governments billions of dollars annually. Inpatients were taken care of at state expense, but outpatients were taken care of under Medicaid and Medicare at federal expense.

Similarly, a victim of its own pharmacological success was the profession of psychiatry itself. Parallel challenges to state commitment laws by trial attorneys, armed with a body of counterrevolutionary antipsychiatric literature, encouraged budget-conscious state governments to shut down state mental hospitals.

As psychopharmaceuticals began to make a major impact, American psychiatry itself was transforming from a psychoanalytic model to a modality that increasingly utilized new therapeutic drugs. This transformation did not occur without a major social reaction to the increasing political power of the new psychiatry. The bigger American psychiatry became, the more it became a target for suspected abuse of therapeutic powers. For example, the once-simple involuntary detention program at what is now Harborview Hospital was eliminated with introduction of adversarial legal procedures for committing the mentally ill. Psychiatry's traditionally guiding principle of *parens patriae* literally died. It was so obvious to those of us in the practice that the patient populations from Massachusetts to Quebec and Seattle were too mentally deranged to take care of themselves. In place of involuntary commitment to address urgent psychiatric issues was a revolutionary new practice called *community psychiatry*, which did not work and which would not have worked for Cho.

The brief period of elation of revolutionary zeal from the community psychiatry movement was decisively defeated. Who were the victors? Certainly not the mentally ill, who, under the guise of having successfully asserted their Fifth Amendment rights to due process, lost the battle for medical care. Those who won were the trial attorneys prospecting for easy cases, construction contractors now flush with millions once earmarked for maintenance of three state hospitals in Washington, lobbyists for the Department of Corrections, and for-profit prison management companies who received rich contracts to warehouse the mentally ill mixed with criminals in the state prisons. Prisons would learn from experience how to manage this new population, both feared by and terrified of felony inmates. The seriously mentally ill could now be called *special offenders* without the system having to mention the *S* word—*schizophrenia*—or *manic depressive illness*.

History has not been, and never will be, kind to the leaders of this counterrevolution, whether legal advocates freeing the insane from their treatment or the administration of the Washington State Department of Health and Human Services. Shockingly, yet not surprisingly so, the nadir of this department's descent into moral bankruptcy was another scandal. It was discovered that its medical director, notorious for rejecting authorization for emergency healthcare interventions, such as appendectomies, in the state's welfare population, had not a single hour of premedical or medical training. We will never know how many medical-surgical patients died or were maimed forever under this person's medical administrative edicts, refusing care to those desperately in medical-surgical need. The Department of Health and Human Services, however, kept him on relatively high salary for a very long time. It was quite apparent from this scandal that the Washington State Department of Health and Human Services was run by bean counters for whom medical expertise was of less value than the ability to keep to a budget so strict that patients in need suffered for it.

It is one thing for state government to question the need for maintaining state hospitals in an era of outpatient pharmaceutical psychiatry. Here the paradox of improving treatments seemed increasingly met with resistance from empowered groups. Some, like Charles Morris (former Secretary of Social and Health Services for the State of Washington), were only concerned about cutting Health and Human Services budgets. Others naïvely believed the antipsychiatric literature of Laings and Szacz, whereas others simply opposed humane treatment of the seriously mentally ill out of either denial of its existence or preference for remaining blind to its existence in family and in the workplace. Not only do we turn a blind eye to Uncle Joe's nighttime solitary drinking and his visits to the bar after work, or to the neighbor boy suspected of killing cats, or even to Junior who took an almost obsessive fascination with tearing the legs off insects or in starting small fires in ashtrays, we look the other way when incipient workplace violence does not target us. As a case in point, the New Haven police were very quick to brand the recent strangulation murder of Yale graduate student and lab researcher Annie Le as workplace violence. And the news pundits, particularly the former prosecutors, will pound the table in fury at the plight of the victim. But how many of them would jump at the chance to climb on board a class action suit to keep a potentially violent mentally ill individual on the street and out of the hospital if that individual did not present an immediate threat of violence? This is what happened to Cho and it is very easy to sink into denial about these potential symptoms of a psychiatric problem.

During the course of the evolution of modern institutionalized psychiatric treatment, more political considerations were laid on by legislators and lobbyists than there were medical requirements. For example, because lawyers tended to see psychiatric institutionalization as a deprivation of patients' rights, they pushed for more stringent involuntary commitment conditions such as imminent dangerousness as opposed to a simple dangerous to oneself or others, threatening behaviors, or past history of violence.

On July 1, 1969, the California Community Mental Health Services Act took effect. It was widely known as the Lanterman–Petris–Short Act, after the names of its sponsors in the legislature. It was abbreviated as LPS. The law restricted involuntary psychiatric hospitalization to a limit of 17 days, unless the individual could be shown to be imminently dangerous. In that case, hospitalization could be extended for an additional 90 days under very strict criteria. One of its sponsors inserted the precedent for timely physical evidence of imminent dangerousness rather than simply threatening behaviors or past history of violence.

Ironically, this legislation was the creation of an unholy alliance of right-wing extremists, including the John Birch Society, advocating termination of psychiatric hospitalization as a means to cleanse our political system of what they were arguing were actual and menacing processes imposed by foreign doctors, meaning, obviously, the psychiatrists themselves. Then there were Southern California conservatives bent upon eliminating threats of leftist-leaning mental health professionals up north in those Berkeley Hills. The so-called psychiatric professionals so visible during nudist therapy days of Esalon Institute in Big Sur were the perceived threats to patient freedom. In those roaring days of the 1960s from Haight-Ashbury to Big Sur, so-called touchy-feely communality was embodied as psychiatric treatment within the context of sensitivity training. Even some police departments were required to take it in order to better understand the good—if not always gentle—protesting spirits of black and white radicals, oftentimes tripping out on psychedelics. And when the executives at IBM were asked to join in executive encounter groups, you knew that pop psychiatry had gone too far.

LPS was a product of the Berkeley School of Family Therapy. Studying the psychosocial interior of the family, this school of therapy was convinced that the cause of schizophrenia lay within the internal dynamics of curably sick families. Popular in the late 1960s, Jay Haley achieved fame in convincing many mental health professionals that schizophrenia was not really a disease of the individual. Accordingly, very liberal politically, and an extension of the popularized sensitivity, group and family therapy movements of the day emanating from Bay Area roots; the Conservative south, embodied by Nixon and Reagan; and the Liberal East Bay area, came together in one of those unique moments of time to draft the LPS Act.

As forensic psychiatry scholar Donald Lunde would testify, it was with the application of LPS that it became impossible to commit somebody for a prolonged period in the State of California, even if the attending psychiatrist knew that the patient was dangerous to himself or to others. The law provided a very limited, very specific numbers of days that one could keep an individual involuntarily committed. Beyond that time, even though a person may continue to be obviously dangerous, the patient must be released.

Like Washington State, California State's tyrannical bean counters were finding ways to divert money from the care of an impotent, seemingly noncaring constituency, the mentally ill and their families and the professionals caring for them, to more popular agendas, such as new state buildings in Sacramento. Demoralized, one of the largest state psychiatric societies, the California Psychiatric Association, stepped aside. At the same time, other mental health disciplines, apparently feeling threatened for their own livelihoods, tepidly endorsed "liberation of the seriously mentally ill" from the protocols of a California Psychiatric Association, the vast majority of whose members were far removed from the fray within their busy private practices.

What does this history have to do with the Cho case? Without overstressing it, when looked at within the context of the *Lessard* case, the screeners and evaluators at St. Albans were more sensitive to being sued by the patient for a violation of his Fifth Amendment rights than they were concerned about his ability to harm himself or others. The larger issue in class action *Lessard* was not that the plaintiff had been misdiagnosed or that she was not dangerous to herself or others but that she had a right to be mentally ill and live in the community as long as she had not committed any crime and was not an imminent threat to herself or others. In other words, even if she were not competent to understand her rights—which she obviously was because she retained counsel to obtain her release—her civil rights under the Fifth and Sixth Amendments still attached because there was no constitutional requirement that a person be sane in order to assert those rights. This seems to be the context within which Cho was evaluated.

In retrospect, one can easily see how each side in the *Lessard* case, which became the law of the land for determining the rules of involuntary commitment, saw the nightmare that the other side posed. For the lawyers representing Lessard, they saw drug-, electrode-, and scalpel-wielding psychiatrists on the rampage, rounding up anyone who dared rant unacceptable utterances into empty space or into the ears of others and then confining the mentally ill but harmless in snake pits where they would rot in their own human waste. Hardly what psychiatrists were doing in the 1960s, but movies such as *Snake Pit* and *Titicut Follies* had made a great impression and were not far from the truth 30 or so years earlier.

For the psychiatrists seeking ways to treat the seriously and dangerously mentally ill, the lawyers were simply young guns asserting rights that simply did not attach. How could a paranoid schizophrenic understand what his or her civil rights were when that patient did not live in the world of reality? These were patients, like Cho, tormented by their own visions, living out nightmares that tortured each minute of their lives. They heard and fought command voices directing them to do, in some cases, unspeakable things. They lived in their own filth as outlaws of their own making because of what was happening inside their minds. Psychiatrists looking upon such suffering knowing that it could be ameliorated were willing to fight the good fight to save these patients. Lawyers wanted to liberate their clients. Psychiatrists wanted to ease their patients' suffering. Each was right, but how to decide who was more right with a bright-line court decision? The court came down on the side of plaintiff Alexandra Lessard. And it was wrong.

The *Lessard* decision was strongly influenced by theories of the psychiatrist, Thomas Szacz, who wrote that psychiatrists were merely arbitrarily defining categories of either eccentric or illegal behavior that should not be medicalized for purposes of diagnosis and treatment. Szacz's theories were legally persuasive in *Lessard*, just as they had been in the Lanterman–Petris–Short Act in California five years earlier. Per Szacz, the judges noted, a diagnostician has the ability to shoe-horn into the mentally diseased class almost any person he wishes, for whatever reason. The judges asserted that persons in need of hospitalization for mental illness should be allowed choice of whether to undergo hospitalization and treatment, unless the state could prove that the person was unable to make decisions about hospitalization because of the nature of his or her illness.

The court did not further define what it meant by "unable to make decisions" or how the state was supposed to establish this deficit. In other words, mental competency had just been declared null and void. The result of this decision was to end, for all practical purposes, involuntary confinement of psychiatric patients because imminent physical harm would be the only excuse the state could assert in order to infringe on a patient's constitutional rights to liberty. *Parens patriae*, or the legal principle of protection of people who cannot protect themselves in absence of imminent dangerousness, was over even though, as any first-year law student or appellate justice might ask, "Where is the concept of *parens patriae* in the United States Constitution?"

We believe that the line of argument in *Lessard* was incorrect insofar as it stressed the petitioner's rights regardless of her illness rather than the petitioner's competency under the law to give or withhold consent. Black letter law, as embodied in the statutory codes of every state in the union, even in basic contracts, makes provision for the necessity of a signatory of a contract to be of legal majority to be able to give consent. Minors, and those deemed to be incompetent, cannot give legal consent. A 10-year-old cannot sign a contract of sale to purchase a car. A 16-year-old, even if he signs such a document, must ratify or affirm it when he reaches the age of majority in order for the contract to be valid.

Similarly, every state law provides for the concept of statutory rape, sex with a partner under the age of consent. Because minors are not of the age to give legal consent, there can be no consensual sex and thus the sexual act in question is rape. In California, for example, if a man has sex with a woman so heavily under the influence of alcohol or a sedative that she is deemed incompetent to resist and therefore is not a consensual partner, it is deemed rape as a matter of law. The law goes so far as to say that a hypnotized party is not a consensual party to a sexual act, and any such sexual act, therefore, is deemed a rape.

Thus, had the court looked at the competency of the petitioner, Lessard, and found that she was incompetent to give or withhold consent, that lack of consent—of which we take notice in parent–child and teacher–schoolchild transactions—might have been sufficient to have kept Lessard committed to allow her to be treated by her doctors.

Because we must look at the case of Cho Seung-Hui in the context of this argument thirty years earlier, we have to look at how the law might protect the individual's rights while placing the individual and his community at greater danger. There must be a humane way of protecting the most dangerous among us from harming themselves, their families, and in the case of Cho, everybody else in sight. Cho Seung-Hui had, as strange as it seems, nothing personal against anyone he killed. They were not even real people in his mind; they were part of a comic book fantasy. They were projections from Cho's internally deranged mind, more likely than not, visibly impaired using modern imaging studies. His demonic characterizations—actually, just real people of all hues, colors and statuses—were not even characters from his life, as originally suspected by police. They were forms of avatars in a schizophrenic video game playing along Cho's neural pathways and dictating what he saw and perceived.

Is the system so broken that those who have taken an oath to protect their patients are prevented from doing so by the very jurisdictions that have licensed them to practice? Has society itself become the absolute reverse of what R. D. Laings hypothesized: the troubled so outnumbered those who can function within a social norm that the entire paradigm has to be shifted? Why was it that trained psychological evaluators and a psychiatrist could not detain Cho for at least another

24 to 48 hours to retrieve background material on him or at least call his parents? And if there is one Cho, whose mental illness is not detectable by the healthcare and criminal justice systems, who could have been pulled back from the brink simply by being detained long enough to get a complete history from his family, might there be others out there ticking away like time bombs on other college campuses? And if there are others, might they be camouflaged within other types of violent cohorts such as gangs and terrorist organizations? Might these places be effective cloaking devices for those who adhere to the group's violent precepts only to act out their own private psychological calling cards of mass destruction even at the sacrifice of their own lives? The answers to this might be unpleasantly surprising.

What do we do with the psychotic when the psychotic threatens the rest of us?

Chapter 8

Cho Seung-Hui, Attachment Disorders, and Pathological Narcissism

Among the many traits of violent offenders, those who melt down into committing mass homicides or inflicting mass destruction upon innocent victims—much like Cho Seung-Hui did at Virginia Tech—are individuals suffering from the severe and oftentimes malignant personality disorder known as *narcissistic personality disorder*. This is potentially one of the most dangerous of psychopathologies because the individual is too self-absorbed to be cognizant of the harm he is causing others.

Rationally, a pathological narcissist may be aware of hurting others, but he may not be capable of empathizing with the suffering he causes. A personality disordered by severe pathological narcissism can step over anyone, causing unimaginable hurt to others, simply because in his universe of his own projection and reflection, he does not see them. In the workplace and in relationships, those with severely narcissistic personality disorders can be dangerous individuals to deal with. But a true pathological narcissist, such as a Ted Bundy, is capable of committing the most horrendous of crimes. He could be considered at the extreme end of the spectrum of malignancy known as the *psychopath*, wherein the capacity for human empathy is completely absent. There is no one in a narcissist's universe but the narcissist, and his gratification is the sole purpose of his existence.

We heard this in Bundy's confessions about his relationships with his victims and in the confessions of Gary Ridgway, the Green River Killer. Bundy described his murdered victims, whom he hid in secluded locations, in almost religious terms.

And Ridgway described his body dump sites as "sacred" places. In other words, the victims became irrelevant to the needs of the killer to experience a transcendental moment. The victims were only an extension of the killers' sexual drives and their needs for gratification.

In his involvement with himself, Cho Seung-Hui demonstrated many of the characteristics of a narcissist in the disintegration of his fragile self to be replaced by a monstrous grandiose identity that not only committed a mass homicide of enormous magnitude, but by blaming his victims for the carnage. He victimized himself to exonerate himself from any guilt for the crime he was about to commit. And we saw this all on the nightly news.

Narcissists are everywhere in varying degrees. In some professions, near-obsessive overinvolvement with the self, projections from the self to reality, and using the self as a prism within which to react is a necessity. Actors learn to be narcissistic, if they are not that way already. Child actors, in particular, have a difficult time adjusting to the real world of daily responsibilities, working at jobs where they are not the center of attention and a simple shopping mall existence after their careers have run their course. In other cases, ask anyone who has had to work for a narcissistic supervisor, someone who has no empathy for others and sees the world as a place in which he or she is served, about what it was like to be under the thumb of a narcissist.

Like most types of syndromes, human deviant or dysfunctional behavior runs along a scale or continuum. At the very end of the continuum sits a psychotic narcissist like Cho Seung-Hui. Cho is dead, however, and only spoke his last words in a manifesto he sent to NBC News in New York. In the case of a young man named Paul Keller, though, we have a well-documented case of narcissistic violence told by a literate individual who is still alive to talk about it.

Keller is the best case of apocalyptic violence caused by narcissistic rage that anyone could ever cite in any study. Many experts would say that schizophrenia is the extreme disintegration of the self. We think that presenting Keller from both the ground level with intimate psychological detail—oftentimes absent—and the theories of the self, from Freud, through Kernberg, Kohut, and Lacan, is unique. This neuropsychiatric anatomy of a narcissist, the crimes he committed, and his effect on those around him are in good contrast to the case of Cho Seung-Hui.

The Paul Keller Case

Within 6 months, Paul Keller, then 26, had committed 96 arsons. One killed three nursing home patients. He had no prior offenses, either as a child or an adult, except for an isolated episode of fire-setting at age 9, which was cleared by the police as curiosity.

Keller had suffered a perinatal injury resulting in cyanosis and incubator care at birth and, unlike siblings, never reciprocated affection with his mother. Perinatal injuries requiring separation from the mother and interfering with critical maternal bonding shortly after birth are often severe impediments to normal neurological and psychological development. Because the human newborn continues neurological development after birth and requires tactile contact with the mother on an almost constant basis for the first few weeks of life, babies who are deprived of this have a difficult time adjusting in early childhood, usually cannot create a psychological border between self and not self without some form of therapy, and often display severe deviant behavior. And so it was with Paul Keller.

At 10 he was diagnosed by a pediatric neurologist as having minimal cerebral dysfunction syndrome, now known as *attention deficit hyperactivity disorder* (ADHD). At 11 he was temporarily placed in a private residential facility for uncontrollable behavior. He was socially awkward and an academic underachiever in childhood without specific learning disabilities. There was a pattern of arrogance and grandiosity in adulthood. Family history is positive only for alcoholism in both grandfathers.

Married at age 22 and divorced 2 years later, adult-onset alcohol and marijuana usage escalated. Six months prior to his arson spree, he presented for neurological assessment for severe headaches. An MRI was ordered but never accomplished. Four months prior to his arson spree, he presented at a mental health center. Psychological testing showed stress intolerance with suicidality, but clinical follow-up was not accomplished. Throughout the year of his fire-setting, he was consuming 15 ounces of 100 percent Southern Comfort and three bowls of "bud" cannabis daily. Three months following psychological assessment, he declared bankruptcy. Just days later, while stopping to urinate off the road, he set his first fire.

Expert testimony at sentencing demonstrated undisputed Axis I diagnoses of attention deficit disorder with associated conduct disorder in childhood; rapid-cycling bipolar mood disorder; and severe, chronic substance abuse disorders. Axis II diagnoses, likewise undisputed, included narcissistic personality disorder with reaction formation to pyromania, along with comorbid social-emotional learning disability.

Dr. Virkkunen, a psychiatrist in Finland, comparing men like Keller to other violent felons, found borderline personality disorder and uniquely lower cerebral spinal fluid levels of serotonin in his study group of arsonists. Many, like Keller, also had explosive behavior associated with alcoholism. Both reactive hypoglycemia and alcohol intoxication were found to be associated with impulsive fire-setting committed during confusional states, particularly in recidivists such as Keller. Possibly because hypoglycemia, also a typical symptom of diabetes, diminishes the patient's judgmental abilities and is sometimes confused with inebriation, it is no surprise that it creates a confused state of mind. In light of this highly specific biological evidence, research was planned to study the psychoneuroendocrinology of Paul Keller. Variations in his metabolism and hormone levels were to be monitored during different psychobiological states, such as sleep, alcohol intoxication, and heightened stimulation. Also, behavioral parameters were to be monitored chronobiologically with supplemental inclusion of brain imaging and pharmacological challenges to find changes occurring from his own body clock (*The Keller Case: Psychopathy or Psychobiological Diathesis?* John A. Liebert, M.D., Alan Unis, M.D., Charles Wright, M.A., Department of Psychiatry, University of Washington Medical Center, Seattle, Washington. Presentation for the International Association of Psychoneuroendocrinology, Seattle, 1994).

As Keller explained in a series of interviews he gave during his post-arrest evaluation and after he was convicted and sentenced to jail:

> Why does my brain tell me to do it. I'm not a criminal. I'm out driving after drinking at the Eagles Club without any intention of hurting anyone. I've just been out there sermonizing about alcohol [before drinking at the Elks, where firemen also gather]. It's disconcerting to me that I was drunk with out-of-control impulse, when I just stop to take a leak and my brain clicked and said, "light it." I reach into my pocket, and, with flip of the Bic to the carpet rolled up. It was good plastic. Took 30 seconds and, boy, the whole thing went! No rhyme or reason. Just a flip of the bic—a bic light. I felt delighted to be sitting there—the only one I stayed to watch. I took photos of that one for my book on history of firefighting. I'm not mean, am I? (Paul Keller, Personal Interview, Snohomish County Jail, February 24, 1993.)

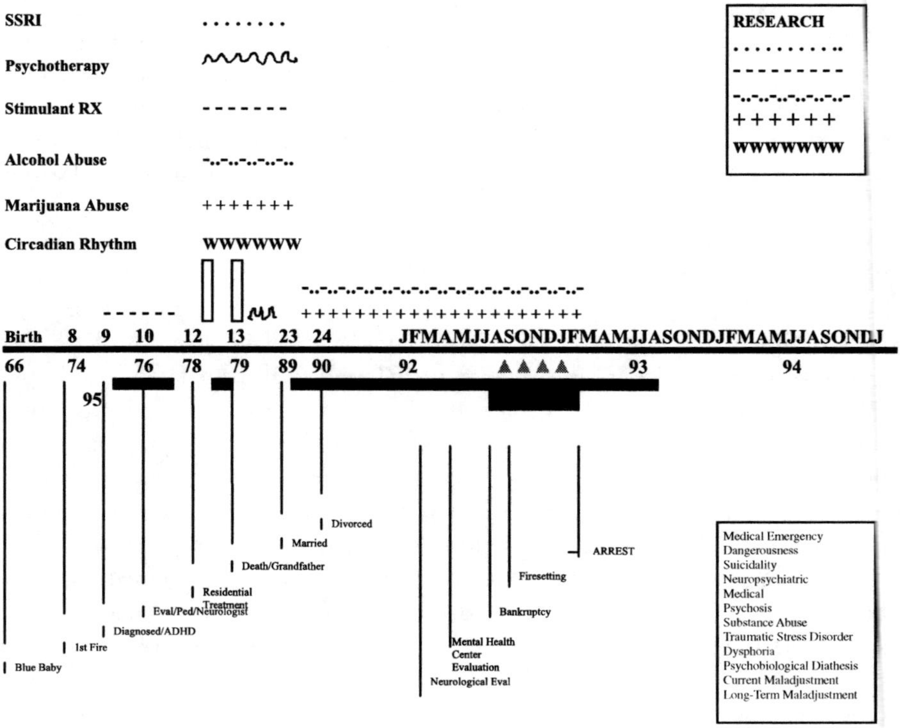

Despite his incipient anger, Keller managed to stagger through adolescence. Moreover, because the Keller family successfully contained and managed his behavior, with residential treatment and private schooling, Keller was never charged as an adolescent with assault, but he fit the lay definition of *rageaholic* (one very prone to rage). Such a person seems to mediate his moods with outbursts of rage similar to the way an alcoholic compulsively binges on alcohol.

Now, what is meant by all of this: narcissistic or borderline personality disorder, childhood development abnormalities that included attention deficit hyperactivity and socio-emotional learning disability, rapid cycling bipolar disorder, and pyromania? Since the evolution of object relations school of psychoanalysis and the work of Bolby on attachment disorders from birth in abandoned, neglected, and abused children, more research interest is being focused on the earliest years of child development—essentially the preverbal years before children can translate feeling states and experience to words. Infant psychiatry is now a subspecialty research field within child psychiatry.

Now that we have the documentary films of nursery behavior, we have a narrower experience-distant chasm between adult behavior and developmental imprinting of such impulse disorders as violence, particularly within the initial dependency state of maternal bonding. *Experience-distant* knowledge of adult clinical behavior and emotional states means that we can see psychological abnormalities during early childhood development and inductively reason that they present in adulthood. *Experience-near* knowledge of clinical psychology and psychoanalysis is less convincing, because it depends on the translation of the patient's language and emotions by an empathic and clinically trained listener, the analyst.

Experience-near knowledge of narcissistic abnormalities will become more important later when attempting to comprehend the apocalyptic explosion of one such human being as Paul Keller. For now, however, we have experience-distant knowledge from nursery documentaries that some mothers engage toddlers in interactive painful behaviors, such as pinching. Watching these nursery documentaries would convince the scientific debunker of developmental psychology that sadomasochism occurs between mother and son before acquisition of language. Can we say that sadomasochism originates from these childhood experiences? Not yet, but common sense and the burgeoning literature on child abuse informs us that such children are at risk for both self-harm and harm to others. Do we all not know that in some ways we reenact the best and worst elements of our earliest years? Alice Miller (1990) wrote about that in *For Your Own Good*, her study of Adolph Hitler and the genesis of what can be called an evil mind.

Alice Miller's work has been applied to the study of the serial killer personality and how parents who torture or abuse their own children manage to train them into thinking that the pain, shame, and humiliation they experienced in childhood at the hands of their parents were ultimately for their own good. Serial killers John Wayne Gacy, Leonard Lake, and possibly Jeffrey Dahmer had very painful childhoods meted out to them by their parents. But in each case, the parent sought to apply that pain and humiliation for the good of the child. These serial killers, all of whom are now dead, carried over the trauma from their childhoods into reenactments in their crimes and post-homicidal activities.

Sigmund Freud learned about how past trauma carries over into the present by treating World War I veterans whose persistent nightmares bewildered him. They had survived to enjoy his pleasure principles. He then theorized their compulsion to repeat their trauma and rewrote his entire psychoanalytic literature. Human beings did not live and suffer just because of blocked pleasure of Victorian morality of the time. People, he theorized, have dual drives or Eros and Thannatos—constantly competing internally for survival and perpetuation of the species, all the while compelled also to return to dust. Why else would combat veterans cling to behaviors and vivid imagery of the horrors they experienced years ago in combat? Answering this question became one of the focal points of psychoanalytic theory in the twentieth century.

The advent of modern psychopharmacology has taken Freud's theories to a point he could only visualize as a trained neurologist in his theoretical writings on psychoanalysis. In the project, Freud foresaw our modern technical discoveries evidencing that the basis of emotion and behavior is programmed into the neurocircuitry of the brain. Medications oftentimes serendipitously discovered to improve the emotionally disturbed patient demanded more finely tuned diagnostics. For example, before the discovery of the mood-stabilizing effects of lithium, it was not important to distinguish the psychotic manic depressive patient from the schizophrenic. Lithium had neglible, if any, effects on correctly diagnosed schizophrenic patients, but it had dramatic mood-stabilizing effects in bipolar disorder. Thus, it became important to ferret out the mood-disordered psychotic from the schizophrenic.

In addition, only recently have psychiatrists believed that major mood disorders, such as depression and manic depressive disorder, started in childhood and therefore needed treatment in earliest years when first evidenced. Again, such diagnostic lag was influenced by treatment. The original antidepressants such as Elavil did not work very well in children, but Prozac did. It has only been in the past couple of decades that we believed that well-known behavioral problems of attention deficit hyperactivity disorder more often than not morphed into adulthood as a lifetime disorder with major disability. Part of this new recognition is modern genetics and higher technology investigations of the brain. The genes are all there from the beginning; few dispute that. Furthermore, little more can be done to change those genes over a person's life span, although biotechnology holds promise for the future in fixing bad genes.

We know, for example, that enormous changes occur in the cellular structure and neuronal networking during both childhood and adolescence. There is strong evidence also that both environmental stresses and traumas, in association with innate timing of chronobiology, alter the manifestations of genetic expression. A child, for example, may not be genetically set to go off when exposed to gang delinquency until at a specific stage of development, whether prepubertal or adolescence. But, when he or she is genetically loaded for socialized delinquency and the gang is the most secure route through youth, environment and natural genetic forces conspire toward peer-determined antisocial behavior. In child psychiatry, this has been traditionally diagnosed as socialized conduct disorder, the known precursor to both antisocial behavior of gangsters and antisocial personality disorder.

We wonder whether O. J. Simpson's violence is embedded in a disavowed or almost dissociated and unremembered ghetto kid from Hunters Point, San Francisco. USC and later professional football, with mentorship from coaches, team support, and public recognition, nurtured the prosocial side of what in the psychology of self is called the *vertical split* of a dissociated self-object. In this case, the self-object was likely running with a violent gang where the rule of the street is "might makes right." For O. J., perhaps he entered USC with such an adaptive defense to threats and deprivation of ghetto impoverishment, but his antisocial persona remained concealed until his football career expired.

This, in a way, is similar to Keller's case. We can see in Paul Keller a uniquely well-documented constellation of problems, oftentimes presenting in adolescents without childhood histories to validate such things as attachment disorder, disruptive behavior, and subtle yet diagnostically valid brain dysfunction. With Paul, however, there is documentation that he was born with his umbilical cord choking him and causing "blue baby" syndrome with fetal distress, requiring intensive newborn care. Subsequently his mother was unable to bond with this child. She had no problem in doing so with his two siblings. The Keller family was not that different. In fact, it was an effective and successful family.

But Paul was different. He had a well-documented disorder of attachment with the unique access back in the 1960s to a rare specialist in pediatric neurology who could correctly diagnose and treat attention deficit hyperactivity disorder. When the Kellers were struggling with his behavioral problems, psychiatry simply did not know that manic depressive disorder frequently erupted early in children like Paul. Similarly, it was not known that a weakened ego emerged early too. This childhood ego was less resilient to external stress, trauma, and regulation of self-destructive behaviors, in his case explosive rage within the family and the devastating impulse to destroy by fire: pyromania.

With the value of hindsight, perhaps the Kellers could have been saved the suffering of struggling to raise a disordered child like Paul, had we known at the time of their efforts to keep him out of trouble that he was likely demonstrating not simply bad behavior but manic depressive disorder, likely genetically acquired within his family lineage. Most such adolescents are still treated as delinquents with some form of restraint, from parental discipline to incarceration or, one step more civilized, for the hyperactivity component of ADHD.

But, in Paul's case, he was likely both hyperactive and manic depressive, in both cases showing signs of disruptive, oppositional, and wrathful behavior within the family. Certainly, there would be outcry from the extreme antipsychiatric movement dedicated to depriving sick kids of effective psychiatric treatments, as well as the opposite extreme excesses of expectations from pharmaceutical agents not effective for every child's problems.

Could the City of Everett, the suffering of arson victims, the Keller family—and Paul himself—have been saved from all of this apocalyptic destruction and tragedy with modern diagnostics? Of course, we will not know, but today, Paul would have likely been treated early with mood stabilizers, as well as stimulants for distractability and Clonidine for hyperactivity. This combination of drugs would more likely than not have muted his disruptive behavior so that more serious underlying developmental personality issues could have been treated, that is, the devastating breach of maternal bonding likely caused by birth injury.

Unlike the Chos, the Kellers had resources and, like the Chos, always demonstrated motivation and willingness to commit to valid treatments. But, how were they to know, when psychiatry itself did not know, what was wrong with boys like Paul? Instead of just the constraints of parochial school, he could have been helped through sophisticated child, adolescent, and adult psychotherapy, both group and individual. There are child psychiatrists in Seattle today who continue to see patients like Paul Keller. A few were actually there when Paul was diagnosed in Seattle with attention deficit disorder and they continue to treat Paul's peers to this day.

These mature child and adolescent psychiatrists assure us that many like Paul can be helped, when treatment starts early enough. He could have developed social skills that might have embedded a sense of empathic concern for other persons, as well as knowledge and expectations of consequences for destructive behavior. Or these same child psychiatrists may have discovered before it was too late the underlying rage in order to prevent his holocaust requiring long-term residential treatment.

Paul was an excellent salesman. So it is not that he could not read people. He simply could not care about them or really comprehend the impact his aggression had on them—particularly his own siblings and parents and later even the elderly and frail in nursing homes, whom paradoxically, he seemed to care for even though they were his victims. Some expired from his pyromania.

We do not know whether the lethal weapon of mass destruction brewing in his psyche could have been redirected and the ultimate holocaust of his terror attenuated by resolving it through family therapy. But we did know about psychological decompensation under stress and psychosomatic manifestations of it. We also knew about self-medicating for decompensation through drug and alcohol abuse and dependence.

Yet, when Paul finally, in his own way—like all of us—presented in dire straits, we simply could not as a clinical community read the telltale danger signs. Shortly before his arson spree, a neurologist, specially trained in psychiatry, ordered an MRI, for what had to be excruciating headaches. Neurologists do not order MRIs for hypochondriacs. He was searching for serious brain pathology. Paul never showed for his MRI and was lost to neuropsychiatric follow-up clinical management. Now we know that this neuropsychiatric presentation was the somatic, or physical, symptoms of psychological disintegration.

Shortly thereafter he presented at a Community Mental Health Center in dire straits. Here a valid Minnesota Multiphasic Personality Inventory, a standard diagnostic tool, proved the point with flashing bright red lights of suicidality and emotional decompensation. Nobody at that center appeared to have known what to do, so he was provided only nutritional counseling. But Keller had already started taking in a fifth of bourbon with Big Gulp cola, to say nothing of high-potency cannabis. As is shown in the research of such urgent psychiatric presentations, he was one of the many decompensating patients for whom alcohol intake is never addressed, even with a documented inquiry.

By then, months of heavy alcohol intake—another flashing red light of emotional decompensation—had caused tolerance. Still presenting himself well, tolerance of severe addiction and his mask of sanity prevented anyone from seeing what his brain was screaming: that he was out of control, telling those around him that he was an atom bomb and not a firecracker.

He tried to connect to a clinical professional, but nobody could get it. And then the impulse he had defended against for so many years by volunteer firefighting, researching the history of firefighting, hanging out with firemen, and even trying to join the fire department penetrated his regulatory controls. Keller had been rejected for firefighting because he had a phobia to masks. Perhaps his phobia was defensive against playing with fire, which he had done dangerously as a small child and which he would do as a young adult. This was psychopathic arson. Keller must be distinguished from the financially motivated professional criminal arsonist, the perpetrators of which are notoriously difficult to find, arrest, and prosecute. The professional arsonist is likely more experienced and trained in explosives and fire.

Paul wore the mask of sanity so well that he literally looked at the front door to the county sheriff's office every day from his own office. As the arson task force went looking for him, he strutted past them, neatly attired in his suit and tie, en route to visit family PR accounts. He made $70,000 per year, not bad for a heavily addicted man with so many psychiatric disorders concurrently running amok. Ironically, one of the sheriff deputies, who was estranged from the department and on medical leave at the time of the arsons, was both a talented artist as well as talented cop. By talking with witnesses to the fires, he was able to draw the most accurate composite likely ever performed in law enforcement history when there were no surviving witnesses to a crime.

This composite was published. Everett, Washington, was not that large a city twenty years ago, so everyone saw it. But Paul, like so many serial killers, did not fit the official profile of a seedy, sexually driven pyromaniac sneaking around the back alleys and living out of a shabby van with only beer and packs of cigarettes to smoke. Between fires, with one blazing behind him en route to start the next one, he was stopped by the police for reckless driving. He was reeling drunk and had just started one side of Everett on fire when he was stopped on suspicion of a DUI. He was released in this traffic stop. He did not fit the profile of an arsonist, even though he fit with an amazing likeness the composite drawing published in the newspapers. Unlike Ted Bundy, Keller never tried to disguise himself. Paul said in private interviews that he could not believe the cops would let him go, but they did. And he set another fire, so that the whole town seemed on fire that night with not a fire engine from the beloved firehouses of his childhood to spare. This, to him, was a demonstration of his sheer omnipotence. One officer said that he was shaving in his sailboat that night. The mirror literally turned bright red; he looked through the porthole behind him to the vista of warehouses on the dock in flames. Having witnessed My Lai, this officer was witnessing the apocalypse or what seemed as such.

Paul's father finally got the message and could hardly miss seeing the obvious likeness between the remarkably accurate composite drawing of the arsonist and his own son. He said that he was not surprised either by the likelihood that it was Paul, so he called the sheriff right across the street from his office. Thankfully, Paul was finally stopped, likely forever, in the least attractive of ways: felony arrest. With family support, he also confessed and the fiery terror in Washington State went dark as fast as it had lit up. A circus of a sentencing finished off the work of authorities. Fatigued officers and the public alike got their piece of Paul. The Kellers went bankrupt. Paul remains incarcerated in state prison, where he is likely to die of old age. Insurance companies paid tens of millions for damaged structures, and fatalities, such as aged residents of nursing homes, were cleared as homicides. And that was it.

This is probably the first attempt to at least try to comprehend what happened, as psychiatric testimony was certainly not welcome at trial. But the Superior Court of Snohomish County spared nothing to obtain a medical evaluation of Paul Keller in order to rule out gross brain disease such as a tumor or extreme epilepsy for purposes of mitigating circumstances. The court provided expert psychiatric evaluators a free reign to hire the best forensic clinical experts available. Accordingly, the community acquired a vast amount of clinical data on Paul Keller that is usually never obtained. There was precious little with Bundy; the Hillside Strangler; George Russell, also called "The Charmer"; and Gary Ridgway, dubbed the "Green River Killer," all high-profile Pacific Northwest killers.

Were we to have had the resources from the court to have done additional testing, it is possible that we would now be looking at an abnormal functional MRI, showing significantly low metabolic activity in the frontal regions of the brain, more on the right than on the left. It is also possible that we would have found abnormal serotonin metabolism, as have been the findings of studies on arsonists in Finland. Maybe one day we will be able to study the functioning brains of arsonist Keller, necrophilic lust serial killer Ridgway, and sadistic lust murderer Kenneth Bianchi, all housed within the penal system of State of Washington. Such studies, however, have no practical forensic value in terms of determining sick versus bad. Insanity, which already failed in the Bianchi case, would not have made it beyond initial pleadings in the Green River case and simply was not a valid consideration for Paul Keller under the statutes of any state. Nor did the findings of Keller's consulting psychiatrists even reach the threshold for mitigating circumstances, possibly ameliorating his life sentence of hard time with placement in the Special Offender Unit of the Department of Corrections.

Keller had no criminal record, either as a child or an adult. He did, however, have an assault, delinquency, and fire-setting history. At age 9 Paul attempted to set fire to a neighbor's vacant house by applying a match flame to the exterior siding. The incident was witnessed by a former Everett fire marshall. Charges were not pressed. On another occasion Paul became angry with a fellow student much larger than he who sat at the desk right in front of Paul. In a sudden fit of rage, Paul stabbed the student in the back with a pencil. Family therapy was not successful. So, at age 11, he was temporarily placed in a private residential facility for uncontrollable behavior.

On another occasion, at age 14, he became angry with some boys living in the neighborhood. One of the boy's parents was employed as an emergency dispatcher. In apparent retaliation, Paul telephoned 911 emergency response and reported that the dispatcher's spouse had suffered a heart attack. The story was completely false. Paul was eventually confronted with making the 911 call but was never criminally charged.

Paul's father said in a private interview, "My son has a history of petty theft. Repeatedly I would be called upon to make good for some items he had attempted to steal."

Paul's mother reported that, from birth, her son never reciprocated maternal affection and, as a result, she could not bond with him. Paul's father reported that the relationship with his mother only worsened with time. "I would often come home from work to find my wife in tears—unable to cope any further with our son's erratic behavior. I was often so frustrated and angry that I may have been harsh with Paul, but never abusive. Paul constantly appeared oblivious to any wrong doing, maintaining that my wife and I always took his brother and sister's side."

Paul reiterated his problem with his mother in a private interview. "My mother blamed psychiatric disorders on me. I was scape-goated. My parents loved me, but they blamed me. And, my brother and sister used it against me. I was the first child. Father was really harsh and would use the belt."

Paul's father reported that his son, Paul, who, up to just weeks before, had been the vice president for sales of the family's growing public relations firm in Everett, Washington, did perform well on the job.

> My son, Paul, is noted to be a relatively successful salesperson, generating nearly $240,000 in gross sales last year for my business … [but] he suffers from extremely low self esteem, although he is very intelligent. He is careless about his personal hygiene such as brushing his teeth. Usually, however, he is very well dressed. When entertaining clients he typically dresses in a suit, dress shirt and tie. Paul is very concerned about appearances, which is also reflected in his adamant desire to drive a nice car. He is sensitive of anything that might reflect badly upon his public image. He attempts to give the appearance of being perfect. (personal communications)

It is odd that Paul Keller's father described a kind of disconnect between his son's ostensibly low self-esteem and slack personal hygiene in contrast to his dressing well and driving "a nice car." Usually, a person who is sensitive about his public image is especially careful about personal hygiene.

His ex-wife's friend supported Paul's father's observation, "Paul would control money, giving his wife a check and then spend money on scanners and clothes. When he went to work for dad, he always bought name brands—expensive stuff, in a variety of styles, usually penny loafer, pull-ons."

In his description of Keller's personality, Paul's father said,

> If something is perceived as reflecting badly of him, Paul can fly into an instantaneous rage, customarily accompanied by horrible verbal abuse. But, he is seldom profane. If confronted, he will escalate verbally, responding in kind. Paul can then just as quickly change his disposition and be very charming. [His mother called her son Jekyll and Hyde.] For instance, if he discovers that a word is misspelled in some advertising he has procured for client, he will scream and rant viciously at our supplier. He can then just walk through the office door and be very calm and collective in a matter of seconds. Paul has always got along famously with elderly people. Despite his temper, he can be very sensitive and tender. He is forever compassionate for the underdog. He loves to watch cartoons, particularly JP Patches. He loves to sing in the choir at his church and has collected 500 gospel cassette tapes. Paul doesn't as a rule self-disclose. From an early age he would lie so convincingly that he would convince us he was right. My wife and I were of the opinion that Paul does not drink alcohol or take drugs. We have, however, recently suspected that we smell alcohol on his breath. … He confided he had visited a strip bar; I don't know of him engaging in that kind of conduct absent this one time.

Again, his ex-wife's friend disclosed this:

> He was very into masturbation. Very possessed with it. He would use her underwear to masturbate. Pornography magazines were all over the house and Rose [Keller's then-wife] would find them and tell him to remove them. He was obsessed with self sex. He would make sexual innuendos to demean her. He wouldn't use sex toys or stuff like that. But, he tried to keep her under his thumb totally—you know, trap her into the house at times.

Dad continued,

> Paul was diagnosed early with hyperactivity, and throughout his life it was best explained by "inappropriate behavior at inappropriate times."

For example, if someone were to fall and be hurt, Paul's typical response would be to laugh. Behavioral problems began to emerge with the birth of my other two children. Paul seemed to continually war with his brother and sister, treating them cruelly and, at times, physically hurting them. On one occasion he spread golf balls across the floor and then induced his one-year old brother, Ben, to walk across them. Ben fell and badly broke his leg necessitating that he wear a partial body cast for an extended period of time. He failed, and continues to fail, to grasp the ramifications of his actions. In Paul's view, everyone is wrong or at fault but him. With his siblings, Paul was, and is, demanding, argumentative and relentlessly taunting, although this has improved. When he entered school, behavioral problems escalated. Paul was caustic with acquaintances to the point of offense. Because of this he never really had any friendships. Paul did not seem to have a single girlfriend in high school. After high school he was popular with some girls. ... His academic record was extremely poor. In class he was disruptive. He often ridiculed other kids. Paul's mother and I were constantly being called to the school due to something inappropriate Paul had done. My wife believes that Paul has a great deal of repressed anger and this may have contributed to a great deal. For example, he is extremely sensitive to even the mention of his "hyperactivity" [diagnosed early by a pediatric neurologist]. Work will induce him to lose control. ... Paul never understood credit, believing he was entitled to money loaned to him; he stole silver dollars from his Grandfather, with whom he was extremely close. ... Paul loved being a security guard after graduating from high school. He was extremely proud of his uniform and car with light bars. He had other jobs, but they seldom worked out. I suspect it was because of inability to get along with others. ... Paul took a job as a bookkeeper with Light Rider Canopy Company in Everett. His involvement with this company turned disastrous, however, when the desk at which he worked caught fire under apparently suspicious circumstances. Paul and the owner are today good friends. Now, Paul works for our family public relations business.

In my own business, Paul's demeanor, with his frequent outbursts, has created many difficult situations. As I've listened to many of his tirades against my employees or suppliers, I have often thought I would fire anyone else for such a thing many times over if he were not my son. In fact, in 1992 I called Paul in to present him with an ultimatum note. The note told him that he was to do a minimum of things or be dismissed from his job. One of these conditions was that he get help for the inability to control his anger. About that same time, his mother likewise had a confrontation visit with Paul on the telephone. She insisted

> that he also get counseling. I think my son probably denies that he needs counseling. In his estimation, it is always some else's fault.

In this statement Paul's father is clearly identifying psychopathology of projective identification, wherein marginally compensated patients will attribute aggression to others in order to justify their own aggression. Object telations theorists believe this primitive psychological defense to be developmental in origin, based on the dynamics of projecting bad introjects from the failures of early childhood nurturing. For example, the pain experienced by the toddler repeatedly pinched by a sadistic mother is incorporated in the developing psyche as painful aggression. The resultant rage toward the mother is then projected within any relationship reactivating this pain. Dependency within intimate relationships is a frequent precipitant for projective identification.

Paul was not abused or deprived by any female, but he constantly blamed his mother and then sadistically controlled and sexually humiliated his wife. Object relations theorists could trace the projection of Paul's rage back to the failure of maternal bonding cited by his mother. He was not deprived, but his mother recalled being unable to nurture Paul right from infancy following his near-death experience from fetal distress syndrome.

His father continued,

> Paul has been going through a difficult period in his life. In the summer of 1989 he met a woman whose uncle is with the Everett Fire Department. She was raped while out of the state in training to be an airline counter attendant. They met in church, and Paul became determined to marry her. Almost immediately after the honeymoon, Paul informed me that the marriage had been a mistake. … The marriage lasted two years before they were divorced. Following the divorce, I think Paul felt very lonely. In July of 1992 he was in financial dire straits. I convinced him that he should file for bankruptcy. For someone obsessed with his pubic image, this was disastrous. The timeline of his crimes shows just how disastrous. For the next few months he terrorized the entire State of Washington, literally sacking and burning indiscriminately.

Father continued,

> He was very depressed. He demanded that no one learn of the bankruptcy. When his car was repossessed, Paul insisted that the family tell everyone that he had wrecked it. Without knowing Paul, it is difficult to comprehend how tragic the bankruptcy process was for him. I believe that I am Paul's best friend. I must say that I also believe that there are moments when my son is in fact capable of committing arson. He can often injure people without realizing the hurt he has inflicted.

> On the day after the press conference announcing the arsonist profile, Paul came into the office late. He said he was sick and had to go home. I later received an answering machine message that said he was going to Yakima to visit with clients. Since that conference, I had the impression that he was fearful and more apprehensive.

Shortly later, viewing a fire from his office, Paul's father would tragically be proven correct in his beliefs about Paul. Following Paul's declaration of bankruptcy, Paul's father gave a portrait of psychological disintegration, actually documented in a valid MMPI that he concurrently took when seeking psychiatric help at the local mental health center.

He said,

> Paul developed a client in Olympia and is currently attempting to enlist a number of funeral home accounts in Yakima. Paul will travel throughout the entire state shooting photographs of fire stations, fire trucks, fires, personal memorabilia and trains. For example, he confided in me that he had been in attendance at some house fires in Lynnwood near his apartment and actually took photographs during the fires. Paul oftentimes would bring these photos into the office and go through them with me. Since I became aware of the arsons, however, it seems to me that Paul has avoided showing me most of the pictures he has taken. He will sort through pictures and then only show me a limited few. This is very uncharacteristic of Paul. In the trunk of his car he carries two yellow emergency lights. On one occasion he also showed me a red emergency light. In addition to the light, Paul maintains a dark yellow fireman's turnout coat in the trunk. For years Paul has been monitoring the emergency radio band at work and will drop everything he is doing and race to fires and other emergency scenes. In the middle of a work day, it is not uncommon to see him race from this office in an attempt to beat the emergency response vehicles to the scenes. While monitoring the emergency calls, his typical response was to discuss it immediately with me, explaining the terminology used by dispatchers and quickly pointing out any mistakes or inconsistencies in the dispatch. Since the arsons started, he doesn't talk about fires anymore. This [new silence from monitoring emergency radio band] is starkly unusual. … Although a sloppy organizer overall, he knows his fire stuff intimately.

According to his ex-wife's friend, "With his wife, Paul was not violent—just mean—verbally. If he got mad, he would call her names like 'whore,' 'bitch'—all names. He wanted a totally submissive wife. Rose wouldn't do it. He felt superior to Rose; he wanted others to believe he was special."

Then came the humiliating injury to his self-esteem. "Paul was not happy about bankruptcy." His wife's friend was understating his state of affairs and his state of mind. "He never let her out during his rages; he would throw up his arms and yell. Just throws 'em up and screams."

Origins of Rage in Pathological Narcissism

Wilhelm Reich conceived of narcissism as being founded on a pathological form of regulation of self-esteem. This problem may be found in both neurotic and psychotic individuals who have exaggerated, unrealistic—that is, infantile—inner yardsticks and constantly seek to be the object of admiring attention as a means to undo feelings of inferiority. Yet, all important psychoanalysts, psychologists, and philosophers have opined on the subject of self through the centuries in asking, "What is the 'I,' and even, is there an 'I?'"

No influential psychoanalyst, however, has ignored the problem of traumatic injuries to the self, for our purposes to be called *self-image*. The differences in clinical thought have heightened with the increasing challenges to classical Freudian psychology by the object relations school of psychoanalysis. The leading theorist in psychology of the self, Heinz Kohut, states,

> Psychoanalytic theory based on drive and conflict theory [Freudian psychoanalytic theory] cannot illuminate the essence of fractured, enfeebled, discontinuous human existence: it cannot explain the essence of the schizophrenic's fragmentation [like Cho], the struggle of the patient who suffers from a narcissistic personality disorder to reassemble himself, the despair—the guiltless despair, I stress—of those who in late middle age discover that the basic patterns of their self as laid down in their nuclear ambitions and ideals have not been realized. Dynamic-structural Freudian psychology does not do justice to these problems of man, cannot encompass the problems of Tragic Man. (Chessick, 1977)

The myth of Narcissus tells the story of a person so in love with himself that his love brought tragedy to his lover and suitor, Ameineus. Ameineus killed himself in desperation and desolation because he could not woo Narcissus, and his blood soaked the earth and up sprang the white narcissus flower from which came the well-known classical narcotic, Narcissus oil. In this timeless myth we can identify Narcissus's stubborn pride in his own beauty, the unempathic hostile and arrogant behavior to others, the primary preoccupation of Narcissus with that other self, his mirroring self-object that would always remain true to him whatever happened and the condensing of death, sleep, *narcos*, and peace. This myth lies at the heart of the definition of the pathology of narcissism and illustrates why the different schools of psychoanalysis take different approaches to the nature of this form of mental illness.

At risk of oversimplification, we might view these differences in psychoanalytic theories in terms of the computer. Freud's comes with three separate operating systems, powered dynamically by the instinctual drives of aggression and sex from the repressed id, the mostly conscious adaptive tools are the ego and the conscience of "guilty man." Guilt emerged through resolving Oedipal strivings in competition with the opposite sex parent and was embodied in formation of the superego. These three dynamic functionalities of the human mind—or operating systems—must network without either excessive leakage or irreconcilable conflict. Originally trained as a pediatric neurologist, Freud described in his project how these structures and their dynamic interactions could ultimately be demonstrated in the neurocircuitry of the brain, thus anticipating modern neuroscience.

The object relations school of Melanie Klein, later modified by Otto Kernberg in his influential writings on borderline psychopathology, magnifies the ego. It is less of a determinate operating system, whose Freudian function was that of mediating demands of the real world, primitive drives of the id, and prohibitions of the superego. In her new computer model we have primarily the self as the dominant or only operating system, its evolving primordial being loaded with introjected software, some of which is "goodness," whereas the other is "badness." Badness becomes destructive aggressiveness toward self or others, whereas goodness creates loving intimacy with self-esteem.

Such downloading, as Freud suspected of the conscience of superego function, forms the self through intimate parenting with introjected experiences of nurturing that can be psychologically poisoning. All of this, we must remember, theoretically occurs before acquisition of language, and this is the dilemma we have in discussing "preverbal," "residual infantile," or "pre-Oedipal" psychic forces. We are trying to discuss a process set in motion prior to the child's ability to organize experience and communicate through language. In theory, it is suspected to be the equivalent of later pathological autistic states; an enormous world of experience is locked into a mind with severely impaired if not paucity of communicative language.

For our purposes, the Object Relations Theory of both Klein and Kernberg are important, because they provide insight into the nature and source of human aggression. The poisonous preverbal introjects can, in these clinicians' behavioral models, be projected out in the form of what they call *projective identification*. In other words, the fire on the inside of a person's psyche is blown outward like a solar flare. The dilemma of experiencing the unjustified rage of borderline psychopathology in adults can be understood as bad introjects from depriving or hurtful parenting, for example, Klein's bad breast being projected onto the caregiver. In clinical theory, it follows that the cure would be the patient's learning in therapy that the caregiver is not either all good or all bad as occurs in "splitting of the object."

If the caregiver appears to be distracted or dozing, for example, the patient can hopefully learn that other human caregivers could do the same without deserving hatred in retribution for absolute neglect. Such hatred, therefore, could be the projection outward of the poisonous introjects from emotional maternal abandonment, as in the mother who is too depressed to care. Expressions of rage toward this caregiver, whether verbal or in violent actions like cutting or switching to a "better," more caring therapist, are then diagnosed and, it is hoped, interpreted as projective identification.

Within the clinical relationship, this process means that the borderline patient has justification for overwhelming aggressive feelings toward the caretaking therapist due to the latter's expression of neglect—momentarily neglectful dozing that has nothing necessarily to do with liking or not liking the patient. Of course, if the caretaker actually does fall asleep or actually does deprive the patient, then the patient most likely has found reenactment of early parental trauma in selection of a bad therapist.

One could make the case for purposes of illustration that, in the first case, the patient doth protest too much in order to allow introjected badness to project onto the caretaker. Switching therapists allows dilution of the primitive rage Kernberg and Klein would trace to introjected badness from failed maternal bonding in early childhood. It also, within this theory, perpetuates defensive splitting of the intimate relational object into goodness and badness.

For such a borderline personality, recognition that goodness and badness exist in the same relational object is intolerable. Splitting allows different people to be all good and all bad. In this way, the borderline patient need never confront her true experience of being mothered—thus exposing the patient to intolerable rage even, theoretically, matricidal in magnitude. Holding the patient while interpreting the source of the rage hopefully results in the therapeutic substitution of the therapist's goodness and stability for this failure of maternal bonding.

At risk of further reductionism and oversimplification, the Lacan school of continental psychoanalysis vigorously disputes the existence of such a high-functioning operating system in the preverbal infant and child, one that can interact with the outside object, thus creating self-objects of the object relations school of psychoanalysis. In Lacan's computer model, the hard drive does not come with Freud's, Klein's, or Kernberg's operating system and is fairly raw or unformatted and is essentially feral and requiring socialization for all programming. Kohut, at the other extreme, finds the naturally unfolding anlage, much like the embryonic development of the human body, of a person's "self" from birth.

Kohut finds this through experience-near attunement to his patient's emotional state in therapy. Such attunement depends on quality empathy, natural to the effective clinician but improved through clinical experience and training. The human mind he finds, therefore, is born with the operating system of the self with active and powerfully unfolding self-image. This inborn self-image—or *imago*—is mirrored within intimate nurturing relations with the parent, "the reciprocal gleam in the infant and mother's eyes." Like any embryonic development, the self evolves naturally. Kohut infers genetic talents to the most damaged of self-images, for example, the celebrity actress, both beautiful and self-destructive, and, like Narcissus, never finding love within a relationship. His theory of destructive behavior resulting from psychological disturbance, however, evolves from early childhood damage to the bipolar self through faulty mirroring.

Kohut's theory of bipolar self includes the pole of the infantile grandiose self, operating with the magical thinking of an adult literally expecting Santa Claus to appear in some form on Christmas, not just wishing but expecting. This grandiose self appears early in therapy as presentations of entitlement, for example, rage over being billed for time with the therapist, which should be gratis. The other pole is the idealizing self, which also shows up in therapy in exaltation of the therapist.

In one instance a patient recently evaluated had several encounters with clinicians following dangerous acts of self-harm through cutting. Each time, she would receive self-destructive medications that would either numb her through opiate dependence or soothe her through Xanax dependence. When she told the last physician that he was the best ever—the only one who understood her—she virtually wrote out her own prescription for opiates and Xanax. She died of an overdose.

It would be Kohut's curative treatment to accept the attribution of "the greatest" for his clinical acumen but kindly and affirmatively prescribe tapering doses of numbing opiates and soothing Xanax. This would not be met with further acclamation of the idealizing self toward him, but gradually the patient would be forced to build internal structure to her own self-image—*imago*—to begin soothing herself and find other means to reduce the emotional pain. It is with such attunement to the grandiose and idealizing self that Kohut is able to visualize the damaged self and begin the repair.

It is also through this means that he sees into the emotional volcano of damaged self and recognizes that trickles of lava through requiring payment and tapering of medications mean a fiery inferno of narcissistic rage. A clearcut example of this volcanic rage can be seen in cases of plastic surgeons being murdered by their patients. Even the most ethical and best of plastic surgeons is at risk.

Of course, this risk is well known in the plastic surgery profession and more often than not leads to presurgical psychological testing to rule out mental instability—more often than not, pathological narcissism, intolerant of imperfect outcomes of cosmetic surgery.

Kohut works on the opposite side of the same coin, mirroring human imperfection, both his and his patient's. Being extremely empathic with his patient, he can see in the clinical field when something said or not said, done or not done injures the grandiose or idealizing self. At that time he makes the interpretation of the injury. With repeated encounters he sees the patient's self, in the form of self-image, strengthening and less vulnerable and fragile with perceived insult to the grandiose self and disappointment in the idealizing self.

Narcissistic rage, therefore, is not equivalent to visualizing blood backing up from a leaky valve in the heart either during imaging or in actual surgery. But through experience-near examination demanding high-quality trained empathic clinical relatedness with the patient, Kohut is convincing with his findings that it not only exists but is as real as an abnormal echocardiogram or direct visualization of the surgical field.

Narcissistic rage, therefore, is known through clinical experience and the operations of empathic successes and failures inside the clinical treatment dyad. The trained and inborn effectiveness of therapeutic empathy, therefore, knows the visually submerged rage as well as the cardiologist correctly predicting an invisible defect in a patient's heart valve. Unfortunately, the lack of hard imaging studies and surgical fields in knowing the bipolar self of pathological narcissism and the human destructiveness of narcissistic rage creates intellectual battles among clinicians, psychologists, and philosophers. For anyone who has had either the experience-near relatedness of a Paul Keller—or even his experience-distant, described by Paul's father—narcissistic rage is a valid entity that leads to understanding of human destructiveness.

Kohut's validation of narcissistic rage as a destructive clinical entity, on the other hand, depends on repeated, intense, and empathic encounters with emotionally disturbed people, oftentimes successful and normal appearing within most social environments. Such validation is hard to prove, however, within the ascetic circles of data-based psychological research or philosophy. For validation, therefore, we can use both the experience-distant data of Paul Keller as reported in his case as well as the experience-near judgments of the serial interviews with him in 1993 and his letters subsequent to the interviews.

In a letter dated September 27, 1994, Paul Keller responded to a newspaper article about him. The reporter focused on his pediatric neurology diagnosis of attention deficit hyperactivity disorder.

He wrote,

> I was complimentary of her style, but also kindly mentioned the following. First of all she called me an academic failure. She certainly has access to the records and I was not thrilled with that. I also felt she could have done a much better job of canvassing the many who know me rather than (as the Arson Task Force did) seek only Mom's input, which we knew presents unique views. I was STUNNED at the lack of broadcast coverage of the August gathering [the sentencing hearing]—Doc, I think you are correct about law enforcement influence over any helpful press in this case. I was displeased with the awards given to the Arson Task Force for these exact reasons, no more, no less. First of all, I confessed the first time of my own volition, and their seemingly successful tactics were actually what we'd call lies that made no impact on the depth of my willingness to cooperate. Furthermore, as we see the sketch—[a remarkably accurate composite drawing performed through interviewing witnesses by a retired Snohomish County Deputy Sheriff] that was pretty good, but we all know that many of the descriptive verbiage [The Arson Task Force's psychological profile] was generic enough to apply to thousands. I suppose what's

> most troubling is them gallivanting around the country spouting their perceived wisdom, when in fact the vast majority of what THEY report as FACT is their opinion. Could the reins on the press be image savers, as the real truth about me would negate all the garbage they preached, and I might add, that the local press has been eager to swallow. Back to the educ. [*sic*] Thing ... why wouldn't she state that I excelled in all fields of study that I saw as applicable, or were of interest to me. Lest we forget, Einstein failed math because he viewed its concept and application differently than the instructor. mhmmmmm I am very curious about the progress in your endeavors re my case and am so very grateful to you.

Margaret Keller, wincing at the memory of Paul as a young boy, remembers sitting with her son at a friend's funeral years ago. Before the funeral Paul Kenneth Keller looked around the hushed room full of mourners and said in a loud whisper, "Man they've gotta do something about this dump. It really needs renovation." Here is the ultimate grandiosity over man's ultimate tragedy—born to die. And his sister told the press, "All his life Paul hurt people by his words and actions, and he didn't know why." This is one description of an emerging narcissistic offender, indifferent to psychological borders and indifferent to the pain he inflicts upon others.

In the following, we can see how well the family and acquaintances of Paul Keller provide uncontested, lay descriptions of lifelong personality traits aligning with minimal variance to all the criteria necessary to diagnose narcissistic personality disorder, utilizing the *DSM IV.* The specific criteria are numbered, followed by statements made by both Paul and family and friends about him.

Narcissistic personality disorder is defined in *DSM IV* as

> A pervasive pattern of grandiosity (in fantasy or behavior), need for admiration, and lack of empathy, beginning by early adulthood and present in a variety of contexts, as indicated by five (or more) of the following:

1. **Has a grandiose sense of self-importance.**

    Compared his academic situation with Einstein's school problems.
    He is irrational and impossible to reason with—thus in fantasy world.
    Disciplinary measures have never worked with Paul—because of this grandiose self.

2. **Is preoccupied with fantasies of unlimited success power, brilliance, beauty, or ideal love.**

    Expressed awe of his power to create a virtual holocaust with just a "flick of the Bic." Photographed the horrific product of his omnipotent power, "Just taking leak."

Overspent on expensive clothing; had to look the best, while not brushing his teeth.
Beat emergency crews to fires, carried emergency lights in car.
Vociferously critiqued dispatchers he monitored on his scanner.
Not realistic. He lies. Lie is untruth with intent to deceive. Pathological lying (pseudologia phantastica: Delbruck, 1900s). Synonymous with mythomania or morbid lying, in which the patient's obvious deceit is noted for chronicity and frequency of the lies and the apparent lack of benefit derived from them. Pathological liars believe their lies to the extent that the belief may approach being delusional.
Does not see things as they really are.
He is unwilling and unable to face the truth about himself.

3. **Believes that he or she is special and unique.**

Bankruptcy was not for men like him.
Only his family could not get along with him.
He is argumentative and needs to be right.
Tells us, the family, that we are the only ones who cannot get along with him.

4. **Requires excessive admiration.**

Marriage was all about him, his sexual prowess, and needs to be The Man.
He related better with older people than peers. He has a tender caring other side but killed them without expressing remorse.

5. **Has a sense of entitlement.**

He blames others and does not want to assume responsibility for his behaviors.
Out of control with spending. He does not earn credit; he is entitled to it.

6. **Is interpersonally exploitative.**

Stole silver dollars from his beloved grandfather.
Sexually degrading to wife, whom he knowingly pursued as a recent rape victim.
He is demanding.
He stole things during childhood.
He is unhelpful and untruthful around the house.
He likes to frighten others.
He is manipulative and tries to both outsmart and out argue.

He teased, irritated, and physically abused his brother and sister throughout childhood.
He picked fights and teased children in school.

7. **Lacks empathy.**

Brother said Paul's reign of terror was the equivalent of shoplifting a grapefruit.
He is oblivious to the pain he causes.
Showed no respect for the mourners at a funeral, audibly debasing the funeral parlor.
He is inconsiderate.
He only thinks of himself and is insensitive to others' needs.
He is intrusive and does not respect others' space.
He does not try to be understanding.
He does not care how I or others feel.

8. **Is often envious of others or believes others are envious of him or her.**

Totally distorted the balance of power among his siblings, believing they were favored by mother.

9. **Shows arrogance, haughty behaviors or attitudes.**

Was so abusive with suppliers for minor errors like misspellings; father would have had to fire anyone but his own son.
He is loud, very impatient, rude, and harsh.
He is very abusive emotionally and verbally,
He's a rageaholic.
He ridicules.
He's extremely impulsive.
He has innumerable inappropriate and unacceptable behaviors.

The excellent alignment between personality traits documented by examiners, family, and friends provides the diagnostic foundation for research of apocalyptic violent rage. After the mass murder suicides of both the events of 9/11 and the Virginia Tech massacre, research is needed more than ever to study the psychoneuroendocrinology of violent offenders. In the case of Paul Keller, as well as Cho, we have the profile of severely abnormal development and disastrous disintegration of the self. This disintegration is associated with well-documented attachment disorder and no juvenile criminal record. The two cases—Cho and Keller—align very well, but they also align with other infamous school mass murders including Columbine, the event that Cho once told his school teacher he wanted to emulate.

Select psychobiological states and behavioral parameters can be monitored chronobiologically with supplemental inclusion of brain imaging and pharmacological challenges, including alcohol. In the case of Keller, for example, it is probably true that his PET scan and functional MRI, both visually reporting regional abnormalities of brain function, would in fact be abnormal and would become even more abnormal upon exposure within a virtualized fire environment. Increasing blood alcohol concentrations would further alter such visualized real-time replications of metabolic brain dysfunction, as would serial samples of spinal fluid serotonin and blood sugars.

Murray (1992) at Harvard coined the neuropsychiatric metaphor for violence, *limbic music*. By this, Murray was reiterating the school of object relations theorists' knowledge of rage by hearing it in the empathic clinical interview. Before we see the final apocalyptic timeline of a Paul Keller, it is important to see the composition of limbic music—the neurochemical scoring, the regional disharmony of brain dysfunction—compositions that are graphically reproducible with metrics.

To extend Murray's metaphor, we need to be able to see meaningful graphical representations of the at-risk state of mind as well as the limbic music of different violent states of mind. What did Keller's functional MRI and PET scan look like when leveraging the flick of a Bic after urinating into a virtual holocaust for an entire city?

Additionally, we can hypothesize that normal controls and volunteers with no history of violence, but with the narcissistic critical personality factors described in Keller's investigation, would all be consistently different and remain stable over time. More complex and difficult—yet demanded by the escalating incidence of personality disorders today—would be the hard testing of brain function during the course of empathic therapy as described by Kohut.

Once again, could Paul Keller have been successfully treated by Heinz Kohut or his equivalent peer through the long and arduous therapeutic course of empathic treatment of his bipolar self? Of the hundreds of violent offenders and severe personality disorders examined, it is likely that Keller was among a small percentage of treatable cases. But all the warning flags of the timeline presented above would have had to be addressed when there was clear recognition. Here was a young man presenting for diagnosis and treatment of the first somatic signs of disintegration from narcissistic injury. Then he presented with robust, objective, and valid psychological test evidence of a declaration of emotional bankruptcy.

Most offenders do not seek help before committing serious felonies. Of course, the warning signs are always there in retrospect. However, when the psychotic is actually capable of sophisticated psychotherapy for addressing his problem, he is too hardened for it to do any good. Let us use the well-known dramatic portrayal of Tony Soprano's therapy as an example of "too little, too late"—or, more likely, getting paid to do the impossible—cracking Tony Soprano's incorrigible criminality.

In *The Sopranos*, Tony's physical collapse is the trigger that sends him into therapy with Dr. Melfi, where he is forced to confront demons that have haunted his past. His current fight for supremacy is with his uncle "Junior," Corrado Soprano, who although the de jure capo, or family boss, is nonetheless a de facto subordinate to his nephew Tony. Junior is supported by Tony's domineering mother, who actually sets up a hit on her own son. Tony actually takes the requisite steps to kill her: an intent to kill combined with stalking the hospital halls with a pillow. His attempted matricide is only prevented by Livia Soprano's stroke, but thereafter, Tony cuts all ties with his mother. Dr. Melfi even suggests that Livia Soprano is dissociated from reality and might even be a narcissist herself.

But *The Sopranos* is a dark comedy in which, evil as they might be, Tony's intentions are still motivated by the need for power in a heavily structured criminal community, well within the context of what we have come to accept as a "Godfather" syndrome, the plight of the overtly and religiously moral individual at work within a completely immoral universe and within a community in which psychotic killers are manipulated, if at all possible, and if not, they are executed as an unacceptable threat. This community was described in the criminal trial of John Gotti, Jr., as "the Life."

Tony is suffering from guilt and sadness. He has guilt because of hatred for his mother and sadness because his mother hates him. Tony cannot openly explore his feelings because within the life—the life in an organized crime family dominated by the law of *omerta*, or silence—any hint that a member is breaking the code is a death warrant. Hence, whatever Tony's feelings are, as he sinks into more frequent and more intense panic attacks, his dealing with them has to be within the same context from which they spring. Therefore, Tony experiences increasing warning signs that a volcano is stirring, whose eruption will shift the tectonic plates of his life and alter the very balance of his confined world. But Tony, in order to survive within the world of organized crime, must be able to look outside of himself with as much acuity as he manages his own feelings of rage. As the Sicilians say, "Revenge is a dish best served cold." Therefore, even though he indulges himself in explosive rage, for the big revenge, such as the execution of FBI informant Sal "Big Pussy" Bonpensiero, Tony is very calculating. A killer, and quite possibly sociopathic, it is still all business. Tony is not an apocalyptic suicidal mass murderer.

Tony Soprano, because his dramatized therapy was the driving part of the show's story line, became a popular psychological hero, a criminal struggling with family issues that go to the heart of his criminality. Not so with real killers, however. Even among the pop-psych community, the self-help counselors shy away from discussing narcissistic personalities because, to be blunt, they simply do not understand the personality mechanics at work. Moreover, the narcissistic personality emerges from a pathology that runs so deep and may have a causality that defies the nonprofessional's attempt to define it. The true violent narcissist—a Ted Bundy, Jeffrey Dahmer, Gary Ridgway—is probably beyond therapy because he has become completely feral with respect to his predatory nature and is best studied and preserved, as harsh as that sounds, as a specimen of "narcissistic zoology."

Like a guided missile that an anti-missile needs to intercept, the best course of treatment for a budding narcissist is to catch one very early, looking at the warning signs of extreme violence, lack of empathy, a selfishness that goes beyond selfishness, and a destructive propensity that seems to defy human logic. Children who exhibit extreme cruelty, especially to animals and other defenseless beings; who have a fascination with starting fires; who erupt into extreme bouts of either self-directed or outward-directed rage; and who seem resistant to any attempts to show them what remorse means are on the road to adult narcissistic behavior and need to be treated early.

It should be pointed out, though, that most narcissists are not episodic offenders or potential mass murderers. Many, particularly those who manage to navigate within the system to their own advantage, can fit their tendencies into the system so that they succeed in ways that others cannot. We have all heard stories of ruthless executives, cruel managers who drain the life out of their subordinates to get ahead, spouses who abuse spouses psychologically, and even sports heroes who are especially brutal. Narcissism can be an impetus to success, but it can also ultimately destroy life. At its most extreme and dysfunctional, narcissism is at the center of what is the psychopathy underlying the rare compulsion of serial killing.

Chapter 9

Best Clinical Practices

Cho Seung-Hui first presented in an emergency room after he was taken into custody by the Virginia Tech police, who responded to a stalking complaint and then Cho's statement to his roommate that he might as well commit suicide. Thus, as Cho drifted further into a violent mental state, the emergency room was the first place where he could have been evaluated, set up for diagnosis, and released into the custody of his family. But the emergency room failed. This is a serious matter because, as healthcare funding in America had precipitously declined over the past forty years, emergency rooms, as underfunded and understaffed as they are, have become ground zero for not just healthcare emergencies but for public safety emergencies as well.

First Encounter: Clinical Assessment in the New Millennium

> Emergency rooms are the new ground zero. Terrorism and bioterrorism are different animals than what we're used to dealing with. Sept 11 showed that emergency departments—not fire departments, not police—are now the first responders of the 21st century. We have to bring front-line disaster planning to hospitals, but it's not there yet. (Auer, 2002)

At the core of missed opportunities in criminal investigations is something called *linkage blindness*, when information in one compartment is not related to information in an adjacent or related compartment so that the big picture is lost. In serial killer investigations, linkage blindness often occurs when one agency does not share relevant information with another agency investigating the same case. As we saw in the Beltway Sniper case, different agencies investigating the same ongoing shooting spree used different computers and, thus, sometimes important clues were lost.

In the Keller case, a police officer released the arsonist right after setting one fire and en route to setting another because he did not fit the federal profile of a serial arsonist. He did, however, fit the publicized composite drawing that was remarkably accurate. In the Cho case linkage blindness occurred when the different first responders did not share valuable background information about Cho or when Cho's special needs medical information never reached the administration at Virginia Tech. Linkage blindness occurred when the psychiatric evaluators at St. Albans did not receive Cho's records from Virginia Tech in time to make a more careful evaluation. Linkage blindness also occurred in the Cho case when no one from either Virginia Tech or St. Albans called Cho's parents for background medical information on their child.

It is easy to minimize first responder information, but it is almost always a mistake to do so. First responders, particularly in episodic offender cases, are usually critically important because first responders on the scene or as investigators usually come into contact with information that is later neglected when more information or clues pile in. Cases tend to get more complicated than they seem and bits of information that can unravel the mystery are often buried beneath subsequent facts.

First responder information is often buried at the bottom of a case file, many times overlooked, and then only rediscovered at the end. This is what happened in the Cho case. It also happens in some serial murder cases, before the police realize that a single homicide case is part of a series. When investigators go back to that early case, as did King County detective Robert Keppel in the Lynda Healy murder, committed by Ted Bundy at the University of Washington, they often find critically important clues fitting the series that were overlook by initial crime scene investigators.

The 9/11 Anthrax Case

What happened in the Cho case and in the Bundy and Jeffrey Dahmer cases also happened in the very well-publicized anthrax case in the days following the 9/11 tragedy. This case, still under investigation, resulted in the humiliation of one of the suspects—later cleared—and quite possibly cost the life of another suspect named Bruce Ivins, probably innocent, who later committed suicide. This is the story of that case and why, because first responder information was not regarded seriously, it is so similar to the tragedy of the Cho case.

The anthrax case of 9/11 is very instructive because of the following similarities that were overlooked.

There was nothing unusual during Dr. Christos Tsonas's ER shift at Holy Cross Hospital in Fort Lauderdale on a June day in 2001, approximately 90 days before the Twin Towers were brought down by two hijacked commercial airliners. As typical of the season, tourists were gone, a breeze off the ocean was welcome, even if warm. Time to begin thinking of scheduling shifts to maximize time outdoors as the humidity and tropical temperatures shoot up. A summer shift for a Florida summer was smack in the middle of the day. That was good. An ER doctor could get eighteen holes in during the cool morning and get a little fishing in before nightfall. One of the bennies of the specialty of emergency medicine—tough and stressful duty when on, but when off, you are off. Days were getting long and hot on Florida's Gold Coast. Other than that, it was the usual quiet, interspersed with crying babies and worried mothers—then punctuated with life-threatening emergencies. The longer it was quiet, it seemed, the more likely it was to get an MCI, or mass casualty incident, to get the adrenalin flowing.

There was nothing unusual either about the two young men who presented for emergency care that day. They identified themselves as pilots, and Dr. Tsonas noted that they were foreign. That was nothing unusual for Florida. They were probably tourists, he later stated. And, they were both well dressed, polite, and healthy in appearance. Ziad Jarrah, age 26, brought his roommate, Ahmed al-Haznawi, age 20, in for an emergency check-up of an infection on his leg. Because his roommate was healthy without any medical history such as diabetes to complicate the presentation, Dr. Tsonas's first clinical encounter with this patient took only 10 minutes.

The lesion on al-Haznawi shin was black and rather ugly in appearance. It was caused, the patient said, by bumping into a suitcase two months earlier. Dr. Tsonas had not seen anything like this before, but this was a chronic condition easily taken care of by a local dermatologist. It was not really an emergency. Because things were quiet in the ER, Dr. Tsonas took care of the problem himself. He cleaned the wound and prescribed the broad-spectrum spectrum antibiotic Keflex. However, inasmuch as the mechanism of injury, also called the patient's *presentation of the cause*, did not really fit the presentation of a localized infection of that ugly a nature, Dr. Tsonas documented it in more detail than he may otherwise have done. Later, this detailed documentation would jar his memory when FBI agents would present him with his Keflex bottle found in the nearby residence of one of the 9/11 hijackers of United Flight 93 believed to be headed for the White House or Capitol, crashing instead three months later in Pennsylvania. This constituted an evidentiary link between the 9/11 hijacking and treatment Dr. Tsonas provided to the two mysterious ER visitors a few months earlier. What did it mean?

Although like all doctors practicing within walking distance of the American Media Inc. (AMI) building later infused with anthrax spores that killed their photo editor, Robert Stevens, Tsonas had boned up on anthrax since the 2001 scare. But he had completely forgotten about the two men who presented early the previous summer. When showed photos by the FBI, he made positive identifications of Flight 93 Hijacker, al-Haznawi, and accomplice, Jarrah, believed to have taken over the controls of United Flight 93 in the final minutes of that epic day. Then, agents gave Dr. Tsonas a copy of his own notes from the emergency room visit, and he read them.

"Oh, my God, my written description is consistent with cutaneous anthrax. I was surprised," he was reported to have said.

That would be what proved a significant understatement about the first clinical encounter of a mid-Atlantic epidemic of anthrax engulfing the events of 9/11 with escalating terror of a foreign attack by weapons of mass destruction.

Dr. Tsonas commented further, "They were well-dressed foreigners. I assumed they were tourists."

Between his unusually detailed notes and vivid clinical image for such a brief ER encounter, he proceeded to describe ulceration of al-Haznawi's shin. The ulcerated lesion, he said, was a little less than an inch wide and blackish, its edges raised and red. He then reported his clinical intervention, having removed the dry scab over the wound, cleansing it, and prescribing Keflex, an antibiotic widely used to combat bacterial infections but not specifically indicated for anthrax. He did not take cultures and had not thought of anthrax, a bacterial infection, which at that time was extremely rare in the United States and unfamiliar to most doctors. After discussing the disease and its symptoms with the FBI agents, and explaining what else could possibly explain the leg wound, Dr. Tsonas was still perplexed.

A spider bite was unlikely, he thought. As for the hijackers' explanation of a suitcase bump, "That's a little unusual for a healthy guy, but not impossible," Tsonas reflected.

In fact, he reportedly considered it unlikely, both at the time he examined al-Haznawi and even more so later, as he studied anthrax. He retrospectively diagnosed the lesion, so peculiar to him back in June, as cutaneous anthrax. Tsonas was later contacted by both federal agents and medical experts, presumably bioterrorism and infectious disease experts from Johns Hopkins School of Medicine.

Dr. Tara O'Toole, Director of Johns Hopkins Center for Civilian Biodefense Strategies, said,

> After consulting with additional medical experts on the al-Haznawi case, I am more persuaded than ever that [Dr. Tsonas's] diagnosis of cutaneous anthrax was correct. This is a unique investigation that has many highly technical aspects. There's legitimate concern the FBI may not have access to the kinds of expertise that could be essential in putting all these pieces together.

Her experts from the Johns Hopkins Center for Civilian Biodefense Strategies prepared a memorandum, circulated among top federal officials, concluding that the diagnosis of cutaneous anthrax was the most probable and cogent interpretation of the data available.

"Such a conclusion, of course, raises the possibility that the hijackers were handling anthrax and were the perpetrators of the anthrax letter attacks" (as reported by NBC, *NY Post*, and brought up on the Senate floor).

A senior intelligence official, who spoke on the condition of anonymity, said that George J. Tenet, director of Central Intelligence, had recently read the Hopkins memo and "that issue had been examined by both the CIA and the FBI. No one is dismissing this. We reviewed the memo and are working with the bureau to insure that it continues to be pursued."

Dr. Tsonas stuck with his retrospective diagnosis, supported by the special group at Johns Hopkins, and questioned, "What were they doing looking at crop dusters?" He was echoing experts' fears that hijackers may have wanted to spread lethal germs as weapons of mass destruction (WMD). "There are too many coincidences," Tsonas asserted in conclusion. They were actually carrying anthrax, had hundreds of thousands of dollars in cash to spend on a crop duster, and actively engaged in a method to inflict a biological weapon on a mass population.

But John E. Collingswood, an FBI spokesman, disagreed, saying that "the possibility of a connection between the hijackers and the anthrax attacks had been deeply explored."

There has never been any further explanation of how this investigation was pursued and why it was abandoned, in contradiction to premonitions of Dr. O'Toole, long-time federal government medical insider, who had served as assistant secretary for health and safety at the Department of Energy from 1993 to 1997.

"This was fully investigated," he stated, "and widely vetted among multiple agencies several months ago. Exhaustive testing did not support that anthrax was present anywhere the hijackers had been. While we always welcome new information, nothing new has in fact developed."

Later referred to as a cavalier and condescending assertion, his basic thesis was also challenged. The terrorists attacking by airplane did not have to have spores on their person to have been directly involved in later bioterror attacks on the media and congress. Apparently suspecting an inside job, possibly motivated by earlier bureaucratic fights for more money to fund bioterrorism, two U.S. federal scientists with access to weaponized anthrax were broadly and prominently presented to the public. One was ultimately cleared but not before successfully suing for defamation of character. The other committed suicide, probably not because of any involvement with bioterrorism but because he was a possible sex offender, had borderline issues with dealing with sexual urge, had been outed to the FBI by one of his female coworkers, and was facing unbearable embarrassment and humiliation. Conveniently for the investigators, dead men don't talk. Politically, the anthrax epidemic coinciding with the events of 9/11 could be left hanging as "unofficially cleared." There have been no more attacks.

Drs. O'Toole and Tsonas certainly are more than well-intentioned practitioners. One had intimate contact with an infected hijacker and retrospectively diagnosed al-Hazwani's ulcer as consistent with cutaneous anthrax. The other had federal experience, professional credentials, and consensus expertise to support that experience-near medical opinion of Dr. Tsonas. For our purposes, the evidence upon which Drs. Tsonas and O'Toole based their conclusions remains uncontested—at least for the public record. Thus, this alleged first bioterrorism case of cutaneous anthrax being diagnosed at Holy Cross Hospital, Fort Lauderdale, in June of 2001 has never been technically cleared by authorities as the earliest alert to subsequent and coordinated attacks on the United States by both unconventional weapons of mass destruction and airplanes.

Alhaznawi entered the United States on June 8, 2001, and moved into an apartment in Lauderdale-by-the-Sea at Delray Beach with Ziad Jarrah, the highjacker who brought al-Haznawi to the Holy Cross ER. al-Haznawi and other hijackers lived and attended flight school near the Boca Raton headquarters of American Media, Inc. In fact, it was widely reported that hijacker Atta's al-Qaeda cell took flight school training in Boca Raton not far from American Media. They even rented apartments from the wife of an editor of *The Sun*, an AMI publication.

The second reported incident with anthrax—whether or not actually the first attack on the United States with WMD—occurred coincidental with the events of 9/11 at the headquarters of American Media, Inc., in Boca Raton, Florida. The 55,000-square-foot office building was completely contaminated with anthrax spores, causing the death of AMI's photo editor, Robert Stevens, on October 2, 2001. Of interest is the fact that this first U.S. victim of the bioterrorism engulfing the events of 9/11 had run an article blasting the Saudi royals. Because the incubation period for anthrax can be 4 weeks or more, the date of the attack cannot be narrowed down to right before 9/11, before the hijackers died. The hijackers lived within walking distance of AMI headquarters in Boca Raton. Although the anthrax proved to be the same strain as that in subsequent letters to the media and congress, it could have been delivered to the building before 9/11.

Because the entire 66,000-square-foot office building was contaminated with anthrax spores, the point of origin for this first attack with WMD remains unknown. Nor do traces of anthrax found in local post offices solve the mystery, because they could have been the result of cross-contamination from American Media's outgoing, rather than incoming, mail. So the attacker could have sent it in a letter or package, or he (they) could have hand-delivered it to the building.

The young Arab flight trainees clustered around Holy Cross Hospital and AMI were hardly lightweights. Authorities in Dubai had detained and questioned Jarrah at the request of the U.S. government before allowing him to continue his journey from Afghanistan to Florida. In October a Delray Beach pharmacist reported informing the FBI of two of the 9/11 hijackers, Mohamed Atta and Marwan al-Shehhi, having presented to his consulting window. They were asking for something to treat irritations on "Mr. Atta's hands." This meant that Atta had come into contact with anthrax as well.

Maureen Stevens, the widow of the AMI bioterroism attack, filed a wrongful death suit that "could embarrass the U.S. government and provide insight into the ongoing investigation of the Fall-2001 bioterrorism attacks." The "embarrassing" lawsuit held that spores "were known to be missing from an Army laboratory at Fort Detrick, MD, as early as 1992 and the litigants accused the government of failing to adequately secure them. 'The bottom line is that a lot of Freedom of Information Act (FOIA) requests were not acknowledged or were not answered or responded to.'"

Her lawsuit was filed in Palm Beach County Circuit Court and named Ft. Detrick–USAMRIID, Battelle Memorial Institute, and other possible sources of the anthrax, such as BioPort Corp. of Lansing, Michigan, a vaccine manufacturer (Bushouse, 2003).

Although we only suggest the possibility that Dr. Tsonas encountered the first victim of the bioterrorism attacks that engulfed the events of 9/11, the coincidences here are overwhelming. It was too many coincidences that became the basis of the cases against Bundy in Aspen Colorado—for example, "pattern,"—and Wayne Williams in the Atlanta Child Murder cases—for example, "theme." Law enforcement was robbed of the opportunity to finally and officially clear this first known bioterrorism attack on the United States when its top suspect of an internally driven bureaucratic plot within our own government committed suicide after his arrest. He could just as likely have committed suicide, however, not because he was complicit in the bioterrorism attack but because he was afraid his dark secret of harboring thoughts of sexual offenses would become public.

Although politically cleared in the consciousness of the public—so desperate for closure of this horror they would likely be settled by any reasonable prosecution—the attacks on America by weapons of mass destruction, coinciding with the Kamikaze-style attacks on New York City and Washington, D.C., remain officially for the public record a mystery. It is reasonable to believe that the FBI decisively cleared these attacks for the criminal record but, for security reasons, cannot reveal the facts. Of interest, however, is the recent National Academy for Science investigation into the chain of bioterror evidence leading to naming of an internal federal terrorist, rather than foreigners, later to attack by air on 9/11.

As reported in the *Washington Post*, August 2009,

> A key congressional critic of the FBI's investigation of the 2001 anthrax attacks called Friday for a broader inquiry into the government's handling of the case, saying he remained deeply skeptical of the bureau's claim that a Maryland scientist acted alone in carrying out the country's worst bioterrorism attack.

> Our government—and specifically, the FBI—suffers from a credibility gap on this issue," Rep. Rush D. Holt (D-N.J.) told an expert panel that convened in Washington this week to begin reviewing the scientific methods the FBI used to link the attacks to Bruce E. Ivins, a microbiologist who worked in the Army's chief biodefense lab at Fort Detrick, Maryland.
>
> Rep. Holt said that the 15-member panel was appointed by the National Academy of Sciences, at the FBI's request, to provide an independent review of the high-tech genetic analysis that ultimately led investigators to Ivins. The review is expected to last up to 18 months.

Regardless of whether the Academy confirms the "lone gunman" conspiracy of a federal mad scientist or does not, such complacency, whether justified or not, cannot stand in the practice of either emergency or disaster medicine today.

> There are going to be more weapons-of-mass-destruction incidents. ... Terrorism means bombs and bullets, and this stuff is not subtle. What do you do if there's a terrorist with a bomb [—or patient infected by germ warfare—] on the stretcher next to you? If you're dead, you're not useful to anyone. ... We are targets, but we're not commandos. (Jonathan Burstein, Director of Disaster Medicine, Beth Israel Deaconess Medical Center, Boston, American College of Emergency Physicians National Conference, Seattle, Washington, October 2002)

Accordingly, when Tsonas's diagnosis, supported by experts at Johns Hopkins, is so authoritatively silenced by the FBI, what are the ramifications? Here is what we can substantiate. Al-Haznawi's roommate, presenting at Holy Cross that June 2001 day, had recently been in Afghanistan. We know that Dr. Ayman al-Zawahiri, a reportedly successful and competent Egyptian internal medicine specialist and current second in command leader of al-Qaeda, had sought anthrax for use against targets in the United States. When Dr. Zawahiri's home in Kabul was examined after the fall of the Taliban, it tested positive for anthrax, thereby establishing the presence of the bacteria in an al-Qaeda compound. We can infer that al-Qaeda had the means as well as the intent of using anthrax, had anthrax in its possession, and was seeking a delivery mechanism. What was that mechanism?

On September 18, 2001, an anonymous party mailed two letters containing dry anthrax bacteria to the *New York Post* and NBC. Two more letters were mailed 3 weeks later to Senators Patrick Leahy and Tom Daschle containing more lethal dosages of the same Ames strain of anthrax. All four letters deliberately connected themselves to the aerial attack by beginning, in bold print, "09-11-01." The last two letters also stated, "We have this anthrax."

For the public record, the FBI did not find the person(s) who mailed the letters, the photocopier on which the messages were reproduced, the equipment for inserting the powdered anthrax into the envelopes, or the laboratory establishment where the anthrax had to have been grown, dried, and processed into micron-sized weapons that aerosolized into a lethal mist. At least, there are no currently known facts to explain this necessary sequence of events associated so intimately with what we now know was a highly sophisticated and elaborately planned attack. In such an orchestrated attack, we know there have to be—and were—clear divisions of specialized terrorists.

Of course, it is possible that the perpetrators and the lab were not within the United States, even though, because the substance had entered the U.S. postal system, it still fell under the jurisdiction of the FBI or U.S. Customs or the postal police. It is still reasonable to assume, however, that the four weaponized bioterrorism letters, like the four aircraft, were part of the same attack; the letters all stated, "Death to America."

Although the anthrax that killed Robert Stevens proved to be the same strain as the subsequent letters, it could have been delivered to the building either before or after 9/11. Most chilling of all is the fact that the FBI determined, based on boarding passes, that 19 conspirators were on the 4 hijacked planes. Both al-Haznawi and Jarrah did not use aliases at Holy Cross ER. It is very possible that al-Qaeda cell members anywhere could have given their boarding passes to other conspirators who had been trained for a suicide mission.

> Since it is not known for certain how many conspirators arrived in America in the spring and summer of 2001, there is no means of excluding the possibility that some conspirators were not aboard the planes. Nor do all the names on the boarding passes match the names of the known conspirators. For example, a person using the identity "Fayed Ahmed" arrived from Jeddah in June 2001 and helped organize the bank accounts, credit cards and other logistics for the 9-11 hijackers. He disappeared after 9/11. His name was not listed on the manifests of any of the flights. There was also a name "Banihammad Fayez" on Flight 175, so the FBI theorized that "Ahmed" had assumed the alias who was on the Flight 175. Or there may have been two individuals: one who did logistics and one who was a suicide hijacker. (Epstein, 2003)

So, we do not know which al-Qaeda operatives were killed. Even more disconcerting is the fact that on September 12, 2001, the FBI identified Abdulaziz Alomari as a hijacker who died on Flight 11. After the FBI published his photo, Abdulaziz Almari came forward in Saudi Arabia and informed authorities that his passport had been stolen in 1995 while he studied electrical engineering at the University of Denver. He even reported this identity theft to law enforcement at the time. "I couldn't believe it when the FBI put me on their list. They gave my name and my date of birth, but I am not a suicide bomber. I am here. I am alive. I have no idea how to fly a plane. I had nothing to do with this."

Obviously a conspirator had obtained his passport and transferred it to an impersonator who resembled him. The impersonator then used the stolen identity to get a visa from the American consulate in Jeddah, obtain a Florida driver's licenses and, on August 28, book seat 8G on AA Flight 11. He then flew to Boston on September 6; drove to Portland, Maine, on September 10; and on September 11 he, or someone else, used the driver's license photo ID to board Flight 11.

At least 15 of the 19 hijackers had Florida connections. Of the 19, three were in the country on expired visas, including Satam al-Suqami, who had a Florida driver's license listing a Boynton Beach address. Boynton Beach is a few miles north of Boca Raton and the AMI target. In the summer, five suspected hijackers on the two planes that crashed into the WTC—Mohamed Atta, Marwan al-Shehhi, Wail M. al-Sheheri, Waleed M. al-Shehri, and Stam al-Suagmi—bought one-month memberships at gyms. Atta and al-Sherihir paid to work out at Delray Beach World's Gym. Delray Beach adjoins Boca Raton. Four of the hijackers on UAL 93 that crashed in Pennsylvania also lived in Florida for several months. Two shared a condo in Delray Beach. They left suddenly Labor Day weekend, the same weekend a group of suspect hijackers living in Vero Beach disappeared.

Seven of the hijackers had Florida driver's licenses or state identification cards. Florida was rich in flight training schools that accommodated foreign students. Three of the hijackers, Saeed al-Ghamdi, Ahmed al-Nami, and Hamza al-Ghadi, lived for several months in the Delray Racquet Club, a condo complex only a couple of miles from AMI Headquarters. None seemed to have jobs, but several were said to be plane mechanics, students, or tourists. Some alleged to work for Saudi Airlines, an allegation that Saudi Arabia firmly denies. Atta was even stopped by a Broward County Sheriff, and he could not produce a driver's license. He was given a ticket, which he never paid, and was released. Atta at the time was on a U.S. government watch list. Despite scant employment histories, they paid as much as $10,000 each for flight lessons and paid $3,000 per month for rent.

The hijackers, while in the U.S., were known to be extremely private, in fact, downright secretive. For three months in the summer of 2001, Charlie Lisa's home in Lauderdale-by-the-Sea, about 20 miles south of Boca Raton, was occupied by two of the hijackers, Amad al-Haznawi and Ziad Jarrah. They moved out without explanation in late August.

Was there a Plan A involving the use of crop dusters to spread weaponized anthrax over Florida or another state? Mohamed Atta sought $650,000 to modify a crop duster, according to Johnell Bryan, a U.S. Department of Agriculture loan officer. Then al-Shehhi, Ahmed al-Ghamdi, Fayex Rashid Ahemed Hassan, and al-Qadi Banihmmad, all known hijackers, tried to get loans from the U.S. Department of Agriculture. Bryan later described Atta as "most persistent and frightening." He said he had just arrived in the United States from Afghanistan,

> to start his dream, which was to go to flight school and get his pilot's license, and work both as a charter pilot, and crop duster, too. He was

> seeking $650,000 for his crop dusting business. He wanted to finance a twin-engine six-passenger aircraft and remove the seats. He said he was an engineer, and that he wanted to build a chemical tank that would fit inside the aircraft and take up every available square inch of the aircraft except for where the pilot would be sitting. (ABC News)

This preliminary application proved to be of major significance within the context of Saddam Hussein's WMD program. Iraq was known to have field-tested anthrax, not only in aerial bombs but also in sprayers of the kind used in crop dusting attached to helicopter, fighter aircraft, and possibly unmanned drones.

AMI's neighborhood, therefore, was literally crawling with these people. To overlook that fact, or play it down, is to either overlook or play down the possibility that they may well have had a hand in the anthrax attack on AMI.

"One of the most intriguing aspects of the FBI's anthrax investigation is the Bureau's apparent disinterest at the presence of so many al-Qaeda terrorists in the immediate vicinity of American Media Inc." AMI CEO David Pecker told CNN. He also said,

> I think this is an attack against America. The World Trade Center was attacked, the Pentagon was attacked and American Media was attacked and I think this was the first bioterrorism attack in the United States. (CNN News)

Steve Coz of AMI said,

> If you just look at the incredible coincidences, you cannot arrive at any other conclusion in my mind other than that this is a bioterrorism attack. (Newsmax)

The inference Pecker was making was that this attack originated from abroad rather than from a perpetrator inside the United States, a Dr. Strangelove from inside our own military medical science institutions. Hence, the Ivins connection that the FBI so desperately pursued was probably a blind alley. But were the FBI investigators deliberately on the trail of a forced lead? That is the biggest question of all, especially when considering the possibility that the weaponization of the anthrax spores could have been done by an ally of the hijackers after 9/11 at an entirely different location.

On September 18, two identical anthrax-laced letters with no return addresses were sent from Princeton, New Jersey, via the main postal center at Trenton, New Jersey, to NBC and the *New York Post*. The photocopied letters contained both a warning and a message in 18-point block print. It warned that an anthrax attack was "next" and advised the letter openers to take "penicillin." These were tips alerting the medical system. The message was "Death to America, Death to Israel, Allah is Great." This anthrax was from the same Ames strain used in the first attack and prepared in dry powdered form.

Because the samples at the U.S. Army Medical Reseach Institute at Fort Detrick or the Centre for Applied Microbiology and Research (CAMR) lab at Porton Downs in Britain were in wet slurry form, someone had to grow and prepare the attack anthrax. So there were at least three roles involved in the anthrax attack: the fit of the sample, which required access to one of the two government labs; the preparation, which required biotech equipment, such as a centrifuge; and a mailer, which required a person in Trenton on September 18. Because this weaponized anthrax was sent to both a national and local news organization accompanied by letters, the attack may have been designed as a media letter.

Then on October 9, the letters to Senators Leahy and Daschle stated, "You cannot stop us. We have this Anthrax." By using the plural *we* and *us*, they implied a conspiracy. These letters contained billions of such spores of the same virulent Ames strain as the second and third encounters. Many spores were as small as one micron in diameter, or 1/20 of a human hair. The tiny size made these virulent spores into aerosol weapons, capable of infecting the entire United States Congress. The difference in the size of the spores in the third and fourth encounters demonstrated that the attack had an operational platform capable of progressively refining and weaponizing the anthrax. The fallout, at a minimum, would be huge. The facility, therefore, had to be constructed to avoid any leakage of spores while they were filtered and moved from glass slides into envelopes.

Because large spores can overcome antibiotics and vaccines, the preparation of the attack anthrax required protection akin to a biosafety level 3 facility, in which lab workers use either moon suits or gloved boxes. The inability of the FBI to find this lab indicated that the lab was either extremely well hidden or located outside the purview of U.S. investigators. We must assume that this conspiracy, whether foreign or internally directed, had either penetrated or was originated from a well-guarded American or British bio-warfare facility with an agent having access to the Ames strain. It had the equipment and technology to create new batches of anthrax, weaponize it, and insert billions of spores in envelopes. It had the means to deliver it anonymously through the mails. It had enough security around its apparatus to remain undetected. Perhaps for this reason the FBI determined that it had to be an inside job. But the alleged suicide of the main suspect may prevent us from knowing, unless—or until—there is another attack with WMD.

Let us hope that the conspiracy expired with the suicide of the FBI's key suspect. But we can assume just as easily that in the terror and confusion of the events surrounding 9/11, this case was never solved, and for purposes of emergency and disaster medicine in this country, Dr. Tsonas's admonitions are heard, whether he was right or wrong. The fact is, if he was wrong, he cannot be proven to be wrong. More likely than not, the pattern and themes of this first bioterrorism attack on America were first identifiably visible at Holy Cross Hospital Emergency Room Fort Lauderdale, in June of 2001.

Because there have been no more attacks since 9/11 and economic forces have now conspired to all but wreck the preparedness of our emergency medical service we are even at greatest risk. By doing so, the market itself has rendered the voices of authority from 2002 to mere echoes. If, as the events of June 2001 imply, emergency rooms are a first-line defense against potential disaster, since 2001 we have diminished their effectiveness.

"We have to be moving the front-line of disaster planning to hospitals, but it's not there yet," said Dr. Auer.

Her colleagues reached consensus that ER physicians need to plan not only for medical response but for heightening of security too. For example, ER physicians should not rely on "nonsecure" cellular phones for communicating critical or confidential information. Screening patients and visitors to the ER—even volunteers—should also be required. Hospitals should have enough gas masks on hand to deal with a possible chemical attack. Hospitals should develop their own stocks of vaccines, antibiotics, and other drugs for a surge of patients, because the federal government may not make its stockpiles available for up to three days. Even then they said that the emergency management system was being asked to gear up during a convergence of troubling trends.

Physicians already feel squeezed by rising liability insurance costs and downsized patient reimbursements, particularly Medicare, considered the financial backup for emergency medical services. Nationwide, there are increasing numbers of ER patients adding to overcrowding. Training and staff costs are significant, but government—local, state, and federal—is suffering revenue shortfalls. To illustrate the point, even after the devastation of 9/11, the federal government was so slow to react to the Hurricane Katrina disaster in New Orleans that it made a mockery of FEMA and drove its director out of his job. And this was a disaster that took no one by surprise because the Army Corps of Engineers had predicted just such a disaster resulting from even a glancing blow of a high-category hurricane on the New Orleans failing dike system.

Looking at the systemic failures of the country's emergency medical system, and in particular the failure of that system in the months before 9/11, we have to ask an inconvenient question. Where does this overview of the anthrax case as first presented to an ER physician and subsequently investigated by the FBI fit into the Cho paradigm that we have been discussing?

First, there are a whole host of similarities, not the least of which is that tragedies resulting in many deaths might have been prevented had systems been in place at the ER and follow-up level to ensure that the emergency room did its job by helping the patient and keeping society safe from dangerous patients. But to do that emergency rooms and the hospitals that staff them have to move away from a reliance on throughput efficiency, the processing of patients through the system as quickly and expeditiously as possible, and, instead, provide care to remediate the patient's condition, identify and red-flag dangerousness, and make sure that the public is protected from that dangerousness. Throughput is oftentimes faster, but quality of care is jeopardized and preparedness for the "expected unexpected"—the Kellers, the Chos, and the al-haznawi—has regressed, rather than progressed.

So, let us take the pre-9/11 Holy Cross case and see how points of entry to our healthcare system can be made smart. This is triage post-9/11. Let us examine the case of Ahmed al-Haznawi and, through this paradigm, the Cho case itself. al-Haznawi was seen by a trained and credentialed professional before Dr. Tsonas encountered him for the first time. This could have been either prehospital care or a triage nurse. For purposes of studying this case within the context of post-9/11 triage and disaster medicine, however, we will call this *prehospital care*.

We do not know whether al-Haznawi was referred for care, but we do know that he was brought in by another person and that his presenting problem had a duration of two months. Thus, by definition, it was chronic. Other than the presenting problem, neither al-Haznawi nor his accompanying friend, Jarrah, showed or complained of anything else but an ulcer on the shin. They were polite, cooperative, and apparently reliable "foreign tourists." They were not outside the norm for this hospital. In fact, Dr. Tsonas did not seem to know where the patient and his friend were from. Nor did he appear to care. And within the context of pre-9/11 triage, he should have not been expected to care, unless the patient presented as severely ill with a potentially exotic disease acquired overseas. In fact, under busy ER conditions, they could have been triaged out due to the patient's apparent youthful good health, lack of anything strange in their behavior or appearance, and most importantly, the lack of urgency. This was a minor injury occurring from a rather trivial accident months ago. It is the responsibility of prehospital triage to rule in all serious medical conditions—rather than ruling them out. It was the responsibility of Dr. Tsonas to rule out anything requiring either intensive or inpatient care.

With the benefit of our post-9/11 hindsight, prehospital screening in a smart point of entry into the healthcare system must first of all establish all the potential problems, in this case localized infection and abscess. Bites and stings could not be ruled out, because the mechanism of injury did not align very well at all with the history of bumping into a suitcase.

The ABCs of emergency triage were assumably normal, thus leading algorithmically to the next tier of both specific and general discriminators. The patient was not highly febrile and did not complain of severe pain. There was no evidence of localized vascular compromise, which could be quickly determined by making certain that the tissue distal to the wound was normal—rather than paler than the other leg and foot—and he had good peripheral pulses.

For al-Haznawi, the emergency was over. Thus, the medical determination next would be to document whether patient was in moderate pain, particularly on joint movement, or showed an inflamed joint. Neither the general discriminator of pain nor the latter two specific discriminators were present. Accordingly, al-Haznawi could have been either referred out for urgent care, to be seen within two hours minimum, or simply requested to wait. In fact, attempts to screen in either significant pain of any kind or fever likely were negative. The absence of these findings, according to the classical rules of triage, could have diverted al-Haznawi for outpatient care of a chronic problem requiring examination with possible clinical intervention within a minimum of four hours.

Dr. Tsonas examined al-Haznawi well within the required 4 hours of maximum secure waiting time for more definitive examination and possible clinical intervention. He discovered an ugly, blackened ulcer unlikely to have been caused by bumping into a suitcase. He could not rule out an insect bite, but with this duration and absence of systemic illness, certainly that restriction would not make a difference in his intervention. He treated the localized infection as uncomplicated without potentially ominous comorbidity.

What were the clues back then of something far more lethal? Working smart in today's high-volume emergency and acute care points of entry into our healthcare system requires knowledge of likelihood of certain diseases presenting in certain ways in certain places. This is epidemiologically informed clinical decision making that all clinicians practice, whether by the book or by the seat of their pants. Tsonas likely thought of a deadly insect or snake bite and ruled them out based on history, chronicity, and peculiar localization without systemic illness. And that was the general discriminator—peculiarity—that Dr. Tsonas would not miss today. not only was al-Haznawi's ulcer not unlikely to have been caused by bumping into a suitcase, but both the patient and his roommate's history was inappropriate. Today, Dr. Tsonas would likely tell us all not to go any further with this patient, because inappropriate history from a patient and collateral informant immediately sets off the alarm. That alarm notifies this ER to quietly secure itself, cautiously approach this patient, and isolate for both contagiousness and a more ominous comorbidity, strange behavior.

So, as described before, if you do not feel secure in determining how mechanism of injury thoroughly explains what you see in that exposed injured body you must ask yourself, what was the source of the history? The source at Holy Cross Hospital ER should have been considered unreliable, the history inappropriate.

You can now assume that absolutely nothing about this history is true.

That brings you back, once again, to the red zone of clinical state of awareness. You are thinking of a deadly destructive process going on.

As stated previously, this is a different era in some ways than that in which Dr. Engels taught—decades ago. First encounters with unknown patients at contemporary points of entry require you at least to observe with all of your senses before embracing the patient in first encounter with a greeting handshake and touching the patient. Here is also where principles of preparedness come into play: universal precautions for contagiousness are invoked for all those in close range of this patient. The collateral informant is separated and isolated. Both patient and collateral should be treated in the red zone. They have been saved medically; now it is time to save yourself and anyone else possible. Both patient and companion are to be considered extremely dangerous until proven otherwise. They could have any exotic infection not endemic to Florida—that is, tropical medicine problem outside the expertise of most ER staffs—or, in our post-9/11 world, early alert as either victims or perpetrators of imminent or ongoing attack with weapons of mass destruction. To minimize such clinical decision making in today's world is simply foolish and absolute medical negligence.

The shock of both the injured or sick dependent and lesion of bioterrorism accompanied by unreliable history leads us to the core subject of emergency psychiatry—human destructiveness. How can we predict with 100% certainty what the result of our treatment will be? We can't. Although it is true that violence and suicide cannot always be accurately predicted, neither can the results of bilateral mastectomy or total resection of the prostate. Such maiming surgeries are hardly less risky clinically than protocols for deescalation of hyperarousal syndromes, including, in the end, humane restraint, whether pharmacological or physical. Encounters with unremitting processes of human destructiveness, just like diabetes, are time determined; there are chronic relapsing cases, latent states, and states of both high acuity and lethality. I will take you through the steps of assessing these presentations with time-determined clinical decision making, concurrently informed by epidemiology.

You already know how the patient presented. These means of presentation tell you much immediately and, as previously stated, the unreliable patient presenting by himself or an unreliable person accompanying the patient—inappropriate history—immediate switching your mind to the red zone of clinical states of awareness—you can assume nothing based on history. The police, however, are different, and they can tell you how out of control your patient is; usually their history leads you again to the red zone of clinical states of awareness. The medics should always be reliable historians and med-surg presentations should fit into specific categories. In this template, pay particular attention to the major problems cited that could have been leads to prevention of disasters in the cases of Cho and al-Haznawi. They are "bites and stings," "mechanism of injury," and "focal inflammation."

It is extremely unlikely that the person with any presentation excluded in this graphic representation of the yellow state of clinical awareness is in fact a patient. That is the importance of always being ready to reassess and to get out of this less vigilant state of clinical awareness. Eye problem and an inappropriate history from parent, caretaker, or significant other is not an urgent presentation; it is a felony assault and an emergency until proven otherwise. Conversely, when you are in the yellow zone of clinical states of awareness—particularly when points of entry are both early alerts for terrorism and targets themselves—you have judged that you are treating an urgently ill patient and not a person presenting fictitiously with other agendas—that is, avoiding prosecution for assault and battery, pursuit by avenging gang, or conning you for opiates. At this time it is imperative to reassess in the red zone; nothing can be assumed valid in this patient and his collateral informant. That goes for Cho, too, when he presented with infestation of mites in the very early stages of escalation of his psychosis; he had no bites or stings, as he alleged. The doctor diagnosed acne. Such inappropriate history demands returning to the red zone and clearing these patients for dangerousness to self and others—in the cases of al-Haznawi and Cho, apocalpytic suicide and mass murder.

Now, instead of localized infection in category blue, this ER ideally would have had strange behavior, verbal and rule out a comorbid presenting problem, high risk of self-harm, and a specific discriminator, high risk of harm to others, and localized infection with unknown risk of contagiousness, remarkably similar at the core of presentation of strange behavior to Cho's presentation at St. Albans of strange behavior, nonverbal. But, al-Haznawi was verbal, and Cho was nonverbal. There is a major difference in how these two patients would be both approached and worked up. We know in retrospect, however, that both would have been approached and worked up differently now.

Table 9.1 is best represented in the literature of "the fuckshouter" and Table 9.2 is best represented in the literature of catatonia and mutism. When approaching the emergency psychiatric patient, there is a very high likelihood of either of these scenarios occurring. Your approach with the patient is of utmost importance, as are your verbal and nonverbal communications and positioning. In this country, three feet is the safest radius to consider before you are perceived to be penetrating the average person's intimate space. Don't touch! And, don't treat a chronic wound that has an inappropriate history and mechanism of injury that do not fit the lesion (Figure 9.1, Table 9.3).

Table 9.1 Strange Behavior, Verbal

1. "May I talk with you?" If patient says "NO," leave area immediately and notify security.
2. Patient considered likely to assault staff. **High Risk**!
3. If considered that patient is noncombative, notify security, have four staff members present and approach patient with caution. • Safe eye contact • Safe interpersonal space • Safe clinician posture • DO NOT touch patient • Prepare patient for any physical exam • Express sympathy • Be polite
4. Maintain airway
5. Maintain adequate breathing
6. Maintain circulation/rule out shock
7. Throw out the W W H H H I M P E S[a]

[a] Withdrawl, Wernickes, Hypoglycemia, Hypoxia, Hypertensive encephalopathy, intracerebral bleed, Meningitis, Poisoning, Encephalitis, Status epilepticus.

Table 9.2 Strange Behavior, Nonverbal

1. "May I talk with you?" If patient says "NO" leave area immediately and notify security.
2. Can't talk patient down and assault risk considered high. **High Risk**!
3. If considered that patient can be talked down, notify security, and have four staff members present and approach patient with caution. • Safe eye contact • Safe interpersonal space • Safe clinician posture • DO NOT touch patient • Prepare patient for any physical exam • Express sympathy • Be polite
4. Maintain airway
5. Maintain adequate breathing
6. Maintain circulation/rule out shock
7. Throw out the W W H H H I M P E S

View Protocols

Pre-Orange

Pre-Yellow

AIDS - HIV	Hepatitis A	Influenza
Chicken Pox	Hepatitis B	Meningitis - bacterial
Common Cold	Hepatitis C	Meningitis - viral
Diarrhea	Herpes Simplex	Mumps
Epiglotitis - or Whooping cough	**Herpes Zoster (VARICELLA)**	Tuberculosis Pulmonary
Measles - rubella	Lice (head, body, pubic)	Wounds
Measles - Congenital	Scabies	

Figure 9.1 Infectious disease protocols.

Table 9.3 Presenting Problems

Mechanism of Injury?					
Abdominal pain	Abdominal pain—child	Asthma	Back pain	Bites and stings	Blood disease
Chest pain	Collapsed adult	Convulsing	Crying baby	Dental problem	Diabetes
Ear problems	Exposure to chemicals	Falls	Headache	History of assault	Irritable child
Limping child	Neck pain	OD or poisoning	Pregnancy	STD	Shortness of breath—adult
Shortness of breath—child	Sick adult	Sick child	Testicular pain	Urinary pain	Worried parent
Burns and scalds	Foreign body	Focal inflammation		Rashes	
Chest/ abdomen wound	GI bleed	Major trauma		Sore throat	
Diarrhea	Head injury	Nasal problems		Vomiting	
Eye problem	Limb problems	Pelvic/vaginal bleeding		Wounds	

Note: OD = overdose; STD = sexually transmitted disease; GI = gastrointestinal.

As stated before by the experts, the staff at Holy Cross were not commandos, but they would have had to discretely notify their own hospital security immediately, assuming that their own security is trained and competent in disaster medicine, a risky wager. If not, it would have been best to have one of those secure communications systems cited by the American College of Emergency Physicians (ACEP) authorities with which to notify the local police, who should be expected to competently respond and notify the appropriate Department of Homeland Security office. Bullies can make their victims so fearful and angry that sometimes the victims of bullying commit suicide to stop the pain, obtain weapons to protect themselves and strike out at their bullies, or go on a vengeful rampage and then kill themselves. It is the responsibility of neither Dr. Tsonas nor any of his ER staff to assume any more than category red and "throw out the GUNS."

So, now, as shown in the mnemonic throw out the GUNS:
G = Guns and weapons
U = Using drugs
N = Need to protect
S = Situation of imminent violence outside

The *G* stands for guns and weapons; it makes a difference what kind of weapon he has in terms of its lethality. Find out from the police whether it is Saturday night special, a combat knife honed for fight, a .357 Magnum, or a shotgun. Such information could tell you about lethality and gives you a clue to type of damage intended. This is first and foremost a police matter. You should not have to be the one to disarm the patient and identify the weapon.

In my experience, ordinary objects in the work space are also very dangerous—for example, the patient's body accelerating as a missile directed at you. In this case it was the lesion itself, an early warning of attack on this nation by unconventional weapons of mass destruction.

Caveat: the legal paperwork written by lawyers for mental patients assumes sanity. Anything can be a weapon, and in the corrections system, gas is one of the most lethal; gas is a plastic baggie containing the inmate's bodily excretions. Crossbows made from milk straws, ballpoint pens, and the elastic waistband of underpants can have deadly accuracy from thirty feet. There seem to be no limits to what man can use as a weapon when desperate, whether rationally so or not. Suicidal precautions require stripping the patient of everything except a hospital gown until cleared for either discharge or admission; that includes belt, razor, pills, and anything that could strangle, cut, or be lethally ingested. Again, the suicidal patient may bring anything lethal to your site, although it may not seem lethal to anyone else.

As we are constantly informed, hospitals have been identified in interrogations of al-Qaeda captives as prime targets for terrorism. One night in Milwaukee, I stopped at the front entrance to baggage at the General Mitchell Field and left my car for less than a minute to look inside for my wife. Turning around, there was a huge Milwaukee cop stooping over my license plate and writing a ticket. I played my doctor card, pleading that I was here on emergency and it was important to understand that I still had a long ways to go to be able to start working right away. He didn't even look at me, "And you need to understand that this is a different world we are in now."

He handed me the ticket, turned his back on me, and walked away. I was angry, but then I decided that this was a pretty good introduction to our post-9/11 world.

Points of entry to our healthcare system must have first alert triggers for attacks with unconventional weapons, as well as for being direct targets. An Israeli hospital has been built underground, where doctors work with protective clothing. If this country becomes Israelized, then we will have to do the same thing to preserve effective triage for mass casualties from attacks with unconventional weapons; such effectiveness is a primary reason for damage in terrorism, as kidnapping of physicians in Baghdad today demonstrates. For any suspicions of lethal weapons in your work site, therefore, do not just hit the facility's code for "man with weapon." or call security about a bomb threat; in this post-9/11 world, I advise you to call the police, notify security, and stop your clinical work on this patient immediately.

All police departments are preparing for terrorism, but hospitals do not seem to even know where to start. Have you been to a code black drill recently?

In 2000, the Hospital Association of Southern California (HASC) determined that a uniform code system was needed after three persons were killed in a shooting incident at an area medical center after the wrong emergency code was called. While codes for fire (red) and medical emergency (blue) were similar in 90% of California hospitals queried, there were 47 different codes used for infant abduction and 61 for combative persons. In light of this, HASC published a handbook titled *Healthcare Facility Emergency Codes: A Guide for Code Standardization* listing various codes and strongly urged hospitals to voluntarily implement the revised codes. In this post-9/11 world, I advise you to call law enforcement directly, preferably on a secure line as advised by American College of Emergency Physcians, because by following the HASC code and announcing over hospital PA, "Code Silver, Emergency Room," the patient and his companion would be alerted to the plot being discovered. They likely would become either extremely violent or flee the scene without a trace of them ever again being found for this ER visit. They could be the most dangerous people any ER staff could encounter during the routine of their work day!

In cases when there is an early alert for an attack by weapons of mass destruction, therefore, it is best to act as calmly as possible, while protecting oneself and the facility. Then notify the authorities via secure and quiet communications unknown to either patient or his terrorist command. Had bioterrorism in fact been suspected in the ER of Holy Cross Hospital that pre-9/11 June day of 2001, ER staff would not have been able to determine whether the facility was being invaded by other terrorists or whether other threats were awaiting them, either inside or outside the facility. As it turned out, the AMI building nearby was the target of a lethal anthrax attack a few months later.

In this case of a first clinical encounter with an unknown patient, the ER staff was flying blind. All they could have known under the best of circumstances is that they had a patient and his companion, both of whom were, more likely than not, giving Inappropriate histories in matter-of-fact manner. The mechanism of injury they described with such poise, more likely than not, did not fit the mechanism of injury and, therefore, this first clinical encounter with an unknown patient and his companion automatically reset the triaging process. Although articulate and seemingly logical in their history of the lesion, they were behaving strangely. But, unlike Cho, they were verbal.

Obvious needle marks or other physical signs of active drug abuse mean that security comes first (see Figure 9.2); they are trained and equipped to examine the active drug user and oftentimes provide insight into their reasons for being in your

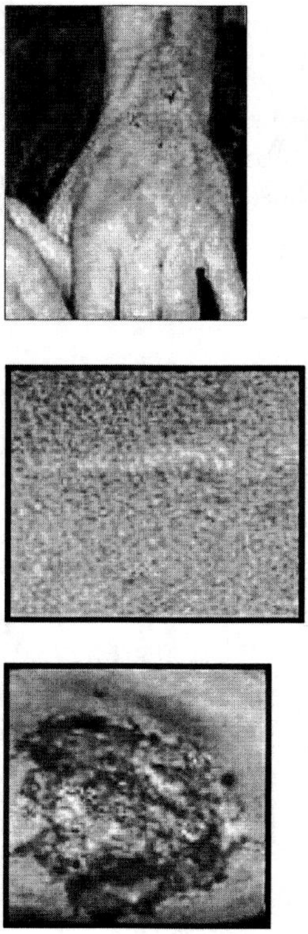

Injecting drug use: injection tracks over veins on the dorsum of the hand. Linear tracks with fibrosis and crusts were created by daily heroin injection into the superficial veins.

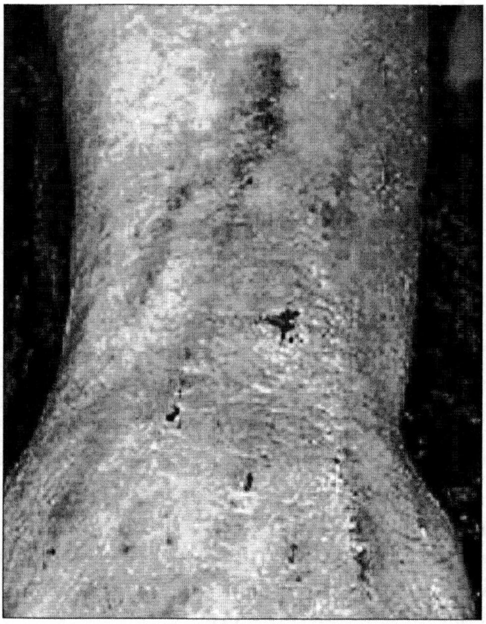

Figure 9.2 Potential drug usage indication.

work site. The risk of being assaulted by a threatening patient on drugs and/or alcohol skyrockets. PCP patients are of particular concern, because they have the paradoxical pathophysiology of extreme hyperarousal and depressed central nervous system circulatory and respiratory regulation.

How can you tell such professional con jobs? Only by following disciplined rules of triage and knowing the epidemiology of your work site. The latter would not have stopped Paul Keller from going on an arson spree, unless a detailed history and high level of attention had been paid to his obsession with the history of local firefighting. Time-determined clinical decision making, however, certainly would not have jumped to nutritional counseling. As in phone triage with that little boy's chemical eye injury, such counseling for Keller's one walk-in visit for psychiatric crisis help is pure quackery.

Throw out the Guns means ruling out possession of weapons. Staff cannot do that. Rule out using drugs. Staff cannot do that. Rule out the need to protect themselves. In this case the patient and his companion will fight to the death we now know and take everyone and everything with them with impunity. Or, more likely, the patient and his companion would try to escape to fight another

GANGS

& the Role of the Hospital Employee

Presented by
The Salinas Police Department Gang Intelligence Unit

Thursday: July 13, 2000 3 p.m. – 6 p.m.
or Friday: July 14, 2000 1 p.m. – 4 p.m.
Place: SEA Center (Old Cafeteria)

CE Contact Hours: 3 NMC Staff: Free

To Register call Educational Services at 755-4177
CLEARLY state your NAME, DEPARTMENT,
RETURN TELEPHONE NUMBER,
and WHICH CLASS you wish to attend.

Figure 9.3 Situation of danger outside.

day. Holy Cross ideally should have ruled out the menace of extremely dangerous accomplices somewhere outside—the *S*, no different in principle from managing young patients in gang-infested neighborhoods. Recognizing immediately their inability to get beyond this emergency psychiatry default, they need to be thinking security and contagiousness (Figure 9.3).

Now keep in mind that aloof and tough-looking guy with poor eye contact; he may not be feeling that tough. In fact, he may feel the need for protection—the *N*—and really be paranoid and terrified of what awaits him outside. Do not just ignore him, but ask whether he is afraid of something. Then, if he says yes, you notify security. In the Holy Cross anthrax case we discussed above, the hijacker's muscleman for the anticipated attack on the White House, the patient's need to protect was evidenced by his collateral informant both accompanying him and lying for him.

That situation he informs you of outside, the *S*, is just the topic for in-service training previously presented in Figure 9.3 notifying staff of workshops to train

Figure 9.4 Weapons protocol.

on gangs on hospital campuses. You also have to remember that gangs oftentimes shoot to maim and not kill and that at certain sites you could be amidst a gang shooting with assailants on campus.

Gangs have no shared conscience preventing them from coming into your work site, whether ER or clinic, when they want another gangster badly enough and may have just wounded him in a drive-by. Your work is now in the way of their work. No, we are not even close to Liberia, where rebels kill patients indiscriminately, yet we are also not Canada, where such threats from armed gangs are extremely unlikely.

Clinical staff is now in the center ring of epidemic violence, making front-line clinical work environment second only to that of policing the streets for a professional taking a risk of serious injury from an assault (Figure 9.4.)

Although statistics demonstrate that an active destructive clinical process can rarely be bisected into harm to others and harm to self, the epidemiology looks at the sentinel act, the one act that determines where the actor will strike; therefore, statistics are either for suicidality or violence. But do not let these separate figures lead you to believe that any of the individuals from these cohorts have not been in both states of mind; likely most have but were simply only clinically trapped in one of them. Statistics robustly support evidence-based response to both danger to self and danger to others as merging states of mind across the same continuum of human destructiveness. Our nosology confuses us in a potentially dangerous way by constantly dividing violence and suicidality. In the real world of such poorly defined nosology, such division is not that simple—in fact, it robustly demonstrates comorbidity of violence and suicidality. So many patients who present as either suicidal or dangerous to others are really dangerous to both themselves and others that I discuss clinical encounters of self-harm and dangerousness as one and the same entity for purposes of first clinical encounters with unknown patients. *Danger to Self* and *Danger to Others* are both legal terms that too frequently miss the combined state of dangerousness to self and to others from the Law of Mother Nature. In fact, there is no man more dangerous to others than a suicidal man, because he intends to kill himself and does not care anymore.

And, when the *N* and *S* evidences potential for gang violence on campus, you call security. In the case of Holy Cross Hospital ER, the situation outside was the premonitory early alert to 9/11; the gang was al-Qaeda.

Ideally, had the classical rules of triage been followed to the letter of the book, these two hijackers would have been identified and investigated. Would the airplane attacks of 9/11 have been prevented? Perhaps. Would the bioterrorism attacks engulfing the events of 9/11 been prevented? Maybe. Would al-Haznawi and his roommate have simply disappeared in those days, having been refused service with efforts by staff obviously made for contagiousness, extreme self-harm, and extreme harm to others? Knowing their stealth, they could just as well have escaped as been apprehended back then. But, the chances for an early alert for the coming attack with WMD may have led to faster and more focused investigation to enhance preparedness for horrors, deaths, and injuries from anthrax that were to follow just a couple of months later. In any event, those responsible for homeland defense would have been alerted to the presence of a WMD on American soil and that the attack on America had begun. It was more than likely, in retrospect, that Dr. Tsonas had encountered the earliest alert to what could have been a progressive testing of increasingly sophisticated bioterror agents and their delivery.

This is where the comparison between Cho and 9/11 becomes so important. Both Cho and the hijackers had made appearances at emergency rooms prior to their attacks. In both cases, had the healthcare professionals followed classic triage procedures and evaluations, both Cho and the hijackers would have been flagged as high risks and referred to security professionals. At the very least, in Cho's case, Virginia Tech would have been notified and Mr. and Mrs. Cho would have been notified. In the case of the hijackers, had they been referred to local police and detained, there is a likelihood that even if higher-ups at the federal level had been asleep at the switch, at a state level, the plot would have been uncovered and dropped like a hot potato into Governor Jeb Bush's lap. But that did not happen in Florida or in Virginia, and look at the results.

Chapter 10

Potential Signs for Dangerous Behavior and Best Practice Solutions

As we studied the Cho case in light of other cases of explosive and suicidal violence, and particularly mass murder, we found that most of these offenders gave off warning signs well in advance of their murders/suicides. Certainly, looking back over Cho's life, we see that there were clear warning signs of dangerousness and menace, signs that even if professionals did not pick up, Cho's teachers, classmates, and roommates did. Can we categorize these signs to cite them objectively in ways that parents, teachers, school and professional counselors, and juvenile authorities can identify them? Most importantly, is there a way that police, the first responders to many of these potentially violent individuals, can spot the warning signs and, at the very least, note them so that later evaluations can take stock of them? We believe the answer is yes, and in light of the warning signs that Cho gave off, the warning signs that Keller displayed, and the red flags raised in the Holy Cross Emergency Room that Dr. Tsongas spotted, violence can be prevented.

Prevalence of Violence

It is an assumption, particularly among officials releasing crime reports to the press and to their constituencies, that most crimes are responsive to economic pressures. Robberies, property crimes, felony murders during robberies, street crimes, domestic violence, and violence stemming from alcohol or substance abuse are the most common types of offenses that tend to rise during periods of economic hardship. However, types of gang violence, serial homicides, certain types of mass murders, school and campus shootings, and episodic sexual offenses tend to be not responsive to economic conditions and are more dependent on the individual's state of mind rather than desperate reactions, even psychological reactions, to economic hard times.

For example, as current economic hard times continue and people lose their jobs, their homes, and their families to divorce, more and more Americans—27 million Americans, according to a recent count—are taking prescription antidepressant drugs. Add to that the number individuals who are taking drugs not prescribed or self-medicating with alcohol, and the total is much higher. Are all of these people potential criminals? Of course not. But the numbers indicate that America is becoming an unhappy nation, and an unhappy population is a breeding ground for certain types of crimes. Daily news reports reveal that individuals of all walks of life in desperate financial straits are doing desperate things, from walking into banks to rob them to trying to extort money from television celebrities. Real unemployment and underemployment in America is over 17 percent and people in previous good times borrowed and spent themselves into tight corners. It is payback time, but a precious few have the resources to pay it back.

For our purposes, regardless of the type of offender—serial killer, mass murderer, episodic sexual offender, suicidal rage offender—psychologically driven violent offenders do give off warning signs prior to their crime sprees. Depending upon how close the offender is to breaking out, the symptoms become increasingly obvious. With respect to Cho, here was a young man who, from the time he was in middle school, was expressing ideations of violence, mass murder, and suicide. He expressed admiration for Kliebold and Harris, the perpetrators of the Columbine High School murders; he wrote violent essays; he wrote violent plays entitled "Richard McBeef" (see Appendix B) and "Mr. Brownstone"; he drew pictures that a professional counselor characterized as evidencing suicidal tendencies; and he told his roommates at Virginia Tech that he was going to kill himself after he had been admonished for stalking women on campus. He was so menacing, his appearance so threatening, that students actually stopped showing up for a poetry class with Professor Nikki Giovanni that he was in because they were afraid. Did Cho have to wear a neon sign to get any more attention?

As another case in point, the nation was shocked by another headline-making mass shooting/suicide in August 2009, this time at a fitness center just outside Pittsburgh, Pennsylvania. A lone gunman named George Sodini walked into the gym with his bags, turned out the lights, and began firing 50 rounds at women working out at the facility. After wounding over 10 people and killing 3 women, he turned the gun on himself and committed suicide. Sodini was described by his neighbors as an antisocial loner, a recluse who had simply stopped talking to people. He worked as a systems analyst in the finance department of a K&L Gates, a local law firm.

Sodini posted on his Weblog (see Appendix B) that he was "never married." He also kept a running commentary on his blog as he tried to muster the courage to wreak his apocalyptic revenge on the women, who, he said, never noticed him. He called his act of murder and suicide his "exit plan."

Sodini wrote in his blog that he had not had a girlfriend since 1984 or a date since 2008. Women, he said, just did not like him. He kept a running commentary on his thought process as he worked himself up to his exit plan.

"Why do this?? To young girls? Just read below. I kept a running log that includes my thoughts and actions, after I saw this project was going to drag on," he wrote.

Sodini started his diary in November 2008, writing, "Planned to do this in the summer but figure to stick around to see the election outcome." And by December 22, now a member of the gym and scouting his future victims, Sodino wrote, "Time is moving along. Planned to have this done already. I will just keep a running log here as time passes. Many of the young girls here look so beautiful as to not be human, very edible. After joining this gym, started lifting weights and like it."

As the chronology progressed, Sodini became more analytical, trying to figure out through his writing—and sounding a lot like Cho—why he was having such a problem with women. Was he alone because he simply was unlikable or was it that the women he met did not measure up to his standards?

"The biggest problem of all is not having relationships or friends, but not being able to achieve and acquire what I desire in those or many other areas," he wrote in a later entry. "Everything stays the same regardless of the effort I put in. If I had control over my life then I would be happier. But for about the past 30 years, I have not."

Sodini lamented his solitude. He wrote that he would see couples together and then bitterly complain that he would go home alone, be alone, and spend the rest of his life alone.

"Every evening I am alone, and then go to bed alone," he reveals. "I see twenty something couples everywhere. I see a twenty something guy with a nice twentyish young women. I think those years slipped right by for me. Why should I continue another 20+ years alone?"

No matter how hard he tried to meet women, he could never connect. In his own words, he says that the women he encounters "don't even give me a second look ANYWHERE."

Toward the end of his blog, he wrote, "Women just don't like me. There are 30 million desirable women in the US (my estimate) and I cannot find one." His final entry on August 3 was "Death Lives!"

He was constantly berating himself, constantly seeing the dark side of life, constantly under the thumb of his older brother who bullied him, acting out a script of defeat over and over again until the only way out was suicide. But Sodini's rage is such that he cannot go out alone. Hence his exit plan. Yet from reading his diary it is obvious that at any point, both with the appropriate medication and intensive psychotherapy, Sodini and all his of his victims could have been saved.

Sodini's Videos

Sodini's online video, again reminiscent of Cho's video that he sent to NBC news, is very revealing. In one segment, he takes his viewers through a tour of his house, showing off his things, his furniture, and his computer. He makes sure that all of us know that he spent $79,000 on his Altima, as if that defines him. Then, in his living room, he wonders why his matching sofa and chair would not be attractive to any young woman who wanted to come over and spend some time. One asks, however, despite the veil of normalcy draped over Sodini and his lifestyle, why is he so intent on showing everyone his things? What is it about him that makes us feel that he is defining himself by external objects, his cave, his lair? But, of course, we are judging him in hindsight, knowing that he is shooting this video as he is planning his mass murder and his own demise.

In the second video that has been released, things have gotten much darker. Although Sodini is talking about his lifestyle, his desire to meet women, to woo them, to have them over at his place, there is an aura of unreality. Sodini cannot relate to women, he admits. Try as he might, the very women he wants to attract seem to look right through him. He admits that he fathered a child years before, but that woman will have nothing to do with him. He has joined a gym, perhaps to relate to women as he plans to carry out his act of public revenge against women. In some ways, the women he says he believes he can relate to actually forestall his plan. But his admission, made calmly near the end, is unmistakable. He has no control over his life, he cannot find a mate or even a friend, he is alone, and he will punish the world for it.

Further investigation will also reveal just how much Sodini's warning signs of violence mirrored other mass shooters and suicidal individuals whose exercise in control ended in their own deaths and the deaths of others. In general, however, the warning signs of violence apply to a whole host of offenders who may lurk just beneath the surface tension of violence needing only a small trigger to start in motion the process of the revenge, in their own minds, that they want to wreak upon their perceived victims.

Warning Signs of Violence

What are the commonalities that potentially dangerous individuals share? What are the warning signs of potential violence that turn up even years before the violence actually occurs?

Ideations of Violence and Violent Fantasies

People who express ideations of violence against others to the point where it is not just wishful thinking might actually be working up the psychological pressure to carry out those fantasies. There is a point, which Cho obviously crossed, when ideations become plans and plans become actions. The harboring of fantasies is not illegal. The expression of those fantasies, particularly in school or workplace situations, is a red flag.

Actual Warnings of Impending Violence

Probably the best example of broadcast warnings was the video posted on the Internet by Kliebold and Harris. It was specific, it was aimed directly at their future victims, and it was in plain sight. Most of the time people mean what they say. Therefore, warnings, specific warnings, of impending violence should be taken very seriously by parents, teachers, healthcare professionals, and juvenile authorities.

Auditory Hallucinations

We think that at certain points close to Cho's final year, he was hearing command voices ordering him to kill. The serial killer known as the Son of Sam also described hearing command voices from a dog, ordering him kill. Auditory hallucinations are one of the signs of schizophrenia and, if commanding the patient to commit violence and left untreated, as in Cho's case, they can, and usually do, lead to some form of violence.

Bullies and Victims of Bullying

In the age of the Internet an age-old tradition carries on digitally just as it still does in schoolyards across the country. Bullies, whether inside the schools, on school busses, or on the street, as we have in the recent Chicago homicides, can torment individuals to the point of death. In the cases in which these professional and very experienced social workers felt the intuitive chill of "white knuckles" from the offenders, three out of four of the offenders actually went on to commit homicides upon their respective releases from detention. The parents of bullies, in many cases, are simply bullies themselves, taking out on their children what they believe is being taken out on them or has been taken out on them. It is, by definition, a vicious cycle that passes through generations, creating more and more victims.

To make matters even worse, exacerbating the prevalence of bullying and its being adapted into new forms of harassment—on Facebook, on MySpace, on Internet Web sites, on e-mail lists, on anything folks can imagine—there are parents of bullies who seem to take a perverse pride in the ability of their children to inflict terror on others. Sometimes, as in one recent Internet bullying case, even the parent herself got involved and, according to the victim's parents, helped drive the young girl to suicide.

Bullying sometimes takes the form of a hate crime when directed at either gays or members of minority racial or religious groups. It can sometimes take the form, as it did in a San Diego, California, high school in March 2001, when Charles Andrew Williams said he had had enough of the bullying and the beating and would put a stop to it once and for all. As in many instances such as Columbine High School and Virginia Tech, Charles Williams made his intentions well known, telling friends in school that he was showing up with guns and confronting the students who were making his life miserable. But even his friends laughed at him, taunted him, goaded him into carrying through on his threats. He did just that, and in a day of rage shot up Santana High School, causing a single fatality and wounding other students.

Parents, of course, responded in shock and offered condolences to the very students whose taunting and physical threats pushed Charles Williams over the edge. The law enforcement authorities, once they had the shooter in custody, simply closed the case. But nobody went back to the root causes. This is where the tragedy began; Cho and Kliebold and Harris said that they were the victims of bullying and ostracism as well. Even Cho's sister admitted that he had been the butt of jokes and taunts, but she called it natural childhood taunting. We wonder, however, just how much of that was playing in his mind as he recorded his video for NBC news in the days before he perpetrated his final act of terror.

Parents and school authorities have it in their power to prevent bullying, to encourage bullies to find other outlets for their aggression, and to examine that aggression. Parents of bullying victims should not give school administrators a moment's rest from their complaints. The lives of their children and the lives of other students are at risk.

Previous Acts of Violence or Sexual Violence

If an individual evidencing other signs of dangerousness has actually perpetrated prior acts of violence, even minor ones, or sexual violence, he may have already crossed the line between harassment and assault. These acts of aggression are all forms of acting out or even mimicking violence. But these can be the very indicators that the person is trying to control an explosive rage by acting out the violence in minor ways, almost like releasing pressure slowly through a valve. At a certain point, though, the pressure will be beyond the capacity of the valve to release.

Chronic Drug or Alcohol Abuse

Substance and alcohol abuse can trigger violence by sapping the offender of any resiliency so that violence becomes a first resort rather than a last resort. Although many drugs have an opiate effect, numbing the individual, alcohol, although a depressant, can have just the opposite effect. Cocaine, too, especially crack cocaine and crystal meth, acts as a trigger to violence because it lowers inhibitions and saps resiliency.

Cumulative Rage

As we have seen both from Cho and from Sodini, rage builds. It is often not an instant trigger that sends a person into murder/suicide but a gradual build until the rage takes over any vestige of rational thought or social inhibition. Other mass killers have also been the victims of their own rage, sometimes even nurturing it with every perceived slight they believe they have received. Rage builds to the point where, as Cho and Sodini described, it overwhelms natural resistance to destroying others and destroying one's self.

Dramatic Mood Swings

Most people normally experience mood swings, often for very simple reasons. When we are tired, we do not have the same resiliency as when we are wide awake. After emotional trauma, such as an accident or a life change, people may be very vulnerable to mood swings that they would normally not have in times of routine daily living. But those who have a high risk of dangerousness can experience mood swings that range across the spectrum from frenzied mania to deep self-destructive depression. For those who experience these types of mood swings, particularly if they grow in intensity, it is a clear sign of impending dangerousness even if not homicidal or suicidal. Irritability and paranoia can be associated with both depressed mood and mania. In Cho's case, grandiose delusions overwhelmed him, but in the case of Sodini, we see a highly functional person succeeding in a complex work environment, while spiraling into the despair of major depression.

Violent Sexual Fantasies and Insatiable Sex Drives

Sexual drives that cannot be satisfied or that are so powerful they overwhelm normal social inhibitions are abnormal. When they reach a point of intensity that compels an individual to violate social rules, even to the point of committing assaults on others, they are a clear sign of dangerousness. When intense sexual drives and fantasies are combined with cumulative rage, as in the case of George Sodini, and a sense of such self-worthlessness and depression that they drive a person over the edge, the prescription exists for mass homicide and suicide. Even the onset of such fantasies that drive a person to take active steps to explore them is an indicator of potential dangerousness. If the person's sexual drives cannot be satiated with normal sexual activity, this is yet another indicator. When all of these drives combine with an all-consuming jealousy of others so that the person, in a paranoid position, objectifies others as enemies, it is a clear red flag that the person is at high risk of perpetrating acts of violence at some point in the near future.

Abnormal Fascination or Obsession with Blood, Gore, and Death

In an age when interactive video games and other forms of violent entertainment can engage people, youngsters, who would normally be repelled at the sight of gore, are gradually inured to it by creating video gore. The different violent video games that train players to spill lots of blood, slash off body parts, and inflict physical damage on opponents also support a rising tolerance for these types of violence. Human beings develop a psychological resiliency to all sorts of stimuli; the infliction of bodily harm is one of them. After all, we train soldiers to kill; we train police officers to overcome their natural abhorrence of violence to shoot repeatedly at targets to stop criminals; we train clandestine agents to kill without any hesitation. So it is that we can train young video game players to kill on a video monitor. In a normal situation, this training might be seen as a prurient form of outlet. But for certain types of individuals such as a Cho Seung-Hui, already wired differently and suffering from a mental illness, this is dehumanizing basic training to spill blood.

Indifference to Life, to Suffering, and to Pain of Other Creatures

Going hand in hand with cruelty to animals, indifference is a sign of a sociopathic nature. We see it evident in narcissistic personalities because pathological narcissism voids the personality of empathy for anyone constantly needing self-aggrandizement. Usually, this type of indifference shows up in children and is a clear sign that something is very wrong and that parents and teachers need to become involved. It is a very early warning sign of potential dangerousness and a clear red flag. In a study of adolescent offenders, experienced social workers were asked to predict future violence based on their sense of dehumanization of the offender subject. Incapacity for empathy, detected by experienced youth workers and clinicians, must be investigated when the opportunity presents, for example, as Wolfgang advises, on the third juvenile offense. Recent violent homicides in Chicago, for example, in which teenagers were beaten to death on the street by packs of other teens for no apparent reason, demontrate a lack of empathy in the midst of blood lust. In Cho's case, as his ideations of violence and self-hatred manifested themselves, his art therapist was able to get him to experience emotion and attach words to the horrors filling the hollows of his mind. In so doing, Cho was able to find a release valve for emotions that could have destroyed him at an earlier age.

History of Arson and Fire Starting

As we have seen from the Keller case, episodic fire-starting, arson, is one of the red flags of dangerousness. A fascination with fire-starting, possibly because of a hard-wired obsession with sexual control, particularly when combined as part of the triad with cruelty to animals and bed-wetting, is associated with indifference to pain and suffering—or, empathic failure—and has been identified as part of the past history of many episodic sexual offenders and is a stop along the way, if not caught early, to homicide.

History of Homicidal Behavior or Manifested Homicidal Intent as a Child

Homicidal behavior may be as simple as throwing rocks at another person with the intent to cause bodily harm. Children express this behavior and parents correct it. However, if the child is serious about hurting another child by throwing rocks at his or her head, if the rocks are substantial enough to cause harm and the offending child is aware of it, or if the child is actually striking another with a rock, that constitutes a battery and may be a manifestation of an intent to kill. Worse, if a person uses an object, such as a stick or club, to strike another with force to cause bodily harm, it is a very serious red flag that the person is dangerous and medical intervention is absolutely required. Children who behave this way, especially repeatedly, need to be sequestered and treated. They cannot be around other children until a psychiatrist gets to the root cause of the behavior, which is often the result of what is going on in the home and possibly combined with some neurological/physiological issue. This behavior, combined with indifference to life, cruelty to others and to animals, striking out at inanimate objects, bed-wetting, and fire-starting, is such an indicator of dangerousness that many psychiatrists would recommend that a state or municipal child services agency intervene to prevent the child from causing harm to others or to himself or herself.

Gathering and Possession of Weapons

If an individual with a background of cruelty and violence, driven by suicidal fantasies and ideations of hurting others, is actively gathering weapons, it is the penultimate stage of murder/suicide. If the person announces his intentions, as Cho obviously did, or keeps a journal in which he states his plans to carry out those fantasies, as Sodini did, then that person may be days or weeks away from the headline-making mass murders whose videos we see on the evening news. People who announce their intentions, usually mean to do what they say. At this point, the lack of intervention by healthcare professionals can be, at least under the laws of many states, negligence or malpractice.

Best Practice Solutions

Education

Insofar as the basics are concerned, probably the best preventive measure for parents of young children is education, raising the awareness of parents to behavioral abnormalities in their children. For kids, even as young as preschool age, who wind up in continual conflicts and who have severe problems socializing with other children, a first step is usually a pediatrician. Parents should not be afraid to talk about a child's violent temper tantrums or a child's use of weapons, such as rocks or sticks, against other children. Unfortunately, however, because parents project their own values, as well as their fears, through their children, honest appraisals of a child's difficulties is usually the last thing parents do.

Many times a child's problems with fitting in, bouts of temper, withdrawal, or other mood disorders have purely physical causes. Vision problems or hearing problems can cause mood swings or an inability to adjust. Childhood-onset, or Type I, diabetes is another cause of mood disorders. By being especially vigilant about watching a child's developing temperament, without being overly anxious, parents are usually the first and primary preventive step.

Warnings to Individuals

Unless a person is psychotic and completely cut off from reality, warnings from teachers, school counselors, or juvenile authorities about violent behavior or violent fantasies uttered to others are another early step in prevention. Too often parents, teachers, counselors, and even juvenile authorities are not aware of red flag indicators of violence and simply ignore them, opting instead for punishment without any method for addressing the specific behavior from a remediation perspective. This is a mistake, because punishment without rehabilitation and remediation can not only make matters worse, it simply ignores the possibility that real medical issues might be at stake.

Enabling Violent Behavior

Many times parents, siblings, spouses, or significant others can make matters worse by enabling the individual's violent personality. Enabling is not only looking the other way, it is feeding the violent individual's fantasy to enhance it. Most obvious is what is often called the *battered wife syndrome*, an enabling relationship in which the wife is either too afraid to confront a violently abusive husband or too afraid to abandon the relationship. As a result, the victim simply submits to the violent abuser's behavior in the hopes that it will somehow get better. It never does. The same situation can apply with parents or grandparents raising a violent youth or codependency in a violent relationship with an alcoholic or substance abuser. Most offenders in prison have been intimately and chronically exposed to brutality within their families of origin, according to Pincus and Tucker (1985).

Community Education

Too few community groups are educated in the prevention of violence and the identification of potentially violent individuals, particularly the police. Police are often front-line responders to violent or potentially violent incidents caused by people with mental illnesses. Individuals making threats, causing a public disturbance, or brandishing weapons may simply be arrested, charged, processed, and later released after a short time in jail only to return to their former lifestyles as angry and as menacing as they were before. Any chance to intervene medically in their lives is lost because the legal system simply did not provide for a diagnosis of a potentially fatally violent cause.

Police and other public safety officers, as front-line first responders, need to be educated as part of a community awareness that potentially homicidally violent individuals are lurking just below the surface tension of society and as pressures on them mount, they could break into the kind of murder/suicide we have seen in the George Sodini Pittsburgh shooting. A high percentage of young offenders booked into jail have obvious scars from gunshot wounds clearly intended to wound, rather than kill. Astoundingly, the system is so dehumanized that such obvious signs of inner-city syndrome are simply ignored.

There is a war going on out there on the streets of America, as we saw plainly in Chicago in the fall of 2009, but either nobody seems to notice or everyone has simply given up on a whole population of youngsters inevitably heading for the third strike that will put them away. But, these violent individuals, now trained inside prison walls, will almost always come back. Such obvious signs of combat wounds such as gunshots and knifing scars must be investigated clinically before the dehumanization process deteriorates and violence escalates.

Carl Bell has found that a significant number of youngsters can get out of this cycle of violence with little or no help (personal communication). What if all of them had help to get out? Too often, the signs of inner-city combat are ignored and the signs of inner-city syndrome are never examined. From my own experience dealing with children growing up in similar inner-city areas to Wayne Williams's hunting ground in Atlanta showed little or no difference in the posttraumatic sequellae of inner-city syndrome; the evidence showed a numbing and dehumanization that not even the omnipresent terror of Wayne Williams could penetrate. Sleep and bed-wetting patterns, for example, were no worse in Atlanta's inner city than they were in other cities where such a monster was not on the prowl.

Municipal and State Child Services and Juvenile Services

Other first responders to children who may exhibit red-flag indicators of violence are child and family services and juvenile justice services, including courts, prosecutors, and police. These are also front-line agencies insofar as they have an early opportunity to spot troubled juveniles, those possibly suffering from varying degrees of mental illness or social trauma, and to intervene in their lives so as to get them help. Juvenile and family court officers without the training to spot the red flags do little more than process psychologically troubled youth along the bureaucratic pipeline. Youths whose lives can be turned around can easily be camouflaged by the huge throughput requirements of the court system, where they disappear only to emerge years later in full-blown homicidal rage. Training these officers in recognizing early indicators of psychosis or red-flag indicators of potential violence will help identify trouble and possibly prevent Cho-like massacres. Wolfgang (1975) clearly shows the economic sense of aggressive clinical diagnostic intervention after the third offense, because it is within that diminishing cohort of young males that the vast majority of future major offenders can be found.

Emergency Room Training

As we have stressed throughout our study of the Cho case, emergency room healthcare workers are simply undertrained and in large measure incapable of identifying emerging symptoms of dangerous psychoses in their admitting procedures. But, even worse, once those symptoms are identified, many emergency rooms have no place to treat these individuals because there are simply no beds available. As a result, many patients in need go untreated even if they are identified as being in need.

A first step is to learn to identify patients in need. Thus, more training is needed. A mandatory second step is to figure out what to do with patients exhibiting psychotic or other clinical signs of dangerousness. And equally mandatory subsequent steps require the assemblage of treatment plans and placement of patients in facilities where they can be helped. All of this takes money, more money than states and municipalities have during these times of crisis. However, there are innovative options coming on line for telemedicine and telepsychiatry.

Telemedicine

Recently, the University of Texas Medical Branch in Galveston has been experimenting with a form of telemedicine to show proof of concept to address different kinds of medical needs. Though these tests involve such devices as wireless pacemakers and will soon involve wireless blood glucose monitors for diabetes patients, it is not far fetched to see psychiatrists monitor levels of antipsychotic drugs in their patients on a daily basis. One can only imagine the success a psychiatrist would have had with a patient like Cho, who certainly needed antischizophrenic drugs to keep him from becoming violent. And drugs that have suicidal ideations as serious potential side effects can be adjusted in patients who suffer from clinical depression. This also opens up the possibilities of what we recommended earlier, telepsychiatry.

Telepsychiatry

Probably one of the most intriguing possibilities is the use of off-the-shelf applications such as Skype to provide video conferencing between a doctor and patient. Mental health professionals as well as physicians can use this remote conferencing application in much the same way they use a telephone. But the video conferencing ability provides for eye contact and face-to-face conversations.

The use of webcams also means that patients who need to be examined for things like sore throats or allergic or physiological reactions to drugs—pimples, hives, eruptions on soft tissue—can scan themselves with a webcam and the images can be transmitted directly to a doctor's monitor. If it looks serious, the doctor can schedule an office visit or send the patient to a hospital emergency room.

Skype, webcams, USB-based monitors, and wireless monitors also fit the model of telepsychiatry, a practice that will allow psychiatrists and their clinical associates in nursing and psychology to monitor and interact with patients at a much lower cost and over a wider area. Even the use of cellular technology combined with video applications on iPhones, Palm Pilots, and Blackberry devices will help psychiatrists deal with patients in the throes of life struggles.

Change Makers

Even as we lament the current state of emergency medicine in general and emergency psychiatry in particular, we believe that help is on the way. Our wish list for telepsychiatry and telemedicine is quickly being addressed by advances in technology. For example, because the old model of the Freudian psychiatrist sitting back and taking notes while a patient talks about dreams and ideations of bizarre sexual practices while lying on a leather couch is as passé as an ashtray on a dinner table, we are looking to the model of a psychiatric practitioner being able to monitor many patients via a datalink hook-up.

A computer-supported diagnostic screen that is both patient and health professions user-friendly can efficiently and uniformly assist triage of patients entering the healthcare system at all points of entry. These now include the corrections system and, via video conferencing, presentations from remote regions, including theaters of combat. But, physicians, nurses, and all other allied health professionals must be on the same page or it will be "garbage in, garbage out." Such a computerized networking system embedding diagnostic screens promotes unity in healthcare creating a complex new management tool known as lean-engineered healthcare solutions.

Such a system must enhance treatment selection and service optimization by integrating disease-specific management for emergency, complex medical presentations, disorganized mental states, and psychic impairment at any point of entry to the healthcare delivery system. This could be accomplished with minimum modifications of the multiform gateway system to American healthcare, whether the patient enters on his own to an outpatient clinic or ER, is directed by phone triage with telehealth video conferencing, or is booked into jail. Like modern retailing, the brick-and-mortar gateway that leads into the healthcare system is likewise becoming a "wired gateway." Video conferencing will be ramped up to leverage scarce professional resources to support care of the neediest populations with bad access to brick and mortar gateways. Nowhere within underserved populations is there more desperate need for such leveraging with telehealth and computerized clinical decision support systems of triage than the 22 percent of people found to have significant psychiatric impairment cross-culturally in well-controlled international studies.

A huge part of the burden on emergency medicine is not just the treatment and patient throughput but the diagnosis itself. Shoddy diagnosis or incomplete diagnosis because of a lack of information impacts the treatment recommendations. Accordingly, at a time of shrinking healthcare budgets, as evidenced by the crisis in California's public healthcare system, we have to implement new technologies to get to a best practices plateau.

Computer-enhanced diagnostics could advance the current art and practice of clinical medicine by supporting selection of both diagnostic and therapeutic technologies in a significantly more objective and effective manner than what is the current state of practice. Studies previously cited from Paul Miller's research at UCLA hospitals have demonstrated poor reliability and alignment between identified signs and symptoms, even at psychiatric emergency centers serving the documented seriously mentally ill patient. Conversely, these studies demonstrate that clinical decision support for helping to identify criteria for diagnosing serious mental illness results in both enhanced accuracy and reliability of diagnosis among examining clinicians. Nonetheless, as Klein states, more must be done to optimize service for this 22 percent of functionally impaired members of our society (Klein et al., 1993).

"For what purpose is differential diagnosis, if not at least partly, to predict clinical course and treatment response?" asks Donald Klein, M.D. He further emphasizes the importance of validity in diagnosis along neuropsychiatric clinical pathways, accounting for nearly all high utilizers and, therefore, one half of all primary healthcare utilization.

> The advent of psychotropic drugs has enormously improved psychiatric care. ... It has been repeatedly shown that the majority of patients with psychiatric illness go undiagnosed, and even if diagnosed, they are inappropriately or ineffectively treated, both by psychiatrists and primary care practitioners. ... The DSM process improved clinicians' abilities to communicate with each other by explicit inclusion and exclusion criteria. Nonetheless, our eventual goal is diagnostic validity, which means that diagnoses have practical value. In this context, the use of one diagnostic criteria set rather than another should lead to a superior ability to prescribe, treat, and render a secure prognosis. Here there has been only moderate progress. A clinician's problem is deciding what treatments to select for a particular patient and how to do it. Diagnosis alone is not sufficient, although usually necessary (Klein, 1993).

The incredible costs of underdiagnosing, with attendant denial of treatment for the complex medical, mentally disorganized, and psychic-impaired patients will eventually demand revolutionary approaches at the points of entry to health services. Whether that point of entry has the form of clinical office, public health services, emergency rooms, or jails can ultimately make no difference, because that is where the at-risk people present for the infrequent opportunity of comprehensive, computer-enhanced diagnostic assessment. Simple artificial intelligence can be a doctor's companion for expanding diagnostic sensitivity while enhancing both the art of medicine with diagnostic specificity that promotes evidence-based pharmacotherapy, as well as selection of diagnostic and invasive procedures. Such modeling must be adaptable to clinicians' needs for making frequent changes in time- and cost-determined clinical decisions to avoid dangerous and destructive cookie cutter stuffing between patient presentation and rigid, superimposed algorithmic pathways. In retracing his insidious deterioration of numerous patients, followed by acute collapse, we came up with a triage algorithm. From the investigation of these cases we demonstrate how medical software can model triage decisions.

Emergency

In progressively screening from highest to lowest levels of lethality, the emergency screen helps prevent patients from leaving the point of entry for follow-up outpatient disposition when screening of a presentation predicts risk of severe morbidity or mortality, violence, or deliberate self-harm. Following immediate clearance of clinical presentations threatening sudden death or acute and irreversible morbidity via easily remembered triage formulas for both single and multiple patient situations, any new patient should immediately be screened for psychiatric emergencies to protect both clinical staff as well as the patient and others in the vicinity from violence. Although it is true that violence and suicide—oftentimes preventable and among the leading causes of death and morbidity in America—cannot always be accurately predicted, neither can the results of bilateral mastectomy or total resection of the prostate. Such maiming surgeries are hardly less risky clinically than humane restraint, whether pharmacological or physical. Prediction of violence can and will be improved—not necessarily through scientific advances but because of current public health demands and medical liability.

Medical/Surgical Approaches

Simply focusing on secondary prevention of at-risk juveniles by epidemiologically informed clinical decision making, supported with the evidence of modern imaging studies, visualizes one iceberg before predictable catastrophic collision. If it were not for progression of conduct disorder in comorbidly attention deficit disordered adolescent males to a malignant form of adult sociopathy defying current corrections efforts, our streets—when curfewed from adolescent reoffenders and drug dealers—should be safe. But, presently nearly 20 million people move in and out of jails in the United States each year, most with past violence-related injuries and high risk of future violent injuries or death. More than one quarter have survived prior gunshot wounds for which statistics demonstrate combat strategies to deliberately wound rather than kill, the nonfatal-to-fatal ratio being 12 to 1 in drive-by shootings.

Of more concern is the fact that 90 percent of illegal acts in juveniles are undetected. Moreover, nonpsychiatric dispositions in the criminal justice system are now, at best, politically expedient, despite the fact that the metro jails are among the largest psychiatric inpatient facilities in most states. Ultimately presentence investigation will have to once again become an integral point of entry into the healthcare delivery system, unless we are prepared to write off a generation of young males, now mostly low-income minorities, and mortgage our children's futures to pay for life and healthcare for millions of men behind bars with three strikes: big business now for corporations.

Conduct disorder in childhood, usually associated with comorbid attention deficit disorder, frequently progresses to antisocial personality disorder (ASD) in adulthood, generating a prevalence of over 6 percent ASD in the population. Research demonstrates that aggression can be reduced in 60 percent of this adolescent population. Chronic depression in the mother, spousal abuse, bad schools, and delayed diagnosis in early childhood—all remedial—predict a bad outcome.

Impairment

Screens for impairment emphasize acuity rather than severity or lethality and enable sophisticated diagnostic tools, now available for selecting effective clinical pathways with frequently misdiagnosed patients—particularly high utilizers. Dissecting presentations of unknown and complex, unremembered patients for subtle comorbidity at all points of entry improves long-term morbidity and mortality as well as the direct and indirect costs of healthcare. After med-surg, neuropsychiatric and the mental states of disorganization in the psychotic, substance abuse, and traumatic stress disorders are ruled out, the diagnostic screen can safely progress to the second large group of high utilizers of primary healthcare services in a cost-effective manner.

Here, consultation liaison psychiatry can significantly impact the dilemma of high utilization. Triage for psychic pain and suffering can divide this enormous patient population between clinical pathways requiring psychiatric treatment and those requiring various forms of effective, nonmedical psychotherapies. This discrimination is enormously important in the macroeconomics of direct and indirect healthcare costs.

Nonpsychotic, ambulatory mood and anxiety disorders are another category of psychiatric care. They, alone, currently afflict 15 percent of Americans every year, 23 percent for varying periods of their lives at an estimated cost of $60 billion per year. Pacific Bell, for example, found that 11 percent of their disability costs were due to nonpsychotic mood disorders. Patients with these disorders utilize over 25 percent of primary care medical services in this country and are usually undiagnosed or almost always denied appropriate psychopharmacotherapy with concurrent psychotherapy.

Adequate psychiatric treatment, 80 percent effective for panic disorder and 65 percent effective for depression, can reduce direct healthcare costs by 15 percent for these patients. This compares with 52 percent effectiveness for atherectomy and 41 percent effectiveness for angioplasty, both of which, on the other hand, were rapidly accepted invasive treatments.

The prevalence of antisocial personality disorder in America today is 3.8 percent. Because false negatives for prediction of dangerousness in this population can be significantly reduced by case detection, the importance of diagnostic sensitivity and accuracy in diagnostic screening with such pervasive psychopathology impacting our society in so many destructive ways can no longer be denied with rationalization of constitutional law. Miss Tarasoff's killer was evaluated and released through official commitment channels. Her murderer's psychiatrist was found liable for not protecting the victim, but he did all the right things constitutionally. Unfortunately for the victim, the psychiatrist, and the psychiatric community itself, a constitutionally correct decision by the doctor simply did not protect anyone, not even the system.

Differential diagnosis within the criminal justice system, where treatable character pathology and reversible neuropsychiatric, posttraumatic, and substance abuse disorders must be differentiated, is currently deemphasized or even devalued. Tragically, that is where many of these people can be properly assessed through presentence investigation or even at booking. The corrections business is booming, even though nobody knows how to correct or even what to correct. To make matters worse, most offenders will be released untreated and uncorrected, despite determinate sentences, because many states reserve the authority to release anyone they so choose to release, if beds are filled and no other corrections disposition is available. Judicial discretion must become the governor's discretion, because the United States cannot really afford to incarcerate 15 million adults, particularly when incarceration has such a minuscule impact on crime.

When we look at the entire picture of warning signs of dangerousness, the ways the system reacts to these warning signs, and the best new methodologies of treatment in light of the warning signs, we become very uncomfortable with the way the future lays out. But our discomfort is not just for the future and the numbers of individuals who will pass through the emergency medical and psychiatric systems, it is whether how we are using our current tools is satisfactory. The frustrating aspect of all this is that all the tools were there for the healthcare professionals at Virginia Tech to use in the case of Cho. When you look at all the evidence, however, even under the harsh bright light of hindsight, you come to realize that Cho's tragedy was not a product of systemic failure. It was a product of human error. And innocent victims had to die for it. The medical profession was put to the test, as it is put to the test every day a psychotic and potentially violent patient walks into an emergency room, and the profession failed. We cannot let this happen again on our watch.

From the cases we have cited here, one can see how our society tolerates sloppiness at points of entry to our healthcare system, too often under the false illusion of preserving individual freedoms. In the case of Cho, his liberty, which he neither enjoyed nor actually had, was so diligently spared that dozens of productive professional and promising young lives were ended in senseless bloodshed. In the memorials to the victims, politicians avoided confronting the real questions and took the issue right back to where it started: denial of mental illness in Cho's act of free will in slaughtering people of no meaningful consequence to him. In fact, not to belabor a point that is well worth belaboring, the governor's panel actually laid the blame on Cho for lying about something he was probably not capable of or even competent to be telling the truth. It was like blaming a blind person for not seeing the tree he walked into because the public health service provided him with neither a cane nor a seeing-eye dog.

The claimed victory over mass murder in the commonwealth's memorial was meaningless tweaking of the law to make it less impossible for mental health professionals to treat the seriously mentally ill and control that small portion so obviously dangerous, like Cho, in the name of consumer choice. Lawsuits were settled around this pronounced victory over death, but then the missing triage notes turned up, provoking more legal actions against the commonwealth.

No doubt this nation has ignored both perversion of rule of law by making civil commitment of the dangerous and seriously mentally ill a mission for our courts equivalent to the Voting Rights Act following the Selma March and lack of preparedness in the wake of 9/11. St. Albans Hospital was so dumbed down by alleged civil liberties of Cho Seung-Hui that it was blinded to frank signs of florid mental illness. Hollywood, Florida's, hospital ER had no early alerts to the terrorists literally crawling around its neighborhood in 2001, yet first response is still a nationwide failure in test after test.

We medical practitioners as a profession fought the losing battle with civil libertarians identifying dissolution of involuntary commitment and state hospitals to humanely care for the seriously mentally ill and protect innocent citizens and family members from its small minority of clearly documented dangerous patients. Yet, in defeat, we willingly take pay checks to do the forensic dirty work of playing legal charades to determine whether a psychotic patient is imminently dangerous or dangerous in the near term—as if it is either possible to do or makes any difference. And, in the case of Cho, the St. Albans willingly went with the collapsing mental health system and legal charades.

We would love to talk about the old days of the country doctor, Marcus Welby, M.D., or even the kindly family practitioner who could see a patient on a moment's notice. We grew up with this kind of medical practice in America in the 1950s. But, as the song says, "Yesterday's Gone," and in its place are insurance-company-run HMOs whose doctors and the hospitals where they practice are dumbed down to the point where they practice medicine by coloring by the numbers. Did anybody even think to question Cho's sudden appearance at St. Albans, transported as he was by the campus police. It was get him a bed, get him a hearing, and get him out the door. Not one phone call was placed to his parents, to an emergency phone number, or to the dean's office that was monitoring him by committee.

Similarly, although Sodini was not overtly psychotic, was there any place he could turn to vent his feelings in a safe way? It is not a crime to be angry or even hostile that you cannot score with the opposite sex. But the brooding, the planning, the methodology to put into action a plan to find a place where you can kill as many people as possible before taking your own life, that is where the line is drawn between unhappiness and psychotic desperation.

If we want to avoid more Cho Seung-Huis trolling the halls of our schools and universities and want to protect ourselves from the Sodinis checking into some sort of public facility with the aim of wiping out its other customers, we have to make emergency psychiatric healthcare more available. We have to convince the courts that their definition of involuntary commitment does not have to resemble that of a Soviet-era Gulag to protect the public. It only has to take into account what the California court took into account in the *Tarasoff* case and look at the consequences of a potentially violent person wreaking havoc on a community of potential victims.

Just like the issues raised by the 9/11 panel, the laws are in place to do the job of protecting us. We simply have to use best emergency medical practices, best law enforcement practices, and common sense to abide by those laws and protect the public. It is our job.

Appendix A

	...			Name	Reason Code	Clinic Code	Provider	Date	Time	ID	SSN	Cancellation Code
1	...			Cho, Seung-Hui	TriagePh	Counseling	SmithM	11/30/2005	09:45 AM	80520	904320691	
2	...			Cho, Seung-Hui	TriagePh	Counseling	BetzelC	12/12/2005	04:45 PM	80520	904320691	
3	...			Cho, Seung-Hui	TriageFF	Counseling	LynchS	12/14/2005	03:00 PM	80520	904320691	
4	...		X	Cho, Seung-Hui	Initial	Counseling	BetzelC	12/12/2005	02:00 PM	80520	904320691	Cancel

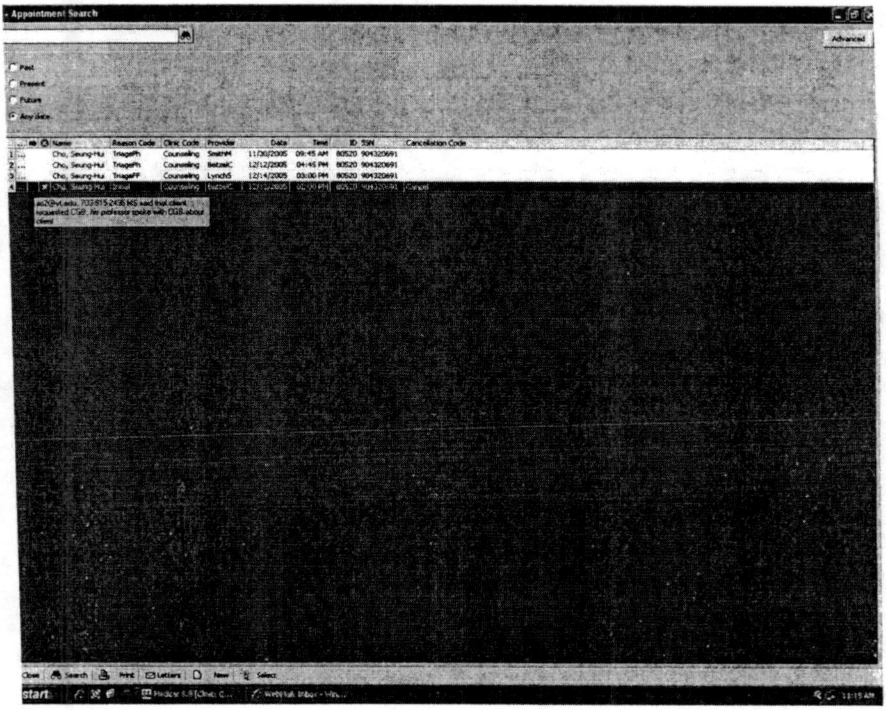

Emily Conway

From: Miller, Robert [rcmiller@vt.edu]
Sent: Wednesday, December 14, 2005 4:24 PM
To: smithcg@vt.edu; aepperso@vt.edu; chgibbons@vt.edu; grooker@naxs.net; Arbuckle, Vicki; Teresa Quesinberry; ccurran@vt.edu; econway@vt.edu; ti3tl7dg@vt.edu; Sandy Ward; Sherry Lynch; Cathye Betzel; Charlotte Amenkhienan; Gary Bennett; Michael Gore; Reliford Sanders; Rita Klein; Zukor, Tevya; Bitsko, Matt
Subject: FW: On Call Report

Fyi in the event this student is seen here

-----Original Message-----
From: Kowalski, Gerard
Sent: Wednesday, December 14, 2005 10:46 AM
Subject: FW: On Call Report

FYI

GJK

Gerard J. Kowalski, Ph.D.
Director of Residence Life
Asst. Professor of Higher Ed. & Student Affairs
109 East Eggleston Hall
Blacksburg, VA 24061-0428
Phone: 540.231.6205
Email: kowalski@vt.edu
Fax: 540.231.5041

From: Smith, Patricia
Sent: Wednesday, December 14, 2005 8:05 AM
To: Chapman, Sarah; Whitley, Carley; Holmes, Margaret; Hart, Janice; Petros, Melanie; Avent, Yolanda; Chadwick, Colin; Kirby, Gail; Kowalski, Gerard; Kuresman, Kia; MacDonald, Chris; Malloy, Alison; Marin, Eileen; 'Matt Grimes'; Miller, Amy; Penven, James; Settle, Rohsaan; Wallington, Evelyn; Wylie, Jonathan; Yancey, Laurica
Subject: On Call Report

On Call Report

Tuesday, December 13, 2005

Residence Life Administrator on Call: Tricia Schwery Smith
Hall Supervisor on Call: Jason Shank

*****Counseling Referral, VTPD, ACCESS, Cochrane*****

*****Counseling Referral, VTPD, ACCESS, Cochrane*****
Resident Involved: Seung Cho (904320691) Cochrane 3032, 232-6213
Staff Involved: Lisa Virga, Cochrane/Harper Graduate Hall Director

Melissa Trotman, Cochrane 3125, 232-4252

8:30 PM – GHD Virga came to my apartment to inform me about Cho who had a history of erratic behavior and counseling-based issues over the course of the semester. AD Settle, GHD Virga and RA Trotman all had extensive familiarity with Cho. Cho's suitemate called VTPD because Cho expressed suicidal ideations and had previously had "blades" in the room. Cho went to the Police Station on his own will to talk to an ACCESS counselor. Trotman and Virga were talking with roommate and suitemates. I called VTPD at 9:47 for an update. At this time, Cho was still in with the counselor. At 10:22PM, Lt Allen called me with an update. The magistrate issued a temporary detention order so Cho was to spend the night at the New River Valley Medical Center for further examination/counseling. Cho expressed that he still had one exam pending today as well. I communicated with both Virga and Trotman after this update.

END OF REPORT

Tricia Schwery Smith
President's & Upper Quad Area Coordinator
Virginia Tech
talktotricia@vt.edu
540-231-3419

From: Smith, Patricia
Sent: Tuesday, December 13, 2005 8:46 AM
To: Smith, Patricia; Chapman, Sarah; Whitley, Carley; Holmes, Margaret; Hart, Janice; Petros, Melanie; Avent, Yolanda; Chadwick, Colin; Kirby, Gail; Kowalski, Gerard; Kuresman, Kia; MacDonald, Chris; Malloy, Alison; Marin, Eileen; 'Matt Grimes'; Miller, Amy; Penven, James; Settle, Rohsaan; Wallington, Evelyn; Wylie, Jonathan; Yancey, Laurica
Subject: On Call Report

On Call Report

Monday, December 12, 2005

Residence Life Administrator on Call: Tricia Schwery Smith
Hall Supervisor on Call: Cyrus Mostaghim

No Report

END OF REPORT

Tricia Schwery Smith
President's & Upper Quad Area Coordinator
Virginia Tech
talktotricia@vt.edu
540-231-3419

ID# 904-32-0691

Patient's Name: ________________

Address: ________________

1. Patient Strengths: ________________

2. Problems Addressed: ________________

3. Progress Made: ________________

4. Aftercare Needs: (Problems Referred) ________________

5. Diagnosis at time of Discharge: ________________

6. Type of Discharge: Regular________ AMA________ Without Consent________

Transferred to: ________________

7. Authorization to Release Information

I understand that:

- By signing this Authorization, I am giving the Health Care Entity permission to disclose confidential health records.
- My treatment, payment, enrollment or eligibility for benefits will not be conditioned on signing this authorization.
- I may withdraw (revoke) this authorization in writing. Withdrawal of this authorization does not affect any disclosure of protected health information made prior to the receipt of written notice of revocation by the custodian of the health records.
- There is a potential that information disclosed may be redisclosed by the recipient and no longer protected by law.
- A copy of this Authorization and a notation concerning the person or agencies to whom disclosure was made shall be included with the original health records.
- I, the undersigned, do hereby authorize Carilion Saint Albans Behavioral Health/Roanoke Behavioral Health to release Treatment Team: Integrated Summary, Nursing Discharge Information and the following information (as checked) to individuals listed below (unless noted otherwise). If applies, Federal Regulations Govern the confidentiality of Alcohol and Drug Dependent Persons (Section 2.31 of P.L. 93.282, 42-CFR Part 2). The Patient or Legal Guardian may revoke this authorization at any time.

Admission History: ✓ Medical Consultation(physical): ✓ Discharge Summary: Sent ✓ Labs: ✓ Other: prescreening

ollow-Up with: Cook Counseling Center Va Tech
ddress: 240 McComas Hall
Blacksburg VA 24061
hone: (540) 231-6557 Fax: ( ) 231-2104
ate: 12/14/05 Time: 3 PM

Follow-Up with: ________
Address: ________
Phone: ( ) ________ Fax: ( ) ________
Date: ________ Time: ________

ollow-Up with: ________
ddress: ________
hone: ( ) ________ Fax: ( ) ________
ate: ________ Time: ________

Follow-Up with: ________
Address: ________
Phone: ( ) ________ Fax: ( ) ________
Date: ________ Time: ________

Signature of Patient or Responsible party: [signature] Date: 12/14/05

Signature/Witness: [signature] Date: 12/14/05

CARILION
Health System
Post Office Box 13727
Roanoke, Virginia 24036-3727
CBASC CFMH CGMH CMC-CRCH CMC-CRMH CNRV BMH
and other Affiliates of Carilion Health System

Carilion Behavioral Health
Treatment Team: Integrated Summary
Adopted: 9/99 Revised: 11/04
Form#181-2082

Patient Identification

10654655

CHO ,SEUNG HUI TDO
MR 236053 PT 10654655
BD: 01/18/1984 SEX: M
ATN DR: MIGLANI, JASDEEP (
ADM DATE: 12/13/05 21Y

I. **Nursing Discharge Information**:

	Date Reviewed	Staff Initials
Diet Instructions Regular	12/14/05	RQ
Physical Activity Instruction and/or Limitations No change	12/14/05	RQ
Relaxation Techniques NA	—	—

II. **Vital Signs**: (obtained 24 hours prior to discharge) BP: 128/63 Temp: 97 P: 69 R: 18

III. **Signs & Symptoms of Present Illness Explained to Patient/Family** (education information given): ✓ Yes ____ No

If no, document: ______

IV. **Discharge Medications Instructions:**

Medication	Dosage	Time
No Medications	prescribed	

Signature: [illegible signature] Date: 12/14/05

V. **Discharge Summary Note**: Patient discharged ambulatory himself to follow up as out patient with VA Tech counseling center. Patient verbalized safety and understanding of discharge plans.

VI. **Discharge Checklist**:

Check	Yes or No	Check	Yes or No
Valuables Returned	Yes	Medications Returned to Patient	NA
Belongings Checked	Yes	Copy of Nursing Discharge Information	Yes

Signature & Title: [illegible signature] Date/Time of D/C: 12/14/05 1400

Signature of Patient or Responsible Party: [illegible signature] Date: 12/14/05

CARILION
Health System
Post Office Box 13727
Roanoke, Virginia 24036-3727
CBASC CFMH CGMH CMC-CRCH CMC-CRMH CNRV CSABH BMH

Carilion Behavioral Health
Nursing Discharge Information
Adopted: 12/99 Revised: 3/04
Form# 181-2027

Patient Identification

10654655
CHO ,SEUNG HUI TDO
MR 236053 PT 10654655
BD: 01/18/1984 SEX: M
ATN DR: MIGLANI, JASDEEP (
ADM DATE: 12/13/05 21Y

CARILION HEALTH SYSTEM
Carilion New River Valley Medical Center
P.O. Box 5
Radford, Va. 24141

DATE OF EVALUATION: 12/13/2005

DIAGNOSIS:
1. Mood disorder.

HISTORY OF PRESENT ILLNESS: The patient is very resistant to discussing how he feels and if he has any symptoms of depression or mood changes. He stated he E-mailed a friend yesterday that he felt like killing himself. The patient states he was just kidding around, but that the friend ended up calling the police and that's why the patient ended up in St. Albans. He says it's all a misunderstanding. The patient denies suicidal ideation, however, he is very non-verbal and did not discuss feelings.

PAST MEDICAL HISTORY: The patient denies any surgical procedure. He denies any history of medical problems. Did not answer if he had any previous depression, he just looks down at the floor. He has no primary M.D. that he has seen in years. ALLERGIES: HE HAS NO KNOWN DRUG ALLERGIES.

FAMILY HISTORY: His mother is healthy. His father is healthy. His sister is 24, they all live in Northern Virginia, he says they are all healthy. Other family history unknown.

SOCIAL HISTORY: The patient is a junior at Virginia Tech studying in English. He wants to be a creative writer. Does not want to go to graduate school. Lives on campus with a roommate. He says they get along okay. He has lived in Northern Virginia for 10 years. Prior to that he lived in Korea. He denies use of tobacco, alcohol or drugs. Occasionally he states he goes to the gym, but otherwise does not discuss what he does for fun. Denies having any hobbies. Does state he is keeping up in school and that his grades are "okay." States he has an exam tomorrow in British Literature.

MEDICATIONS: Current medications are Ativan 1 milligram p.o. every six hours p.r.n. anxiety.

REVIEW OF SYSTEMS: The patient denies problems with eyes, ears, nose and throat, denies any respiratory problems such as shortness of breath or cough. Denies any cardiac chest pain. Denies any GI symptoms such as nausea, vomiting, diarrhea or constipation. Denies any problems with musculoskeletal issues such as pain or weakness of the extremity. Denies any changes with his skin or any problems. Denies any changes in his weight or increased thirst or increased urination. Denies confusion, dizziness, visual changes. His last eye exam was two years ago. Denies any recent history of head injury or accident or drug use.

Patient: **CHO, SEUNG HUI**	Acct#: 10654655	MR#: **236053**
Date of Birth: 01/18/1984	Admit Date: 12/13/2005	Room#: SA02
Attending: JASDEEP (BOBBY) MIGLANI	Discharge Date:	Service: TDO

Physical **Page 1**

CARILION HEALTH SYSTEM
Carilion New River Valley Medical Center
P.O. Box 5
Radford, Va. 24141

PHYSICAL EXAMINATION: Vital signs: 158.6, 5'8", blood pressure 128/63, pulse 69, respirations 18. Physical exam, patient very non-verbal, very quiet, sits in the chair looking down at the floor, does not blink. Often does not answer questions, or perhaps shakes his head yes or no. When he does speak, it's very slow, very soft spoken. No smile, no laughter, no crying. Patient does not blink. The patient speaks so softly it's almost difficult to hear him. Eyes, pupils equal, round and reactive to light, extraocular movements intact, funduscopic exam appears within normal limits. Did stress that patient needs to get an eye exam since it has been two years since he's had an eye exam. Ears, nose and throat, within normal limits. Patient has very healthy teeth. Neck is supple, non-tender, thyroid within normal limits. Chest clear to auscultation anteriorly and posteriorly. Heart regular rate and rhythm. Abdomen, bowel sounds X4, soft, non-tender, no rebound, no organomegaly appreciated. Femoral pulses normal, peripheral pulses normal, no swelling of the lower extremities. No scars noted. The patient denies tattoos. Neurologic exam, cranial nerves II-XII was within normal limits with negative Romberg. Patient is able to follow all instructions and does so deliberately and slowly.

LABORATORY DATA: Patient's labs essentially look within normal limits including CBC, urinalysis, liver function test and chemistry panel. Patient has full range of motion of all extremities and strength appears to be 5/5. He has 2+ deep tendon reflexes of all extremities.

ASSESSMENT:

1. Mood disorder. Very difficult to get a verbal history from this patient regarding signs of a mood disorder or depression. Patient to be treated by Dr. Jasdeep Miglani who has suggested he can be treated on an outpatient basis with counseling.
2. Patient in need of an eye exam as it has been two years since his last eye exam.
3. Patient to be treated by Dr. Miglani and hopefully have some intervention in therapy for treatment of his mood disorder.

FNP

LOUISE R. COATS, N.P.

12/20/05

JASDEEP (BOBBY) MIGLANI, M.D.

LRC / MEDQ
Job: 907798
DD: 12/14/2005 12:00:49

Patient: **CHO, SEUNG HUI**
Date of Birth: 01/18/1984
Attending: JASDEEP (BOBBY) MIGLANI

Acct#: 10654655
Admit Date: 12/13/2005
Discharge Date:

MR#: **236053**
Room#: SA02
Service: TDO

Physical

Page 2

CARILION HEALTH SYSTEM
Carilion New River Valley Medical Center
P.O. Box 5
Radford, Va. 24141

DT: 12/14/2005 12:52:23

cc: Jasdeep (Bobby) Miglani, M.D.

```
DISPLAY RESULTS                              PATIENT PRIORITY RESULTS FORM
10654655      CHO ,SEUNG HUI                       SABH      SA02 1      TDO
 SABH         ORDER/OCCR #:        8001
----------------------------------------------------------------------------PAGE      1
RESULTS FOR TEST: TPC1            WERE ENTERED ON 12/14/05   AT   14:12
OBSV CD NAME        VALUE      UNIT    ABN   REFERENCE RANGE        DATE        TIME
T3 UPTAKE           40.8       %             (32-48.4)            12/14/05    06:20
T4                  5.9        ug/dL    L    (6.09-12.23)         12/14/05    06:20
FREE THYROXN        6.0        ug/dL         (5.93-13.13)         12/14/05    06:20
 Calculation of the FTI has changed effective 8-17-04 and now uses the
   Thyroid Hormone Binding Ratio as recommended by the American Thyroid
   Association.
```

```
DISPLAY RESULTS                              PATIENT PRIORITY RESULTS FORM
10654655      CHO ,SEUNG HUI                       SABH      SA02 1      TDO
 SABH         ORDER/OCCR #:        9001
----------------------------------------------------------------------------PAGE      1
RESULTS FOR TEST: TSH             WERE ENTERED ON 12/14/05   AT   14:12
OBSV CD NAME        VALUE      UNIT    ABN   REFERENCE RANGE        DATE        TIME
TSH                 1.278      uIU/mL        (0.34-5.60)          12/14/05    06:20
```

```
DISPLAY RESULTS                              PATIENT PRIORITY RESULTS FORM
10654655      CHO ,SEUNG HUI                       SABH      SA02 1      TDO
              ORDER/OCCR #:      11001 ORD PARTY:
----------------------------------------------------------------------------PAGE      1
RESULTS FOR TEST: UDRG            WERE ENTERED ON 12/14/05   AT   11:41
OBSV CD NAME        VALUE      UNIT    ABN   REFERENCE RANGE        DATE        TIME
AMPHETAMN,UR                                 (NEG)                12/14/05    06:00
 NEG Cutoff Concentration     1000 ng/mL
BARBITURT,UR                                 (NEG)                12/14/05    06:00
 NEG Cutoff Concentration      200 ng/mL
BENZODIAZ,UR                                 (NEG)                12/14/05    06:00
 NEG Cutoff Concentration      200 ng/mL
CANNABINO,UR                                 (NEG)                12/14/05    06:00
 NEG Cutoff Concentration       50 ng/mL
COCAINE,URIN                                 (NEG)                12/14/05    06:00
 NEG Cutoff Concentration      300 ng/mL
OPIATES,URIN                                 (NEG)                12/14/05    06:00
 NEG Cutoff Concentration     2000 ng/mL
PCP, URINE          NEG                      (NEG)                12/14/05    06:00
   Cutoff Concentration       25 ng/mL
```

DISPLAY RESULTS PATIENT PRIORITY RESULTS FORM
10654655 CHO ,SEUNG HUI SABH SA02 1 TDO
ORDER/OCCR #: 11001 ORD PARTY:
--PAGE 2

RESULTS FOR TEST: UDRG WERE ENTERED ON 12/14/05 AT 11:41

OBSV CD NAME	VALUE	UNIT	ABN	REFERENCE RANGE	DATE	TIME
PCP, URINE	NEG			(NEG)	12/14/05	06:00

This drug screen is intended only for medical management of patients. The results should not be used for medicolegal purposes. The specimen was collected and processed without documentation of the chain of custody. The results have not been confirmed by an alternate method. For information regarding the availability and ordering of medicolegal drug testing, call CCL client services.
CROSS REACTIVITY, YIELDING A POSITIVE RESULT, MAY OCCUR WITH OTHER DRUGS.
CONTACT CLIENT SERVICES FOR INFORMATION AT 981-7157 OR 1-800-653-2205.

CARILION CONSOLIDATED LABORATORY (CNRV)
ROANOKE, VIRGINIA

NAME : CHO,SEUNG HUI DX: DEPRESSIVE D/O NOS AGE: 21Y SEX: M
MR# : 236053 ADMISSION: 12/13/2005 DR : MIGLANI,JASDEEP B
ACCT#: 10654655 RM#: SA02 1 SABH

HEMOGRAM

TEST:	WBC	RBC	HGB	HEMOGLOBIN CAPILLARY	HCT	MCV	MCH	MCHC
UNITS:	K/uL	M/uL	g/dL	g/dL	%	fL	pg	g/dL
LO-HI:	4.8-10.8	4.5-5.3	13.0-16.0	11.5-13.5	37-49	78-98	27-31	33-37
12/14 * 0620	5.9	5.53 H	16.3 H		49.0	88.6	29.5	33.3

HEMOGRAM

TEST:	RDW	PLT	MPV	NEUT	LYMP	MONO	EOS	BASO
UNITS:	%	K/uL	fL	%	%	%	%	%
LO-HI:	11.5-14.5	130-400	7.4-10.4	42-75	21-51	2-13	0-10	0-2
12/14 * 0620	12.8	224	8.0	51.2	39.5	6.4	2.3	0.6

HEMOGRAM

TEST:	NEUT NO.	LYMP NO.	MONO NO.	EOS NO.	BASO NO.	PERFORMING LAB
UNITS:	K/uL	K/uL	K/uL	K/uL	K/uL	
LO-HI:	1.8-7.7	1.0-5.0	0-0.8	0-0.4	0-0.2	
12/14 * 0620	3.1	2.3	0.4	0.1	0.0	

BASIC METABOLIC PANEL

TEST:	SODIUM	POTASSIUM	CHLORIDE	CO2	GLUCOSE	BUN	CREAT	ION GAP	B/C RATIO
UNITS:	MMOL/L	MMOL/L	MMOL/L	MMOL/L	MG/DL	MG/DL	MG/DL		RATIO
LO-HI:	135-145	3.5-5.3	98-110	21-31	70-110	6-20	0.5-1.4	2-11	12-20
12/14 * 0620	135	3.8	100	30	101	15	1.0	5	15.0

BASIC METABOLIC PANEL

TEST:	CALC OSM
UNITS:	MOS/KG
LO-HI:	275-301
12/14 * 0620	271 L

CHO,SEUNG HUI SS# : 121-37-7551 RM#: SA02 1 SABH
MR# : 236053 ADMIT: 12/13/2005 DR : MIGLANI,JASDEEP B
ACCT#: 10654655
RPT PRINTED: 12/14/2005 11:25 CHART COPY CUMULATIVE SUMMARY PAGE: 1

CARILION CONSOLIDATED LABORATORY (CNRV)
ROANOKE, VIRGINIA

NAME : CHO,SEUNG HUI	DX: DEPRESSIVE D/O NOS	AGE: 21Y SEX: M
MR# : 236053	ADMISSION: 12/13/2005	DR : MIGLANI,JASDEEP B
ACCT#: 10654655		RM#: SA02 1 SABH

******************************** PROFILE CHEMISTRY ********************************

DATE:			12/14/05
TIME:	NORMALS	UNITS	*0620
T PROTEIN	6.0-8.3	G/DL	7.0
ALBUMIN	3.2-5.5	G/DL	4.2
GLOBULIN	1.7-3.9	G/L	2.8
A/G RATIO	0.7-2.3	RATIO	1.5
T BILI	<1.3	MG/DL	1.0
ALK PHOS	42-121	IU/L	56
ALT	10-60	IU/L	17
AST	10-42	IU/L	22
CALCIUM	8.5-10.7	MG/DL	9.2

************************************* THYROID *************************************

TEST:	T3 UPTAKE	T4	FREE THYROXINE INDEX	TSH
UNITS:	%	ug/dl	ug/dL	uIU/mL
LO-HI:	22.5-37.0	6.09-12.23	5.93-13.13	0.34-5.60
12/14 * 0620	PEND	PEND	PEND	PEND

**************************** ALCOHOL AND DRUG SCREENS ****************************

TEST:	AMPHETAMINE	BARBITURATE	BENZODIAZEPINE	CANNABINOIDS	COCAINE
UNITS:					
LO-HI:	NEG	NEG	NEG	NEG	NEG
12/14 0600	PEND	PEND	PEND	PEND	PEND

----------------------------- ALCOHOL AND DRUG SCREENS -----------------------------

TEST:	OPIATES	PCP
UNITS:		
LO-HI:	NEG	NEG
12/14 0600	PEND	PEND

CHO,SEUNG HUI	SS# : 121-37-7551	RM#: SA02 1 SABH
MR# : 236053	ADMIT: 12/13/2005	DR : MIGLANI,JASDEEP B
ACCT#: 10654655		
RPT PRINTED: 12/14/2005 11:25	CHART COPY CUMULATIVE SUMMARY	PAGE: 2

CARILION CONSOLIDATED LABORATORY (CNRV)
ROANOKE, VIRGINIA

NAME : CHO,SEUNG HUI DX: DEPRESSIVE D/O NOS AGE: 21Y SEX: M
MR# : 236053 ADMISSION: 12/13/2005 DR : MIGLANI,JASDEEP B
ACCT#: 10654655 RM#: SA02 1 SABH

********** URINALYSIS **********

TEST:	SPECIMEN	COLOR	APPEAR	SP GRAV	PH	PROTEIN	GLUCOSE
UNITS:							MG/DL
LO-HI:				1.005-1.030	5.0-7.0	NEG	NEG
12/14 * 0600	URINE	YELLOW	CLEAR	>1.030	6.0	NEG	NEG

---------- URINALYSIS ----------

TEST:	KETONE	BILI	BLOOD	UROBIL	NITRITE	LEUC ESTERASE	RBC	WBC
UNITS:	MG/DL			EU/DL			/HPF	/HPF
LO-HI:	NEG	NEG	NEG	0.2-1.0	NEG	NEG	0-2	0-5
12/14 * 0600	NEG	NEG	NEG	0.2	NEG	NEG	NONE SEEN	NONE SEEN

---------- URINALYSIS ----------

TEST:	SQ EPI	MUCUS	BACTERIA
UNITS:	/LPF	/LPF	/HPF
LO-HI:		NSN	NSN
12/14 * 0600	FEW EPIN	NONE SEEN	NONE SEEN

---FOOTNOTES---
EPIN (NSN TO FEW)

CHO,SEUNG HUI SS# : 121-37-7551 RM#: SA02 1 SABH
MR# : 236053 ADMIT: 12/13/2005 DR : MIGLANI,JASDEEP B
ACCT#: 10654655
RPT PRINTED: 12/14/2005 11:25 CHART COPY CUMULATIVE SUMMARY PAGE: 3

Appendix B: Richard McBeef

By Cho Seung-Hui
Richard McBeef

ACT ONE

SCENE 1

(It is morning. The sun is s shining through the windows of the kitchen. John enters the kitchen, grabs a cereal bar, and opens it. Richard I~lcBeef is sitting in the kitchen with his legs crossed reading the newspaper.)

RICHARD
Hey John.
(He forces a smile at him.)

JOHN
Whats up, Dick!

(He frowns.)

RICHARD
Try dad.

JOHN
You aint my dad and you know it, you Dick.

(John chews on the cereal bar angrily.)

RICHARD
Come on, John. Sit down. 1~e need to have man-to-man talk.

(Richard pulls a chair next to him from under the table.)

JOHN
Mantoman up your assl bud!

(John sneers Lhen proceeds to the living room and turns on

the TV. Richard follows him, sits down, and faces him.)

RICHARD
I may not be your biological father, but Im your new father. We live under the same roof. We really need to get along. Come on, son, give me a chance.

(Richard gently rests his hand on John's lap.)
hand on Johns lap.)

JOHN
What the hell are you doing! (John slaps Ricahrds's hand.)

JOHN (Cont'd)
What are you, a Catholic priest! I will not be molested by an aging balding overweight pedophilic stepdad named Dick! Get your hands off me you sicko! Damn you, you Cathloic priest. Just stop it, Michael Jackson. Let me guess, you have a pet named Dick in Neverland ranch and you want me to go with you to pet him1 right?

(He sighs and ignores the comment.)

What is it you want from me, what do you want me to do? Why are you so angry at me --

JOHN
Why am I so angry at you! Because you murdered my father so you can get into in my morns pant!

RICHARD
Now hold on right there mister. It was a boating accident. I did everything I could to try to save your father.

JOHN
Bullshit! Are you always full of slAt, McBeef? I can see that you are by the extra fat you have packed on! You MURDERED my father and covered it up! You committed a cons irac . Just like what the overnment has done to John Lennon and Marilyn Monroe.

RICHARD
WHAT? WHAT?

(Frowning, he catches a glimpse of an old tabloid titled The Cover-up of Marilyn Monroe and John Lennon! !)

JOHN

You once worked for the government. As a janitor, at least. You hated the fact that my niom was with my dad. You knew my morn was too good for my father. So you took him out and stole her, you son of a bitch~

RICHARD

St

JOHN

No, DickJ You shut the hell u and listen to me.

RICHARD

You-

JOHN

Me what[You want me to stick this remote control up your ss, buddy~ You aint even worth it man. This remote was five bucks. You are such a --

RICHARD

NOW THATS ENOUGH.

(Richard raises his hand to strike his stepson, but before he does Johns mom comes down the stairs.)

SUE

Oh my godL Whats going on?

(She covers and hu s John and ushers him to the other end of the couch.)

What are you doing to m son! You said ou would have a nice chat to get on terms with him. And this is what I catch you do~ What kind of stepfather are you? Pretending to be nice to hi~ with a take smile on your chubby facet Tell me, what were you trying to do to him. You were about to hit him! Damn you, Richard!

RICHARD

He was

SUE

I dont want to hear it~ (Sue tells John to go up to his room. But he observes the spectacle half way up the staircase.)

RICHARD

I swear Sue! I tried talking to him. He called me a son of a bit

SUE

How dare you[John would neverNEVER -- say such a thing, my poor little pocey pooey boy! He lost his father just a month ago. Show some compassion! Some stepfather!

JOHN

He tried to touch my privates.

SUE

(She gasps)

Holy shxt! Oops. Sorry John. Dick, You son of a b

(She peeks at John. She a r aches Richard and sla s Richard in the head multiple times. Taking off her shoes, she hits him hard.)

RICHARD

(He brushes Sue with his large arm and build.)

Sue Sue Sue. Listen to me!

(continued)

Appendix C: The Sodini Transcript

George Sodini

Age 48

DOB 9/30/1960

DOD 8/4/2009

5-10, 155 lbs

Never married

Pittsburgh, Pennsylvania, USA

Why do this?? To young girls? Just read below. I kept a running log that includes my thoughts and actions, after I saw this project was going to drag on.

November 5, 2008: Planned to do this in the summer but figure to stick around to see the election outcome. This particular one got so much attention and I was just curious. Not like I give a flying —— who won, since this exit plan was already planned. Good luck to Obama! He will be successful. The liberal media LOVES him. Amerika has chosen The Black Man. Good! In light of this I got ideas outside of Obama's plans for the economy and such. Here it is: Every black man should get a young white girl. … Kinda a reverse indentured servitude thing. Long ago, many a older white male landowner had a young Negro wench girl for his desires. Bout' time tables are turned on that —— . … LOL. More so than they dig the white dudes! Every daddy know when he sends his little girl to college, she be … real good. I saw it. "Not my little girl," daddy says! (Yeah right!!) Black dudes have their choice of best white —— . You do the math, there are enough young white so all the brothers can each have one for 3 or 6 months or so.

December 22, 2008: Time is moving along. Planned to have this done already. I will just keep a running log here as time passes. Many of the young girls here look so beautiful as to not be human, very edible. After joining this gym, started lifting weights and like it. Much info about weight programs, diet, etc., on the web. Or anything for that matter. Instead of TV I can Google for hours to relax. TV and most movies are dull.

December 24, 2008: Moving into Christmas again. No girlfriend since 1984, last Christmas with Pam was in 1983. Who knows why. I am not ugly or too weird. No sex since July 1990 either (I was 29). No ——! Over eighteen years ago. And did it maybe only 50–75 times in my life. Getting to think that a woman now would just, uh, get in the way of things. Isolated. I have extra money and enjoy traveling, too, with my 25–30 days of vacation. LA was the best! But going alone is not too fun. Invited to a party on Christmas day tomorrow. Seems about 15–25 people will actually show. I like her parties; I can meet new people and talk. Got the next 8 days off. I should have exit plan done and practiced by then. I know nothing will change, no matter how hard I try or what goals I set.

December 28, 2008: Glad I stayed around. All these days off are great. I will shoot for Tuesday, January 6, 2009, at maybe 8:15. I have list of to-do items to make.

December 29, 2008: Just got back from tanning, been doing this for a while. No gym today, my elbow is sore again. I actually look good. I dress good, am clean-shaven, bathe, touch of cologne—yet 30 million women rejected me—over an 18- or 25-year period. That is how I see it. Thirty million is my rough guesstimate of how many desirable single women there are. A man needs a woman for confidence. He gets a boost on the job, career, with other men, and everywhere else when he knows inside he has someone to spend the night with and who is also a friend. This type of life I see is a closed world with me specifically and totally excluded. Every other guy does this successfully to a degree. Flying solo for many years is a destroyer. Yet many people say I am easy to get along with, etc. Looking back, I owe nothing to desirable females who ask for anything, except for basic courtesy—usually. Looking back over everything, what bothers me most is the inability to work towards whatever change I choose.

As police investigate this case further, digging into Sodini's life, the reasons why he might have been a loner, and how he was able to function at the law firm where he worked for the past ten years, we will learn more about what took Sodini over the edge. But his Web diary reveals that he complains most that he cannot exercise control over his life. For a person who believes that he cannot exercise control, the ultimate moment of control is murder and then suicide.

> December 30, 2008: While driving I radio surfed to a talk show. The caller was a 30ish black man who was describing the despair in certain black communities. According to him, life is cheap there because you are going to die anyway when you get old. It is the quality of life that is important, he said. If you know the past 40 years were crappy, why live another 30 crappy years then die? His point was they engage in dangerous behavior which tends to shorten the lifespans, to die now and avoid the next 30 crappy years, using my example. The host got sarcastic and ended the call instead of trying understanding his point. Agreement wasn't necesary. I put music back on. But it was an interesting, and useful point for me to hear.
>
> December 31, 2008: My anger and rage is largely gone since I began lifting weights. Lifting drains me but I still have energy. Somebody else suggested running but that did not help me. I guess strenuous exercise is necesary for a man. So I just learned that now at 48. Maybe 30 years later than I would have liked. My dad never (not once) talked to me or asked about my life's details and tell me what he knew. He was just a useless sperm doner. Don't know why, find it fun talking to young kids when I visit someone. Brother was actually counter-productive and would try to embarrass me or discourage my efferts when persuing things, esp girls early on (teen years). Useless bully. Result is I am learning basics by trial and error in my 40s, followed by discouragement. Seems odd, but that's true. Writing all this is helping me justify my plan and to see the futility of continuing. Too embarrassed to tell anyone this, at almost 50 one is expected to just know these things. I hope it doesn't snow on Tuesday. Just thought of that. The crowd will be thin so I would postpone. ——!
>
> Now that I am on the topic of family and people I know, I might as well make a summary of sorts to show where things stand. This is New Years Eve I have time, no date tonight of course, so:
>
> Honorable mention:
>
> Tetelestai Church in Pittsburgh, PA—"Be Ye Holy, even as I have been Ye holy! Thus saith the lord thy God!", as pastor Rick Knapp would proclaim. Holy ——, religion is a waste. But this guy teaches (and convinced me) you can commit mass murder then still go to heaven. Ask

him. Call him at [phone number]. If no answer there, he should still live at [address]. In any case, guilt and fear kept me there 13 long years until Nov 2006. I think his crap did the most damage. Their web site: http://www.tetelestai.org.

Mum—The Central Boss. [address] Don't piss her off or she will be mad and vindictive for years. She actually thinks she's normal. Very dominant. Her way and only her way with no flexibility toward everyone in the household. A power and control thing. People outside the immediate family like her. Why are people vicious with their closest ones? She is the Boss above all other Bosses.

Michael Sodini—A Boss, my brother (Mike Sodini) [address]—Always the big bully, twice the size of most others. When he bullied or harassed someone, it was the other person who "deserved it." It was always about him. Way to self absorbed, too. Still is. Used to like to embarrass guys in front of their girlfriends. Lots of other —— . Kind of guy you actually loved to hate. The biggest, most self-centered jag-off I know. He took those bullying "skills" into the business world and is doing good financially. He is a big wheel only in his mind. Most people can see thru all his manipulation. He calls only when he wants something.

Sherry—sister—More of a victim than anything. Copes by exercising much control over her adult children. We used to be close until her control of L & D caused a conflict. Never the same after.

David—neph, sis's son (girlfriend Mallory Squires). Good young guy, though.

Lisa—niece, sis's daught. Attractive, smart, emotional—all good YW qualities.

Idiots:
Andy Pulkowski—I have been in barrooms and church groups. The worst people by far are the religious types. Especially a right-wing, stiff-faced fundie like Andy. A condescending, demeaning, passive-aggresive person. Frigid, rigid, linear and totally inflexible. Being a very serious person, he cannot hide his frown-lined face. He better not try to smile; lest his face might crack. I knew children of parents who grew up in strict religious homes. Religion has a certain stink to it of guilt, shame, fear, and that moral standard that always contradicts the natural tendencies and desires of a person. Therein lies the conflict.

Young person cannot experiment with things to decide on their own and establish their own parameters. So they tend to cut loose and really rebel much worse than the average young person. Ma and Pa never know what goes on. They easily BS their parents because they want to believe their little one is an angel. Andy has a young daughter Bethany Pulkowski away at college, High Point University. I saw her picture on his desk. She's your basic, attractive, young girl. Please reread my entry made on Nov 5th. That's only one thing she can do. You Andy types out there need to further strengthen your strict resolve and do more of the same thing! Because those girls were great when I recall my college years! She is someone's (or many guy's) little —— now, I am sure.

Another point about Andy. How can someone be cold, vicious, sarcastic and generally nasty ALL THE TIME and then make the claim about their church life and how good they are? Total hypocritical idiots.
That's all for now. That felt good.

Let's continue …
January 5, 2009: Was at the gym to lift. Very crowded. Tomorrow should be good. There is a woman there that gives me a certain look every time I am there. I decided to walk over and make a comment about the crowds but she left when I finished the exercise. Better that I do not get sidetracked from tomorrow's plan anyways. Life is just playing games. One or two dates with her, then the end. No matter how many changes I try to make, things stay the same. Every evening I am alone, and then go to bed alone. Young women were brutal when I was younger, now they aren't as much, probably because they just see me just as another old man. I see twenty something couples everywhere. I see a twenty something guy with a nice twentyish young women. I think those years slipped right by for me. Why should I continue another 20+ years alone? I will just work, come home, eat, maybe do something, then go to bed (alone) for the next day of the same thing. This is the Auschwitz Syndrome, to be in serious pain so long one thinks it is normal. I cannot wait for tomorrow!

January 6, 2009: I can do this. Leaving work today, I felt like a zombie—just going thru the motions. Get on the bus, get the car, drive home. … My mind is screwed up anymore, I can't concentrate at work or think at all. This log is not detailed. It is only for confidence to do this. The future holds even less than what I have today. It is 6:40pm, about hour and a half to go. God have mercy. I wish life could be better for all and the crazy world can somehow run smoother. I wish I had answers. Bye.

It is 8:45PM: I chickened out! —— ! I brought the loaded guns, everything. Hell!

April 24, 2009: Early last month, we had our second general layoff. I survived. First one was in November. When I began 10 years ago, that used to be a nice place to work. I understand the need to reduce staff when times sour, but this is out of proportion to the economic problems at this time. The economy is shrinking by about 4–5%. They decided not to pay Christmas bonus—for staff that amounts to about 8% of yearly pay. Well, OK. Plus no yearly "merit" raise, another 3.5%. That totals to about 11% cut. Plus two layoffs of 5% staff in each case. Do the math. I know this firm is using this downturn as an excuse to take advantage of a bad situation and kill jobs UNNECESSARILY. The second layoff people who actually did work were let go. We all need to pick up the slack so the company can cut beyond what is necessary. Wasn't going to mention it, because of all this —— , it is K&L Gates, the large law firm headquartered here in Pittsburgh. Just call it K&L Gates Corporation. Most people there are OK and I would never have a shoot 'em up there. They paid me for 10 years, so far!

Then is when I take care of things. I don't have kids, close friends or anything. Just me here. If you have nothing, you have nothing to lose. I enjoy writing these entries, I have no plans to go back and edit or even read most stuff already written. If you get bored, just click that "x" at the top, right corner of your browser. Bye.

May 4, 2009: I was so eager to do this last year. The big problem on my mind now is that my job will end soon. One project is being transitioned to another. The other one I am solely responsible, but is being fast tracked to production. I estimate maybe a month. I am not ready for the job market. I am ok what I do, a .NET software developer. Not at the top of the class, but I do a good job. I survived two general layoffs and other little layoffs they are having but keeping quiet about. I hear things.

The problem is I feel too good now to do this but too bad to enjoy life. I know I will never enjoy life. This is an over 30 year trend. Some people are happy, some are miserable. It is difficult to live almost continuously feeling an undercurrent of fear, worry, discontentment and helplessness. I can talk and joke around and sound happy but under it all is something different that seems unchangable and a permanent part of my being. I need to realize the details of what I never accomplished in life and to be convinced the future is merely a continuation of the past—WHICH IT ALWAYS has been. I am making a list of items that will provide motivation to do the exit plan, it won't be published. I always had hope that maybe things will improve especially if I make big attempts to change my life. I made many big changes in the past two years but everything is still the same. Life is over. Even though I look good, dress well, well groomed—nails, teeth, hair, etc. Who knows.

What is it like to be dead? I always think I am forgetting something, that's one reason I postponed. Similar to when you leave to get in your car to go somewhere—you hesitate with a thought: "what am I forgetting?" In this case, I cannot make a return trip!

I like to write and talk. Ironic because I haven't met anybody recently (past 30 years) who I want to be close friends with OR who want to be close friends with me. I was always open to suggestions to what I am doing wrong, no brother or father (mine are useless) or close friend to nudge me and give it bluntly yet tactfully wtf I am doing wrong. A personal coach or someone who knows what he is doing would be perfect. Money is highly secondary for a solution.

May 5, 2009: To pull the exit plan off, it popped into my mind to just use some booze. I want to do this before I get laid off, for reasons not worth mentioning but don't seem to have the ——. After the gym, I stopped at Shop N Save and got a fifth of vodka and a small bottle of Jack Daniels. I haven't had a drink since September 1, 1988, just over 20 years. It doesn't matter now, I need to use it to take the edge off of carrying out the exit plan. I will be taking some every now and then to get used to it and see if the alcohol effects will embolden me. Weed would be fun to try again. I don't know who has any. Life is over, who cares? I just need to use common sense, can't drink and drive, etc. This idea just hit me at a point in time and I immediately acted on it. Same thing happened when I decided to go back to Pitt full time, first day was Monday, May 8, 1989, and to buy the house that closed on Friday, September 30, 1996, to name two examples I remember so well.

The list idea yesterday is working. I carry it in my wallet and add to it. I am feeling too good to do carry this out, but too bad to enjoy ANYTHING. My life's dilema.

May 6, 2009: I started the JD. About one ounce with some tea to get me started. No big deal.

May 7, 2009: Went to the gym and did mostly cardio. My heart rate was 117 just from walking on the treadmill at 3.4. This should be done a few times a week for maybe 15 mins or so to keep the heart active. I sprinted a few times to push the limits.

May 18, 2009: I actually had a date today. It was with a woman I met on the bus in March. We got together at Two PPG Place for lunch. The last date for me was May 1, 2008. Women just don't like me. There are 30 million desirable women in the US (my estimate) and I cannot find one. Not one of them finds me attractive. I am looking at The List I made from my May 4th idea. I forgot about that for several days. That tells me where I stand. These problems have gotten worse over a 30 year period. I need to expect nothing from me or other people. All through the years I thought we had the ability to change ourselves—I guess that is incorrect. Looking at The List makes me realize how TOTALLY ALONE, a deeper word is ISOLATED, I am from all else. I no longer have any expectations of myself. I have no options because I cannot work toward and achieve even the smallest goals. That is, ABOVE ALL, what bothers me the most. Not to be able to work towards what I want in my life. I believe I deserve that. I read recently it is called "self efficacy," but who knows. Is that more psychobable?

May 25, 2009: I was invited to a picnic, and I went. An older woman there, out of the blue, asked if I liked high school. Then quickly asked if I was picked on very much. Interesting why she would ask that. But, thanks, I already know what the problem is, but a solution eludes me.

May 29, 2009: Another lonely Friday night, I'm done. This is too much.

June 2, 2009: Some people I was talking with believed I date a lot and get around with women. They think this because I showed an email I got from a hot woman to the department gossip, but it didn't work out. All this is funny. Actually, I haven't had sex since I was 29 years old, 19 years ago. That's true.

June 5, 2009: I was reading several posts on different forums and it seems many teenage girls have sex frequently. One 16 year old does it usually three times a day with her boyfriend. So, err, after a month of that, this little —— has had more sex than ME in my LIFE, and I am 48. One more reason. Thanks for nada, b——! Bye.

July 4, 2009: Wow, already late evening. I stayed in all day. Can't believe there was NOTHING to do today. No parties or picnics. WTF. No need to leave now.

July 20, 2009: Been a long time since last write. Everything still sucks. But I got a promotion and a raise, even in this —— Obama ecomomy. No more grunt programming. Go figure! New boss is great. He tactfully says when you did something wrong or complements on good things. Never confused with him. But that is NOT what I want in life. I guess some of us were simply meant to walk a lonely path. I have slept alone for over 20 years. Last time I slept all night with a girlfriend it was 1982. Proof I am a total malfunction. Girls and women don't even give me a second look ANYWHERE. There is something BLATANTLY wrong with me that NO goddam person will tell me what it is. Every person just wants to be —— nice and say nice things to me. Flattery. Oh yeah, I am sure you can get a date anytime. You look good, etc. —— . Awwww, wait. I can just start being self-righteous and say I live a good, clean life. I am holy, that's all Rick Knapp stuff. Hear that you —— : I Am Just Good!

July 23, 2009:

Wow!!

I just looked out my front window and saw a beautiful college-age girl leave Bob Fox's house, across the street. I guess he got a good lay today. College girls are —— . I masturbate. Frequently. He is about 45 years old. She was a long haired, hot little hottie with a beautiful bod. I masturbate. Frequently. Some were simply meant to walk a lonely path in life. I don't usually look out, but just happened to notice. Holy —— . I have masturbated since age 13. Thanks, mum and brother (by blood alone). And dad, old man, for TOTALLY ignoring me through the years. All of you DEEPLY helped me be this way.

I wish I can go back to 1975 and fix things. Awe, that wont work, big BULLY BROTHER would assert his —— . He was twice my size. He never messed with guys bigger than 5′10″, or so. He is a —— at heart. Remember, Michael is my brother (we have common parents, that's all) is still a BOSS. Repetition only for emphasis: HE IS ONLY A BULLY, even at 50ish! Never forget that! Because he exudes confidence. People believe —— if delivered WITH CONFIDENCE. Get it??

On the same thought, things occured to me today. Michael NEVER had an attractive girlfriend. Debbie, Barb, Kim, ... then I lost track. Not to say I had any (except Pam, who was about a 7.25). He married a Chinese-descent, petite woman with no body, no —— , no chest and no personality. She never laughs or smiles, neither does he. But she is highly intelligent and an excellent cook. I can testify to that! She home bakes her own DELICIOUS wheat bread! But who cares about that type of small bull crap? Mike even mentioned when we were visiting dad that "she's not very attractive."

I don't know where I am going with this. I am getting tired, feels good to write and get it all out.

On still another thought, I had 20+ years of sobriety and achieved nothing about friendships, girlfriends, guys, etc. Zilch. What a waste.

Bye, for today.

August 2, 2009: The biggest problem of all is not having relationships or friends, but not being able to achieve and acquire what I desire in those or many other areas. Everthing stays the same regardless of the effort I put in. If I had control over my life then I would be happier. But for about the past 30 years, I have not.

August 3, 2009: I took off today, Monday, and tomorrow to practice my routine and make sure it is well polished. I need to work out every detail, there is only one shot. Also I need to be completely immersed into something before I can be successful. I haven't had a drink since Friday at about 2:30. Total effort needed. Tomorrow is the big day.

Unfortunately I talked to my neighbor today, who is very positive and upbeat. I need to remain focused and absorbed COMPLETELY. Last time I tried this, in January, I chickened out. Lets see how this new approach works.

Maybe soon, I will see God and Jesus. At least that is what I was told. Eternal life does NOT depend on works. If it did, we will all be in hell. Christ paid for EVERY sin, so how can I or you be judged BY GOD for a sin when the penalty was ALREADY paid. People judge but that does not matter. I was reading the Bible and The Integrity of God beginning yesterday, because soon I will see them.

I will try not to add anymore entries because this computer clicking distracts me.

Also, any of the "Practice Papers" left on my coffee table I used or the notes in my gym bag can be published freely. I will not be embarased, because, well, I will be dead. Some people like to study that stuff. Maybe all this will shed insight on why some people just cannot make things happen in their life, which can potentially benefit others.

Miscellaneous:

1. Probably 99% of the people who know me well don't even think I was this crazy. Told by at least 100 girls/women over the years I was a "nice guy." Not kidding.
2. Lee Ann Valdiserri had my baby in early 1991. Haven't seen her since she was about four months into it. I knew her sister, Chris, from high school.
3. Net worth slightly more than $250K, (after all debt) as of end of 2008.
4. Death Lives!

References

ABC News, Johnell Bryan interview. http://abnews.go.com/WNT/story?id-130304+page=1

ABC News, http://abcnews.go.com/US/story?id=7052272&page=1"\t"_new

ABC News, http://abcnews.go.com/Health/VATech/story?id=3050483&page=1

Associated Press. Virginia Korean Community Still Reeling. April 22, 2007. http://www.nytimes.com/aponline/us/AP-Virginia-Tech-Koreans.html. Retrieved September 16, 2008.

Auer, N., Presentation to the National Conference of American College of Emergency Physicians, Seattle, Washington, October, 2002.

Aursnes, I., Tvete, I.F., Gaasemyr, J., & Natvig, B. Suicide attempts in clinical trials with paroxetine (Paxil) randomized against placebo, *BMC Medicine.*, 3, 14, 2005.

Bergeron, M.A. Comments on Virginia Panel, *Behavioral Healthcare*, 28(8), 14–21, 2008.

Bonnie, R., *Psychiatric News*, 43(7), 21, 2008.

Boyd, D., The conceptual development of EMS systems in the United States, Part II. *Emergency Medical Services*, 11(2), 26–35, 1982.

Bushouse, K., Security at issue in widow's case, *Sun-Sentinel*, September 28, 2003.

Chessick, R., *Intensive Psychotherapy of the Borderline Patient*, Jason Aronson, 1977.

CNN News http://cnn.com/2001-10-10/health/anthrax_1_anthrax-strain-ernesto-blano-fbi-agents/ *eMedicine* Psychiatry. http://www.chall.com/cme-emergency-medicine-psychology.php

Entsminger, K., A missed opportunity to strengthen treatment laws, *Behavioral Healthcare*, 28(8), 14–21, 2008.

Entsminger, K. Statement, January 25, 2008. http://www.treatmentadvocacycenter.org/index.php?option=com_content&task=view&id=114

Epstein, E., Anthrax Letters & 9/11, http://edwardjayepstein.com/teamb/2.htm

Halleck, S., in *Violence and Criminal Justice*, Eds., D. Chappell & J. Monahan, Lexington Books, New York, 1975.

Kelly, G.A., *The Psychology of Personal Constructs*, Norton, New York, 1955.

Kessler, R. et al., Lifetime and 12 month prevalence of DSM-III psychiatric disorders in the United States: Results from the National Comorbidity Survey. *Archives of General Psychiatry*, 51, 1994.

Kitzrow, M.A. The mental health needs of today's college students: Challenges and recommendations. *NASPA Journal*, 41, 167–181.

Klein, D., Clinical psychopharmacological practice: the need of developing a research base. *Archives of General Psychiatry*, 50, 1993.

Leighton http://www.deepdyve.com/lp/sage/august-b-hollingshead-and-fredrick-c-redlich-social-class-and-mental-P00Xl1WVQ1

Levin, A., Virginia's commitment law raises many questions, *Psychiatric News*, 43(7), 21, 2008.

Liebert, J. Attitudes of Psychiatrists in Washington State Towards Third Party Coverage for Psychiatric Disorders: Is There Any Consensus?, Washington State Psychiatric Association, 1982.

Liebert, J. Unity in Healthcare the Toyota Way: Can Lean Engineering Fix North American Health Care?, *Bulletin of King County Medical Society*, 87(2), 9–24, 2007.

McLean, D. & Shankar, V. Virginia Tech Strives to Move Beyond Shooting "Horror" Reopen. Bloomberg. Accessed September 16, 2008.

Millet, A., *For Your Own Good*, FS&G, New York, 1990.

Monahan, J. in *Violence and Criminal Justice*, Eds., D. Chappell & J. Monahan, Lexington Books, New York, 1975.

Murray, G.B. Limbic music, *Psychosomatics*, 33, 16–23, 1992.

Nasrallah, *Current Psychiatry*, 7(3), 19, 2008.

Stanley, J., http://www.treatmentadvocacycenter.org/BriefingPaper/www.semissourian.com/article/20090330/NEWS01/703309940

National Commission on the Causes and Prevention of Violence, *Rights in Conflict, Bantam*, New York, 1968.

Newsmax, http://archive.newsmax.com/archives/articles/2002/8/15/172539.shtml

Palsgraf v. Long Island Railroad Co., 248 N.Y. 339, 162 N.E. 99 (N.Y. 1928).

Pincus, J.H. & Tucker, G.J. *Behavioral Neurology*, 3rd ed., Oxford University Press, New York, 1985.

Rachlin, S. With liberty and psychosis for all, *Psychiatric Quarterly*, 48(3), 410–420, 1974

Report of the Virginia Tech Review Panel, Commonwealth of Virginia. http://governor.virginia.gov/TempContent/techPanelReport.cfm. Retrieved September 16, 2008/

Schulte, B. & Craig, T. Unknown to Va. Tech, Cho had a Disorder, *Washington Post*, August 27, 2007.

Szacz, T., Myth of mental illness. *American Psychologist*, 15, 113–118, 1960.

Tarasoff v. Regents of the University of California 17 Cal. 3d 425, 551 P.2d 334, 131 Cal.Rptr. 14 (Cal. 1976).

Time Magazine. A Family's Shame in Korea. *Time Magazine*, April 22, 2007. http://www.time.com/time/world/article/0,8599,1613417,00html. Retrieved September 16, 2008.

Torrey, E.F. Letter to the Editor, *New York Times*, April 27, 2007.

Torrey, E. F., *The Insanity Offense: How America's Failure to Treat the Seriously Mentally Ill Endangers Its Citizens*, Norton, 2008.

University of Wyoming, http://onlinelibrary.wiley.com/doi/10.1111/j.1745-9125.1986.tb01502.x/abstract

USA Today, http://www.usatoday.com/news/nation/2008-05-05-citiesready_N.htm

Webster, S. & Terek, D. A hidden health epidemic. *The Detroit News*, November 26, 2000.

Wolfgang, M., in *Violence and Criminal Justice*, Eds. D. Chappell & J. Monahan, Lexington, New York, 1975.

Index

D

J

K

L

M

N

Q

R

S

V

W